Notable American Unitarians 1936-1961

Edited by

Herbert F. Vetter

Harvard Square Library
www.harvardsquarelibrary.org

Designed by Andrew Drane

Notable American Unitarians 1936-1961

Published by Harvard Square Library
www.harvardsquarelibrary.org

ISBN: 978-0-6151-4784-0

Contents

Arts

Business

Education

Government

Health

Human Rights

Literature

Natural Sciences & Engineering

Philanthropy & Service

Philosophy

Religion

1   James Luther Adams
10 E. Burdette Backus
25 John Nicholls Booth
33 Ralph Wendell Burhoe
42 Paul N. Carnes
56 J. Raymond Cope
70 A. Powell Davies
75 John H. Dietrich
83 Frederick May Eliot
88 Samuel Atkins Eliot
96 Arthur Foote II
98 Henry Wilder Foote
100 Stephen H. Fritchman
103 Max Gaebler
107 Dana Greeley
108 Donald Szantho Harrington
111 Vilma Szantho Harrington
113 John Hayward
115 Clara Cook Helvie
118 John Haynes Holmes
120 Duncan Howlett
122 Homer A. Jack
124 Charles Rhind Joy
131 Walter Donald Kring
135 John Howland Lathrop
142 Duncan Littlefair
148 Rowena Morse Mann
177 Kenneth Leo Patton
181 Leslie T. Pennington
187 Robert Raible
190 Curtis W. Reese
217 Dorothy T. Spoerl
228 Von Ogden Vogt
238 Earl Morse Wilbur
241 Edwin H. Wilson
243 David Rhys Williams
245 George Huntston Williams
248 Conrad Wright

Social Sciences

72 Karl W. Deutsch
138 Alfred and Elizabeth Lee
151 Edward S. Mason
164 Ashley Montagu
204 Arthur Schlesinger
215 Herbert A. Simon
219 Vilhjalmur Stefansson
231 Caroline Farrar Ware
253 Quincy Wright

Notable American Unitarians

PREFACE

"American Unitarianism's great book" is the citation penned in 1923 to celebrate the work by Cooke published by the American Unitarian Association in 1902—*Unitarianism in America: Its Origin and Development.*

George Willis Cooke's celebration at the beginning of the 20th century of the 75th anniversary of the American Unitarian Association—which was founded in 1825—was followed by several later publications. In 1925 the 100th anniversary of the AUA was observed by publication by Beacon Press of *Our Unitarian Heritage* by Earl Morse Wilbur of the Starr King School for the Ministry in Berkeley, California. This book, which was prepared at the request of the AUA Department of Education for the use of young people, contained 80 pages in four chapters on "Unitarianism in America."

In 1952, volume two of Wilbur's magnum opus—*The History of Unitarianism*—was published by Harvard University. Though concentrated on Europe, it did include a section on America, but Wilbur's story ends in 1900, and was not identified as celebrating the 125th anniversary of the American Unitarian Association.

The 150th anniversary of the AUA was celebrated in a well illustrated book—*A Stream of Light: A Sesquicentennial History of American Unitarianism*—published by the Unitarian Universalist Association and edited by Conrad Wright, the historically unexcelled historian of Unitarianism in America. The Professor of American Church History at Harvard invited four other scholars to unite with him in telling the story: Charles Forman, Daniel Walker Howe, David B Parke, and Carol R. Morris. This book is the most adequate and the most meticulously accurate tale of this liberal religious denomination.

Notable American Unitarians, begun online in 2000, is a celebration of Unitarianism by the First Parish in Cambridge, Massachusetts. Sustaining support has come from the Unitarian Universalist Funding Program of the Unitarian Universalist Association and from various cosponsors of the project.

Cosponsors are:
Unitarian Church of All Souls, New York, N.Y.;
First Unitarian Society, Madison, WI;
The First and Second Church of Boston;
The First Parish in Cambridge;
Unity Church - Unitarian in St. Paul, MN;
The First Unitarian Universalist Church of Austin, TX;
The Evangelical Missionary Society in Massachusetts, Weston;
The Follen Church Society, Lexington, MA;
The James Luther Adams Foundation;
The Main Line Unitarian Church, Devon, PA;
Freda Carnes,   .
one Anonymous,
Jan and Lowell Steinbrenner,
and the A. Powell Davies Memorial Fund of All Souls Church, Washington, D.C.

Project advisors are:
Gloria Korsman, Andover-Harvard Theological Library;
Conrad Edick Wright, Massachusetts Historical Society;
and Conrad Wright, Harvard Divinity School.

A color illustrated edition of this book is available online at www.harvardsquarelibrary.org

Herbert F. Vetter
Cambridge 2007

JAMES LUTHER ADAMS:
THEOLOGIAN OF POWER (1901-1994)

By George Kimmich Beach, Faculty of Divinity Memorial Minute, Harvard University

James Luther Adams — "JLA" as he came to be affectionately known — was born in Ritzville, Washington, in 1901, the son of James Carey Adams, an itinerant Baptist preacher and farmer, and Leila Mae Bartlett. When his father, who later joined the Plymouth Brethren, went on his Sunday preaching circuit, young Luther (as he was called in the family) often went along, taking his violin to accompany the hymns. His childhood experience of fundamentalist Christianity and of farm life deeply influenced his development, and became a source of the storytelling for which he later became renowned. At age 16, when his father fell seriously ill, he dropped out of high school in order to help support the family. Among other jobs, he worked for the Northern Pacific Railroad, acquired speed shorthand, and soon rose to the position of secretary to the regional superintendent. To his boss's astonishment, he turned down the lucrative offer of promotion in order to further his education — his "deprovincialization" — he often called it. In 1920 he entered the University of Minnesota, while continuing to work nights in the railroad yards.

After a phase in which he radically rejected all religion, Adams came to recognize it as his passion—and ministry as his calling. He entered Harvard Divinity School in 1924 with the intention of becoming a Unitarian minister. In his autobiographical essay of 1939, he recounted his transitions from the "premillennarian fundamentalism" of his youth, to "scientific humanism" (as expounded by John Dietrich in Minneapolis during his college years), and then to liberal Christianity. He recalled the words of an influential teacher, Dr. Frank Rarig, who once told him that his problem was that he had never heard of a "self-critical religion." The entire quest of Adams's professional career may be seen as transformative responses to his childhood religion in two basic respects: first, his quest as a theologian for "an examined faith" — a faith subject to self-criticism and growth — and second, his quest as an ethicist for a faith that "takes time seriously" — a faith that seeks to embody its ethical commitments in history.

In 1927 Adams was ordained and installed as minister of the Second Church (Unitarian) in Salem, Massachusetts. In the same year he and Margaret Ann Young, an accomplished pianist and graduate of the New England Conservatory in Boston, were married. Margaret went on to study social work and actively promoted social reform movements. During more than fifty years together, they raised three daughters and shared musical and other interests. They hosted weekly informal evening gatherings in their home, a place for communal support and discussion among theological students, during his years of teaching theology. Margaret died of cancer in 1978.

1

During his pastorates in Salem and, subsequently, in Wellesley Hills, Massachusetts, Adams pursued graduate studies in comparative literature at Harvard. In 1937 Adams joined the faculty of the Meadville Theological School, a Unitarian seminary in Chicago, as professor of religious social ethics. In 1956 he returned to Cambridge to become the Edward Mallinckrodt, Jr., Professor of Christian Ethics at Harvard Divinity School. By the force of both his personality and his ideas Adams deeply influenced a generation of students for the ministry (in many denominations) and doctoral students in ethics and society.

In 1968 he retired from Harvard, becoming Professor *Emeritus*. At the 350th anniversary of Harvard in 1986, he was awarded a medal for distinguished service to the University.

Adams died on July 26, 1994, at the age of 92.

CONRAD AIKEN:
UNITARIAN PRODIGY POET (1889-1973)

By Richard A. Kellaway, Minister Emeritus, First Unitarian Church in New Bedford, Massachusetts

Conrad Aiken was born in Savannah, Georgia. In his childhood Aiken experienced considerable trauma when he found the bodies of his parents after his physician father had killed his mother and committed suicide. He was brought up in Massachusetts from the age of eleven by a great-great-aunt.

Before entering Harvard, Aiken was educated at private schools and at Middlesex School, Concord. At Harvard he shared a class and developed a close friendship with T. S. Eliot, with whom he edited the *Advocate*. After working as a reporter, Aiken devoted himself entirely to writing, having also a small private income. Of the many influences Aiken acknowledged, the writings of Freud, Havelock Ellis, William James, Edgar Allan Poe, and the French Symbolists are evident in his work. Freud considered Aiken's *Great Circle* a masterpiece of analytical introspection.

Aiken's first collection of verse, *Earth Triumphant*, appeared in 1914, and it made him known as a poet. He was a contributing editor to *Dial*, which led to a friendship with Ezra Pound. Aiken's essays, collected in *Scepticisms* (1919) and *A Reviewer's ABC* (1958), dealt with the questions provoked by his commitment to literature as a mode of self-understanding.

Aiken's adult life was marked by trans-Atlantic journeys. In 1921 he moved from Massachusetts to England, settling in Rye, Sussex. He married Jessie Mac-Donald, a Canadian, in 1912; the three children of that marriage—John, Jane Aiken Hodge, and Joan—all became published authors. Conrad Aiken later married Clarissa M. Lorenz in 1930 (divorced in 1937). In 1933 he sailed again for Boston, and then spent two years in Rye (1934-36), writing "London Letters" to *The New Yorker*. He returned to New York and Boston, and traveled in Mexico, where he married the artist Mary Hoover. They returned to Rye in 1937, but moved to the United States after the outbreak of World War II.

In 1930 Aiken received the Pulitzer Prize for his collection *Selected Poems*. Aiken wrote most of his fiction between the 1920s and 1930s, including novels *Blue Voyage* (1927), in which he used interior monologue, and *King Coffin* (1934). He also wrote short story collections: *Bring! Bring!* (1925) and *Among the Lost People* (1934).

After staying two years in Rye, Aiken settled in 1947 in Brewster, Massachusetts. He was a consultant in poetry at the Library of Congress from 1950 to 1952. In 1953 he published *Collected Poems*, which included the masterwork "Preludes to Definition" and "Morning Song of Senlin." Aiken's autobiographical narrative, *Ushant* (1952), depicted his friendships with Malcolm Lowry, Eliot, and other figures he knew.

Aiken received a Pulitzer Prize, National Book Award, and Bollinger Prize in 1956, a Gold Medal in Poetry from the American Academy of Arts and Letters in 1958, and a National Medal for Literature in 1969. He died in Savannah on August 17, 1973.

Aiken's psychological penetrations and verbal richness never received the wide recognition they deserved in spite of the several awards the author received. His trans-Atlantic life mode made it difficult for the public to decide whether he was an American or an English author. Because as a critic, he always tried to tell the truth as he saw it, he did not always endear himself to literary colleagues. His shyness prevented him from doing public readings and led him to reject all offers of honorary degrees—including one from Harvard. Indeed, he resigned from the College as an undergraduate, partially because his election as Class Poet would have required him to speak in public.

Aiken's maternal grandfather, William James Potter, was the minister of the First Congregational Society (Unitarian) of New Bedford from 1859 to 1892. In 1971, Aiken wrote: "What could have been more natural, as I grew older, that in my preoccupations as to the content of the poetry I should turn to the teachings— for they were more teachings than preachings—of my grandfather. I regard all my work, both verse and prose, as in a way a continuation of his work—the finding of the truth about man, and man's mind, and of man's place in the universe, and the telling of it as accurately and beautifully as such themes deserved."

He never joined a church. However, when his wife, Mary Hoover Aiken, jokingly listed him as Episcopalian on a hospital admission slip, he was furious and insisted that he was a Unitarian. She reports that the two volumes of Grandfather Potter's sermons accompanied them on all their journeys and that they were once lent to Eliot.

About his religious views, he once said: "Yes, I suppose I'm a naturalistic humanist if I'm anything—that and an evolutionist. I am against all forms of supernaturalism, dogma, myth, church—primarily, I believe in the evolution of consciousness as something we're embarked on willy-nilly, the evolution of mind, and that devotion to this is all the devotion we need."

UNITARIAN NOTE

Conrad Aiken's poetry is deliberately built on the foundation of the philosophy of Heraclitus expressed in such presocratic fragments as these:

—This world, which is the same for all, no one of the gods or men has made, but it ever was, is now, and ever shall be an everliving Fire, with measures of its kindling, and measure going out.

—Fire lives the death of air, and air lives the death of fire; water lives the death of earth, earth that of water.

—All things come into being and pass away through strife.

Conrad Aiken affirms the all too often hidden Heraclitean heritage of the American Unitarian faith: faith in the everliving cosmos which is our home, faith in reason as a way to reliable knowledge, and faith symbolized by sacred fire, such as that dancing in a flaming chalice.

ARTHUR ALTMEYER:
MR. SOCIAL SECURITY (1891-1972)

Arthur Altmeyer, who was a member of the first Unitarian Society of Madison, Wisconsin, is known as the person who did more than anyone else to shape the institution that administered the Social Security Program of the United States. He worked closely with fellow Unitarian, U.S. Representative Thomas Eliot of Massachusetts, to draft the enabling legislation.

Altmeyer was born in DePere, Wisconsin. He obtained a B.A. from the University of Wisconsin in 1914 and subsequently taught high school and was a high school principal. He then became a statistician, advancing to chief statistician and later executive secretary of the Wisconsin Industrial Commission. After being awarded his Ph.D. from the University of Wisconsin in 1931 and writing two books, in 1933 he was summoned by President Franklin D. Roosevelt to Washington, where he became chairman of the Social Security Board in 1937. Altmeyer's retirement from government service in 1953 ended an era of shaping the nation's social insurance program. He remained active in social welfare policy, however. He served as an advisor to foreign governments and in 1954 was elected president of the National Conference on Social Work.

"Arthur Altmeyer was part of the President's Committee on Economic Security that drafted the original legislative proposal in 1934. He was a member of the three-person Social Security Board created to run the new program, and he was either Chairman of the Board or Commissioner for Social Security from 1937-1953. Although he believed that public administration was a vitally important activity, he was also one of the principal conceptual and philosophical spokesmen for social insurance in America, and much of the policymaking during Social Secu-

rity's founding decades was formulated by Altmeyer. Along with a mere handful of others, Arthur J. Altmeyer is responsible for the Social Security program as it exists in America today" - DeWitt.

A Legacy of Dedication

The following is adapted from Never a Finished Thing: A Biography of Arthur Joseph Altmeyer *by Social Security Administration historian Larry DeWitt:*

Altmeyer was a modest, serious, and dedicated career public servant. In 1916, he married Ethel Thomas, his former high school history teacher who was four years his senior. They remained married for 56 years, until Altmeyer's death in 1972. Although they had no offspring, the Altmeyers' concern for the welfare of all members of society was evidenced in their chosen professions of striving for the public good.

When Franklin D. Roosevelt ascended to the office of President of the United States of America in 1933, he inherited a country shattered by the economic devastation of the Great Depression. Before that catastrophe, "there was no precedent for a social insurance system in United States law." President Roosevelt vowed to give the American people once again a sense of security and, therein, hope for a better future.

Altmeyer, during his nearly twenty years of leading the charge for the Social Security program during the Roosevelt and Truman presidencies, was instrumental in ensuring that this new social welfare policy would be designed, administered, and legislated as comprehensively and efficiently as possible. Originally conceived as a means to help provide financial stability for the elderly in retirement, Altmeyer's advocacy and devotion eventually led to the expansion of Social Security's coverage to orphans, widows, unskilled laborers, and the self-

employed. Although his desire to also have Social Security supply health insurance coverage and disability benefits was never fully realized during his tenure, Altmeyer persevered in championing the ideal of a broad, fair social insurance program.

On January 19, 1973, three months after his death, the Social Security Administration headquarters in Baltimore, Maryland were renamed in honor of Altmeyer. Then Social Security Commissioner and former colleague, Robert Ball, noted:

> It has always seemed to me that the contribution Arthur Altmeyer made to the development of the social security program was very specific and personal. He did more, much more, than oversee the building up of an efficient organization. He imprinted on the evolving program and on the administration and in the people who were with it a set of values that are still operative and that have been largely responsible for the success and widespread acceptance and support that the social security system enjoys.

Thus, "Mr. Social Security," as Altmeyer came to be known, helped to forge one of the world's most enviable government programs and left behind an incomparable legacy of dedication.

The First Decade in Social Security

The following is abridged from Arthur Altmeyer's August 1945 report as Chairman of the Social Security Board:

On August 14, 1935 the Social Security Act became law. Probably never before in a corresponding period of time has legislation done as much to establish a groundwork of economic security for families in the United States as in the years following President Roosevelt's message of June 8, 1934, in which he said to Congress: "Among our objectives I place the security of men, women, and children of the Nation first."

Today some 40 million people are insured. Even so, social insurance is new in the United States and incomplete in coverage and scope. As coverage is extended, it will go far toward cutting down poverty and insecurity.

Recall some of the remarks made about social security in 1935 and 1936: It was unconstitutional, unworkable, a first step toward communism. It would destroy individual enterprise and initiative. Actual experience quickly belied all such charges. The program has worked—better in some respects than its sponsors dared hope. The United States was far stronger, freer, and richer than it could have been if the alarmists who opposed such legislation had had their way. Freedom to be sick or hungry is not a freedom to be prized.

Social security does not endanger the moral fiber of the Nation. Enlightened self-interest, as well as common humanity, requires that we set a floor beneath which human beings in our civilization shall not sink. Only in that way can an industrialized society preserve political democracy and a competitive economy in accordance with our traditions. In these first 10 years we have laid the foundation for that effort.

BLANCHE AMES AMES: ARTIST AND WOMEN'S RIGHTS ACTIVIST (1878-1969)

By Heather Miller, writer and editor

Born in Lowell, Massachusetts to a prominent family, Blanche Ames was one of six children. Her father — who had been a general in the Civil War and a U.S. Senator and governor of Mississippi — and her mother took an active role in their children's education.

At Smith College, Ames was class president and pursued diplomas from both the College and the School of Art, earning an A.B. in 1899. One year later she married Oakes Ames (unrelated), an instructor in botany at Harvard. Their marriage was a highly successful collaboration in home and family building, art, science, technology and politics. They were Unitarians who belonged to the Unity Church of North Easton.

Between the years 1900 and 1910 they had four children. In 1910, they designed and constructed an impressive stone mansion located in North Easton, Massachusetts. The house was surrounded by 1500 acres called Borderland, which the family farmed. Today Borderland is a State Park.

As an artist, Ames is known for her drawings of orchids, which she produced over a period of fifty years to accompany her husband's ground breaking scholarly work in orchidology. Little was known about the *Orchidicae*, one of the largest plant families, before Oakes Ames's thorough study and classification of them. In search of further identification and knowledge of orchids, Blanche traveled with her husband on expeditions to Florida, the Caribbean, the Philippines, and Central and South America. Thanks to his scholarship and thousands of her minutely observed drawings, the *Orchidicae* is now the best researched and classified of all the large plant families. The Ames' cumulative work was published in the seven-volume *Orchidicae: Illustrations and Studies of the Family Orchidicae*. The couple also jointly developed the Ames Charts, using watercolors to illustrate the phylogenetic relationships of the major plants useful to humans. The chart is used to this day.

Blanche Ames, a Republican, was a deeply political person and an outspoken feminist who lobbied for suffrage and for women's right to birth control. In 1916 she cofounded the Birth Control League of Massachusetts, affiliated with the national group led by Margaret Sanger. She was vocally critical of the Catholic Church's prohibition of birth control. When the ban on dissemination of birth control information was upheld, Ames reacted by suggesting that women take the matter into their own hands. She encouraged mothers to teach birth control methods to their daughters. To help them, she created formulas for spermicidal jellies and provided instructions on how to make a diaphragm by using such everyday objects as a baby's teething ring.

Ames's involvement with the Birth Control League of Massachusetts came to an end, however, when she quit in outrage at a fundraising advertisement for the league. In the advertisement, the league used the fact that 250,000 babies had been born that year to families on welfare to persuade taxpayers to support birth control.

Blanche Ames Ames was also well known as a witty pro-suffrage political cartoonist. In all of her political endeavors, her husband actively supported her.

In 1941, Ames became a member of the corporation of the New England Hospital for Women and Children which was run entirely by women for women and children. In 1952 due to financial difficulties, the board of directors opened itself to the possibility of hiring male staff. Ames vigorously fought to maintain the hospital's almost hundred year-old charter. In 1952, as president of the board, Ames successfully spearheaded a massive fundraising effort that raised sufficient funds to ensure an exclusively female staff and administration for the hospital.

Ames's imagination extended to inventions and engineering. She designed and engineered dams and ponds throughout the 1250-acre Borderland estate. During World War II, she invented and received the patent for a method of trapping propellers of enemy airplanes using strings held by balloons.

Ames is notable not only for the breadth of her interests and activities, but also for her longevity. At the age of 80, prompted by her anger at a suggestion in John F. Kennedy's *Profiles in Courage* that her father was a carpetbagger politician in Mississippi, she wrote the biography of her father, General Adelbert Ames. Also, at the age of 90, Blanche received the patent for her invention, "the antipollution toilet."

Blanche's daughter, Pauline Ames, explained her mother's productivity by stating, "For her to have an idea was to act." Blanche Ames lived for nineteen years after her husband's death before succumbing to a stroke at her home, Borderland, at the age of 92.

MELVIN ARNOLD:
PUBLISHER (1913-2000)

By Alexandra Arnold Lynch, his daughter

Melvin Luxton Arnold was born August 13, 1913, the fifth of seven children, one of whom died in infancy, to Daniel and Letitia Luxton Arnold. His father was an electrician, and the family lived in modest circumstances in Portland, Oregon.

Mel's inquiring mind developed early. As a young boy, he was severely punished by his fundamentalist father for asking, "Who created God?" As he grew up, he found interesting and stimulating friends in the neighborhood. The father of his best friend, Tom Perry, was a basement inventor and scientist, who challenged the boys to experiment and question.

Like many young men in the hard economic years of the Great Depression, Mel worked his way through high school. He had an after-school job with the *News Telegram* as a night reporter on the police beat. After graduating from Franklin High School, he worked for the paper as a full-time reporter.

When his salary was increased by one dollar to sixteen dollars a week, he felt financially secure enough to marry his high school sweetheart, Valerie Hendricksen. Their only child, Alexandra, was born in December 1933.

With his family to support, Mel never had the opportunity to go to college. He was self-educated and read omnivorously for the rest of his life. He bought books as he could afford them, underlining as he read, making marginal notes and frequently writing summaries for his files. "Feed your mind!" he told his daughter, and made sure she always had good books to read.

Mel's responsibilities grew at the *News Telegram*, and his early contacts with the members of the civic and service clubs developed into important friendships. Among the most socially active citizens were Portland's liberal ministers, including Dr. Richard Steiner of the First Unitarian Church, who became a good friend and mentor.

In the years leading up to World War II, Mel was an account executive with a major advertising agency in Portland and then director of advertising with Portland General Electric. His association and experience with energy issues led to an executive position in the publications division with Standard Oil, N.J. at the headquarters in New York.

In 1946, at the urging of his friend Dr. Richard Steiner, he accepted the offer from the Unitarian Association to become director of Beacon Press and *The Christian Register*.

As the war was coming to its end, he foresaw the potential healing power of Albert Schweitzer's philosophy of "Reverence for Life." Schweitzer's books were no longer in print, and his publisher in England was not interested in new editions. Mel decided to go to Africa and ask Dr. Schweitzer personally for permission to publish his works in America.

This was a turning point, both for Mel and for Beacon Press. Schweitzer's enthusiastic acceptance and encouragement gave Mel the confidence to pursue other distinguished authors. For Beacon, it was the beginning of development from a church-based program into a nationally respected publisher of scholarly books.

In 1947, Mel and Charles R. Joy spent several weeks at the Schweitzer Hospital in Lambarene. They co-wrote *The Africa of Albert Schweitzer*, which was published jointly by Beacon Press and Harper & Brothers in 1948. The public interest in Schweitzer that developed was phenomenal. *Life Magazine* even hailed him as "The Greatest Man in the World" in a three-page photo essay.

When Melvin Arnold retired in the early 1970s, he and Val decided to return to their home state, where they bought a home and three acres on the Applegate River in southern Oregon.

He died April 13, 2000, at the age of 86. Valerie, his wife of 67 years, died a few months later. In 2005, they are survived by daughter Alexandra, her husband Douglas Lynch, grandsons John and Jason, and great-grandsons Duncan and Noah.

Beacon Press — The Growth of an Idea

By Walter Donald Kring

This article, abridged from the Christian Register, *April 1956, was written when the author was chairman of the AUA Division of Publications and President of Beacon Press.*

The past ten years of the Beacon Press have been inextricably bound up with the director of the division, Mr. Melvin Arnold.

The Beacon Press had been a small, highly respected publishing house printing hymnals, religious education material, ministers' sermons and books: far above average in quality, but far below average in sales. From this very important but meager beginning developed Beacon Press of today. In 1948, the Beacon catalogue had 19 titles on its backlist; the spring 1956 catalogue had 321.

Today the Beacon Press is known by many as one of the most courageous presses in America.

In the issuing of the new Beacon "quality paperback" series, the Press has gained additional stature. Beacon was the third house to enter this field, and the first to introduce the "library-sized" paperback. Thus far, Beacon Press has published 26 paperback titles, many of them already part of college supplementary reading lists.

E. BURDETTE BACKUS:
A HUMANISTIC MINISTRY IN INDIANAPOLIS
(1888-1955)

By Edd Doerr, Executive Director, Americans for Religious Liberty

Burdette Backus was my introduction to Unitarianism in 1951 when I was a college undergraduate in Indianapolis. He had read something I had written and sent me an appreciative note inviting me to visit All Souls Unitarian Church in Indianapolis.

I found Backus to be a forceful but gentle man, brilliant but not arrogant, at once a thinker and an activist. His writing, his work, and his life are to me among the finest expressions of the best in both Humanism and Unitarian Universalism, and illustrate the very considerable overlap between these two traditions.

Edwin Burdette Backus was born in Blanchester, Ohio, on December 27, 1888. His father, Wilson Marvin Backus, was a leading Universalist minister. His mother, Estelle Campbell Backus, also a Universalist minister, tragically died bringing Burdette into the world.

After serving in the Universalist ministry for several years, Wilson Backus moved into the Unitarian fold and served in Minneapolis as the humanist predecessor to John Dietrich.

After graduating from the University of Michigan in 1909, Burdette followed in his parents' footsteps and headed for Meadville Theological Seminary, where he earned his B.D. in 1912. He pursued graduate studies at Oxford, Harvard, the University of California, and universities in Berlin and Jena, Germany. He was awarded a D.D. in 1940 by Meadville.

Burdette's first parish was in Lawrence, Kansas, where he met his future wife, Irene Garrett, a Phi Beta Kappa graduate of the University of Kansas. In 1917 his father was called to serve a Unitarian congregation in Erie, Pennsylvania, but ill health forced him to resign and Burdette was called to replace him the same year. Burdette went on to serve Unitarian congregations in Los Angeles, Des Moines, and the Chicago Humanist Society, before being called to the Thomas Paine pulpit of All Souls Unitarian Church in Indianapolis.

Burdette served the Indianapolis congregation from 1938 until his retirement at the end of 1953. The Ku Klux Klan had been a powerful force in Indiana not too long before Backus's arrival in the state and a John Birch Society was founded there. During the McCarthy Burdette had to face a serious challenge from an influential faction in the congregation that did not like his humanism (Backus, like his predecessor Frank C. S. Wicks, was a signer of the 1933 Humanist Manifesto) or his support for the American Civil Liberties Union and the Mental Health Association. The majority of the congregation supported Backus; the minority, worried that newcomers and possibly "Communists" and African Americans might "infiltrate" the church, pulled out and formed a new congregation, which did not last very long. Burdette was hurt by the affair but did not allow it to sour him or to dampen his sense of humor or optimism.

Backus was a spellbinding speaker, though without a hint of bombast or flashiness. His pulpit addresses and his weekly fifteen-minute radio broadcasts — inspirational, thought-provoking and gentle — influenced a great many and contributed to the founding of new Unitarian congregations in Indiana.

Burdette was much more than a preacher. He was active in the ACLU and played an important part in the formation of the Indiana Society for Mental Hygiene and he served for many years as president. He served on the board of the Indianapolis Children's Bureau and on the Indiana White House Committee on Child Welfare. In September 1945, he preached an important sermon on the Illinois McCollum "released time" lawsuit, which resulted in an important U.S. Supreme Court precedent in 1948 supporting the principle of church-state separation.

Burdette was a lifelong naturalistic humanist. He was one of the 34 signers of the 1933 Humanist Manifesto, along with such eminent Unitarian ministers as John H. Dietrich, Curtis Reese, Edwin H. Wilson, Raymond B. Bragg, and Lester Mondale, and such philosophers as John Dewey.

A fitting tribute to Burdette was that of his fellow minister and American Unitarian Association president Frederick May Eliot: "If you were to take a poll of the Unitarian ministers throughout the country on the question of who stands highest both in the matter of fundamental respect and also of heartfelt affection, I have no doubt that Burdette Backus's name would lead all of the rest."

BEN H. BAGDIKIAN:
JOURNALIST FOR SOCIAL JUSTICE (1920-)

Ben H. Bagdikian has been a reporter and editor, author of books, former assistant managing editor for national news of the Washington Post, and former dean of the Graduate School of Journalism at the University of California at Berkeley. He is the author of several books, three of them published by Beacon Press: In the Midst of Plenty: The Poor in America, The Media Monopoly, *and* Double Vision: Reflections on my Heritage, Life, and Profession. *His life deserves our celebration for its dramatic disclosure of thousands of pages of top-secret Pentagon papers revealing the years of official lying about the Vietnam War. He is likewise the unstilled sounder of astounding facts about the dangerous concentration of power of the media monopoly in our electronic epoch.*

by Ben H. Bagdikian

I have lived a life of perpetual education, aided by my journalism career and deepened, of course, by living through most of our traumatic twentieth century. Though it was never a conscious choice, the core of my work has been a concern with social justice issues. Most of the crucial decisions in my life have been the result of impulse and intuition rather than rational analysis.

I came to the United States as a four-month-old refugee from terror, grew up in the Great Depression, and when confronted with Hitler, abandoned my adolescent devotion to pacifism and survived World War II.

My parents, four older sisters, and I were all born in Turkey, an Armenian minority in the old Ottoman Empire. My father was a professor of chemistry in an American college in Tarsus—a college strongly influenced by Boston Congregationalists. I was born during a massacre of Armenians and, as an infant, was carried by my father, mother and four older sisters through an excruciating escape over frozen mountains. Once in this country, my father accepted an invitation to become the pastor of a large Armenian Congregational Church in Cambridge, Massachusetts.

A powerful impact on me was my Uncle Fred. He had the talent of enjoying life regardless of his circumstances. My closeness to him led to my realization that there are cads and heroes up and down the social and economic scale. I learned also from my father. He had undergone seismic eruptions in his personal and family life without losing his vigor and ability to create a fulfilling life.

In the end, all this background plus undeserved good luck has given me a sufficiently happy professional and personal life to endure the inevitable times of tragedy and anger.

I graduated as a premedical student from Clark University in Worcester, Massachusetts, where I also edited the campus paper. I was on my way for an appoint-

ment interview at a laboratory when, on an impulse, I walked into a newspaper office, was hired as a reporter and never turned back.

World War II intervened, and after three years as an aerial navigator, I worked as a reporter in Providence, Rhode Island. It was here that I became a member of the beautiful First Unitarian Church of Providence, where, for the first time, I could listen to sermons without mentally dismissing half of what was preached. I went to Washington as a correspondent, and soon left daily reporting in favor of political stories. My 13 years of covering civil rights and poverty in the Deep South were both rich and frustrating.

Frustration at the sins and omissions in our news media during these periods led me to do parallel reporting and criticism of our standard reporting. A Guggenheim Fellowship permitted me to spend a year in the Library of Congress reading the history of American journalism. It enriched my knowledge and affected my views as a media critic.

I knew from both journalism and covering politics that mainstream news has a powerful influence on the actions of political leaders. The agenda in the news and the national agenda dance around each other. But the news concentrates on the words and actions of people with titles, the view from the top. Only lately have a few of the better newspapers and standard magazines begun to see the view from ordinary homes.

I moved to Berkeley, always having been in love with the San Francisco Bay Area, where I wallowed in its beauty, its life of the arts, and its contrarian impulses. I continue the undeserved good luck that has buoyed my life. My wife, Marlene Griffith, and I are close to the generations below us, our surrogate grandchildren, and their wise parents. I have no personal complaints.

But I see a future for the human race that requires a level of official and corporate wisdom and intelligent self-interest that is lacking. The planet is not yet safe. It suffers from the kind of greed that ignores not only global warming but an even more immediate bomb ready to detonate — the terrible gap between the rich and the poor, the technologically proficient and the majority left behind, the overfed and the starving; and the arrogance of our only superpower, my country, that sees only as far as the next election or tomorrow's Dow Jones Industrial Index.

Modern communications is the fuse to our bomb. People in the most desperate circumstances can see television and know that there are privileged places in the world where, unlike their own lives, most babies don't die in their first year of life, most diseases have adequate medicines, most people have food and housing in excess. I await our surrogate grandchildren to take over. I only hope the world is willing to wait for them.

SARA JOSEPHINE BAKER: UNITARIAN PUBLIC HEALTH WORKER (1873-1945)

By Marsha Lakes Matyas, The American Physiological Society

History of the Times

In the late 1800s and early 1900s, infectious diseases were a major concern of both physicians and researchers. In larger cities such as New York and Boston, sanitation was poor. Preventative medicine was almost unknown. There were no public health nurses and few large-scale public health programs or policies. It was also a time of social change. Women were marching in the streets to gain the right to vote. Certainly, female physicians were a rarity at this time; they accounted for less than 1% of all physicians. Few medical schools were open to women.

Josephine Baker's Personal Background

Josephine Baker did not intend to become a physician. At the age of 16, she was preparing for studies at Vassar when her father died of typhoid fever. In order to support her mother and family, she decided to study medicine, instead. She knew of only one school that would accept women: the Women's Medical College of the New York Infirmary for Women and Children, founded by Drs. Elizabeth and Emily Blackwell.

After finishing medical school, Josephine Baker interned at the New England Hospital for Women and Children in Boston and worked at an out-clinic in one of Boston's worst slums. There she learned how poorly medical science was serving the crowded city populations.

Working at the Department of Health in New York

At the turn of the century, Dr. Baker began her life's work with the New York Department of Health as a medical inspector. Her first job was to examine children in a public school. Her work in the schools led to the establishment of a citywide school nurse program. The program worked so well that cases of head lice and the eye infection trachoma — once extremely prevalent in the schools — dropped to nearly zero.

Josephine Baker helped to establish some of the first programs in preventative medicine and public health. In order to curb the enormous death rates among infants in the city, Dr. Baker used school nurses in the summer of 1908 to visit the homes of newborns to teach mothers how to take care of their babies. There were 1,200 fewer deaths that summer than the previous one. Soon after, the Division of Child Hygiene (later the Bureau of Child Health) was established and Josephine Baker was appointed its chief.

Her other accomplishments include: a long and successful battle to allow midwives to be licensed by the city; the development of a foolproof dispenser for administering silver nitrate to newborns' eyes to prevent gonococcal infections and subsequent blindness; the development of a newborn formula by adding water, calcium carbonate, and lactose to cow's milk; and the controversial development of the Little Mothers Leagues, where eight- to nine-year-old girls were taught how to take care of younger children while their mothers were working to earn a living. Many protested that the Leagues were "enslaving the young girls so their mothers could be irresponsible, go to the movies, or get drunk."

It is difficult to realize today how innovative and radical these programs were. In testimony before a Congressional committee, one physician opposed Baker's Little Mothers Leagues, stating, "If we're going to save the lives of all the women and children at public expense, what incentive will there be for a young man to go into medicine?" When the Bureau of Child Hygiene was formed, a petition was signed by more than 30 Brooklyn physicians and sent to the mayor demanding that the bureau be abolished because "it was ruining medical practice by its results in keeping babies well." Dr. Baker told the mayor that the letter was a compliment to the Bureau. There was no doubt that some social norms were about to change!

One of Josephine Baker's most famous professional tasks was tracking down Mary Mallon ("Typhoid Mary") in 1907. The way Ms. Mallon's case was handled raises some interesting questions even today about conflicts between personal rights and public health.

Finally, Baker served as an officer, consultant, or board member for a number of professional associations, most notably as president of the American Child Hygiene Association and president of the American Medical Women's Association. She published five books and over 200 articles during her professional career. In 1939, her autobiography, *Fighting for Life*, was published.

Reprinted with permission from Women Life Scientists: Past, Present, and Future, Marsha Lakes Matyas and Ann E. Haley-Oliphant, Editors (Bethesda, MD: American Physiological Society, 1997)

EMILY GREENE BALCH: NOBEL PEACE LAUREATE (1867-1961)

By Heather Miller, writer and editor

Emily Greene Balch, a member of the first generation of American women to attend college in significant numbers, had three groundbreaking careers: social reform, the teaching of economics at Wellesley College, and international political activity. She devoted her life's work to the coming of "an age in which the unlikeness of other races will be conceived as much of an asset as the unlikeness of wind and string instruments in a symphony."

Born in 1867 to a prosperous family of liberal Unitarian persuasion, Balch grew up in Jamaica Plain, Massachusetts, with a belief in dynamic good will, hard work, and hope as a discipline as well as a theological virtue.

She received her A.B. in Greek and Latin as a member of Bryn Mawr's first graduating class in 1889. The faculty, discerning in her extraordinary beauty of moral character, awarded her their highest honor, the European Fellowship. This allowed Balch to study poverty alleviation policies for a year at the Sorbonne, an experience she found disappointing because her research never brought her into contact with poor people themselves.

On her return from Paris in 1892, Balch was determined to join the emerging female social reform movement in Boston. In that year, she founded Boston's first settlement house, Denison House in Jamaica Plain, where she lived for several months as its head. During that time, she began what would become a lifelong friendship and working relationship with Jane Addams.

Balch decided she would be of greatest use to the social reform movement as a teacher who might instill the social reform drive in the growing numbers of women attending college. To prepare for a college-teaching career, she studied at the Harvard Annex (later called Radcliffe), the University of Chicago, and for one year at the University of Berlin.

In 1900, Balch began her 18-year career at Wellesley teaching a course in sociology. Her subsequent courses reflected her own practical experiences as a reformer.

In the early twentieth century, many Americans favored immigration limits for Slavic Europeans. Balch combined a settlement worker's interest in immigrants with academic discipline. She took a sabbatical and lived in Austria-Hungary and in Slavic neighborhoods in the United States in order to research the conditions of Slavs in the "Old" and "New" worlds. Balch's years of research resulted in her major work, *Our Slavic Fellow Citizens* (1910). In 1913, Balch became Welles-

ley's chair of the Department of Economics and Sociology.

Balch was an outspoken, active pacifist throughout the First World War. She joined the American delegation to the International Congress of Women at The Hague (1915). She met with President Woodrow Wilson and unsuccessfully attempted to gain his support for the ICW's plan for continuous mediation as an alternative to battle.

In 1918, Balch was dismissed from the Wellesley faculty — ostensibly for her long absences on behalf of the ICW, but in fact for her anti-war views. She began writing for *The Nation* and, in 1919, founded the Women's International League for Peace and Freedom with Jane Addams. As a WILPF member, Balch contributed to the first public criticisms of the

Versailles Treaty and championed inclusion of minorities, expansion of member nations and democratization of the WILPF's structure.

Her accomplishments reflect a broad interest in world and human affairs and an abundance of energy. She organized the third International Congress in Vienna in 1921. In that year, she became a member of the Society of Friends (Quakers), in part because of its unwavering pacifist philosophy. She was a supporter of peace education at several of the WILPF's summer schools. In 1926, under a special mission for WILPF, she traveled to Haiti to investigate conditions there and recommended withdrawal of American troops and self-government of the Haitian people. She was the first to propose internationalization of Antarctica, which came to pass.

Deeply disturbed by Hitler's Germany, she reluctantly made an exception in her pacifist position and supported U.S. involvement in the Second World War. During the war years, when she was between the ages of 72 and 78, she helped relocated Japanese-Americans who had been forcibly interned in concentration camps.

For her extraordinary contributions to world peace, she became the third woman to win the Nobel Peace Prize in 1946. Her close friend Jane Addams had been the second.

Although she had many friends, she insisted on living alone and never married. In her old age, lack of money forced her to live in a nursing home in Cambridge, Massachusetts. She remained intellectually active, and was in close and constant contact with a loving extended family and a supportive network of friends. She died in Cambridge in 1961 at the age of 94.

The American Unitarian Association presented Balch its 1955 Unitarian Award for Distinguished Service to the cause of Liberal Religion, stating, "Miss Balch's Unitarian background, her present Quaker and Unitarian affiliations, make it especially appropriate that she be honored ... when the quest for peace in a nuclear age demands recognition and encouragement."

In 1996, Wellesley College, the Jamaica Plain Unitarian Church, and the International League for Peace and Freedom jointly held commemorations of the 50th anniversary of the Nobel Peace Prize Winner.

ROGER BALDWIN:
FOUNDER, AMERICAN CIVIL LIBERTIES
UNION (1884-1981)

Roger Baldwin, when reflecting on his life, said that in his early years he not only regularly attended the Unitarian Church in Wellesley Hills, Massachusetts, he also helped to teach in the Sunday school and even listened to the preacher. He added, "I would say that social work began in my mind in the Unitarian Church when I was ten or twelve years old, and I started to do things that I thought would help other people." In 1981 a memorial service at the Community Church of New York, Unitarian Universalist, celebrated the ninety-seven years of Roger

Baldwin's vigorous and sometimes contradictory life.

The definitive biography, Roger Baldwin and the American Civil Liberties Union, *published by the Columbia University Press in 2000, was written by Robert C. Cottrell, the author of the following sketch.*

By the mid-1930s, Roger Nash Baldwin had carved out a well-established reputation as America's foremost civil libertarian. He was, at the same time, one of the nation's leading figures in left-of-center circles. Founder and long-time director of the American Civil Liberties Union, Baldwin was a firm Popular Fronter who believed that forces on the left side of the political spectrum should unite to advance progressive causes. Baldwin's expansive civil liberties perspective, coupled with his determined belief in the need for sweeping socioeconomic change, sometimes resulted in contradictory and controversial pronouncements.

Raised in the Boston suburb of Wellesley Hills, Baldwin's ancestral roots were rich and comfortable. Baldwin had parents who considered themselves "agnostic Unitarians." Baldwin attended Harvard College during the period when the Progressive movement unfolded. Afterwards, Baldwin heeded the advice of his father's attorney and confidante, Louis D. Brandeis, to seek his fortune in the Midwest, where he entered the field of social work.

As the period of direct U.S. involvement in World War I approached, Baldwin ended up in New York, where he became a leading figure in the American Union Against Militarism. Concerned about the plight of wartime dissidents, Baldwin eventually headed the National Civil Liberties Bureau. In a display of solidarity with wartime resisters, Baldwin deliberately violated the Selective Service Act, which resulted in a celebrated trial and confinement in prison. In 1919 he took to the road as a laborer, before returning to New York and his new wife, lawyer Madeleine Z. Doty. The following January Baldwin helped set up the ACLU, which became involved in a series of noteworthy cases, including those involving Sacco and Vanzetti, John T. Scopes, and the Scottsboro Boys. ACLU attorneys helped reshape American constitutional law. All the while, Baldwin continued to back a number of left-wing endeavors.

Baldwin's ideological stance underwent an alteration starting in the mid-thirties, the byproduct of personal and political developments. Baldwin became increasingly disturbed by events in the Soviet Union, where purge trials were being undertaken, and by politically troublesome accusations leveled at the ACLU by the House Committee on un-American Activities.

Baldwin became less happy with the Popular Front approach and concerned about the very existence of the ACLU after the Nazi-Soviet Non-Aggression Pact in August 1939. The following spring, in an effort to stave off criticisms, Baldwin orchestrated a campaign to revise the ACLU charter. Henceforth, those affiliated with totalitarian organizations could not serve on the ACLU board. In the meantime, the ACLU wrestled with the issue of internment of Japanese-Americans and Japanese aliens, which had been demanded by the U.S. military. In contrast to many of his longtime colleagues at the ACLU, Baldwin continued to challenge such violations of civil liberties, but also sought to maintain good relations with the federal government.

During the postwar period Baldwin's respectability and celebrity status mounted. In 1947 General Douglas MacArthur arranged for Baldwin to serve as a civil liberties consultant in Japan. Accolades poured Baldwin's way in late 1949, when he announced his intention to resign as director of the ACLU.

For the next several years, Baldwin sought to work for international human rights. He visited South Vietnam, where he both criticized the repressive regime of Ngo Dinh Diem and termed him "a charming idealist but tough on dissenters." In Puerto Rico, Baldwin remained close to Governor Luis Munoz Marin, a former fiery socialist; the jailed independence leader Pedro Albizu Campos; and the cellist Pablo Casals, among others. In India, Baldwin maintained an old friendship with President Jawaharlal Nehru and his family.

Baldwin also maintained an office in the secretariat building of the United Nations and continued as a consultant for the International League for the Rights of Man. In a moving tribute, Margorie M. Bitker quoted Baldwin as affirming, "The rule of law in place of force, always basic to my thinking, now takes on a new relevance in a world where, if war is to go, only law can replace it."

JOHN BARDEEN:
DOUBLE NOBEL LAUREATE SCIENTIST (1908-1991)

The following is adapted from www.physics.uiuc.edu/People/jbardeen.html, 1995:

John Bardeen was born in Madison, Wisconsin, on May 23, 1908. His father, Charles Russell Bardeen, was the first graduate of the Johns Hopkins Medical School and founder of the Medical School at the University of Wisconsin. His mother, Althea Harmer, studied oriental art at the Pratt Institute and practiced interior design in Chicago. He was one of five children.

John received his elementary and secondary education in Madison. He studied electrical engineering at the University of Wisconsin, receiving a B.S. in 1928 and an M.S. in 1929. The three years 1930-33 were spent doing research in geophysics at the Gulf Research Laboratories in Pittsburgh, Pennsylvania. In 1933, he returned to graduate studies in mathematical physics at Princeton University, where he received his Ph.D. in 1936. The three years 1935-38 were spent as a Junior Fellow of the Society of Fellows of Harvard University, where he worked with Professors J. H. Van Vleck and P. W. Bridgeman. He taught at the University of Minnesota and the Naval Ordinance Laboratory in Washington, DC, before, in 1945, joining the newly formed research group in solid state physics at the Bell Telephone Laboratories in Murray Hill, New Jersey. It was there that he became interested in semiconductors and, with W. H. Brattain, discovered the transistor effect in late 1947. He left Bell Labs in 1951 to become Professor of Electrical Engineering and Physics at the University of Illinois, Urbana.

At Illinois, Bardeen established two major research programs: one in the electrical engineering department dealing with both experimental and theoretical aspects of semiconductors; and one in the physics department, which dealt with theoretical aspects of macroscopic quantum systems, particularly superconductivity and quantum liquids. The microscopic theory of superconductivity, developed in collaboration with L. N. Cooper and J. R. Schrieffer in 1956 and 1957, has had profound implications for nearly every field of physics, from elementary to nuclear particles and from helium liquids to neutron stars. During his sixty-year scientific career, he made significant contributions to almost every aspect of condensed matter physics, from his early work on the electronic behavior of metals, the surface properties of semiconductors, and the theory of diffusion of atoms in crystals, to his most recent work on quasi-one-dimensional metals. In his eighty-third year he continued to publish original scientific papers.

During this period, Bardeen maintained active interests in engineering and technology. He began consulting for Xerox Corporation in 1951 when it was still called Haloid. Bardeen worked with Xerox throughout their spectacular development, and later served on the Xerox Board of Directors. He also consulted with General Electric Corporation for many years and with several other technology firms.

John Bardeen was elected to the National Academy of Sciences in 1954 and the National Academy of Engineering in 1972. He served on the U.S. President's Science Advisory Committee from 1959 to 1962 and on the White House Science Council in 1981 and 1982.

Bardeen shared the 1956 Nobel Prize for Physics with W. H. Brattain and W. Shockley for research leading to the invention of the transistor, and he shared the 1972 Nobel Prize with L. N. Cooper and J. R. Schrieffer for the theory of superconductivity. He received the distinguished Lomonosov Award of the Soviet Academy of Sciences in 1987. In 1990, he was named by *Life Magazine* as one of the 100 most influential people of the century.

Other achievements include a hole-in-one in a golf tournament held at the Champaign Country Club. He was an active member of the Unitarian Church in Urbana, Illinois.

BÉLA BARTÓK:
COMPOSER (1881-1945)

By Peter Hughes, Editor of the Dictionary of Unitarian Universalist Biography

Béla Bartók, the great Hungarian composer, was one of the most significant musicians of the twentieth century. Owing to his passion for ethnomusicology, his music was invigorated by the themes, modes, and rhythmic patterns of the folk music traditions he studied, which he synthesized with influences from his contemporaries into his own distinctive style.

Bartók grew up in the Austro-Hungarian Empire; his birthplace, Nagyszentmiklós, became part of Romania. A smallpox inoculation gave the infant Béla a rash that persisted until he was five years old. Because of this, he spent his early years in isolation from other children, often listening to his mother playing the piano. Béla showed precocious musical ability and began to compose dances at the age of nine.

At Pozsony, in Slovakia, Bartók studied piano under distinguished teachers and taught himself composition by reading scores. Under the influence of composer Ernö Dohnányi, four years ahead of him in school, teenage Bartók wrote chamber music in the style of Brahms. In 1899, Bartók attended the Academy of Music in Budapest, where he heard a performance of Richard Strauss's *Also Sprach Zarathustra*, which showed him, as he later recalled, "there was a way of composing which seemed to hold the seeds of a new life." Combining his new enthusiasm for Strauss with his youthful Hungarian nationalism, in 1903 Bartók produced his first major work, the symphonic poem, *Kossuth*.

Bartók began a career as a concert pianist, performing in 630 concerts in 22 countries during his life. In 1907 he became a piano instructor at the Budapest Academy. During more than 25 years there, Bartók compiled notable teaching editions of the works of Bach, Mozart, and Beethoven.

In 1904, Bartók overheard Lidi Dósa, a Székely Hungarian woman from Transylvania, sing the song *Piros alma* ("Red Apple"). This encounter was the beginning of Bartók's lifetime fascination with folk music. Bartók went on to study the folk music of Romanians, Slovakians, Serbs, Croatians, Bulgarians, Turks, and North Africans as well as Hungarians. In 1906, while visiting Algeria, Bartók had a vision of how he might begin to order scattered folk tunes of the world. Afterwards, the main task of his life was to collect, analyze, and catalogue major portions of the world's folk music.

Bartók's multi-ethnic interests caused him trouble, especially after World War I. Areas in which Bartók had previously been free to do research were no longer open to him. Moreover, he endured criticism at home for his "unpatriotic" interest

21

in peoples of nations hostile to Hungary.

In 1907, while studying music in Transylvania, Bartók first became acquainted with the Unitarian Church. Bartók had been brought up as a Roman Catholic, but the ethical legalism taught at school drove him away from his early faith. Bartók thought life's meaning was not directed towards immortality or the afterlife, but to have a zest for life, i.e., a keen interest in the living universe." He stated, "If I ever crossed myself, it would signify 'In the name of Nature, Art, and Science.'"

In 1909 Bartók married Márta Ziegler. Their son, Béla Jr., was born in 1910. Bartók declared his conversion to Unitarianism on July 25, 1916, and joined the Unitarian Church in Budapest. Béla Bartók Jr. later wrote that his father joined the Unitarian faith "primarily because he held it to be the freest, most humanistic faith."

Bartók's personal philosophy was stoic and pessimistic. His sense of spiritual isolation translated into music, including *The Wooden Prince*, 1917, and *The Miraculous Mandarin*. His two violin sonatas, 1921 and 1922, and the *Dance Suite*, 1923 helped establish him as an important modern composer. His third and fourth string quartets, from 1927 and 1928, in Bartók's most abstract and concentrated style, are among the works most often cited as masterpieces by music critics. Much of the music for which Bartók is remembered was written in the 1930s, often in response to commissions from abroad.

After divorcing his first wife in 1923, Bartók married a student, Ditta Pásztory. They had a son, Péter, born in 1924. Bartók did not like the fascist régime that governed Hungary during the inter-war period. As the European political situation worsened, Bartók sailed for America with his wife. One attraction of the U.S. for him was the opportunity to study a collection of Serbo-Croatian folk music at Columbia University.

On September 26, 1945, Bartók died in a New York hospital with his wife Ditta and his son Péter each holding one of his hands. A statue of Bartók stands in front of the Second Unitarian Church in Budapest.

WENDELL BERGE:
TRUST BUSTER, WASHINGTON D.C. (1903-1955)

The following eulogy is from the Christian Register, November 1955:

Former Assistant Attorney General and head of the Justice Department's antitrust division, Wendell Berge died in Washington of a heart ailment on September 25. He was chairman of the board of trustees of the All Souls Unitarian Church, Washington, D.C.

The Washington Post in an editorial, said: "The death of Wendell Berge takes from Washington one of its most public-spirited lawyers and a man who made a notable record in antitrust enforcement."

Mr. Berge was a native of Lincoln, Nebraska, and was from an active Democratic family (his father, who had Populist "leanings," was narrowly defeated while running for governor in 1904). He took his undergraduate diploma at the University of Nebraska and his Bachelor of Law from the University of Michigan.

After a brief period of practice in New York City, he went to Washington in 1930 at the invitation of John Lord O'Brian, prominent antitrust lawyer, then head of that division under Herbert Hoover. In 1941, President Roosevelt named Berge Assistant Attorney General, in charge of the criminal division of the Justice Department. In 1947 he returned to private practice in Washington.

Mr. Berge consistently argued that monopoly would ruin free enterprise and that competition must be preserved. He wrote *Cartels: Challenge to a Free World* and *Economic Freedom for the West.*

UNITARIAN NOTE

Why I Believe in Unitarianism: by Wendell Berge, appeared in the Christian Register *in May 1946.*

Unitarianism offers the opportunity for a positive and buoyant faith in the possibilities of man to create a richer, fuller life for himself and his fellows, for this and succeeding generations. It offers a challenge to assure an immortality here on earth for man and his world. The opportunity is for man, and the challenge is to him. Thus religion for the Unitarian is a dynamic force that elevates life to a place of greater dignity. Because it does not require rejection of any demonstrable acts, and indeed invites inquiry and adventure, the Unitarian way of life prevents inner conflicts between religion and the known facts of life.

It seems to me that the spirit of freedom in which Unitarians approach their religion is needed if religion is to survive as any kind of force in the affairs of men. Given such freedom, the church could perform a vital role in leading men's thinking to the ways of peace and well-ordered human relationships. Traditional Christianity certainly has failed to provide the moral leadership men need—to which failure the war and the present confusion are tragic witnesses—but there may yet be time to save ourselves if we can sweep aside the trappings that have encumbered men's minds and spirits, and fare boldly the challenge of the present crisis. The advance of Unitarianism offers hope to those who believe in man's infinite possibilities.

PAUL BLANSHARD & MARY HILLYER BLANSHARD: FIGHTERS FOR SOCIAL JUSTICE (1892-1980 & 1902-1965)

By Henry Hampton, Information Officer, Unitarian Universalist Association, and later TV Producer, "Eyes on the Prize"

The following is abridged from Challenge: For Unitarian Universalist

Leaders, UUA, 1965:

Both Paul and Mary Blanshard have spent most of their lives in the midst of controversy. From the 1920s when they worked as "organizers" in the hazardous early days of unionizing, through their exposing of rackets in New York City and the storm that erupted when Paul Blanshard took the Catholic Church to task for its infringement on the separation of church and state, they have successfully run the difficult course of political, social and religious liberalism.

The granddaughter of Alexander Pope Wilder, president of the Kansas Universalist Convention, and niece of Louis Parkhurst, one of the donators of Star Island, Mary Blanshard had deep roots in the liberal tradition. Born in Brooklyn in 1902, she moved to Kansas at an early age.

Returning to New York in 1920, she became actively involved with the League for Industrial Democracy and was arrested more than once for her efforts with unions. It was during this time she met Paul Blanshard, the Education Director for the League. Mary Blanshard became Executive Director of the Unitarian Fellowship for Social Justice in Washington. Over her lifetime, she was a member of many political and religious groups and peace and civil rights organizations.

Both Mary and Paul Blanshard had definite ideas about what Unitarian Universalists must do to survive and flourish in our age: The issues of war or peace, a solution to the race question, and the separation of church and state, in that order, were the most critical issues facing the world. They thought Unitarian Universalists were especially fitted to defend our basic constitutional guarantee of religious freedom.

The following is by Jeanette Hopkins, Editor and University Publisher:

Paul Blanshard was a person of great courage and daring, whose pen was his principal weapon in his fight for social justice.

Paul and his twin brother, Brand Blanshard, Yale professor of philosophy, were born on April 27, 1892. Their conservative parents died early, their mother in a fire on their farm in Ohio, followed by their Congregationalist minister father. They were raised in poverty by their stern paternal grandmother. The twins graduated from the University of Michigan in 1914, both Phi Beta Kappa, both known for fierce and brilliant debating skills. Paul performed an abortive stint as an ordained Congregational minister, serving at the Maverick Church in East Boston and in Tampa. He studied briefly at Harvard, and then at Union Theological Seminary, but abandoned a ministerial career after only two years. In mid-life he became a

Unitarian and joined All Souls Unitarian Church in Washington, D.C.

Restless for a more public and more secular arena than the ministry, Blanshard became a labor organizer for the Amalgamated Textile Workers Union; led a strike in Utica, New York; spent 30 days in jail for contempt of an anti-picketing injunction; founded the Rochester Labor College; wrote his first book, *An Outline of the British Labour Movement* (1923); then became field director for the League for Industrial Democracy. He toured Soviet Russia and China, and worked on and off for *The Nation*. After supporting Norman Thomas's bid for the presidency, he became executive director of New York City's Affairs Committee, which helped oust Mayor Jimmy Walker, and wrote (with Norman Thomas) *What's the Matter with New York* (1932). In 1937, he became Commissioner of Investigations and Accounts for Fiorello LaGuardia, responsible for the political demise of many Tammany officials. After night-time study at Brooklyn Law School and a 1937 LL.B., he practiced law in New York with Arthur Garfield Hays' firm, and, in the Second World War, served with the State Department as an advisor on Caribbean Affairs. Blanshard "retired" at 53 to begin what became two decades of research and writing on the Catholic hierarchy and ecclesiastical power.

His next, and most noted book, *American Freedom and Catholic Power,* was turned down by ten publishers before the Unitarians' Beacon Press took it on. The book was published in 1949, its thorough research never overturned despite rigorous public onslaughts led by the church. Eleanor Roosevelt, John Dewey, and Albert Einstein praised the book, but it was banned from New York schools. Although most media refused to advertise it, the book became a bestseller.

His next book, *Communism, Democracy, and Catholic Power* (1951), was also a bestseller. Blanshard published 15 books in total, including *The Right to Read* (1955), *God and Man in Washington* (1960), and *Personal and Controversial* (1973), an autobiography.

JOHN NICHOLLS BOOTH:
FROM MAGICIAN TO MINISTER (1912-)

By John Nicholls Booth

Much against my wishes or control, when I decided to enter the Meadville Theological School in Chicago in 1940, an account of it filled newspapers from coast to coast. Why? At the age of 27, I was surrendering the occupation of a prominent, skilled professional magician for the probable relative oblivion and uncertain remuneration of the ministry. This was considered news!

I am the eldest son of two English-born parents, Sydney Scott Booth and Margaret Nicholls Booth. My father was studying for the Unitarian ministry when I came into this world. In 1928, our family, increased by the arrival of two brothers, moved permanently from the United States to Hamilton, Ontario. My mother and I, during my high school and McMaster University years, would trudge six miles roundtrip through snow, rain and starry nights to evening services in the Unitarian Church, a large, empty Victorian-style home. Always active in the youth club, I eventually was named continental vice president of the Young Peoples' Religious Union.

After graduating from McMaster in 1934, during this nation's worst depression, I decided to make my hobby the art of conjuring. After 17 months with a one-hour, high-school assembly program, I developed a 10-minute largely sleight of hand act for nightclubs and hotel room shows. Fortunately, I climbed rapidly and played many of the finest hotels and nightclubs in this country and Canada. I wrote two books for the profession—*Forging Ahead in Magic* and *Marvels of Mystery*—both of which became classics.

Through all those years, a vision of becoming a minister haunted me. Finally, in 1940, I enrolled in the Meadville Theological School, the seminary of my father 30 years earlier. In just over two years, I completed my studies and my thesis, *The Quest for Preaching Power*, which was published by the Macmillan Company. Much to my astonishment and that of my homiletics professor, it became a first alternate choice of the Religious Book Club.

I was to remain happily settled in Unitarian Universalist churches for the next 33 years. During my conjuring career, I had met my wife of 41 years, Edith Kriger, on the steamship *Nieuw Amsterdam*. She was a passenger and I was booked professionally as a performer.

My first pastorate was in Evanston, a Chicago suburb. Pamphlets explaining Unitarianism were, I felt, inadequate for inquiring outsiders. So I sat at my typewriter and wrote one titled, *Introducing Unitarianism*. Denominational headquarters accepted it, and I was told the 39-page work became the most requested pamphlet up to then in Unitarian history. For many months in the mid-forties, I rode the "elevated" train into Chicago's Loop to present over WBKB the first series of talks on television by a clergyman in the USA.

During our first two years in Evanston, we were living above a store and wondering how we could supplement my meager minister's salary. Edith suggested I should try to secure a limited number of dates on the national celebrity lecture platform. After a rocky start, I finally became a major speaker, limiting myself to 35 dates a year, across the country.

Unitarians were often considered outside the pale by many traditional laypersons and clergy, so it was a cause for some eyebrow-raising when I was the first Unitarian made president of the interfaith Evanston Ministerial Association. Two ministers, a Lutheran and a high Anglican, resigned over this. After a six-year pastorate, I resigned my church position out of sheer fatigue.

In 1948-49, I was designated Asiatic Correspondent for the *Chicago Sun-Times* and represented the *Christian Register* on a trip around the world. I interviewed and photographed the prime ministers of Japan, China, Thailand and India, the governors of Hong Kong and Singapore, and the president and three former presidents of the Philippines.

An unforgettable experience was finally receiving permission to trek into then-forbidden Tibet. With five Sherpa porters, I crossed the border from Sikkim into Tibet, allegedly the ninth American in history allowed to do so. My kodachrome slides of the difficult journey not only constituted the first travelogue in color on TV (NBC), but also became the initial basis of a future part-time career as a cinematographer while still a busy clergyman.

I embarked upon my second parish ministry in Belmont, Massachusetts. At the same time I wrote my next book, *Fabulous Destinations*, describing the events of that wonderfully tumultuous year mainly in the Far East. Published by the Macmillan Company, it became a Travel Book of the Month Club #1 selection.

With the blessings of the Boards of successive churches, I was able to shoot, lecture nationally, and have exhibited on television, my eight documentary-type feature films, one produced roughly every three years during vacation and/or sabbatical time. These projects (1954-1975) took me to Africa, India, the South Seas, South America, Britain and Spain, as well as the USA.

One picture, *East from the Khyber Pass*, was projected on television worldwide. Another, *Morocco*, caused the pleased King to decorate me with the Order of Ouissam Alaouite Cherifien.

In 1967, my portrait was hung in the prestigious Cinematographers' Wall of Fame.

Terminating my Belmont pastorate after eight quiet, pleasant years, I spent 17 months in Asia making two films: *Golden Kingdoms of the Orient* (India, Kashmir and Nepal) and *Indonesia: Pacific Shangri La* (Java, Bali, Sumatra and Borneo).

My fourth and last full-time settled ministry—seven years—was in Long Beach, California. Within a short time I was defending the city librarian before the city council against a group determined to eliminate classic or liberal books it did not like from the library system. I led the largest civil rights march in Long Beach history.

Retired now at the age of 88, I can look back upon four basic careers that produced 17 published books and hundreds of magazine and newspaper articles, and I tried as a magician, cinematographer, lecturer, and Unitarian clergyman to bring people together in a more just, enjoyable, and harmonious society.

CHESTER BLISS BOWLES: GOVERNOR & DIPLOMAT (1901-1986)

By Edric Lescouflair, Harvard College '03

Chester Bowles was born in Springfield, Massachusetts, on April 5, 1901. He and his parents were active in the Springfield Unitarian Church. His grandfather, Samuel Bowles, was editor of the *Springfield Republican*, in which he voiced support for liberal causes.

Bowles attended Choate School in Wallingford, Connecticut, and later the Sheffield Scientific School at Yale, from which he received his B.S. in 1924. He would often voice his regret that he had not pursued a liberal education.

Because of ideological differences with his cousin, who published the family newspaper, he took a job as a copywriter at a New York advertising agency, the George Batton Company. Bowles's creativity and ease in interacting with the media quickly impressed Batton. In 1929, he started a similar agency with William Benton, also a Yale graduate. Despite the Great Depression, the business flourished and was a multimillion-dollar corporation by the mid-1930s.

Monetary success alone did not satisfy Bowles; he truly felt the need to change the world for the better on a large scale. He used his influence to convince mega-corporations, such as Proctor & Gamble and Maxwell House, to slash prices while improving product quality. Although his salary was $250,000 by 1941, he was searching for another job.

He was offered the position of director of the Office of Price Administration in Connecticut, and accepted. His ambition, however, required a greater role in public service. The opportunity for national service occurred when President Franklin D. Roosevelt appointed him general manager of the Federal Price Administration in 1943. Although the task would not be easy, Bowles realized that he could ameliorate the lives of Americans all across the nation; he oversaw 70,000 employees and 500,000 volunteers.

The Truman years began with Bowles as the director of the Office of Economic Stability in 1946. In that same year, he wrote his first book, *Tomorrow Without Fear*, in which he claimed that Americans had "so to plan our lives, so to use our great productive power for the benefit of all of us, that we and all the world's people shall move steadily toward that tomorrow ... for which all mankind yearns."

Connecticut would be his adopted home state, and he entered the gubernatorial race in 1946, but lost, only to run again in 1948. The second time around he defeated Republican James C. Shannon.

During his time as a politician Bowles was also heavily involved with the United Nations. His service reached an international scale when he was appointed as a delegate to the United Nations Educational, Scientific, and Cultural Organization in Paris. Unlike many other leaders, Bowles knew the importance of being in contact with those whom he was trying to help. He worked for the UN Appeal for Children in Europe and traveled across the continent documenting the conditions of his day. The UN work caused him to identify a new mission: to convince Americans that the only way for the U.S. to remain prosperous was to spread prosperity and democracy around the world. The first case study for Bowles of the lack of prosperity in a massive democracy was that of India, the nation to which he was named ambassador in 1951.

Bowles's stay in India was unique because he refused to separate himself from the people and took pains to live among them. He went as far as to ride a bicycle to work every day, and to send his children to public school in India.

In 1953 Bowles resigned to write a book about the liberal democratic beliefs that so influenced his public service, such as equality of races and the need to uplift the disadvantaged. He also served in the House of Representatives from Connecticut's second district.

The Kennedy administration did not accept Bowles as readily as previous administrations, primarily because he was willing to speak out on what he considered to be abuses of power. He was appointed U. S. Undersecretary of State, but was relieved of that post in 1963, at which point he again became the United States Ambassador to India. In 1963, he wrote *The Makings of a Just Society*, in which he concentrated on ways to empower less developed nations such as China, India, and African and Latin American states.

After suffering a stroke, Chester Bliss Bowles passed away in 1986. Although he was never an active adult member of a Unitarian congregation, his liberal religious practice of faith in action was decisive. Chester Bowles practiced a truly global human faith dedicated to strengthening international prosperity and unity in the world.

RAY BRADBURY:
WRITER (1920-)

Abridged from the 2000 National Book Foundation Medal Award Presentation

Steve Martin, Master of Ceremonies:
Each year the Board of Directors of the National Book Foundation confers a special award upon an individual who has enriched our literary culture through a life of service or a corpus of work. The National Book Foundation Medal for Distinguished Contribution to American Letters will be presented tonight to Ray Bradbury.

Novelist, short story writer, essayist, playwright, screenwriter, and poet, Ray Bradbury was born in Waukegan, Illinois, 80 years ago. He grew up in Illinois and Arizona, and his family moved to Los Angeles in 1934, where Mr. Bradbury has lived ever since.

He married Marguerite McClure in 1947. They have four daughters: Tina, Ramona, Susan, and Alexandra. Ray Bradbury's first published story appeared when the author was 18 years old.

Since that time, how can we even begin to count all of the ways in which Ray Bradbury has etched his indelible impressions upon the American literary landscape? There are few modern authors who can claim such a wide and varied province for their

work, spanning from the secret inner-worlds of childhood dreams, to the magic realism of everyday life, to the infinite expanses of outer space.

Half a century ago, *The Martian Chronicles* was published, and soon thereafter, *Fahrenheit 451* (by the way, in Europe that would be "*Centigrade 283*"), the quintessential book lovers' book written in nine days; and then *Dandelion Wine, I Sing the Body Electric, The Illustrated Man, The October Country, Something Wicked This Way Comes*. (By the way, the original title was *Look Out, Here Comes Something Wicked*.) Ray Bradbury's prodigious and seemingly never-sleeping imagination continues to delight us.

Response by Ray Bradbury:

Thank you. Thank you. Thank you. Thank you very much. Well, here I am. I have one good eye, one good ear, one good leg, and there are other things missing, but I'm afraid to look.

The library's been the center of my life. I never made it to college. I started going to the library when I graduated from high school. I went to the library every day for three or four days a week for 10 years, and I graduated from the library when I was 28.

When it comes to a novel like *Fahrenheit 451*, I don't know how many of you know, but I wrote it in the library, the basement at UCLA. This is 50 years ago. I had no money to rent a proper office. I had a large family at home, and I needed to have a place where I could go for a few hours. I was wandering around the UCLA campus, and I looked down below, and I listened, and down in the basement I heard this typing. So I went down in the basement of the UCLA library, and by God, there was a room with 12 typewriters in it that you could rent for 10 cents a half-hour. And there were eight or nine students in there working away like crazy, so I moved in there one day with a bag of dimes, and I began inserting dimes into the machine and the machine released the typewriter, and you'd have half an hour of fast typing.

Can you imagine what it was like to write *Fahrenheit 451* in the library, where you could run upstairs and feel the ambience of your beloved writers; and you could take books off the shelf and discover things that you might want to put in your book as a quote and then run back down and finish writing another page. So over a period of nine days I spent $9.80, and I wrote *Fahrenheit 451*.

A young editor came along who was starting a new magazine and needed material. He said, "I have very little money. I've got $400. Is there something you could sell me for $400?" I said, "Yes, I have this novel, and I'd like to have it published in the magazine before it comes out in book form," and he said, "I will take it." So I sold *Fahrenheit 451*, and it appeared in the second, third, and fourth issues of *Playboy*.

But a wonderful thing happened concerning one of my first books. Back in 1949 my wife was pregnant, and we had absolutely no money in the bank. Our friend Norman Corwin, the great radio writer, producer, director, a dear friend, said to me, "Ray, why don't you come to New York and let the editors see your face and maybe you'll sell something there."

So I got on the Greyhound bus, four days, four nights to New York. Have you ever done that on the Greyhound bus? Don't. Don't. Those were the days before air conditioning and toilets. I arrived at the YMCA, the Sloan House, moved in there for $5 a week and proceeded to show my short stories to editors all around New York City, but nobody wanted my short stories. They said, "Don't you have a novel?" I said, "No I'm a sprinter."

But finally I had dinner my last night in New York with Don Congdon and Walter Bradbury, no relation of mine. Walter Bradbury at Doubleday. And sitting at dinner that night he said to me, "Ray, what about all those Martian stories you've been writing in the pulp magazines during the last 10 years? Don't you think they would make a novel if you wove them together in some sort of tapestry and called it *The Martian Chronicles*?" I said, "Oh my God." He said, "What do you mean?" I said, "I read *Winesburg, Ohio* by Sherwood Anderson when I was 24, and I said to myself, 'Oh God, wouldn't it be wonderful if someday I could write a book as good as this but put it on the planet Mars.'"

I made an outline, I named some characters, but I forgot all about it, and suddenly here was Walter Bradbury suggesting to me a possible novel I'd written without knowing it. So he said, "Do an outline. Come tomorrow to the Doubleday offices, and if I read your outline and like it, I'll give you $750."

I stayed up all night at the Y. I wrote the outline. I took it to him the next day, and he said, "Yes, this is it. Here's $750." He said, "Now do you have any other material that you could give me that we could kid people into thinking it was a novel?" And I said, "Yes, I have a short story about a man with tattoos all over his body, and at night when he dreams he perspires and the tattoos on his body come to life and tell their stories." And he said, "Here's another $750."

So in one day I sold *The Martian Chronicles* and *The Illustrated Man* for $1,500. I was rich. And that's, you know, 53 years ago, and money went a long way then. It paid for our rent for the next two years. Our rent was only $30 a month. It paid for our baby. Babies were cheap back then. It cost $100 for our baby. And it was a down payment on a little tract house when we moved inland further. The book came out, and there were very, very few reviews. In fact, only one. I was in a bookstore. I bumped into Christopher Isherwood. I did not know him. I grabbed a copy of my book; I signed it and gave it to him. I thought, Oh Christ, you know, I know he's thinking, One more book to read. Oh God.

But three days later Christopher Isherwood called me and said, "Do you know what you've done?" I said, "No, what have I done?" He said, "You've written a remarkable book, and I'm going to be the book editor and writer for *Tomorrow Magazine* next October, and this will be my first review." So he did a three-page review of *The Martian Chronicles*, which introduced me to the intellectual world and saved my soul.

So that was the only review. But he introduced me to Gerald Heard and finally my hero, Aldous Huxley, at tea one day. I hate tea. My God, I hate tea. And you have to pretend to like tea when you're sitting with Aldous Huxley. And Mr. Huxley leaned forward during tea, and he said, "Do you know what you are?" And I said, "No, what am I, Mr. Huxley?" He said, "You're published. You're a poet." I said, "Is that what I am? Is that what I am." Aldous Huxley was telling me that I was a poet, and I had yet to write one decent poem. I was working at it but it didn't come right, so I put all my poetry into my books.

So through Isherwood, I met a lot of wonderful people, and over the years slowly, slowly, slowly, *The Martian Chronicles* came into being. I wrote a whole series of essays and short stories and one day woke up and saw that I'd written a novel, and that's still around.

Along the way people said to me, "Ray, when are you going to do a screenplay?" Because I love motion pictures. I've seen just about every one ever made. A lot of the bad ones and a lot of the wonderful ones over and over again. I said, "Yes, there's one man I'd love to work for, that's John Huston," and I knew that I wanted to work for him. Well, I gave John all of my books of short stories one day in 1951, and he wrote back from Africa where he was making *The African Queen*, and he said, "Yes, I agree with you, someday we'll work together. I don't know on what."

The day finally came. I came home from a bookstore one day, and my wife said, "John Huston just called. He wants you to come to his hotel." I went to John Huston's hotel. I walked into his room. He put a drink in my hand. He sat me down, and he leaned over, and he said, "Ray, what are you doing during the next year?"

I said, "Not much, Mr. Huston. Not much." And he said, "Well, Ray, how would you like to come live in Ireland and write this screenplay of *Moby Dick*?" And I said, "Gee, Mr. Huston, I've never been able to read the damn thing."

He'd never heard that before, and he thought for a moment, and then he said, "Well, I'll tell you what Ray. Why don't you go tonight, read as much as you can, and come back tomorrow and then tell me if you'll help me kill a white whale."

So I went home that night, and I said to my wife, "Pray for me." She said, "Why?" I said, "Because I've got to read a book tonight and do a book report tomorrow."

Luckily I was at the right age to read the book. I was 33 years old. I'd tried when I was younger. It just didn't work. But what I saw there is a part of myself, the gift of metaphor.

All the early writers in America—Melville and Poe and many of the others—wrote in metaphorical style. You could remember their stories. I raced through the book. I didn't read it. I looked at all the metaphors, and I came back the next day, and I said, "Yes, I'll do it."

I went to live in Ireland for the better part of a year, and it was hellish work. Terrible work, because I read some sections of the novel over 100 times. Some sections 200 times. Some sections 300 times. Other sections not at all, because you're looking for the metaphor. You're finding a way to combine things and put them together.

And finally, after seven months of hard work, a day of great passionate relaxation came to me. I got out of bed one morning in London, and I looked in the mirror, and I said, "I am Herman Melville." I sat down at the typewriter, and in eight blazing hours, I wrote the last 40 pages of the screenplay, and it all came out right; for that one day, for a few hours, the ghost of Melville was really in me.

Was really in me.

I ran across London, and I threw the screenplay into John Huston's lap, and I said, "There, I think it's finished." And he read it, and he said, "By God, start the cameras."

Now it's time to wind this up and to show my appreciation for this magnificent Medal. My moment with Herman Melville in many ways is equal to what has occurred to me in my lifetime. I've researched my life. I've looked into myself. I've tried to find me. Along the way I've located myself.

Text abridged from http://raybradbury.com/awards_acceptance.html.

UNITARIAN NOTE

Ray Bradbury is a self-confessed Unitarian Univesralist.

RALPH WENDELL BURHOE:
RELIGION IN AN AGE OF SCIENCE (1911-1997)

By Philip Hefner

Ralph Wendell Burhoe was a twentieth-century pioneer who interpreted the importance of religion for a scientific and technological world. While Burhoe followed an unconventional academic path, beset by Depression-era economic difficulties that prevented him from attaining any earned degrees, his intellectual and organizational achievements were recognized in 1980 when he was awarded the Templeton Prize for Progress in Religion. In a ceremony in London, at Buckingham Palace, the founder of the prize, noted financier Sir John Marks Templeton, said of Burhoe, "He is not only a scientist and a theologian; he is a missionary for a new reformation, a reformation which may be far more profound and revolutionary than the reformation led by Martin Luther.

Born in Somerville, Massachusetts, on June 21, 1911, Burhoe attended Harvard from 1928 to 1932, but dropped out before he could complete his degree. In 1935-36, he spent eighteen months in theological study at Andover Newton seminary. Shortly after he was married in 1932 to Frances Bickford, they retreated to a log cabin on the side of Mount Washington to "meditate upon their situation." His search in these years, as during his long lifetime, was to find "ontological and rational supports for the sacred meaning of his life." Those supports were eroded, Burhoe believed, for himself and for many persons, by the alienation that separated the traditions of meaning and value carried by humanity's religions from the knowledge attained by science and applied in technology.

After he left formal studies in 1936, Burhoe became assistant to the director of Harvard's Blue Hill meteorological observatory, a position he held until 1946. He was active in the American Meteoreological Society and founded the journal *Metereological Abstracts*. From 1947 to 1964, Burhoe served as the first executive officer of the American Academy of Arts and Sciences. This position brought him into contact with the finest scientists of the time. He was instrumental in establishing the Academy's journal, *Daedalus*, and its Committee on Science and Values.

Convinced that science did not threaten the wisdom of traditional religion, but rather reinforced it, Burhoe developed an extensive theoretical framework to explain how religion emerged within the evolutionary process. His system of thought included the concept of God as demonstrated through the processes of natural selection, which, however, did not depend entirely on brutal competition. In fact, he saw trans-kin altruism, or love, as the central factor that enabled human culture to survive.

The nub of his theories was the recognition that in the brain, genetic evolution converged with culture and its evolution. Culture carries the information that transforms the "ape-man" into a genuine human being. And it is the religious traditions that have carried core information about how humans can live together and thereby reach their full evolutionary potential. Burhoe believed that religion was humanity's best hope for achieving peace.

In their totality Burhoe's theories presented a comprehensive explanation of how traditional religion could be translated into serious scientific theories. Although this explanation was never recognized as the scientific advance that Burhoe envisioned, it was warmly received by some of the leading scientists who knew Burhoe, and it attracted many of them to his work and to conversation with religious thinkers.

A number of these scientists, including those who were members of the Academy Committee on Science and Values, were responsible for that committee's becoming, in 1956, the nucleus of the Institute on Religion in an Age of Science. This Institute was the first of a number of enterprises founded by Burhoe. These include *Zygon: Journal of Religion and Science*, 1966, which under Burhoe's editorship became a renowned interdisciplinary vehicle. The Center for Advanced Studies in Religion and Science was established in 1972. In 1988, Burhoe founded the Chicago Center for Religion and Science, in cooperation with the Lutheran School of Theology at Chicago. A collection of Burhoe's essays was published in 1980 under the title, *Toward a Scientific Theology*.

The Society for the Scientific Study of Religion, of which he was a founder, bestowed on him its first Distinguished Career Achievement Award in 1984. He was a fellow of the American Association for the Advancement of Science, the American Academy of Arts and Sciences, and the World Academy of Arts and Letters.

UNITARIAN NOTE

Ralph Wendell Burhoe was long active in the life of Unitarianism's historic Arlington Street Church, Boston. When a professor at the Unitarian Universalist Meadville Lombard Theological School from 1964-1974, he was an active member of the First Unitarian Society.

EDWARD C. BURSK:
HARVARD BUSINESS REVIEW EDITOR (1907-1990)

The following biography is reprinted courtesy of the Baker Library, Harvard Graduate School of Business Administration:

Edward Collins Bursk, born in Lancaster, Pennsylvania, in 1907, graduated from Amherst College (A.B. 1928) and Harvard (M.A. 1929) intending to spend a lifetime teaching Latin and Greek. His first teaching position was at Dartmouth College (1931-1933), but the Depression caused him to return to Lancaster to take over as President and General Manager of J. H. Bursk & Company, a family firm which distributed sugar. He returned to teaching in 1941 at Franklin & Marshall College and moved to Harvard Business School in 1942 as an instructor. He was promoted to assistant professor (1943) and associate professor (1946), becoming full professor in 1954.

Bursk joined the *Harvard Business Review* staff in 1943 as managing editor and became editor in 1947, retaining the position until 1971. In addition, he edited and coedited a number of books, including *Getting Things Done in Business* (1953); *The World of Business; How to Increase Executive Effectiveness* (1954); *Human Relations for Management* (1957); *The Management Team* (1955); and *Business and Religion* (1959). In 1964 he appeared as moderator in an eight-part television series jointly sponsored by Harvard and WGBH entitled "Marketing in the News." Bursk was a highly active consultant, speaker, and board member during his career at Harvard Business School. Married and the father of three sons, Bursk lived in Cohasset, Massachusetts, and became professor *emeritus* in 1978.

OBITUARY

When Edward C. Bursk died in 1990, a memorial service was held at the First Parish Unitarian Church in Cohasset, Massachusetts, where he was long active and earlier served as moderator. The following words were published in The Boston Globe:

Edward Collins Bursk, editor of *Harvard Business Review* from 1946 to 1972 and professor emeritus of marketing at the Harvard Business School, died Monday at his home in Cohasset. He was 82.

The monthly publication broadened its coverage during Mr. Bursk's tenure and increased its circulation from 2,000 to 150,000. He retired in 1989 after 47 years as a professor at the school.

A member of the Council of Economic Advisers during the Kennedy administration, Mr. Bursk was an advocate of international competitive cooperation. In 1958, he founded the International Marketing Institute of Boston, which trains foreign businessmen, and became its educational director.

Mr. Bursk wrote *Text and Cases in Marketing; a Scientific Approach* (1968) and *Modern Marketing Strategy* (1972). He was a coeditor of the four-volume *World of Business* (1964), a collection of writings dating to biblical times...

During the 1960s he served as chairman of Browne & Nichols School of Cambridge and as moderator of the "Marketing on the Move" series on WGBH-TV (Channel 2).

Mr. Bursk was a member of the Cohasset Golf Club and the Badminton & Tennis Club of Boston. He and his wife have three sons, Edward C., John H., and Christopher.

HAROLD HITZ BURTON: MAYOR, SENATOR AND SUPREME COURT JUSTICE (1888-1964)

By Thomas Blair, Harvard College '03

Harold Hitz Burton was born into a Unitarian and Republican family in Jamaica Plain, Boston, the son of a civil engineering professor at the Massachusetts Institute of Technology. Young Harold lived with his mother in Switzerland, but she died when he was seven years old. After attending public schools in Boston, Burton matriculated at Bowdoin College, from which he graduated *summa cum laude* in 1909. He was both a member of Phi Beta Kappa and quarterback of the football team. He proceeded directly to Harvard Law School and by 1912 had a law degree, a wife, and two tickets to Cleveland, where he believed it would be easier to establish a law practice than in the East. Burton and his wife, childhood friend Selma Florence Smith, settled happily in Ohio and raised four children.

In 1925 he established his own firm: Cull, Burton & Laughlin. Burton decided to run for mayor of Cleveland. He won, was twice reelected, and remained mayor until his 1940 election to the U.S. Senate. As mayor, Burton gained a reputation for returning economic well-being to Cleveland's citizens by combating organized crime and developing employment programs. In the Senate, Burton became known as generally liberal in international affairs and conservative in domestic ones. He served as moderator of the American Unitarian Association, representative of all Unitarian parishes in the United States and Canada.

The highlight of Burton's political career came in 1945, when the retirement of Justice Owen Roberts left an open seat in the United States Supreme Court. For Truman, Burton proved an ideal choice: a moderate Republican with whom Truman had served on a Senate special committee. The Senate unanimously approved Burton's appointment in under 24 hours.

As a justice, Burton gained a strong reputation for his hardy work ethic and humble adherence to his legal ideals. He was known for working eighty or ninety hours each week, eating at his desk and leaving his judicial chambers for little more than requisite social functions. He tended to vote in favor of government control of social matters and against government control of economic ones. Notably, he tended to advocate racial integration and to oppose the aggrandizement of union power and antitrust legislation. His particular opinions, however, varied from case to case.

Brown v. Board of Education was, perhaps, the most significant case tried by the Court during Burton's tenure. In this famous case, the nine justices unanimously decided against the constitutionality of racial segregation in public schools.

Diagnosed with Parkinson's disease in 1957, Burton retired from the Court the following year. Burton then served for four years in the D.C. Circuit Court until his death. By all accounts, Justice Burton was deeply admired as a public servant.

UNITARIAN NOTE

I believe in advancing religious liberalism because I believe that God is at the foundation of life, and the truest possible understanding of God is the best road to peace and progress on earth. I regard religious liberalism as but another name for search for the truth in the field of religion wherever that truth may be found.

My religious faith rests upon two great Commandments—"Thou shalt love thy God with all thy heart, and with all thy soul, and with all thy mind" and "Thou shalt love thy neighbor as thyself." The Golden Rule translates these into action. It is our first duty to put that faith to daily practice among ourselves and with all nations.

From "Why I Believe in Advancing Unitarianism" by Harold Hitz Burton, The Christian Register, 1946

HUGH CABOT:
SURGEON & MEDICAL REFORMER (1872-1945)

Beginning in his youth, Hugh Cabot's varied interests included music, activities in the Unitarian Church, and outdoor endeavors. The following celebration of his life, (published in Urology *50.4, 1997), is an abridged form of an article written by four of his colleagues: W. Scott McDougal, David Bloom, Harry Spence, and Gretchen Uznis.*

The Early Years—Childhood, Education, and Professional Training

Hugh Cabot and his identical twin brother Philip were born in 1872 in Beverly Farms, Massachusetts. They grew up with five older brothers in a household in which structure and discipline were not strictly enforced. Hugh's father, James Elliot Cabot, was a close friend of the great American philosopher Ralph Waldo Emerson. Perhaps influenced by Emerson, Hugh developed an inclination to speak pungently and bluntly no matter what the consequence.

In addition to his earthy self-expression, Cabot acquired leadership qualities and a spirit of independence during his early years. His interest in the out-of-doors was kindled by his father, an excellent naturalist.

Cabot was educated at the Boston Latin School and Harvard College. Elected to Phi Beta Kappa and Sigma Xi, he graduated in 1894. He went on to Harvard Medical School, graduating Alpha Omega Alpha and cum laude in 1898. He was appointed to the surgical service at the Massachusetts General Hospital (MGH) as a "House Pupil."

Practice in Boston and Wartime Experiences

On completion of formal training, Hugh entered surgical practice with his older cousin, Arthur Tracy Cabot. In 1902 Hugh married Mary Anderson Boit, and they had four children. A paper Cabot published in the *Boston Journal* in 1904, "The Interrelation of Medicine and Surgery in the Treatment of Gastric Ulcer," gave an early glimpse of his larger-than-average view of medicine, which extended across the artificial boundaries of specialties. Except for 1919, Cabot never again missed a year of publication in his career.

During his years of practice at the MGH, Hugh Cabot recognized the need for separating genitourinary surgery from general surgery. In 1910 the trustees at the MGH voted to establish a genitourinary outpatient service, with Cabot, at 38 years of age, as surgeon in charge. Cabot rose to the rank of Clinical Professor of Genito-Urinary Surgery at Harvard Medical School.

By the second decade of the 20th century, Cabot had developed a substantial reputation as a surgeon and educator. He began to compile his clinical experience for his book, *Modern Urology*, first published in 1918.

In 1916 the global conflict that was to become World War I was well underway. Cabot organized the Harvard Medical Unit before the United States entered the war, becoming honorary lieutenant colonel in the Royal Army Medical Corps (1916-1919) and commanding officer of the No. 22 General Hospital of the British Expeditionary Forces (1917- 1919). When the war ended, Hugh returned to the MGH, but in 1919, at 47, Cabot left Boston to become professor and director of surgery at the University of Michigan.

The Ann Arbor Years

In 1921, the university regents turned to Cabot as the next dean of the medical school. Cabot's organizational ability, innovative ideas, and love of teaching were given full expression in Ann Arbor. He oversaw the building of a modern university teaching hospital and assembled a faculty of outstanding specialists in the various medical and surgical fields.

Cabot's ideas regarding the organization and purpose of the new university hospital eventually caused him difficulty. Private practitioners were threatened by his economic concepts, and in September 1928, a committee recommended that university regents abandon the "full-time" concept at the hospital and prohibit the admission of private patients to the university hospital. Cabot remained adamant in his demand that physicians devote full time to the practice of medicine and the facility be open to all patients from the state. The regents forced Cabot's resignation in 1930.

The Mayo Clinic and Retirement

Cabot's good friend William Mayo encouraged him to come to the Mayo Clinic. Cabot arrived in June of 1930 as professor of surgery and head of a surgical section. In Rochester, Cabot was a respected clinician at a clinic that operated in accord with his paradigm of medical economics. The 1937 edition of *Physicians of the Mayo Foundation* listed 158 items in Cabot's bibliography.

In 1936, his wife, Mary, died. In October 1938 he married Elizabeth Cole Amory, a vivacious widow 30 years his junior. That same month found him in Washington, DC, testifying for the government against the American Medical Association and the District of Columbia Medical Society in their actions in restraint of trade against a cooperative known as the Group Health Association of Washington.

Hugh Cabot remained at the Mayo Clinic until 1939, when he retired and returned to Boston. He resumed private practice but mainly immersed himself in medical reforms and public affairs. In 1940 he published, *The Patient's Dilemma: The Quest for Medical Security in America*. Cabot continued to advocate group practice of medicine and budgeted prepayment systems to alter the fee system of private medical practice that he condemned as antiquated. He also became chairman of the Massachusetts State Committee for Russian Relief and supported the newly formed American Euthanasia Society.

Hugh Cabot died of a heart attack in August of 1945 at the age of 74. After his death, friends raised money to establish a penicillin plant in Russia in his memory.

A key figure in the formative years of the 20th century specialty of urology, Hugh Cabot was also a visionary in medical education, medical practice, medical economics, and sex education.

IDA M. CANNON:
FOUNDER OF MEDICAL SOCIAL WORK (1877-1960)

By Heather Miller, writer and editor

Ida Cannon was responsible for establishing the first social work department in a hospital in the United States. Convinced that medical practice could not be effective without examining the link between illness and the social conditions of the patient, Cannon diligently worked at creating the field of medical social work. During her long career, she worked as a nurse, a student of sociology, a medical social worker, Chair of Social Services at Massachusetts General Hospital, she was the author of a seminal book in the medical social work field, consultant to hospitals and city administrations throughout the United States, and professor and designer of a training curriculum for medical social workers. Cannon saw the emergence of medical social work as part of the Progressive movement, because it sought to humanize medical practice.

She was born in Milwaukee, the third of four children. She completed her nursing education at the City and County Hospital in St. Paul. After working as a nurse for two years, she began studies in sociology at the University of Minnesota. It was there that Cannon heard a lecture given by Jane Addams about the living conditions of the poor that would change her life. Her three subsequent years as a visiting nurse for the St. Paul Associated Charities deepened her understanding of the connections between poverty, occupation and disease.

Realizing the need for an education in social work to add to her training and experience as a nurse, Cannon enrolled in the Boston (Simmons) School of Social Work. It was through her brother, Walter, that Cannon met Richard Clark Cabot, who was developing a program in hospital social services at Massachusetts General Hospital. This was to be the first organized social work department in a hospital in United States history.

Ida Cannon began in the social services department as a volunteer and soon became the department's head worker. With Cabot, Cannon systematically studied patients presenting industrial diseases in Massachusetts General Hospital. In 1915, Cannon was made chief of the Social Service Department, a position she would hold for thirty years until she retired in 1945. The outstanding success of the social service department brought about its integration into the inpatient services of Massachusetts General Hospital.

Ida Cannon's work at Massachusetts General Hospital constituted only a fraction of her professional commitments. Determined that medical social work departments exist in every hospital, Cannon traveled around the country giving speeches and meeting hospital directors and staff. In order to professionalize medical social work, she developed a specialized training program that combined medical and social work expertise. She advised institutions and hospitals around the country on how to create their own medical social work departments.

Cannon authored the seminal text of the medical social work field, *Social Work in Hospitals: A Contribution to Progressive Medicine*. She helped to establish the American Association of Hospital Social Workers and served as president from 1920 to 1922. Cannon represented her profession as a delegate to the White House Conference on Child Health and Protection in 1930 and 1931.

In recognition for her labors in successfully building the medical social work field, she was awarded an honorary Doctor of Science degree from Boston University and an honorary Doctor of Humanities degree from the University of New Hampshire.

Ida Cannon lived until the age of 80 when a stroke made it necessary for her to be cared for in a nursing home in Watertown, Massachusetts. She died there three years later. She was remembered by friends and loved ones for her extraordinary warmth and generosity of spirit.

WALTER BRADFORD CANNON: EXPERIMENTAL PHYSIOLOGIST (1871-1945)

By Eric Lescouflair, Harvard College '03

Walter Bradford Cannon was born in Prairie du Chien, Wisconsin, on October 19, 1871. From his early years, he exhibited acumen in the biological sciences. As a youngster, he read about the debates between traditionalists and Darwinists, especially those involving William Wilberforce, bishop of Oxford, and Thomas Huxley. During his high-school years the perceived conflict between science and religion so affected him that he eventually announced that he no longer believed in the ideals of the Calvinist church, the faith of his family.

At this difficult time in his young life, Cannon found friendship in the person of Samuel McChord Crothers, a Unitarian minister who had had a similar experience and who advocated the "freedom of the human soul." He would subsequently adhere to the Unitarian faith. Cannon's interest in science and liberal religion only increased as he immersed himself in the writings of Charles Darwin, James Martineau, and James Freeman Clarke.

Cannon entered Harvard College in 1892. Because of his interest in the biological sciences, he decided to pursue a preparatory course for medical school. By 1896, Cannon had been accepted at Harvard Medical School. He started working in the lab of Henry Pickering Bowditch during his first year and investigated swallowing and stomach motility using the X-ray technique. The results of his research were published in the first *American Journal of Physiology* in 1898. In 1900 Cannon received his medical degree, joined the American Physiological Society, and became an instructor in the Department of Physiology at the Harvard Medical School.

Cannon married a longtime friend, Cornelia James, on June 25, 1901. In 1902 Cannon became an assistant professor of physiology, and upon Bowditch's retirement, Cannon took on the roles of George Higginson Professor of Physiology and chair of the department, a position he would hold until 1942.

Cannon's research became more involved at the beginning of the 20th century, particularly at the outset of World War I. From 1914 to 1916, he served as president of the American Physiological Society and concentrated on traumatic shock, a major issue for soldiers, writing *Bodily Changes in Pain, Hunger, Fear, and Rage* in 1915. In 1923 his *Traumatic Shock* postulated that traumatic shock was caused by blood being drained into the dilated capillary region, a phenomenon for which he coined the term exemia. The treatment of shock, he argued, should concentrate on reinstating normal circulation. Also well documented is his research on the sympathetic nervous system and neurochemical transmission of nerve impulses. He also discovered the adrenalin-like hormone, sympathin.

Cannon exhibited his unusual integrity in accepting an invitation to address the International Physiological Congress in Leningrad in 1935. He stated, "During the last few years how profoundly and unexpectedly the world has changed. Nationalism has become violently intensified until it is tainted with bitter feeling. The worldwide economic depression has greatly reduced the material support for scholarly efforts. What is the social value of the physiologist or biochemist?" He went on to decry the recent university closings and general lack of attention to proper education. In 1943, he defied Soviet-American tension by receiving the presidency of the American Soviet Medical Society in 1943.

Those close to Cannon knew of his humanitarian nature. Among the causes he espoused were the Loyalist struggle in Spain and aid to the Chinese. As a Unitarian, he felt that it was his duty to speak and act against what he identified as injustice. When he died on October 19, 1945, Dr. S. B. Wolbach, a pathology professor, offered in tribute that Cannon was "competent in the highest degree to appraise character and achievement, praise often came from him, condemnation rarely—and was never expressed at large. His geniality, quick wit, and delightful sense of humor enlivened any group he chanced to join and made him the best of companions on all occasions."

PAUL N. CARNES:
UNITARIAN UNIVERSALIST PRESIDENT (1921-1979)

Paul Carnes was a native of Indiana. He graduated with honors from Indiana University and was a member of Phi Beta Kappa. Following his graduation from college, he served as a platoon leader in the First Infantry Division during World War II. He was captured by the Germans in the early days of the Tunisian campaign—on Christmas Day, 1942—and remained a prisoner of war for 29 months, until his liberation by the Russian Army in 1945.

Upon his discharge from the Army, he enrolled in the Harvard Divinity School, where he received his S.T.B. Degree with honors. After years of serving Unitarian congregations primarily in Youngstown, Ohio; Memphis, Tennessee; and Buffalo, New York, he was elected President of the Unitarian Universalist Association.

REMEMBRANCE AND THANKSGIVING
The First Parish in Cambridge, Massachusetts, March 20, 1979

Recollection

by Dana McLean Greeley, D.D.

Paul was a born minister, and I think that he was a born president. Brief as his occupancy of that office was, it spanned three papal administrations in Rome, and was only eleven months shorter than John Kennedy's residence in the White House. His death is a major tragedy, but the mystique of his personality and his ministry has challenged us and quickened us to renewed vitality. We have had him, even though we have lost him.

He was one of a very small group that pushed me to run for the presidency 21 years ago. And since I first knew him, I have stood in admiration of his strength and his humility, his conviction and his tolerance, his courage and his compassion. He was as thoughtful as he was eloquent, and as patient as he was resolute. He had an inspiring presence, and a commensurate appreciation of the worth and work of others. His dream for us will be a guiding star still, and his commitment to our cause, and his genuine ecumenism as well, will be examples for us as we carry forward the work that, with this whole life, he has begun.

In Appreciation

By Rhys Williams, D.D.

In gathering now to honor the life and spirit of Paul—husband, father, friend, pastor, leader, and exemplar of the good and the true—we are compelled by the strength, intensity, and warmth of his personality to reflect on the power and inspiration of his life on all of us gathered here, and on so many others across this continent and in other lands.

"Here was a man to hold against the world, a man to match the mountains and the sea. The color of the ground was in him, the smack of elemental things." Close was he to earth and sky, and close, too, to the needs of earth's people. This closeness to what matters in human living was reflected in his commitment to social justice, to being on the cutting edge of progressive change when he saw a dangerous drift backward or perceived a vacuum in responsible leadership.

This closeness was witnessed by his concern for the whole person. Thus whether in a prisoner of war camp or in his church or with his colleagues, he moved beyond statistics and expectations in order to talk with an individual in an empathetic, sharing way, while stirring each with hope and promise.

This was shown in his dedication to truth, to upholding the right of free speech, to a directness that knew no sham, to a recognition of our mortality and the democracy of death, to a readiness to deal candidly with people and be candidly dealt with by them. It was indicated by his sense of balance, his ability to see several sides and seek a common, positive solution for all problems, to find the grace of self-forgiveness while expecting much of himself. It was demonstrated by his belief in the "ecstasy of the possible," culminating in knowing that universal love

43

is our greatest good.

But beyond all these was the fullness of his personhood—the great reservoir of his being, his humor that overflowed to bring light to others, his enjoyment of music and singing, his statesmanship and churchmanship, his powerful prophetic preaching, his sense of style and grace.

BROCK CHISHOLM: DIRECTOR-GENERAL, WORLD HEALTH ORGANIZATION (1896-1971)

By Eric Lescouflair, Harvard College '03

George Brock Chisholm, former moderator of the American Unitarian Association, was born on May 18, 1896, in Oakville, Ontario. At the outbreak of the First World War, he joined the Canadian Army, in which he served as a cook, sniper, machine gunner, and scout. Chisholm's leadership skills and cool demeanor under pressure brought him much acclaim, including a Military Cross for heroism at a battle outside of Lens, France.

In 1917, Chisholm returned to Canada a quasi-legend. At this juncture in his life, he decided to pursue medicine, which had been his passion ever since his uncle had given him a toy doctor's set when he was a boy.

Equipped with an M.D. from the University of Toronto, Chisholm specialized in psychiatry during an internship in England. He then went into general practice for six years. Beginning in 1931, he studied at the Yale School of Human Relations, where he concentrated on the mental health of children, concluding that, "Children must be free to think in all directions irrespective of the peculiar ideas of parents who often seal their children's minds with preconceived prejudices and false concepts of past generations. Unless we are very careful, very careful indeed, and very conscientious, there is still great danger that our children may turn out to be the same kind of people we are." Chisholm inevitably earned a reputation as a controversial, unconventional speaker.

Soon thereafter, Chisholm once again involved himself in the affairs of the Canadian military, this time to study the psychological aspects of soldier training in the Second World War. He was named Brigadier Deputy Adjutant-General and rose to become Director General of the Medical Services of the Canadian Army. The Canadian Government, made aware of the importance of wellness by Chisholm's efforts, created the Deputy Minister of Health position in 1944, which he immediately occupied.

In July of 1946, he became the Executive Secretary of the Interim Commission of the World Health Organization, based in Geneva, Switzerland. The WHO became permanent in April of 1948, with Chisholm at the helm. He was now in

a position to redefine the world's definition of health. WHO stressed the idea that health had as much to do with mental wellness as with physical wellness. By extension, Chisholm maintained, the well-being of humanity depended on the emotional health of the world's collective population.

WHO regulated disease nomenclature, sanitation, and quarantine. The organization was tested in 1947 by an Egyptian cholera outbreak. Relying on its stated preference for international solutions, the Interim Commission of WHO notified Egypt's neighbors as to the best procedures to take in order to prevent the spread of the disease, including quarantine precautions. A vaccine was distributed efficiently to the people of the affected area.

Characteristically, Chisholm brought his message to a world audience by stating, "The world was sick, and the ills from which it was suffering were mainly due to the perversion of man, his inability to live at peace with himself. The microbe was no longer the main enemy; science was sufficiently advanced to be able to cope with it admirably. If it were not for such barriers as superstition, ignorance, religious intolerance, misery and poverty."

Brock Chisholm was married to Grace McLean Ryrie on June 21, 1924, and they had two children. Dr. Chisholm died on February 4, 1971, in Veterans' Hospital in Victoria, Ontario.

GRENVILLE CLARK:
WORLD PEACE THROUGH WORLD LAW
(1882-1967)

By J. Garry Clifford, Professor of Political Science at the University of Connecticut, Storrs (Courtesy of Dartmouth College Library)

He was a tall, strong-framed man, with a rugged face, jutting eyebrows, and a great square jaw. He was the personification of tenacity, but his eyes were known to twinkle, and his measured voice often chuckled. New Englander by temperament, aristocrat by birth, Harvardian by education, lawyer by profession, and citizen by vocation, Grenville Clark was perhaps the least-known of the Americans who helped shape the course of the Twentieth Century. "He is that rare thing in America," his close friend Felix Frankfurter once wrote, "a man of independence, financially and politically, who devotes himself as hard to public affairs as a private citizen as he would were he in public office." His work spanned war and peace, education, politics, and the law, and he well deserved the title "statesman incognito."

Clark was born in New York City in 1882, heir to a banking and railroad fortune. Educated at Pomfret and Harvard (where he was Phi Beta Kappa and a

Law School graduate), he married Fanny Dwight in 1909. He was a member of the ultra-exclusive Porcellian, Somerset, and Knickerbocker Clubs. In 1909 he and fellow law-school classmates set up a small law office in New York; within a few years the firm grew into one of the most prestigious in the country.

Clark's public services were many and varied. His first important undertaking involved the famous military training camps for business and professional men at Plattsburg, New York. Clark approached General Leonard Wood, after the sinking of the *Lusitania* in 1915, setting in motion a practical campaign to prepare the country for war. Out of these training camps came the idea of selective service in 1917.

After the war (in which Clark won the Distinguished Service Medal for his work in the Adjutant General's office), he returned to his Wall Street law practice. He worked so hard that in 1926 he suffered a breakdown from nervous exhaustion. Health problems forced Clark to curtail much of his legal work and devote himself to the more flexible demands of public service.

This decision to concentrate on public work crystallized in 1931 when Clark joined the Harvard Corporation. That same year he and Archibald Roosevelt organized the National Economy League, which for the next several years worked to balance the federal budget. Clark was a watchful critic of the public scene during the 1930s. He supported the New Deal and took a deep interest in civil rights, particularly those treated by the first ten amendments to the U.S. Constitution. He became Harvard's spokesman on matters of academic freedom. Expanding this interest, Clark went to the leadership of the American Bar Association in 1938 and persuaded President Frank Hogan to create an ABA Committee of the Bill of Rights.

The coming of World War II prompted Clark to bring about a revival of the Plattsburg movement. Gathering together his associates, Clark formed, in the spring of 1940, a National Emergency Committee of the Military Training Camps Association, and in the next three months he wrote, publicized, and accomplished the passage of the Selective Training and Service Act.

World War II was also a time when Clark thought about peace. His initial effort was a pamphlet entitled *A Federation of Free Peoples*. He came back to the question of the "peace" in 1944 when Secretary Stimson told him to "go home and prevent World War III." The result was Clark's most important public undertaking, namely, the quest for world government. Clark criticized the United Nations Organization as outlined at the Dunbarton Oaks and San Francisco Conferences. For the next several years Clark was unofficial leader of the United World Federalists. He wrote books and gave speeches. His collaboration with Harvard Professor Louis B. Sohn began during this period, an association that culminated in 1958 in the magisterial treatise *World Peace through World Law*.

Unsuccessful in reversing the momentum of the Cold War, Clark nonetheless enjoyed moderate influence. His phone calls to John McCloy during the Cuban Missile Crisis, and his contacts with the Vatican, which led to Pope Paul's visit to the United States in 1965, are two cases in point.

Civil rights also occupied Clark's time and energies after 1945. Clark was an outspoken critic of Senator McCarthy in the 1950s, and he became involved in the celebrated case of Dr. Willard Uphaus, a Christian pacifist who was jailed when he refused to "name names." Nor did Clark confine himself to free speech. So distressed was he by the plight of blacks in the South, Clark personally raised some $80,000 in bail money for defendants in the Montgomery and Birmingham "freedom ride" cases in the early 1960s. This effort led to the so-called "Clark Plan" for guaranteeing legal expenses for defendants in civil rights cases, as well as a personal bequest of $500,000 from Clark and his wife to the NAACP Legal Defense Fund.

Clark's last years were difficult. His beloved wife, Fanny, died very painfully. His own health, never robust, deteriorated. The world situation, was dominated by Vietnam, missile crises, and overwhelming armament burdens. At home, the cause of civil rights made headway too slowly. Yet Clark was a congenital optimist, so he continued to work.

When the Missile Crisis in 1962 failed to galvanize the United States and the Soviet Union toward real and lasting disarmament, Clark formed the World Law Fund, which he endowed with some $750,000 to begin the process of long-range education. Several times his friends nominated him for the Nobel Peace Prize. He did not win, but he deserved the award.

He died in January 1967 at age eighty-four.

UNITARIAN NOTE

Grenville Clark's daughter, Louisa (Mrs. Patrick Spencer), notes that her father was married at the First Church in Boston, with the Rev. Charles E. Park officiating; he was active in the Dublin Community Church in New Hampshire, where Rev. Lyman V. Rutledge was the Unitarian minister.

JOSEPH S. CLARK, JR.: UNITED STATES SENATOR AND MAYOR OF PHILADELPHIA (1901-1990)

By Thomas Blair, Harvard College '03

Joseph S. Clark, Jr. was a lifelong member of the Unitarian Society of Germantown in Philadelphia, where he was born in 1901. He attended Middlesex School in Massachusetts, matriculating at Harvard in 1919. Clark graduated *magna cum laude* with a special award for his leadership as a student athlete, and went on to earn an L.L.B. degree from the University of Pennsylvania in 1926.

Clark's legal career in Philadelphia took off quickly. He joined the Air Force in World War II, however, in which he became a captain and was, in his own words, "pushed gently upwards to a soft and delightful staff job with the rank of colonel." As such, he traveled all over the world, and earned the Bronze Star, the Order of the British Empire, and other medals.

Despite his extraordinary success in the military, Clark returned to domestic affairs, campaigning for Democratic candidates before joining the fray himself. "I have been very busy," Clark wrote to his Harvard classmates at the time of their twenty-fifth reunion in 1948, "practicing all kinds of law and trying to raise a family." Clark was not to become any less busy in the years that followed, as victories in mayoral and congressional elections saw him deeply entrenched in politics.

Clark's first victory came in 1952, when he overturned a longstanding Republican hold on Philadelphia politics by winning the mayoral election. Clark battled corruption in local government throughout his time in office, taking on Republicans and Democrats alike as he dismantled the city's "political machine." Remembered as a "high-minded reform mayor," Clark introduced to his office such revolutionary notions as refusing to accept personal gifts and insisting that he would only remain in office one term, lest concern for reelection should make him preoccupied with unimportant issues. "In his first month in office," one journalist recalls, Clark "received a portrait of himself, 25 passes to a sportsmen's show, a colored photograph of the Liberty Bell, season passes to two theaters, and a pass for the city transportation system. All were returned to the donors."

Clark held to his promise to remain in office only one term, but his political career continued. In 1956, Clark inspired an end to the Pennsylvanian tradition of electing Republicans, ascending to the United States Congress. Hailed by the United Press as a "political Jack the Giant Killer," Clark remained an ardent Democrat; he was reelected in 1962, but failed to win in 1968.

He moved on to become a professor at Temple University the following year. In the remaining twenty years of his life, Clark served as president of the World Federalists, U.S.A., continuing his involvement in local, national, and international politics. Honored with degrees from Temple University, Harvard University, Haverford College, and the University of Pennsylvania, Clark left the legacy of Members of Congress for Peace through Law, an organization he founded while in office. The legacy for which he is best remembered, however, is his dedication to reform in a corrupt community—the work of an honest politician.

STANLEY COBB:
NEUROLOGIST AND PSYCHIATRIST (1887-1968)

By Benjamin V. White, M.D.

Stanley Cobb was a uniquely creative man. Possessing the mind of a natural scientist, which in his youth had been formed through exposure to wildlife and by the study of ornithology, and with medical training in human and comparative anatomy, neuropathology, neurohistology, clinical neurology, and finally psychiatry, he was able to piece together fragments of these sciences into an imaginative understanding of the nervous system. In the doing, he added several important building blocks to the foundational structure of the modern neurosciences. He attempted to correlate the physical and the behavioral aspects of the human condition in order to understand better the underlying causes of disease and treat the patient as a whole.

A severe handicap, which nevertheless creatively motivated Stanley Cobb's entire life, was his stammering, which he believed dated from the stressful birth of his sister Beatrice when he was four. The stammering interrupted Cobb's schooling and social life. On the other hand, his solitude made it possible for him to develop his interest in nature. Moreover, it was his curiosity about the origin of his stammering that later led him into the medical neurosciences.

Cobb attended Harvard Medical School and married Elizabeth Mason Almy in 1915. After his marriage, Cobb's stammering improved considerably. The Cobbs moved to Baltimore, where for the next three years Stanley was to work in physiology and psychiatry.

When he arrived on the Boston scene in 1919, Cobb saw private patients and was a psychiatric consultant at Massachusetts General Hospital. He also did research in the physiology laboratories of the Harvard Medical School.

Cobb built a neurological unit at Boston City Hospital — a remarkable achievement. It became the leading center for scholars of varying disciplines to cooperate in studies of the nervous system. In 1934, Cobb left again for MGH.

For a number of years Cobb took an active interest in the Boston Psychoanalytic Society.

Cobb was receptive to opportunities to welcome other psychoanalysts on his staff, affording psychoanalysis respectability at a time when it was almost an underground cult in Vienna. He saw psychoanalysis as one approach to the incredibly complex relations of mind, body, and environment and was effective in establishing psychoanalysis as an academically recognized empirical science.

In addition to influencing the nonpsychiatric members of the medical profession through psychiatric consultations, emergency care, joint research projects, clinical teaching, and work on the curriculum committee at Harvard, Cobb from 1935 through 1959 published each year a review of neuropsychiatry in the *Archives of Internal Medicine*. Other writings for the general medical public appeared during the thirties, included an article on shock therapy.

The demands upon Cobb during the late thirties were taking their toll. The rheumatoid arthritis, from which he had suffered for many years, gradually became more crippling, yet he continued with such activities as sailing, skiing, watercolor painting, and the study of nature.

When Cobb retired in mid-1954 after twenty years as psychiatrist-in-chief at the Massachusetts General Hospital, he focused on avian neurology and worked with the Museum of Comparative Zoology at Harvard and the department of student health at the Massachusetts Institute of Technology. During retirement Cobb published more than sixty papers. The full impact of Cobb's work was to be apparent in the future, when psychiatric wards spread throughout the country and psychiatry became a respected specialty of medicine.

UNITARIAN NOTE

When Stanley Cobb died on February 8, 1968, a service was held in the Memorial Church in the Harvard Yard. Officiating were the Reverend Ralph Helverson, minister of the First Parish (Unitarian) Church in Cambridge, and the Reverend Charles Price, the University Chaplain. Stanley Cobb and his wife were members of the First Parish Church in Cambridge (Unitarian).

ARTHUR D. CODE: ASTROPHYSICIST AND SPACE AGE ASTRONOMER (1923-)

An Autobiography

I was born on August 13, 1923, in Brooklyn, New York, and attended an Episcopal Church in the area. That was fine as a child, but as I began to find my place in the world, organized religion and doctrine did not fit in. Around 1960 I learned of and joined the First Unitarian Society of Madison, Wisconsin. I appreciated the openness and intellectual atmosphere of the Society and believe that our children benefited from this foundation. Although I no longer live there, we continue to support the society and to enjoy long-standing associations we formed there.

My first astronomical adventure was viewing a solar eclipse from the roof of our six-story apartment in 1930. When I started high school, books by the British astronomers James Jeans and Arthur Stanley Edington captured my imagination. My future was set: I was going to be an astrophysicist, and the University of Chicago was the place for me. After my first year at the university, however, the United States entered World War II. I enlisted in the Navy and was sent to Radio Material School. My training brought me back to Chicago, where I married Mary Gould, a coed at the University of Chicago, in 1943. We have had a rich and interesting life and raised four children of whom we are proud.

While in the Navy, I took exams, which enabled me to pursue graduate work

after my discharge from the service. Through Otto Struve, director of the Yerkes Observatory at Williams Bay, Wisconsin, I was accepted for graduate work in astronomy. Each day was new, productive, and exciting.

When I left Yerkes Observatory, I went to the University of Virginia, where I started a photometry program and constructed a photoelectric photometer before returning the next year to the University of Wisconsin. There my research focused on quantifying the measurements of the brightness of stars and galaxies. Of particular interest were the hot blue stars that make up the spiral arms of our galaxy.

To extend our study of the galaxy, Ted Houck, a Wisconsin graduate student, and I traveled to South Africa, where I obtained spectra for classification, and Ted carried out photometric observations of the blue stars. Ted worked at the Cape Observatory in Cape Town and I at the Radcliffe Observatory then located outside Praetoria. We met once a month at new moon at the Harvard Observatory's Boyden Station outside of Bloemfontain. The sky was exceptionally dark there, and we took sky camera images in many wavelengths. The center of our galaxy is located nearly overhead at this site, and the photographs obtained were for many years in great demand for books and magazines.

Later, upon becoming a tenured professor at Cal Tech, I was able to use the Palomar 200-inch telescope, then the largest in the world. Also at Cal Tech, physicists were making great inroads into the understanding of elementary particles. Murray Gell-Mann conceived of quarks, the building blocks of protons an other elementary particles, and Richard Feynman pioneered quantum electrodynamics, ideas intimately entwined with the start of the Big Bang Universe. Both received Nobel Prizes. On the astronomical side, it was discovered that the very atoms from which we were made were formerly in the center of some star in the past history of our galaxy.

In December 1957 Sputnik was launched. I realized that telescopes would be put in space, and astronomers should be involved. When the National Academy of Sciences sent out a letter soliciting proposals for the 100-pound satellite, I was prepared to accept an appointment at the University of Wisconsin as director of the Washburn Observatory and to start a space astronomy program aimed at developing an ultraviolet photometric space telescope. We started the University of Wisconsin Space Astronomy Laboratory, which still carries out astronomical space experiments.

The Orbiting Astronomical Observatory (OAO) was launched on April 8, 1966, from Cape Kennedy, but apparently the batteries exploded. After nine years of intense research, the failure was deeply felt. Although some scientists and engineers left the project after the disaster, OAO II was launched on December 7, 1968. This first observatory in space operated successfully for four years, opening up an entirely new era of astronomical investigations.

Sometimes, when I paddle down a winding river where the currents have swept the bank free of any sign of civilization, or ski through the forest with only pristine snow before me, I feel as though I am discovering a new land never before seen. Of course many have been there before me. That is how I felt as the new data came in from OAO: I was standing someplace viewing something that no one had ever seen before. In this case, however, it was true that no one else had been there before. This is the reward for the effort and the reason it was worth the risk. Another bonus of embarking on such adventures is the camaraderie that develops between all those who share the adventure. It is so satisfying to see the accomplishments that can be achieved by teamwork.

HENRY STEELE COMMAGER: AMERICAN PUBLIC INTELLECTUAL (1902-1998)

By Neil Jumonville, William Warren Rogers Professor of History, Florida State University

Although Henry Steele Commager is remembered chiefly as a prolific American historian who taught at New York University, Columbia University, and Amherst College, he also lived a notable public life outside the gates of scholarship. His academic credentials included more than forty books that he wrote and edited, visiting positions at Cambridge and Oxford, and the Gold Medal of the American Academy of Arts and Letters—none of which saved his scholarly position from some erosion by criticism from a later generation of historians.

What remains important in Commager's influence is found as much in his journalistic essays and reviews as in his scholarly books. From the beginning of his career he was able to bring together the worlds of scholarship and public discourse. When only 26 years old, Commager had already teamed with Samuel Eliot Morison to write *The Growth of the American Republic*, the most respected American history survey of its time. At the same moment, Commager dove into the world of cultural journalism. In 1928 Commager began reviewing books for the *New York Herald Tribune*; the editors found his first attempt so good that he was given 24 more books to review that year and compiled 234 more reviews for the newspaper within a decade.

This combination of an active intellectual life interwoven with academic duties was the pattern for Commager's life. He frequently contributed articles to magazines such as *Saturday Review*, *Atlantic*, the *New Republic*, the *Nation*, and *Harper's*; he even wrote a biweekly column for the *Senior Scholastic*, a magazine for high-school students. Commager nearly single-handedly provided the lead essays for the *New York Times Magazine* from the late 1940s to the mid-1960s. During his career he published over 700 articles, most of them aimed at the general public, and most of them on the historical context of contemporary social issues.

Clearly, Commager was what we now call a public intellectual. In addition to his magazine articles he kept up a crushing schedule of lecturing around the country on political and social matters—denouncing McCarthyism, explaining why the United States did not belong in a war with Vietnam, or warning against an

abuse of American power in the Nixon administration. His schedule was enough for a half-dozen people: teaching, writing newspaper and magazine columns, editing a series of books, collaborating on textbooks, doing research on his historical projects, flying here for political lectures or there to give the government historical advice, being interviewed by reporters, doing a radio talk-show, being filmed for a special program for CBS or PBS, giving Congressional testimony. Sometimes he flew to a dozen spots around the country in a month to address audiences, as though he were a secular itinerant preacher. Commager believed that it was his responsibility, whether by writing in magazines or standing at a podium, to address what his friend Nevins called that "one democratic public—the public to which Emerson and Lincoln spoke."

His was a vision of the historian's role that recalls the public lives of nineteenth-century historians such as George Bancroft. A scholar should be a generalist, in this view—an exhorter as well as an interpreter. The historian's badge was not a license to retreat to the archive away from the pain of the world; instead, it was an obligation to join in current debates and to propose solutions that might be divined from the experience of history.

Commager's first book, published in 1936, was a biography of the nineteenth-century Unitarian minister Theodore Parker. If most histories and nearly all biographies are also autobiographies, it is certainly true of Commager's *Theodore Parker*. In the transcendentalist Parker, Commager saw his own passion for mounting the stage and addressing a national congregation about the problems at hand.

Because of Commager's own commitments, particularly his concerns about civil liberties, it is fitting that his best-known campaign was against McCarthyism. Many Americans incorrectly interpreted Commager's defense of dissenters as the words of a leftist who sympathized with communists. As a result, his lectures were occasionally cancelled, and a publisher warned that one of his textbooks might be discontinued by high schools.

Commager published what became a part of the canon of early American Studies volumes. In *The American Mind*, he searched for a common bond of commitment to principles of democracy, opportunity, pragmatism, and intellectual freedom in American culture. Commager was happy to stay his course in the face of hostility and indifference. To describe Commager's legacy, we can borrow the words of historian Richard Hofstadter once used about Charles Beard: "Some scholars," Hofstadter noted, "choose to live their lives, usefully enough, amid the clutter of professional detail. [He] aimed to achieve a wisdom commensurate with his passion, and to put them both in the public service. No doubt he would rather have failed in this than succeeded in anything else."

UNITARIAN NOTE

An active ally of the American movement and its Beacon Press, Commager at times for many years would fill the pulpit of the Unitarian Society of Amherst, Massachusetts.

WILLIAM DAVID COOLIDGE: INVENTOR, PHYSICIST, RESEARCH DIRECTOR (1873-1975)

By C. B. Suits, Director of General Electric Research Library.
The following is abridged from the Biographical Memoirs of the National Academy of Sciences.

Tungsten, X-rays, and Coolidge form a trinity that has left an indelible impression upon our life and times. The key word in this triad is Coolidge, for his work brought the element tungsten from laboratory obscurity to the center of the industrial stage and gave the X-ray a central role in the progress of medicine throughout the world.

William David Coolidge was born in Hudson, Massachusetts, near Boston, on October 23, 1873. His father was a shoemaker who supplemented his income by running a farm. His mother was a dressmaker in her spare time. Coolidge attended a grade school about a mile from town, where one teacher presided over the six grades. He enjoyed fishing baseball, hiking, skating, and photography. After a brief stint manufacturing rubber garments in a local factory, Coolidge graduated valedictorian from Hudson High School

In the fall of 1891, Coolidge entered MIT, then known as "Boston Tech," on a state scholarship.

The period was one of growing interest in science and engineering, and opportunities for engineering graduates were numerous in industry. Coolidge studied electrical engineering, and was an excellent student. He came under the instruction of Professor Willis R. Whitney, which turned out to be the start of a long and happy relationship.

By the time Coolidge graduated in 1896, he sensed that engineering practice was not what he wanted; he had a greater interest in his science studies and the research orientation of his laboratory work. Therefore, he took a position as an assistant in physics at MIT. The following year, he obtained a grant to do graduate work at Leipzig.

After graduating with a doctorate *summa cum laude*, Coolidge took a teaching position at MIT in the fall of 1899. The following year he became a research assistant in the chemistry department, where he remained for five years. To Coolidge's complete surprise, Dr. Whitney, who worked in an adjacent laboratory, offered him a job at the new General Electric Research Laboratory. The laboratory was at the time achieving a modicum of credibility and prestige in its industrial trial setting because of the success of its early work.

Coolidge was devoted to his research work, but not to the exclusion of social contacts. In 1908, he married Ethel Woodward, the daughter of the president of a local bank. A daughter and a son were born to this marriage. Early in 1915, Ethel became seriously ill and died at the hospital in February of that year. A year later, Coolidge married Dorothy Elizabeth MacHaffie, who was employed by Coolidge to help with the children at home.

Lamp research and experimentation were proceeding apace in the U.S. and in Europe during that period. Coolidge first got into the lamp filament problem by way of tantalum, but he quickly switched to tungsten. After three years of painstaking research on this intractable metal, a process was developed by means of which tungsten was made sufficiency ductile at room temperatures to permit drawing through diamond dies. Lamps made with ductile tungsten filaments appeared on the market in 1911, and they have dominated the lighting industry ever since. Coolidge and the laboratory gained great stature as a result of this work.

Coolidge was appointed assistant director of the laboratory and, in 1914, he was awarded the Rumford Medal of the American Academy of Arts and Sciences, the first of a long series of medals and honors that marked his career.

Roentgen had announced his discovery of X-rays in 1895, an event that created worldwide interest. As Coolidge got into the study of X-rays, he found that the three principal parts—the cathode, the anode, and the "vacuum" environment—were sources of erratic performance. Coolidge installed a heated tungsten filament in an X-ray tube with a tungsten disk anode. This tube was heated and outgassed until all evidence of gas ionization disappeared. The tube became the first stable and controllable X-ray generator for medical and dental use, and it rapidly replaced gas-filled tubes in this country and throughout the world.

Prior to the U.S. entry in World War I, the laboratory became involved in war work. Coolidge found that sealed rubber binaural listening tubes provided excellent range for submarine detection. This device went into service on U.S. and British vessels as the "C" Tube. The Coolidge tube was adapted to a field X-ray unit for use

in World War I, and it became a major medical tool in field hospitals.

In 1932, Coolidge became director of the laboratory; he retired after World War II. In retirement, Coolidge retained an active interest in X-ray research and continued to receive recognition in the form of awards and medals for the impressive work of his career. He died on February 3, 1975, at the age of one-hundred-and-one.

UNITARIAN NOTE

William David Coolidge was a member of the First Unitarian Society of Schenectedy, a group of famed Unitarian researchers at General Electric who worked closely with Charles P. Steinmetz.

J. RAYMOND COPE:
MINISTER IN BERKELEY (1905-1988)

By Merv Hasselmann

The more one knows about the Dr. J. Raymond Cope's 22-year ministry, the better one understands why so many who knew him esteemed him so highly. Cope came to the First Unitarian Church of Berkeley in 1946 from a Salt Lake City pastorate, with a background in philosophy, teaching, and social service, as well as ministerial work. He served there until his retirement —the big church on the hill was his crowning glory.

Cope had character, charisma, modest friendliness, and intellectual ability combined with openmindedness, inventiveness, and willingness to progress. He was sincere, but could always take a humorous approach to himself. He was not above doing a church maintenance or carpentry chore. To him, religion was a great and enduring human need. His concepts of God, morality, forgiveness, and conscience were taken over intact by many. Cope's sermons were interesting and challenging. Neither Humanist, Theist, nor Deist, he minimized differences between members' philosophies and maximized what they had in common. Cope could inspire and lead the young as well as adults and the elderly.

New Horizons, New Heights

One of the first activities under Dr. Cope's inspiration was a series of lectures on philosophy, which resulted in a permanent Philosophers' Club. After only three years in Berkeley and at 43 years of age, Cope was invited to give the 1949 May Meeting (national Unitarian convention) sermon, a once-in-a-lifetime honor. His title: "Modern Man in Search of a Soul."

In 1950, Cope became chair of a local nonprofit radio station. That same year the church cooperated in a group therapy experiment with the University of California's psychology department experts; the church continued with a group therapy program of its own. Cope continued his activities vigorously until his retirement, became prominent in civil rights, marched at Selma, was an opponent of the war in Vietnam, and was an organizer of Ministers Mobilization.

Defeat of the Levering Act

Early in the 1950's, the State of California extended control over the religious activity of citizens by requiring the Bible to be read fifteen minutes a day in all classrooms. Cope advised the congregation that this law should be protested. Then in 1953, the Levering Act required that all teachers and college faculties sign a loyalty oath. In 1954, churches were notified that ministers must sign the loyalty oath or their churches would be subjected to additional taxation.

The First Unitarian at Berkeley stood firm and paid the tax, refusing to have the minister sign a loyalty oath. With the cooperation of three other California churches, two of them Unitarian, the church took the matter all the way to the Supreme Court where the Levering Act was declared unconstitutional. The taxes that had been paid were refunded with interest.

Building the Second Church

In the 1950s the church was bursting at the seams. Having paid off the mortgage on the first church and, following the settlement of financial and legal negotiations with the University of California, the congregation went into action on plans for a building in a new location. In 1955, building and landscaping architects were engaged, and surveying was begun. An original design and located high on the Berkeley hills, the new church offers a magnificent panorama of the Bay.

A 22-Year Period of Great Vigor

During the 22 years of Cope's pastorate, congregation participation rose to a crescendo. In 1952, so many helped that the church was redecorated on a weekend and the Parish Hall in a day. By 1965 twenty volunteers helped the paid staff on a regular basis and seventeen active committees reported to the annual meeting. "War babies" swelled the Sunday school, and a new building was erected —plus an addition to the main building. A custodian's cottage was added, a fountain was added in the Atrium, and the cottage at Inverness was modernized.

After Dr. Cope's resignation at 62, the socio-political developments of the 1960s continued, resulting in considerable turmoil within the church family, particularly between the younger activists and the middle-aged and elderly. It is possible that Cope foresaw such effects and, despite his experience and momentum, thought that a younger minister could surmount or channel them more effectively than he.

—*Abridged from* The Unitarian Universalist Church of Berkeley: A History by Merv Hasselmann *(1981)*.

NORMAN COUSINS:
EDITOR AND WRITER (1915-1990)

By Kenneth Read-Brown, Minister of Old Ship Church, Hingham, Massachusetts

The lifelong concerns of Norman Cousins—writer, editor, citizen diplomat, promoter of holistic healing, and unflagging optimist—were large indeed: world peace, world governance, justice, human freedom, the human impact on the environment, and health and wholeness. During a lifetime that spanned most of the twentieth century, the central concerns of Cousins's life were also among the most important issues facing the human race. His primary platform for promoting his views was as editor of *Saturday Review* for the better part of forty years. He was also the author of a dozen books and hundreds of essays and editorials. Besides having been notably active in a variety of peace organizations, he was, in his in later years, on the faculty of the University of California at Los Angeles School of Medicine.

Norman Cousins was born in Union Hill, New Jersey, on June 24, 1915. Growing up, he was both a fine athlete and a fine writer. He graduated from Columbia University Teachers College in 1933 and began his career as writer and editor with brief stints at the *New York Evening Post* and *Current History*. In 1940 he became executive editor of the *Saturday Review of Literature* (later *Saturday Review*), becoming editor just two years later at the age of twenty-seven. In the course of his tenure, *Saturday Review* grew from a small and struggling literary magazine to a weekly forum of ideas with a circulation of over 600,000.

During World War II Cousins was a member of the editorial board for the Overseas Bureau of the Office of War Information. He came to believe that enduring world peace could only be achieved through effective world governance. When the United World Federalists was founded in 1947 Cousins served as one of its vice presidents and later as president. To generate support for world government he made more than 2,000 speeches both in the United States and around the world.

Cousins's concern for peace and human well-being was more than an abstract idea. His concern, for example, for the victims of Hiroshima, following a postwar visit to that devastated city, became quite personal. He arranged, with funding from *Saturday Review* readers, for medical treatment in the United States for twenty-four young Japanese women who came to be known as the "Hiroshima Maidens." *Saturday Review* readers also supported the medical care of 400 Japanese children orphaned by the atomic bomb. In the 1950s Cousins and his wife legally adopted one of the "Maidens."

A few years later, again with the support of *Saturday Review* readers, Cousins helped create a program for thirty-five Polish women who had been victims of Nazi medical experiments during the war.

During the 1950s Cousins was outspoken in his criticism of atmospheric nuclear testing. In 1957 he was among the founders and became the first cochairman of the National Committee for a Sane Nuclear Policy (SANE). In the early 1960s he became an unofficial citizen diplomat, facilitating communication between the Vatican, the Kremlin, and the White House, which helped to lead to the Soviet-American nuclear test ban treaty. Upon ratification of the treaty in 1963, President Kennedy publicly thanked Cousins for his help with the treaty, and he was also the recipient of the United Nations Peace Medal.

In the 1960s Cousins had an experience that changed his life and that reinforced some of his deepest convictions concerning the nature of the human being. Stricken with a crippling and life-threatening collagen disease, Cousins followed a regimen of high doses of vitamin C and of positive emotions (including daily doses of belly laughter), all in consultation and partnership with his sometimes skeptical physicians. He chronicled his recovery in the best-selling *Anatomy of an Illness as Perceived by the Patient: Reflections on Healing and Regeneration*, published in 1979. When Cousins had a heart attack fifteen years following his earlier illness, he wondered whether it would be possible to recover from two life-threatening conditions in one lifetime, but he was determined that he would. Once again Cousins recovered, and once again he chronicled his experience in a book, *The Healing Heart: Antidotes to Panic and Helplessness.*

The last years of Cousins's life, following his retirement from *Saturday Review* in 1978, were spent as a faculty member of the University of California at Los Angeles School of Medicine. During the last year of his life, Cousins received additional awards, including the Albert Schweitzer Prize for Humanitarianism and the Japan Niwano Peace Prize.

Norman Cousins died on November 30, 1990, having lived twenty-six years after his doctors first diagnosed heart disease.

UNITARIAN NOTE

Though not a member of any Unitarian congregation, Cousins did at times attend services at the Unitarian Church in Westport, and he donated the pulpit of that church "In memory of Albert Schweitzer."

GARDNER COX: ARTIST (1906-1988)

By Robert Taylor, literary and art critic of The Boston Globe

In "The Painter of Modern Life" Baudelaire describes the artist as a passionate spectator "amid the ebb and flow of movement, in the midst of the fugitive and the infinite." Gardner Cox called this preliminary act of sustained observation his "fly on the wall" technique; his initial step in creating a portrait was to study the subject interacting with the environment. As a portraitist he regarded the mysteries of identity amid the fugitive flux of time, but he would not have been so distinctive an artist if he did not also have a visionary sense of the fantastic and the infinite.

Unquestionably Cox's best-known work was in portraiture. He did more than 300 portraits, from General George C. Marshall and Supreme Court justices to tender domestic images. The portraits of Gardner Cox are not validations of power; they are too serious for flattery; they do not serve as mere decor or as routine commissions from banks, universities and wealthy individuals; and though he was a realist with an obligation to likeness, the portraits allude and suggest rather than submit to the exigencies of practical representation.

The tension between getting a good likeness and making a good picture accounts for the haunting quality of many of his pictures—the Felix Frankfurter portrait at Harvard Law School, where a few loosely-brushed strokes constitute a background for the head like the visible emanation of mental activity; the Dylan Thomas, painted in a burst of enthusiasm after hearing the poet deliver the first reading of "Under Milk Wood" at the Fogg Museum, yet capturing his tragic vulnerability; the profile portrait of Robert Kennedy which, like the Dylan Thomas, sounds an eerily prophetic dark note (now in the National Portrait Gallery, the picture antedated Kennedy's assassination by a few weeks), where the subject is isolated, almost engulfed by space.

Each portrait by Gardner Cox constituted a complex skein of relationships between painter, sitter and spectator. Growing up in a world where John Singer Sargent dominated portraiture, Cox had obviously looked long and hard at Sargent, but the portraiture of the young New Englander was to have nothing about it of Sargent's paste-jewel society panache; it was more in accord with the introspective spirit of art's mid-century. The subjects of Gardner Cox are usually placed in abstract spaces and define themselves through a gesture or a formal interplay of color relationships. They express what they are rather than who they are; the social accessories are kept minimal; the inner self is reciprocal with the outer likeness.

The difference between a Gardner Cox portrait and one that only documents is the difference between poetry and prose. Not every artist, however fluent, can paint a portrait. Patently the task requires empathy with people, a psychological instinct and a compelling touch of curiosity. But giving visual life to someone else also requires an imagination that affords the appropriate image. Gardner Cox's portraits may seem remote from the forms and textures of his visionary personal statements; one is objective realism, the other an alternate universe of shadowy images, slight distortions and near-surrealist juxtapositions. In fact, the inward fantasy of this universe overlaps the other. The face is a mystical landscape no less than the stellar panoramas of the invented compositions.

From the start of his career achieving universality was a major objective. That career commenced formally rather late when, in 1936, the 30-year-old Gardner left his father's architectural firm to devote himself to art full-time. Painting had long been a passion; Gardner's mother was a gifted artist who had studied in Paris, and even in the Depression he found an audience. People liked his work, and he could make a living. On a painting trip with friends, he usually painted a single leaf, the papery veinings meticulously rendered.

The range of Gardner's portraits, from Robert Frost to Elizabeth Bancroft Schlesinger, from the granddaughter of Owen Wister to Dean Acheson and Gov. Michael Dukakis, suggests the trust in which his sitters placed him. His concern for someone else's sensibility translates into the quiet conviction of the portraits.

UNITARIAN NOTE

Gardner Cox was a member of the First Church in Cambridge (Unitarian Universalist).

BERNICE BROWN CRONKHITE: RADCLIFFE COLLEGE GRADUATE DEAN (1893-1983)

By Barbara Norton, Former Director of the Radcliffe Alumni Association

Bernice Brown Cronkhite had a tremendous impact on Radcliffe and its development, serving for thirty-six years, longer than any other senior officer—first as vice president and dean and later as the first dean of the Graduate School. Earlier, she had been an undergraduate and graduate student.

I knew her best when I became director in 1978 of the Cronkhite Graduate Center, at the corner of Brattle and Ash Streets. Bernice was then retired and in her mid 80s. She would speak of the three ages of woman: young, middle-aged and truly remarkable. She was the latter as she continued to enjoy visiting the building, recalling how it came into being, and occasionally meeting with resident students, who found her greatly to be admired. She was always poised, in command of a situation with a ready anecdote and a fund of well-informed conversation.

My earliest recollection of her goes back to the summer of 1938. She was then dean of the Graduate School. Her office was next to admissions, where I typed form letters—an interim job after my own June graduation and a chance to improve my shaky typing. Memories are of a fashionably dressed and dignified lady rushing to appointments or picking up a speech someone more accomplished than I had typed.

Bernice had abundant credentials, with a Ph.D. in international law, a year of study in Brussels under a distinguished professor of international law, and a year at Yale Law School, which helped her prepare for the graduate degree. Incidentally, she was the Belgian professor's first female student, and as she points out in her memoir, "Yale Law School had never admitted women, but they decided to admit me." Another year abroad on fellowship gave her the opportunity to attend early meetings of the League of Nations in Paris and later in Geneva, when that became League Headquarters. She greatly regretted that the United States never joined the League. On her return, she worked for a time for the Boston Women's Municipal League, which trained women for civil service jobs.

Bernice was a scholar and administrator, as well as a woman who loved stylish clothes. She was also fond of interior decorating and landscape design at her homes in Cambridge and Harvard, Massachusetts. She once told me that, as a child, her father had given her a free hand in planning her own room. Years and years later, when I visited her for tea, I discovered that she changed the look of her living room each summer, covering furniture upholstery with light slip colors.

During her busy life as dean, she met Leonard Cronkhite, who became chairman of Atomic Instruments in Cambridge, when both served on a committee to set up arrangements for an exchange between American and British students. They were married in 1933. When Leonard was still courting Bernice, I remember a mutual friend's telling me that when she and Bernice were on a trip together, Leonard pursued her with red roses at strategic overnight stops.

Bernice's dream as graduate dean was a residence for female graduate students, who often had lonely lives in cramped and unattractive apartments. She promoted her cause with vigor, and Radcliffe-owned land on Ash Street became the site of the Graduate Center. The cornerstone was laid in 1955, and the dedication took place the following year. When I was director of the Center from 1978 to 1982, men were also residents. Radcliffe seminars and public procedures programs had their headquarters there, and countless meetings, conference and social events filled the attractive first-floor rooms.

These are just a few glimpses of Bernice Cronkhite. She held national and international appointments and knew scores of people in the academic world and beyond—for instance, Henry Ford, diplomats, and former students who established distinguished careers. Perhaps one of her most unexpected friendships was with a gypsy called Nation who first came to help with housekeeping. Early on, Nation Cooper disclosed that because of her gypsy upbringing she had never been to school and could not read or write. Bernice proceeded to teach her and found her efficient and intelligent. They became lifelong friends. Bernice Cronkhite genuinely liked people and reached out to them in ways that made a difference, helping them establish enduring connections and creating for herself a life full of joy and friendships.

UNITARIAN NOTE

Bernice Brown Cronkhite was a member of the First Parish in Cambridge (Unitarian Universalist).

E. E. CUMMINGS:
POET AND PAINTER (1894-1962)

By Malcolm Cowley, Interpreter of Literature and Society

e.e. cummings grew up a Unitarian. His life embodied endless conflict between radical individualism and faith in love. The following selection reveals the volcano of his uniquely creative soul.

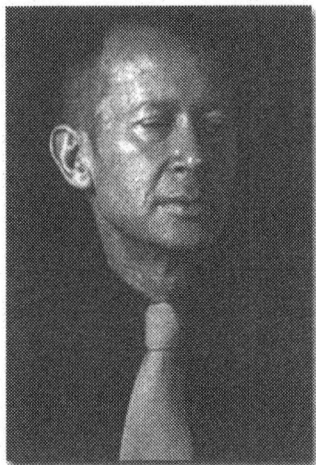

Edward Estlin Cummings was born and brought up on a quiet street north of Harvard Yard. I think it was T.S. Eliot who said that life there was so intensely cultured it had ceased to be civilized. Edward Cummings, his father (Harvard '83), had been an instructor in sociology, but had then become a clergyman, preaching in Boston as the assistant, the colleague, and finally the successor of Edward Everett Hale at the South Congregational Society, Unitarian.

Cummings attended a public high school, Cambridge Latin. Sending him there was apparently one of his father's democratic ideas, and another—when the son went on to Harvard, Class of '15—was to have him live at home for the first three years. That encouraged his bookish habits and cut him off from college life. Cummings joined nothing but the Musical Society and the board of *The Monthly,* a literary magazine that had published some of his early poems. At commencement he was awarded a degree *magna cum laude*, with honors in Literature, Greek and English. He was also chosen to give the Disquisition and shocked his classmates and their parents—those who listened—by speaking on "The New Art," with examples from Amy Lowell and Gertrude Stein.

In the autumn after his postgraduate year, Cummings went to New York, where he spent three months at the only office job he was ever to hold. The experiment having failed by reason of pure boredom, he went to work seriously on his drawing and painting. By the time Congress declared war on April 1917, Cummings was on his way to France as a volunteer in the Norton-Harjes Ambulance Corps.

On the old *Touraine* of the French Line, he met William Slater Brown, another New Englander, with whom he spent a month in Paris. Finally they went to the front, where Brown talked about war weariness in letters to friends (as well as in one to anarchist Emma Goldman). A French censor reported his remarks to Lieutenant Anderson, who said that Brown was a dangerous character and that Cummings should be arrested too. The friends were shipped off to a detention barracks. Confined with men of all nations, mostly illiterate, all used to living outside the law, Cummings found that he liked some of them vastly more than he liked his college classmates.

After the Armistice, Brown and Cummings rented a Greenwich Village apartment that became a model of squalor. He was painting "all the time," Brown says, but was also writing hundreds of poems. The critics were severe: they condemned his fleshly realism, his experiments with typography, and his custom of using a small "i" for the first-personal pronoun. But the more his work was condemned by critics, the more it was admired by younger writers.

Cummings led the revolt against Victorian standards, especially those prescribing chaste language and chaste behavior. In his poetry, there is respect for rebels of all sorts. There is compassion for outcasts. There is finally the deep strain of anti-intellectualism, a prejudice against scientists and "prudent philosophers" who poke and prod the earth, combined with praise for a child's direct vision, which sees the earth as "mud-luscious" and "puddle-wonderful."A new book of poems, *VV* (which he also called "ViVa"), appeared in 1931 and was a mild disappointment to his readers. There is a growing bitterness in the satires directed against politicians, generals, and run-of-the-mill people. In 1931 he made a trip to Russia—a shattering experience.

The New England tradition to which the poet returned was that preached by Ralph Waldo Emerson—the tradition of the autonomous individual standing before God (or the Oversoul), living by universal laws in harmony with nature, obeying an inner voice. Where Emerson was essentially a Neoplatonist, Cummings was a scoffer in his youth, then more and more a Christian.

Cummings lived into the late summer of 1962 and continued working to the last day. He wrote twelve books of poetry, including one that appeared after his death (*73 poems*, 1963), but not including collected or selected works. The books contain 770 poems in all, an impressive output for a lyric poet. His career, if not his opinions, had been remarkably self-consistent. Poet and painter—and nothing else—he remained to the end.

    —*Abridged from "Cummings: One Man Alone,"* Yale Review, *Courtesy of Yale University© and the Literary Estate of Malcolm Cowley.*

On a visit to Tucson, Arizona, e.e. cummings had a mystical experience while walking in the desert, where he encountered a strange cactus-like plant: he touched one spine and jumped "spiritually 40 miles." His journals are full of references to "le bon Dieu" and frequent prayers for help in his creative life (such as "Bon Dieu! may I some day do something truly great. amen."). He also prayed for strength to be his essential self ("may I be I is the only prayer—not may I be great or good or beautiful or wise or strong"), and for relief of spirit in times of depression ("almighty God! I thank thee for my soul; & may I never die spiritually into a mere mind through disease of loneliness"). His basic religious feelings were in tune with his Unitarian upbringing. His concept of God was that of a comprehensive Oneness together with a sense of the presence of this Oneness in nature. He expressed this belief most clearly in a sonnet that combined both prayer and an awareness of the Divinity of the natural world:

I thank You God for most this amazing
day: for the leaping greenly spirits of trees
and a blue true dream of sky; and for everything
which is natural which is infinite which is yes

(I who have died am alive again today,
and this is the sun's birthday; this is the birth
day of life and of love and wings:and of the gay
great happening illimitably earth)

how should tasting touching hearing seeing
breathing any—lifted from the no
of all nothing—human merely being
doubt unimaginable You?

(now the ears of my ears awake and
now the eyes of my eyes are opened)

—*From* E. E. Cummings Revisited *by Richard S. Kennedy*

MERLE E. CURTI:
AMERICAN SOCIAL HISTORIAN (1897-1966)

By Allen F. Davis, Professor of History and Director of Public History, Temple University

Merle E. Curti was a pioneer in the development of intellectual history and one of the founders of the American Studies Association. A transitional figure in American historiography, Curti was one of Frederick Jackson Turner's last students and a close friend of Charles Beard. Born in Nebraska and educated at Harvard, Curti taught at Beloit, Smith, Teacher's College, Columbia, and from 1942 to 1968 at the University of Wisconsin.

Each summer he returned to his beloved, restored farmhouse in Lyme Center, New Hampshire. It was here and at Baker Library at near-by Dartmouth College that he did much of his writing. He also taught in Japan, Australia, and India, and he lectured many times throughout Europe, where his work is well known. Of all the honors bestowed upon him, including many honorary degrees and the Pulitzer Prize, he was perhaps most proud of the Order of the Northern Star awarded him by the Swedish Government in 1965.

Curti was strongly influenced by John Dewey's instrumentalism, and that influence permeates *The Growth of American Thought* (1943) and much of his other writing. He traced the social history of ideas and the relationship of ideas to society. *The Growth* may seem encyclopedic and difficult to read today, but at the time it was published, along with Ralph Gabriel's *The Course of American Democratic Thought* (1940), it helped to establish intellectual history as a field of study, and after the war it became an indispensable guide for American Studies scholars. There is no "Curti School" of history. His eighty-six Ph.D. students wrote on dozens of topics, and he never tried to enforce an interpretation or insist on a particular approach. His bibliographical knowledge in a dozen fields was legendary.

He wrote several books on the peace movement, including *Bryan and World Peace* (1931) and *Peace or War: The American Struggle* (1936), and he helped to establish Peace Studies as a field of scholarship. The American Peace Crusade (1929) was based on his dissertation, written after Arthur Schlesinger Sr. (who had replaced Turner at Harvard) rejected his first effort, which was apparently a junior version of *The Growth of American Thought*. He wrote on the history of education; in fact, *The Social Ideas of American Educators* (1935) remains one of his most important books. His history of the University of Wisconsin, done in 1949 with Vernon Carstensen, is still one of the best college histories ever written. In addition to books on American philanthropy abroad and on philanthropy and higher education, his article, "American Philanthropy and the American Character," *American Quarterly* X (Winter, 1958): 420-437, is the best place to begin to learn about a field that is just now attracting American scholars.

Curti not only wrote intellectual history, he was also one of the leaders in attempting to apply social-scientific methods to the study of history. He chaired the Committee on Historiography of the Social Science Research Council (that included, among others, Charles Beard, Thomas Cochran and Jeanette Nichols), which produced the famous "Bulletin 54" *Theory and Practice in Historical Studies* (1946). More important he tried to apply social-scientific methods and statistical analysis to the study of Trempealeau County in Wisconsin. His book, *The Making of an American Community* (1959), tried to test Turner's theories about democracy, and it remains an important pioneer work in social history.

Curti was the co-author (with Willard Thorp and Carlos Baker) of a collection of documents, *American Issues* (1950), the first such collection in American Studies. He was also the co-author with Paul Todd of a high-school text, *The Rise of the American Nation*, which is still in print and still being attacked in some circles as too liberal. Curti was often attacked, especially in the 1950s, for his liberalism, his relativism, and for his defense of unpopular causes. He was always proud that in one such attack a right-wing critic denounced the dangerous, radical ideas of "Beard, Becker, and Curti." He thought he was in excellent company. He was not afraid to speak out in defense of freedom of speech and to denounce loyalty oaths, anti-intellectualism and McCarthyism, as he did in his presidential addresses to the Mississippi Valley Historical Association (1952) and the American Historical Association (1954).

Curti was not a dramatic lecturer, nor a charismatic teacher. He influenced through his wide-ranging mind, his vast knowledge, his varied and innovative scholarship and his tolerance for all points of view. He offered sympathetic support to hundreds of students and to a great many others who demonstrated any intellectual curiosity about the human condition and the American scene. In retirement he kept up a huge correspondence with friends and former students, even with some scholars he had never met. And he continued to read widely in the most recent scholarship and the latest fiction. Even in the last few years, his letters to me praised or criticized books that I had never heard of or had not gotten around to reading.

Merle Curti was a member of the First Unitarian Church of Madison, Wisconsin, whose Meeting House was designed by Frank Lloyd Wright.

—Courtesy of American Studies Association's ASA Newsletter, *June 1996*

CYRUS DALLIN: AMERICAN SCULPTOR (1861-1943)

—From www.dallin.org/pages/dallinbio.html.

Cyrus Edwin Dallin was born on November 22, 1861, in Springville, Utah. His talents at sculpting and art were recognized at an early age, and he was sent to Boston at the age of 19 to study at the sculpture school of T.H. Bartlett.

In 1883, Dallin entered a competition to develop an equestrian statue of Paul Revere. Among the other entrants was Daniel Chester French. No entries were selected, but Dallin persisted in trying to obtain the commission. This began a 58-year endurance trial to get the work made (and paid for). During those 58 years Dallin made seven versions of *Paul Revere*. A timeline with photos of the seven versions is in the Revere room of the Dallin Art Museum.

In Boston, he gained the respect of the other famous artists of his day, including Augustus St. Gaudens and John Singer Sargent, who became a close friend. (Sargent's sketch of Dallin's Portico is a treasured artifact of the Dallin Museum.) He became internationally famous, and his works were widely duplicated and collected.

In 1891 he married a Boston woman, Vittoria Colonna Murray, who was a successful writer. They raised three children: Bertram, Arthur, and Lawrence.

In 1900, at the age of 39, Dallin moved to Arlington, Massachusetts, which remained his home for the rest of his life. As a result, Arlington is now the home of many of his works. He was also busy throughout his life creating war memorials, statues of statesmen, generals, and mythic figures. Dallin

created more than 260 sculptures during his life.

Among his most beloved works are those celebrating Native Americans. When Dallin was a boy, American Indians were often depicted as brutal savages. Dallin was among the first to see a more transcendent character, and conveyed this in his many Native American sculptures. His *Appeal to the Great Spirit* may be the most famous and copied example, but there are dozens of other works that are admired for their humanity and classicism.

Dallin's prolific output continued until the end of his life. In 1940 he finally saw his *Paul Revere* statue erected in Boston. By now the work was famous, with copies installed in schools across America. Dallin contributed substantially to the cost of casting and installing the Boston "original," Boston's city fathers having failed to fulfill their financial commitments.

Dallin died at home on November 14, 1944, a week shy of his 83rd birthday.

UNITARIAN NOTE

The Dallin family, which included three sons, was affiliated with the First Parish in Arlington, Massachusetts—the Unitarian church where the life of the sculptor was celebrated in 1944. The church, which was organized in 1733, is just across the street from the new Cyrus Dallin Art Museum in Arlington Center.

MABEL WHEELER DANIELS: COMPOSER (1878-1971)

By Madeline Goss

Until comparatively recent years there have been only a few women composers, either in this country or abroad, and most of these have confined themselves to the smaller forms. Mabel Daniels has so far been one of the few women who have composed for orchestra and whose works have been played on important symphony programs.

Born in Swampscott, Massachusetts, Daniels spent most of her life in and around Boston. Music was a daily part of her early environment: One of her grandfathers played the organ, and the other directed a choir, while both parents sang in Boston's Handel and Haydn Society chorus.

She was given piano lessons at an early age and often made up pieces to play (when ten years old she wrote a Fairy Charm Waltz). She also had a fine soprano voice, and this was what really started her on a musical career. At Radcliffe she sang in the Radcliffe Choral Society and took leading parts in the college operettas. Soon she was made director of the Society and began writing music for the operettas. Daniels graduated from Radcliffe *magna cum laude*.

By the time she had finished college Mabel Daniels knew that composing was to be her life's work. For a time she studied composition and orchestration with George W. Chadwick in Boston. Then, she went to Germany to work with Ludwig Thuille. When she tried to join the score-reading class at the Royal Conservatory in Munich, the director was frankly upset—no woman had ever before presumed to ask admittance. After long and weighty consideration, he finally gave his consent. After two winters spent in Germany, Daniels came back to Boston, where she joined the Cecilia Society—a chorus of mixed voices.

Every creative artist—whether painter, sculptor, writer, or musician—dreams of a retreat where he or she can work undisturbed. Edward MacDowell, America's first great composer, discovered such a retreat in the wooded hills of New Hampshire. At MacDowell's death his widow dedicated her life to the project they had planned together. The wooded acres of their New Hampshire farm were turned over to a Memorial Association, and largely through the personal efforts of Mrs. MacDowell, who toured the country giving concerts to raise the necessary funds, the colony gradually took shape: Old farm houses were transformed into eating, sleeping and recreation buildings, and small studios were built, scattered through the woods. A group of working artists, recommended for their talent and promise and chosen by a special committee from a large number of applicants, gathered there each year, and many important works have sprung from this fruitful environment. It would be difficult to estimate the influence that the McDowell Colony had on cultural development in America.

During the colony's early years, a festival was put on each summer in the forest-encircled amphitheater. Mrs. MacDowell— always interested in promising young composers—learned of Mabel Daniels's *The Desolate City* (an early choral work for baritone and orchestra) and was so struck by it that she asked her to direct a performance of the piece at the pageant. This was Daniels's first important composition. The following year she was invited to return as a colonist, and after that most of her music was written at the colony. The lovely New Hampshire woods inspired one of her most widely played compositions. *Deep Forest*, a "delicately imaginative work."

Daniels was a member of the American Composers' Alliance, an honorary member of Phi Beta Kappa, and an alumna trustee of Radcliffe College. She was awarded an honorary M.A. degree from Tufts College and a Doctor of Music Degree from Boston University. When Radcliffe College planned a celebration for its fiftieth anniversary in 1929, President Comstock invited Daniels to compose a choral work in honor of the occasion. For this, she wrote *Exultate Deo*, which became her best-known work. Among her other compositions are *Peace and Liberty* and *Pirates' Island.* Miss Daniels's most important work is *The Song of Jael*, which shows a use of modern idiom.

In her music Daniels retained the best of the old, but constantly experimented with new forms "Real music should be more than a crossword puzzle," she insisted. "It must have something human in it." It was this human quality that made her own work noteworthy.

—*From* Modern Music-Makers: Contemporary American Composers *published by E.P. Dutton and Company, New York, 1952.*

UNITARIAN NOTE

Mabel Wheeler Daniels was a celebrated member of Boston's Arlington Street Church, whose pulpit was long filled by William Ellery Channing.

A. POWELL DAVIES:
MINISTER IN THE CAPITAL (1902-1957)

The following is abridged from a statement by the A. Powell Davies Memorial Committee of All Souls Church (Unitarian), Washington, DC.:

"Religion is not something separate and apart from ordinary life. It *is* life—life of every kind viewed from the standpoint of meaning and purpose: life lived in the fuller awareness of its human quality and spiritual significance."

Probably no words of A. Powell Davies better express the universality and simplicity of his religious faith. Minister of All Souls Church in Washington from 1944 until his death in 1957, Dr. Davies rose to prominence as one of America's most forthright, courageous liberal spokesmen. His influence was felt not only in his own church and community but reached out into national and international areas of concern. Whether it was a question of racial injustice in the District of Columbia, the unfair methods of Congressional committees, or the needs of the underfed and underprivileged in Asia—he spoke out simply and courageously.

Powell Davies was born in Birkenhead, England, and spent many vacations on his grandfather's farm in Wales. He loved to listen to the family's spirited discussions in the large household, where the growing boy found stimulation for his already active and adventurous intellect. Proud as he was of his Welsh heritage, Davies early was fascinated with America—its founding principles, its opportunity, and, as he foresaw, its inevitable position of world leadership. After completing his theological studies at the University of London and a brief pastorate in a Methodist church nearby, he came to the United States in 1928 with his wife, Muriel Hannah Davies.

Always an unconventional preacher, even within Methodism, Davies, follow-

ing a four-year pastorate in Portland, Maine, in 1933 became minister of the Community Church of Summit, New Jersey, where he remained for 11 years. During this period, through magazine articles and numerous public addresses, Davies became known as an astute analyst of national and international affairs. His first book, *American Destiny*, published in 1942, argued that America must take leadership in a world that has become a single, vast, reluctant community.

In September 1944, Davies became minister of All Souls Church in Washington, D.C. From this pulpit and in many addresses throughout the country, he continued to champion American founding principles. He vigorously opposed racial injustice, censorship, abuses of Congressional investigating committees, persecution of public servants, the activities of Communist and pro-Communist groups, miscarriages of justice, and petty police tyrannies. The *Washington Post* commented that Davies was "militantly in the forefront of every assault upon intolerance and racial discrimination and injustice."

All Souls Church became an effective force for social action. The collection on one occasion of more than 90 tons of canned goods for overseas relief, the shipment of school supplies to the children of Hiroshima in 1947, the widely publicized pledge to no longer patronize segregated restaurants in the District of Columbia, the founding of the integrated Columbia Heights Boys Club in cooperation with the Unitarian Service Committee—all these are examples of the religion-in-action that he inspired. A longtime student and vigorous opponent of communism, he early saw the moral issues at stake and took forthright positions while many were still confused. He was equally clear as to the menace of McCarthyism, and fought it resolutely.

Meanwhile, during Dr. Davies' ministry, All Souls Church, heir to a long and distinguished history, was experiencing its greatest growth. So many people attended the Sunday morning services that the overflow heard the service over a public address system in an adjoining hall. Seven new congregations were formed in the Washington area, and until they called their own ministers, four of these groups heard Dr. Davies's sermons by direct wire. At the time of Dr. Davies's death, the *Washington Post* said: "Powell Davies was at once the spiritual leader and goading conscience to his congregation—and to the whole community."

In addition to these activities, Davies found time to write numerous books. *Man's Vast Future: A Definition of Democracy*, was translated into seven languages for distribution overseas. Other books were: *The Faith of an Unrepentant Liberal, America's Real Religion, The Temptation to be Good, The Urge to Persecute,* and *The Language of the Heart: A Book of Prayers*.

In a posthumous award, Americans for Democratic Action called Davies "a universal citizen." His universality was perhaps his outstanding characteristic. "The world," he said, "is now too dangerous for anything but truth, too small for anything but brotherhood. Our neighbor whom we must love as we love ourselves is anyone whatever and everyone whatever throughout the world."

KARL W. DEUTSCH:
INTERNATIONAL POLITICAL SCIENTIST
(1912-1992)

The following is a Memorial Minute adopted by the Faculty of Arts and Sciences, Harvard University (Samuel Beer; Stanley H. Hoffmann; Samuel P. Huntington; Robert O. Keohane, Sidney Verba; Jorge I. Dominguez, chairman):

Karl Wolfgang Deutsch, Stanfield Professor of International Peace, Emeritus, was born in Prague in 1912 and died on November 1, 1992. He received his first university degree from the Deutsche Universitaet in 1934 and a law degree from Charles University in 1938, both in Prague. Shortly thereafter, he emigrated from Czechoslovakia. In 1939 he was awarded a fellowship to study at Harvard, from which he received a Ph.D. in 1951. During World War II, he worked for the Office of Strategic Services and took part in the 1945 San Francisco conference that resulted in the founding of the United Nations. He taught at M.I.T. from 1945 to 1956 and then at Yale until 1967, whereupon he returned to Harvard as a Professor of Government.

Deutsch's dedication to social science was linked to a moral passion for improvement in the world. His dissertation and first book, *Nationalism and Social Communication*, remains a landmark work on its subject. Born to a Sudeten German family in the Austro-Hungarian Empire, Karl wrote the book as an attempt to understand why the world of his youth was destroyed by war, racism, and fratricide. Karl studied the forces of nationalism, searching for its roots as well as for its effects. This was no mere scholarly project: Karl said that political science should be considered a branch of medicine, for the purpose of understanding and doing politics well was to prevent death and relieve suffering.

Deutsch's greatness as a social scientist was due to his erudition and his ability to develop new concepts that led to insights into fundamental issues, such as nationalism and political integration or disintegration within and among states. He devoted much of his career to the effort to link theory with evidence systematically and, preferably, quantitatively.

Karl developed the concept of social mobilization, the process whereby people become uprooted from their traditions and become available for new patterns of communication and behavior, and he identified quantitative indicators to study it in most countries of the world. Deutsch sought also to specify the background conditions for the political integration of what he called "security communities" in the North Atlantic world.

An author or co-author of fourteen books and hundreds of scholarly articles, Deutsch was perhaps most proud of his book, *The Nerves of Government*. Deutsch noted that the book aimed to reorient "political thought toward a greater interest in seeing government and politics as potential instruments of social learning, of social and economic development, and of intellectual and moral growth."

Deutsch was elected President of the American Political Science Association, of the International Political Science Association, and of the Society for General Systems Research. He received honorary doctorates from seven universities in the United States, Germany, and Switzerland. He was a member of the U.S. National Academy of Sciences. For about two decades, he was perhaps the main international figure in political science.

But Karl was much more than that. He was a teacher to thousands of students at universities all over the world. He exploded with ideas. He was demanding of his students; his shortest reading list was five hundred pages per week. When students complained that he expected too much, he replied with grin: "Would you rather that I should expect too little?"

Karl was a missionary. It was not enough to understand politics; it was important to do so with purpose, commitment, and vision. He traveled ceaselessly, as a prophet might, to teach others about the scientific study of politics and about the humane practice of politics. He did so with a sunny disposition and a warm smile. Karl was also a passionate and persistent champion of peace, both during the Vietnam War and over the question of nuclear weapons. To say that Karl Deutsch was eloquent is a bit like saying that Shakespeare was a pretty good playwright. Whether in front of community groups or undergraduates, many would hear Karl as St. Paul is said to have heard God on the road to Damascus.

Karl Deutsch, the eternal optimist, was never punctual, but was always ahead of his time.

UNITARIAN NOTE

A member of the First Parish (Unitarian Universalist) in Cambridge and a contributor of various articles to *The Christian Register*, Karl Deutsch also edited the "Seeds of Thought Series" of the Beacon Press and wrote a booklet, *Faith for Our Generation*, published by American Unitarian Youth. His several articles for the *Unitarian Register* include "The Atom and Disarmament" in October 1946 and an article on the creative opportunity before our church published in November 1943.

JOHN DEWEY:
A COMMON FAITH (1859-1952)

By Max Otto

John Dewey was not a member but was a close friend of the Unitarian movement. The memorial service celebrating his life was held at a church with a long-distinguished Unitarian heritage, the Community Church of New York. Dewey's Unitarian philosopher friend, Max Otto of the University of Wisconsin, was the speaker. His words are reprinted below:

Toward sundown on the first day of June, the thing happened that had to happen sooner or later. The life of John Dewey came to a close. He had remained singularly active, not only in body but in mind and heart and spirit, more than a score of years after reaching the officially designated termination of professional effectiveness and the traditionally announced ending of the possibility of finding life enjoyable. But it is not granted to any man to live forever.

It is being said in newspaper reports, in editorials, in conversations across the country, that such a life cannot end; that John Dewey lives on and will live on down the long stretch of time. In one sense this is profoundly true. In another sense it is not true at all. John Dewey's impact upon affairs, upon public education, the sciences, philosophy, religion, the enterprises of politics, of business, of labor, has been so pervasive and penetrating that men and women in the most various walks and ways will continue to think and act, unknowingly when not knowingly, under the persisting influence of his initiating genius.

But he himself is gone. The never failing source which he was of original insights and novel perspectives, of fresh ideas and new methods creatively responsive to changed conditions—this has been taken away.

John Dewey lived his philosophy. His stature as a crusader, who poured his incredible gifts and energies into the struggle to improve the lot of mankind, equaled his stature as a philosophic thinker and educational pioneer. A progressive in every sense of the word, he took his place at the front with the most daring of those who sought to build a new political party for the people of America. He gave vigorous support to social movements designed to provide hope and greater opportunity and dignity for the underprivileged of our country and the world beyond our shores.

The following is abridged from A Common Faith *by John Dewey (New Haven: Yale University Press, 1934):*

The idea of God, or, to avoid misleading conceptions, the idea of the divine is, one of ideal possibilities unified through imaginative realization and projection. But this idea of God, or of the divine, is also connected with all the natural forces and conditions—including man and human association—that promote the growth of the ideal and that further its realization. We are in the presence neither of ideals

completely embodied in existence nor yet of ideals that are mere rootless ideals, fantasies, utopias. For there are forces in nature and society that generate and support the ideals. They are further unified by the action that gives them coherence and solidity. It is this active relation between ideal and actual to which I would give the name "God."

A clear and intense conception of a union of ideal ends with actual conditions is capable of arousing steady emotion. It may be fed by every experience, no matter what its material. In a distracted age the need for such an idea is urgent. It can unify interests and energies now dispersed; it can direct action and generate the heat of emotion and the light of intelligence. The function of such a working union of the ideal and actual seems to me to be identical with the force that has been attached to the conception of God in all the religions that have a spiritual content; and a clear idea of that function seems to me urgently needed at the present time.

One reason why personally I think it fitting to use the word "God" to denote that uniting of the ideal and actual which has been spoken of, lies in the fact that aggressive atheism seems to me to have something in common with traditional supernaturalism... exclusive preoccupation of both militant atheism and supernaturalism with man in isolation. For in spite of supernaturalism's reference to something beyond nature, it conceives of this earth as the moral center of the universe and of man as the apex of the whole scheme of things. It regards the drama of sin and redemption enacted within the isolated and lonely soul of man as the one thing of ultimate importance. Apart from man, nature is held either accursed or negligible. Militant atheism is also affected by lack of natural piety. The ties binding man to nature that poets have always celebrated are passed over lightly. The attitude taken is often that of man living in an indifferent and hostile world and issuing blasts of defiance. A religious attitude, however, needs the sense of a connection of man, in the way of both dependence and support, with the enveloping world that the imagination feels is a universe. Use of the words "God" or "divine" to convey the union of actual with ideal may protect man from a sense of isolation and from consequent despair or defiance.

JOHN H. DIETRICH:
RELIGION WITHOUT GOD? (1878-1957)

By Mason Olds, Unitarian Universalist Minister

John H. Dietrich was born in 1878, on a farm near Chambersburg, Pennsylvania. Dietrich's parents were simple, uneducated farm people, his father being a fairly successful sharecropper. His family professed the Reformed faith, which had originated with Ulrich Zwingli, the Zurich reformer in the sixteenth-century Protestant Reformation. It was a rural minister who suggested that young John, who was a good student, become a minister.

In 1893 he entered Mercersburg Academy, where he managed to crowd four years' work into three, while walking eight miles a day to and from the Academy and doing farm chores. Dietrich still managed to graduate as valedictorian of his class in 1896. In 1900 he graduated from Franklin and

Marshall College in Lancaster, Pennsylvania.

The following fall he obtained a position as private secretary to the multimillionaire, Jonathan Thorne, of New York. During this time Dietrich occasionally went with the Thornes to religious services at All Souls Unitarian Church in New York City. When he had saved enough money to return to school, Dietrich entered the Eastern Theological Seminary of the Reformed Church, which was affiliated with his alma mater.

After his graduation from seminary in 1905, Dietrich became minister of St. Mark's Memorial Church in Pittsburgh. The Bernard Wolffs, who financially supported the church, were determined that Dietrich resign. A committee recommended that Dietrich be indicted for heresy, hoping that he would resign before the actual trial, which was set for July 10, 1911. Dietrich refused to defend himself and was "defrocked." This occurred in spite of the continuous support of his board of trustees and the members, generally, at St. Mark's.

The minister of the First Unitarian Church in Pittsburgh, Dr. Walter L. Mason, recommended that Dietrich be invited into ministerial fellowship with the American Unitarian Association. Dietrich became the minister of the First Unitarian Society of Spokane, Washington. When he arrived he had a congregation of about sixty; when he left in 1916, he had a congregation of over fifteen hundred.

During his Spokane ministry, Dietrich lectured on comparative religions, and as a result, he began to question even his liberal view of Jesus as the greatest spiritual leader of all history. He came to believe that the world owed a great debt to Buddha, Confucius, the Hebrew prophets, and the Greek philosophers. He also accepted the "scientific method" as the most effective means for arriving at truth.

Though long familiar with the humanism of the Renaissance, Dietrich came across the word "humanism" in a different connotation through an article by Frederick M. Gould, an ardent advocate of August Comte and his Positivism, or what has been loosely termed the religion of humanity. It struck a responsive note in Dietrich; this "humanism" would be a good name for his interpretation of religion in contrast to theism. Leaning confidently upon the background of Renaissance humanism, Dietrich drew certain elements of meaning from it and fused them with his own more social concept of this term. More and more Dietrich moved to a kind of "naturalistic humanism" and away from liberal theism. In this move, he was going beyond the arms of conventional Unitarianism.

In 1916, Dietrich became the minister of the First Unitarian Society of Minneapolis and built it into a large, vibrant, and effective institution. As his congregation progressively swelled, Dietrich began broadcasting his services over the radio, which brought a strong reaction from both Roman Catholic and Protestant clergymen, who were convinced that Dietrich's opinions were dangerous to the community and that some of their members were staying away from their churches to listen to him.

Many of Dietrich's addresses were used to combat the movement to ban the teaching of evolution in the public schools. "The Humanist Pulpit," which contained individual addresses of Dietrich, was published every month.

In 1941 Dietrich moved to Berkeley, California, where he continued to read and think and to deliver an occasional address. A friend who visited Dietrich in a nursing home just before his death, reported that Dietrich, then in his eightieth year, was standing by the side of his bed teaching himself Italian and eagerly discussing the existential humanism of Jean-Paul Sartre. The "father" of American religious humanism died on July 22, 1957.

—*Abridged from* Religious Humanism in America: Dietrich, Reese and Potter *(Washington: University Press of America, 1978).*

UNITARIAN NOTE

In correspondence with Warren Allen Smith, who compiled *Who's Who in Hell* (2002), Dietrich wrote: "My philosophy and religion have undergone a complete revision. My utter reliance upon science and reason was a great mistake. Its negative side, cutting itself off from all cosmic relationship, was and is very short-sighted. I have come to accept a kind of naturalistic theism."

JAMES DRUMMOND DOLE: ENTREPRENEUR (1877-1958)

The Rev. Charles Fletcher Dole (1845-1927) served for more than forty years as pastor of the First Unitarian Church in Jamaica Plain, Massachusetts. His son, James Drummond Dole, studied agriculture at Harvard's Bussey Institute and traveled to the Sandwich Islands in 1901, where he is credited with establishing the Hawaiian pineapple industry.

From the records of the 25th anniversary class book of the Harvard College Class of 1899, published in 1924:

Following my inclination toward an agricultural pursuit and the lure of Hawaii, then recently annexed to the United States, I landed in Honolulu on November 16, 1899; within two weeks I found the town quarantined for six months by an outbreak

of bubonic plague. I bought a government homestead of sixty-four acres, twenty-three miles from Honolulu, and on August 1, 1900, I took up my residence thereon as a farmer—unquestionably of the "dirt" variety. After some experimentation, I concluded that the land was better adapted to pineapples than to peas, pigs or potatoes, and accordingly concentrated on that fruit. Growing Hawaiian pineapples created the necessity for a market, and in order to enlarge the market to the entire United States (and other countries) and to extend the marketing season throughout the entire year, a cannery seemed necessary. I started my first pineapple plants in the spring of 1901, our company was incorporated in December of that year, and in the summer of 1903 we put up our first season's pack of 1893 cases. In 1923 we packed 2,038,671 cases, or 43,497,828 cans. The period between has been one of repetitive cycles of more land, more pineapples, more canneries. Our plantings in 1923, if extended in a straight line, would have made a double row from New York to San Francisco.

The game has been a very interesting one, taking in practically all the fascinating and troublesome agricultural operations, various transportation questions, and constantly changing manufacturing, marketing and financial problems. I have been particularly interested in trying to organize our business in such a way that every employee, so far as possible, may feel that his interest is that of the company, and vice versa. I don't claim to have reached this point, but the recipe seems obvious; the Golden Rule, at least in the Confucian form, and preferably in the Christian version, backed up by the quotation from Micah, "What doth the Lord require of thee but to do justly and to love mercy and to walk humbly before thy God."

In answering the question as to my hobbies and recreations, I may say that I am the worst golf player in the Hawaiian Islands, but will try to match fish stories against any member of the Class.

From the records of the 50th anniversary class book published in 1949:

In looking back over fifty years, most if not all of my "satisfactions" of life are the result of teamwork. I name a few:

A happy home life, five fine children, and eleven grandchildren. In business perhaps my greatest satisfaction was in the *esprit de corps* and teamwork of the Hawaiian Pineapple Company organization that was built up during my leadership.

I derive satisfaction from seeing the dream of my prospectus of 1901 come true, "Expand the market for Hawaiian Pineapple to every grocery store in the United States"; from the enjoyment by millions of a wholesome and palatable food; from my part in the too-long delayed development that made it possible for the public, who didn't eat all the pineapple production of the 1930-33 depression years, to drink the surplus and put the industry by 1934 on a balanced basis; a little, from sundry agricultural and manufacturing developments in which I played a minor part; from seeing the need for a quick and efficient way to get pineapple juice out of a can and having the American Can Company develop, within six months of my request, the answer in the form of what is now known as the beer can opener (two years before canned beer hit the market).

In August, 1948, I discontinued connection with the Hawaiian Pineapple Company as director and chairman. I am still working on new things and as from early years, trying to use scientific approaches. I am devoting much of my time to certain food and food equipment developments that seem to merit attention. I am distressed at the parlous state of the world, at the imminence, at least in India and China, of the possible proof that Malthus was no idle dreamer, and at the apparent lack of human capacity to organize mankind for the safe and humane guidance of atomic energy.

EMILY TAFT DOUGLAS:
UNITED STATES REPRESENTATIVE, ILLINOIS
(1899-1994)

From the Biographical Directory of the U.S. Congress:

Emily Taft Douglas of Illinois recognized the dangers of fascism during the mid-1930s and dedicated her public career to the cause of collective security against aggression and the establishment of a permanent machinery to insure international peace. The daughter of sculptor Laredo Taft, she was born in Chicago on April 10, 1899, and graduated with a Ph.B. from the University of Chicago in 1919. Following study at the American Academy of Dramatic Art, she worked in the theater and by 1926 was the star of *The Cat and the Canary* on Broadway.

In 1931 she married University of Chicago professor Paul H. Douglas, who at the age of fifty enlisted as a Marine private in 1942 and later was elected to three terms as Senator from Illinois. Disturbed by the rise of fascism in Europe and by the Italian invasion of Ethiopia, she returned from a trip abroad in 1935 to organize and chair the Illinois League of Women Voters' department of government and foreign policy. In 1942 she became executive secretary of the International Relations Center in Chicago.

In February of 1944 Illinois Democrats chose Douglas as their nominee for the state's at-large seat in the House of Representatives. In the general election, Douglas, who ran as a supporter of Roosevelt's foreign polices, faced Republican Stephen A. Day, one of the staunchest isolationists in the House. Despite the formidable opposition of the *Chicago Tribune* and its powerful publisher, Colonel Robert McCormick, she defeated Day by over 191,000 votes.

Shortly after the opening of the seventy-ninth Congress and in her first House vote, Douglas opposed the establishment of a standing Committee on Un-American Activities. She also helped rescue former Vice President Henry Wallace's chances to become Secretary of Commerce by acceding to the demands of Wallace's opponents and voting for legislation to withdraw the Reconstruction Finance Corporation's lending bureau from the jurisdiction of the Commerce Department.

During her term in the seventy-ninth Congress, Douglas served on the Committee on Foreign Affairs and was widely recognized as a specialist in the field. She joined several committee colleagues on a visit to Europe in August 1945 to inspect the work of the United Nations Relief and Rehabilitation Administration. Along with California Representative Jerry Voorhis, she proposed legislation to put the United Nations in charge of international programs for arms control and the abolition of atomic weaponry. She also called for greater federal support for libraries, particularly those in rural and low-income areas, and cosponsored a public library service demonstration bill.

Weary and frustrated by wartime controls and shortages and the strains of demobilization, voters in the midterm elections of 1946 ousted fifty-four House Democrats, among them Douglas, who lost to William G. Stratton. Following her husband's election to the Senate in 1948, she served on the legislative committee of the Unitarian Fellowship for Social Justice and as the Continental Moderator of the American Unitarian Association. Douglas also wrote a book for juveniles, a biography of Margaret Sanger, and a book of biographical essays on famous American women. She was a resident of White Plains, New York, until her death on January 28, 1994.

UNITARIAN NOTE

Emily Taft Douglas, who has been nominated as moderator, highest lay office in the American Unitarian Association, long has been active in Unitarian affairs. She is a member of All Souls Church (Unitarian), Washington, D.C, and a member of the Board of Contributing Editors of *The Unitarian Register*. She is active in the Unitarian Fellowship for Social Justice. In 1955, she was presented a Diamond Jubilee award by the General Alliance of Unitarian and Other Liberal Christian Women.

—*From an article in the* Unitarian Register, *February 1958*

PAUL H. DOUGLAS:
UNITED STATES SENATOR (1892-1976)

Paul Douglas, who identified himself in his autobiography as both a Unitarian and a Quaker, served as a trustee of the Abraham Lincoln Center (Unitarian) in Chicago. He was active in both All Souls Church (Unitarian) in Washington, DC, and the Cedar Lane Unitarian Church in Bethesda, MD. The following celebration of his life is drawn from an article in the Illinois Historical Journal *(Volume 83, Summer 1990) written by Edward L. Schapsmeier, Distinguished Professor of History at Illinois State University.*

Paul Douglas was born in Salem, Massachusetts in 1892, but the contours of his character were formed in the backwoods of Maine, where he was raised by a kindly stepmother. Young Douglas was forced by circumstances of poverty to work his way through Bowdoin College, from which he graduated in 1913 with

a Phi Beta Kappa key. After securing a master's degree at Columbia University in 1915, he did a year of post-graduate work at Harvard University and then earned a Ph.D. in economics at Columbia in 1921. He taught at the University of Illinois, Reed College, and the University of Washington, before accepting an appointment at the University of Chicago. He soon gained a professional reputation as an excellent teacher, a productive scholar, a humanitarian, and a civic activist. In 1927 Douglas became intrigued with the communist experiment going on in the Soviet Union. But after visiting Russia on a trade union mission and observing the aftermath of Lenin's dictatorial powers, he rejected Marxist economic theory. Instead, he turned to socialism tempered by the pacifism and humanism of the Quaker faith he had espoused since 1920.

Douglas campaigned for Norman Thomas in the 1932 presidential election but gradually became a supporter of the New Deal as Roosevelt began to implement genuine social reforms. He published a number of books agitating for enactment of New Deal legislation.

In Chicago, Douglas moved in both socialist and Democratic Party circles. In 1935 his friends urged him to run against Democratic Mayor Edward J. Kelly. When the Republicans refused to endorse him as their nominee, Douglas withdrew his candidacy. He ran in 1939 for the Chicago City Council as an Independent Democrat. He won and served as an alderman until 1942.

Paul Douglas's gradual gravitation towards true membership in the Democratic Party was hastened by his participation in Chicago politics, but it was his own conversion from pacifism to interventionism that propelled him to join the ranks of Franklin Roosevelt's supporters. After hearing Benito Mussolini announce Italy's invasion of hapless Ethiopia, Douglas had

been shocked into the conclusion that "isolationism was impossible and pacifism self-defeating against dictators." Douglas, who had once opposed the Reserve Officers' Training Corps, began to drill regularly with the volunteer Home Defense Unit at the University of Chicago. He also became an active member of the Committee to Defend America by Aid to the Allies.

In 1942 Douglas tried to win the Democratic nomination for the United States Senate but failed to gain the support of the Cook County Democratic machine. Douglas thereafter enlisted in the Marine Corps as a private. When discharged from service in 1946, Douglas was a wounded and decorated lieutenant colonel who had served heroically in the First Marine Division at Okinawa and Peleliu, where he was awarded the Purple Heart. He underwent five operations on his injured left arm, but its functional use was never restored.

By 1948 Colonel Jacob M. Arvey had succeeded Mayor Kelly as chairman of the Cook County Democratic organization and was willing to slate Professor Paul Douglas as the party's senatorial candidate. Thus, he began his eighteen-year Senate career as a true, regular Democrat. He spoke out forcefully for Truman's containment policy and fought for the Fair Deal as he had for the New Deal.

When the United States became involved in the Korean War in 1950, Douglas applauded America's military efforts on behalf of South Korea's right of self-determination against the communist invaders from the north.

During Douglas's three-term career—which spanned the presidential administrations of Truman, Eisenhower, Kennedy, and Lyndon Johnson—he was a forceful champion of civil rights, social welfare programs, public housing, extension of Social Security (including Medicare), federal aid to education, concern for the environment, and legislation beneficial to labor unions. Known as an uncompromising idealist, Douglas marched to his own drumbeat.

ABIGAIL ADAMS ELIOT:
NURSERY SCHOOL MOVEMENT PIONEER
(1892-1992)

By Paula Robbins, editor and author

Abigail Adams Eliot was a pioneer of the nursery school movement—she is best known for her work with young children and for teaching other people to work with young children.

As her name suggests, she was a member of two of the most illustrious Unitarian families of New England: the Adamses and the Eliots. Abby Eliot, as she was called, was born in Dorchester, Massachusetts, on October 9, 1892, the third child of Rev. and Mrs. Christopher Rhodes Eliot. Her father was the minister of the Meeting House Hill Church in Dorchester for thirteen years. Following a year of study at Oxford, he became minister and social worker of Bulfinch Place (Chapel) Church, one of the mission churches of the Benevolent Fraternity in Boston's West End. Abby attended Radcliffe College, graduating in 1914.

Eliot began her career as a social worker with the Children's Mission to Children. Quickly disillusioned with social work, she studied at Oxford for the academic year 1919-20 and, upon her return, was invited by Mrs. Henry Greenleaf Pearson to establish a nursery school in Boston. The Women's Education Association then sent her to study at the McMillan Nursery School in London for six months. Returning in January 1922 to join the Ruggles Street Day Nursery in Roxbury, Eliot also continued her formal education, earning a M.Ed. from the Harvard Graduate School of Education in 1926 and a doctorate in 1930.

As the nursery school movement grew, Eliot was part of the leadership that formed the National Association for the Education of Young Children and the National Association for Nursery Education. In 1933, she was their representative to the Federal Works Progress Administration, which provided funds to nursery schools for children in unemployed families and jobs for teachers. Later, she became responsible for the program in the New England states. During World War II she consulted on the provision of day care for the children of war workers under the Lanham Act.

In 1951 the Nursery Training School (later the Eliot-Pearson School) became affiliated with Tufts University and moved to the campus in 1954. In 1952 Eliot retired as head of the school she had founded and moved with her friend Anna Holman to Pasadena, California, to found a Nursery Training School at the Pacific Oaks Friends School.

Upon their return from California in 1954, Eliot and Holman moved to a house on Main Street in Concord, Massachusetts, on the Sudbury River, where they lived together until Holman's death in 1969. In Concord Eliot assisted in the First Parish Sunday School and taught for three years at the Brooks School. She also assisted in the formation of the Walden Clinic, now known as the Eliot Community Mental Health Center, and Belknap House, a boarding house for the elderly. In 1961 she became the unpaid Director of Development for the Eliot-Pearson School. She raised funds to build the Children's School and the administration building. In 1964 the school became the Eliot-Pearson Department of Child Study at Tufts University, which in 1981, began to award the Ph.D.

Of her Unitarian faith, Eliot said, "Religion has always been an important part of my life—a subconscious influence, as well as a conscious directive." She proudly affirmed that she was "born and bred a Unitarian" and that she had "always gone to church nearly every Sunday."

Abby Eliot lived her last years at Rivercrest in Concord because of her failing eyesight. Her brother, Frederick May Eliot, was minister of the Unitarian Church in St. Paul, Minnesota, and then President of the American Unitarian Association (AUA) between 1937 and 1958. Dr. Martha May Eliot, her sister, was chief of the U.S. Children's Bureau and worked for UNESCO and the World Health Organization (WHO).

FREDERICK MAY ELIOT: UNITARIAN PRESIDENT (1889-1958)

By Judge Lawrence G. Brooks, Chairman of the Board of Directors of the American Unitarian Association

Abridged from "Frederick May Eliot as I Knew Him" in the 1960 issue of The Proceedings of the Unitarian Historical Society (13, Part 1).

I was in close contact with Frederick Eliot during the last sixteen years of his life. I saw him as a man, a writer, a preacher, and as President of the American Unitarian Association.

Frederick May Eliot was born in Dorchester, Massachusetts, where his father was minister of the Unitarian church. Frederick was the oldest of three children of Christopher Rhodes Eliot and Mary May Eliot, the other two being Dr. Martha May Eliot and Abigail Adams Eliot, both of them persons of distinction. I remember Frederick's father well. Like many of his generation, he wore a beard, which by the time I knew him was completely white. In his later years he lived near my parents on Francis Avenue, Cambridge, where he built a house on part of the estate known as Shady Hill, which was formerly owned by Charles Eliot Norton.

Frederick attended the Prince Grammar School

in Boston, and the Roxbury Latin School, from which he entered Harvard College. He graduated with honors in 1911. His academic interest, at that time, was government. He received a traveling fellowship and went abroad to study the governments of European cities.

Had it not been for the Reverend Samuel McChord Crothers, it is quite likely Frederick would not have entered the ministry. This is where his Unitarian ancestry undoubtedly came into play. It was a good background for the persuasive Dr. Crothers to argue for the ministry. At any rate, instead of continuing in government, Frederick entered the Harvard Divinity School, from which he graduated in 1915.

Following his ordination as a Unitarian minister, he became assistant, for two years, to Dr. Crothers at the First Parish in Cambridge. In 1917 he was called to Dr. Crothers' old church in St. Paul, Minnesota. There he remained, with the exception of a few months when he was chaplain in the armed services, until called to the presidency of the American Unitarian Association twenty years later.

While Frederick was still in St. Paul, Unitarians became concerned over the obvious lack of progress of Unitarianism in the United States. The denomination appeared to be existing on a glorious past, certain prelude to decline.

To forestall this, the American Unitarian Association in 1934 created a Commission of Appraisal, and appointed Frederick May Eliot its chairman. He took the assignment very seriously. When, largely as the result of his fine work as chairman, he was called to the presidency of the A.U.A., Eliot felt it his duty to accept the call. It was as if all his Unitarian preacher ancestors spoke to him and bade him carry the Unitarian banner. It was a challenge in a time of crisis, which a man of courage could not refuse.

History records the results of his presidency. During the twenty years of Frederick's incumbency (1937-1958), adult membership in the denomination increased 75%; Church School membership almost trebled. In the last ten years, forty new churches have been established, over two hundred fellowships have been organized, of which a dozen have become churches (included in the forty). Indeed, to use a current expression, the Unitarian population has "exploded" and the machinery, more especially the American Unitarian Association, has been hard pressed to meet the challenge with ministers, buildings and other services.

Now what were the capabilities which contributed to Frederick Eliot's stature? To start with, he had a splendid inheritance, spiritually and morally. He possessed a superior intellect, which he constantly cultivated. He was executive by nature and enjoyed administrative work. His early life in Boston, followed by the twenty years in St. Paul, were an admirable combination which gave stimulus to an alert and inquiring mind. His retentive memory enabled him to store up what he read and heard. He had an unusual gift for public speaking. I never saw him read a speech or even use notes.

Frederick was tremendously interested in what he called liberal religion. One reason was his apprehension of what he thought to be the growing influence of orthodoxy in the United States and Europe. The other reason was his awareness of the growing dissidence in orthodox denominations—a curious paradox. He knew that the actual number of Unitarians was not found in the church roster but in the hearts and minds of thousands of individuals who, though tied to orthodoxy by inheritance or for social reasons, yearned for a faith free from creed and dogma.

Because Frederick so earnestly advocated liberal religion for those capable of understanding it and benefiting from it, and because he wanted to marshal the liberal forces into a united group, he favored close union between all liberal faiths, especially between Unitarians and Universalists, but not excluding non-Christians. He would welcome liberal Jews, Hindus, Moslems, for example, into such a church. This breadth of vision dismayed some Unitarians who feared for the survival of our denomination in any such religious cosmopolis.

Frederick May Eliot's life was full and varied. He had time, in addition to other duties, to serve as chairman of the Board of Trustees of Mount Holyoke College and on the Boards of Proctor Academy and Hackley School and for a period, like his father before him, as Chaplain to the Massachusetts Senate. For forty years he was dedicated to the advancement of Unitarianism. He literally was a soldier in this cause and he did not spare himself. This involved his battling sometimes with the right wing, sometimes with the left, and occasionally with both at once. His more difficult battles were with the conservative elements in the denomination. These encounters were harassing to his spirit. They made his constant struggle with financial problems more difficult because, as is frequently the case, the financial resources were with the conservatives. Their financial help was vital for the effective operation of the American Unitarian Association, but sometimes given not too generously.

All this and other labors took their toll of Frederick Eliot. It was a great shock, but not a great surprise to me, when word came of his sudden death. To conclude the metaphor of the soldier, Frederick truly died on the field of battle. He was just entering the courtyard of All Souls Unitarian Church in New York to attend a meeting when he died.

MARTHA MAY ELIOT:
SOCIAL PEDIATRICIAN, CHILDREN'S BUREAU
CHIEF (1891-1978)

By William M. Schmidt, M.D.
Courtesy of the Schlesinger Library, Radcliffe Institute, Harvard University

Address at the Harvard University Memorial Church, 1977

I met Dr. Martha Eliot first in 1941, thirty-six years ago, not long after she had had her fiftieth birthday. I had just come to join the Children's Bureau to work on regulations relating to health hazards for young workers, a field that was new to me.

For more than fifty years Martha May Eliot took a leading part in the development of health services for mothers and children. She was concerned for children of all countries of the world, and worked for them in the great international organizations: the League of Nations, United Nations Relief and Rehabilitation Administration (UNRRA), the United Nations Children's Fund, and the World Health Organization. At home, here in the United States, her own country, she used her vision and vigor in the United States Children's Bureau, at Yale Medical School, Harvard School of Public Health, and the Massachusetts Committee for Children and Youth, as well as in many governmental and non-governmental agencies and committees.

Her entire career was a fulfillment of a decision and commitment made early in her life. At Radcliffe she determined to study medicine. She has related that having learned that Professor Sedgwick was working to create a school of public health, she went to seek his advice. When he suggested that she should aim to become a laboratory technician, she asked him what advice he would give her if she were a man. "Study medicine," he said. "It was what I wanted to hear," she said.

While in the second year of medical school at Johns Hopkins in 1915 (she was 24 years old) she wrote to her family that she had a strong feeling that she should take every opportunity to take part in social work. "You see," she wrote, "even if I am studying here, and if I should practice, I want to keep attached to the social end of it; in other words, to be some kind of a social doctor—though what kind I don't know."

Dr. Edwards A. Park invited her to become his first resident pediatrician in the new department of pediatrics he was establishing at Yale. It was there that Dr. Eliot moved into social pediatrics with her study of rickets.

The question Dr. Eliot undertook to study was whether a program could be designed and carried out which would afford protection to every child on a community-wide basis. It was one thing to know that a child in an enlightened family, under excellent health care, could be protected from rickets. She wanted to know if all the children, even in a poor neighborhood, could be equally protected. She proved that they could. This was an important step in the history of the disappearance of rickets. Her three-year demonstration in New Haven was also a model of a community health center approach to meeting child health needs.

While continuing at Yale, Dr. Eliot became a member of the Children's Bureau staff, commuting frequently to Washington until 1935, developing the Division of Child Hygiene, and keeping in touch with what was being done under the Sheppard-Towner Act, which was the first Maternity and Infancy Act. She collaborated in the drafting of the children's sections of the Social Security Act.

Dr. Eliot's work for children through international organizations began in 1935 when she was an alternate delegate for Grace Abbott to a conference of the League of Nations, in Geneva, on child welfare. The next year she took part in a conference on infant and child nutrition of the Health Organization of the League. After that conference she seized the opportunity to visit seven European countries and to study their ways of providing health and welfare care for mothers and children. During the Second World War when England was under air attack, she went to London with a delegation from the United States to see how the British were handling civil defense, and especially caring for children's needs. She was called upon to serve with the U.S. delegation to the International Health Conference in 1945, where she and Dr. Brock Chisholm won the support needed to have the constitution of the World Health Organization include child health as one of its major responsibilities. She was the only woman to sign the constitution of the World Health Organization. She has been referred to by its present Director General as one of the brilliant pioneers of international health. Her work for UNICEF, surveying the situation of children in some thirteen European countries in 1937, and working on agreements between the governments and UNICEF, was a great achievement.

We shall remember Martha Eliot as one of the great pioneers of maternal and child health; as one of the early advocates of a national health program; as one who worked for the welfare of children, believing that child health and child welfare were inseparable. She had the highest honors from her peers in her professional associations, and from many universities and other organizations. We shall remember that she did indeed become, as she had hoped and planned when she was still a medical student, a "kind of social doctor" — a great social doctor.

SAMUEL ATKINS ELIOT II:
FIRST PRESIDENT OF THE UNITARIANS
(1862-1950)

By Elizabeth Curtiss, Unitarian Universalist Minister and Educator
Courtesy of the Dictionary of Unitarian Universalist Biography

Samuel Atkins Eliot II (1862-1950) was the first President of the American Unitarian Association (AUA) to be given the power of an executive; he held this office from 1900 to 1927. A member of one of 19th century New England's most accomplished families, Eliot vigorously expanded the denomination's identity through application of the then-new "scientific management." Many of Eliot's innovations in governance and patterns of authority can still be seen in today's Unitarian Universalist Association (UUA).

Samuel Atkins Eliot was the third generation of his family (and the second of his name) to grasp the helm of a major institution with the intention of improving its operation. Sam's paternal grandfather, the first Samuel Atkins Eliot, pursued public cultural interests ranging from membership in King's Chapel to co-founding Boston's premier choral society, the Handel and Hayden Society. A conscientious businessman, grandfather Eliot served as mayor of Boston from 1836 to 1850. Dr. Charles William Eliot, the mayor's son and Sam's father, briefly taught college chemistry before becoming president of Harvard University.

The AUA President was born in Cambridge, Massachusetts. His father, widowed when Sam was six years old, did not remarry until 1877. Rather than attending any school, Sam spent his childhood in the company of his father and the tightly knit Harvard faculty. Their guidance allowed Sam and his brother, architect Charles Eliot, to enjoy individual educations. In 1885 he entered Harvard Divinity School, where his grandfather, Samuel Atkins Eliot, had once studied as well.

Eliot graduated in 1889 and accepted the call to Unity Church in Denver, Colorado, evangelizing two new liberal churches, in Colorado Springs and Salt Lake City. He married Frances Hopkinson and the couple soon prepared to welcome the first of their seven children. Sam scandalized many of his Denver neighbors by joining his wife to wheel baby carriages and play outside with their children.

In 1892 Eliot returned east to occupy the prestigious pulpit of The Church of the Savior, Brooklyn, New York. In 1894 he began serving on the Board of Directors of the AUA. In 1898, he was elected to the AUA's highest executive office, as its Secretary, and left the Brooklyn pulpit for full time denominational work. In 1900 the AUA conferred executive powers on its hitherto quiescent presidency and elevated Eliot to the expanded position.

The AUA's first executive president envisioned his task as the restoration and expansion of a religion, which was a great offshoot from Christian Europe's Reformation.

During his 27 years as President, he created a Department of Ministry, which assisted congregations with selection of candidates for ministry, and a Department of Social Justice, which enacted his vision of liberal religion as a unified political force in secular society.

Eliot tirelessly advocated business method in congregational organization. He believed Unitarianism's best hope for the future lay with congregations associated with suburban communities and universities. He proposed to position denominational presence at the local level by creating what are now our district executives and offices. To ensure ministers in the west, he instituted a new seminary, which has become Starr King School for the Ministry.

After his presidency, he served a single pulpit (Boston's Arlington Street Church) for the remainder of his career.

Beginning in 1899, Eliot worked to further ties between the Unitarians and Universalists. He believed that they were each tending liberal faiths whose martyrs had created a great and liberal religion.

"I am sad to have retired"

by Arthur Cushman McGiffert, Jr., biographer and son-in-law

"I am sad to have retired," Eliot wrote to a friend shortly after he became minister *emeritus* of Arlington Street Church, "but I was never busier and have to paddle hard to keep my head above water."

Ten years after his resignation from the presidency of the AUA, the latter undertook an appraisal of its methods and form of organization. The Commission of Appraisal commended itself to Eliot because its members were not "rainbow chasers or fabricators of dreams. They dealt with things immediately practical."

He was one of the founders of the National Association for the Advancement of Colored People and of the Urban league, became a trustee of Tuskegee Institute and put Booker T. Washington on the map as a wise and reliable leader of his race.

In 1943 Eliot accepted an invitation to help start an agency to assist Jewish children who were the victims of German Nazism. What he described as his "happy association with synagogue and temple" ran back to the very beginning of his ministry. While still a Divinity School student, he preached in the Temple Emmanuel in San Francisco. When he was ordained in Denver, a young rabbi stood with him and took part in the service.

"In recognition of distinguished service to the cause of liberal religion," the American Unitarian Association in May 1950 presented Eliot with the Second Annual Award—just five months before his death. The occasion marked the fiftieth anniversary of his election to the Association's presidency, the one hundred and twenty-fifth anniversary of the Association's founding, and the fiftieth anniversary of the International Association for Liberal Christianity and Religious Freedom which he had organized.

He "slipped away" on October 16, 1950, in his 89th year. A tablet placed by the Arlington Street church in Eliot's memory reads:

Preacher   Administrator

Civic Servant and Friend

Abridged from Pilot of a Liberal Faith, *by courtesy of Beacon Press.*

Eliot Edited the four volume Heralds of a Liberal Faith,*published by the American Unitarian Association (Volume 1-3, 1910; Volume 4, 1952).*

THOMAS H. ELIOT:
LEGISLATOR AND EDUCATOR (1907-1991)

Thomas H. Eliot was born in Cambridge. He was the grandson of Charles W. Eliot, a president of Harvard University. Mr. Eliot's family includes also William Greenleaf Eliot, a founder of Washington University, and the poet T.S. Eliot. Over the years, Mr. Eliot wrote articles for many professional journals and general-interest magazines and was author of a leading college textbook, Governing America: The Politics of a Free People. *In addition, Mr. Eliot served as a trustee of the St. Louis Council on World Affairs and New England chairman of the United Negro College Fund. The chief draftsman of the Social Security Act, as well as the first General Counsel for the Social Security Board of the United States, he was the son of Samuels Atkins Eliot, the first president of the American Unitarian Association.*

FROM THE SOCIAL SECURITY ARCHIVES

In 1933, Thomas H. Eliot, together with many of his youthful fellow graduates from Harvard Law School, went to Washington, becoming Assistant Solicitor of the Department of Labor under Frances Perkins. Later, she appointed him Counsel for the Committee on Economic Security, which drafted the social security bill. After serving as General Counsel for the Social Security Board, he returned to Massachusetts, taught at Harvard, was elected to Congress from Massachusetts, joined the faculty of Washington University in St. Louis in 1952, and served as Chancellor of that institution during the period 1962-71. The problems faced in the drafting of legislation which could withstand constitutional challenges in the U.S. Supreme Court are the core of Mr. Eliot's presentation. He reports how the Court's earlier decisions on grants-in-aid provided the basis for the old-age assistance program and several other grant-in-aid programs in the 1935 Act; how the decision upholding tax offsets was used as the basis for the unemployment insurance legisla-

tion once the policy decision of State responsibility and administration had been made; and how events unrelated to social security may have had an impact on the Court's upholding the constitutionality of the old-age insurance program.

FROM THE ST. LOUIS POST-DISPATCH, OCTOBER 16, 1991

Thomas H. Eliot, as Washington University chancellor, led the school to national academic prominence and helped it weather the student protest era. Mr. Eliot headed Washington University from 1962 until his retirement in 1971. Earlier, he represented his home state of Massachusetts in Congress and was a federal labor official, playing a key role in the drafting of the Social Security Act and the lobbying for its passage. After leaving Washington University, he became president of the Salzburg Seminar in American Studies, holding that post until 1976. In that position, he divided his time between Salzburg, Austria, and the seminar's U.S. office in Cambridge. Mr. Eliot joined Washington University in 1952 as chairman of its political science department. In 1958, he became the Charles Nagel Professor of Constitutional Law and Political Science. In 1961, he became dean of the College of Liberal Arts and vice chancellor, dean of faculties. As the school's 12th chancellor, he was credited with completing the school's transformation from an institution of primarily local renown into one with a national reputation. He achieved that in part by bringing well-known scholars in various fields to join the university's faculty and by attracting substantial financial support from the Ford Foundation and other private groups. During Mr. Eliot's tenure, the school's full-time faculty grew from 600 people to more than 1,100. Fourteen major buildings were completed, and construction was begun on three more.

WILLIAM EMERSON: M.I.T. DEAN OF ARCHITECTURE (1873-1957)

From The Unitarian Register, *Midsummer MCMLVII*

The man responsible for development of the Unitarian Service Committee, Dr. William Emerson, died May 4 at the age of 83.

Dr. Emerson was chairman of the USC when it was a standing committee of the American Unitarian Association, from 1940 to 1948. When the USC was

incorporated in 1948, Dr. Emerson became president and served until 1953. He was honorary president from 1953 to the time of his death.

Under Dr. Emerson's leadership, the USC program was established. He is considered the man most instrumental in the development of the committee and its "moving spirit."

In 1949, Dr. Emerson was presented the first annual AUA award for "distinguished service to the cause of liberal religion." In 1956, the USC presented him an award for this outstanding service.

Born October 16, 1873, Dr. Emerson received his A.B.

degree from Harvard University in 1895; studied architecture at Columbia University, 1895-97, and at *Ecole des Beaux Arts, Paris*, 1897-1901, and received an honorary doctor of the arts degree in 1939 from Harvard.

An architect, Dr. Emerson specialized in the design of bank buildings and model tenements. As chairman of the educational committee of the American Institute of Architects, he was known for his contributions to architectural education.

Joining the staff of Massachusetts Institute of Technology in 1919, Dr. Emerson was professor of architecture, chairman of the faculty, and dean of the school of architecture. Upon his retirement in 1939, he was appointed dean emeritus of the MIT school of architecture.

During World War I, Dr. Emerson served as director of the Bureau of Construction of the American Red Cross in Paris, and was presented the Chevalier Legion of Honor by the French government.

The noted architect was advisory architect of Radcliffe College; a life member of the corporation of MIT; former chairman of the corporation of Simmons College; president of the Boston Society of Architects, 1940-42; former vice-president of the Society Beaux Arts Architects; elected honorary Phi Beta Kappa, Harvard, 1928; president of the Association of Collegiate Schools of Architecture, 1921-23; and vice-president of the Byzantine Institute, 1935.

Dr. Emerson devoted himself to collective security by supporting the League of Nations Association, by helping to organize and serving as chairman of the Committee to Defend America by Aiding the Allies in 1940, and by serving as president of the American Association for the United Nations.

SOPHIA LYON FAHS: LIBERAL RELIGIOUS EDUCATOR (1876-1978)

By Edith Fisher Hunter, author

The life of Sophia Lyon Fahs was a remarkable journey from the heart of evangelical Christian orthodoxy to a leadership role in a revitalized religious liberalism, a revitalization due in large part to her role as an innovative religious educator.

Born in China on August 2, 1876, the child of Presbyterian missionaries, Sophia Lyon graduated from Wooster College in Wooster, Ohio, dedicated to becoming a foreign missionary.

In June 1902 she married Charles Harvey Fahs. Because of his health problems, the young couple could not go immediately into the mission field, but moved instead to New York City. Sophia continued her studies, now at Columbia University's Teachers College, another intellectually exciting place where John Dewey would join the faculty in 1904.

Between 1905 and 1914 five children were born to Sophia and her husband, and as she herself later wrote: "The children who joined our family circle were not merely the object of my educational efforts, they were the most potent source of my own education. In a vital sense, the children were unwittingly my major teachers." Since her husband's health continued to be a problem, all thought of going out as foreign missionaries was abandoned.

In between bearing children, coping with their frequent illnesses and the death of two of them, Sophia Fahs was busy in her field. As she hammered out her increasingly liberal theology and its implications for religious education, she found herself drawing less exclusively on the Judeo-Christian tradition and more on the natural sciences, on the religion of primitive people, and on other world religions. She had discovered that primitive people developed their religious ideas as they reacted to the natural world around them. What if today's children were allowed to express freely their reactions to the same primary phenomena -- birth and death, sun and moon and stars, dreams, shadows, wind and rain? Should not children's inescapable confrontations with and reflection on these realities be the beginning of their religious education rather than Bible stories about people of long ago and far away?

In 1923 she enrolled as a Bachelor of Divinity student at Union Theological Seminary. The Union School of Religion had taken over the experimental Sunday School at Teachers College, and Sophia Fahs was soon a teacher there. She also became a Lecturer in Religious Education on the Seminary faculty. However, word of her innovative ideas and practices in the school at Union soon brought her into direct conflict with the Union Seminary authorities.

Riverside Church was built right across the street from Union, specifically to provide a pulpit for Harry Emerson Fosdick, the champion of Modernism. Its Sunday School was to be forward looking and experimental, and by 1933 Sophia Fahs had been invited to try out some of her ideas there. The courses developed at Riverside by Sophia Fahs and her coworkers would prove to be the core of the curriculum she would develop for the Unitarian denomination between 1937 and 1965.

By 1937, her shift from a Bible-centered curriculum to a child-centered approach that embraced "the latest scientific findings" in all fields of human endeavor was complete.

The Unitarian churches had long been wrestling with many of the problems that perplexed Sophia Fahs. In 1837, 100 years before she took up her work with the denomination, the prophetic Unitarian preacher, William Ellery Channing, speaking before the Boston Sunday School Society, urged his listeners to have faith in the child and to see as the challenge"not to stamp our minds irresistibly on the young, but to stir up their own, not to tell them that God is good, but to help them to see and feel his love."

In 1935, Ernest Kuebler was appointed secretary of the Unitarian Department of Religious Education, and he was instrumental in hiring Sophia Fahs in 1937. Almost immediately titles in yet another curriculum, "The New Beacon Series," began to appear. Not only was Sophia Fahs the Editor of these materials, she was in the majority of cases the author or co-author as well.

With every book, a teacher or parent guide was provided with ideas for artistic and dramatic activities, and with bibliographies of resource materials. Sophia Fahs always maintained that it took more research and preparation to teach children than to teach adults. She co-authored a book to explain the philosophy behind "the here and now" stories for the youngest children, *Consider the Children How They Grow*. She also fostered the production of new song books to accompany the curriculum.

In 1952, Sophia Fahs took the time from her editorial duties to write the book that presented the underlying philosophy of The New Beacon Series, *Today's Children and Yesterday's Heritage, A Philosophy of Creative Religious Development*. In 1965, *Worshipping Together with Questioning Minds* was published, summarizing her experience in "leading children in worship."

Membership in the Unitarian churches, which had been shrinking for years, began to grow by leaps and bounds and new congregations and fellowships sprang up all around the country. Beacon curriculum books came into use not only for Unitarian religious education but also by other denominations, and by some private schools as well as by parents who were not Unitarian. In February 1959, at the age of 82, Sophia Fahs accepted the invitation of one of these new churches, the Montgomery County Unitarian Church of Bethesda, Maryland, to be ordained into the Unitarian ministry. It was a booming church with the largest church school in the country.

Sophia Lyon Fahs completed her remarkable life journey on April 14, 1978, at the age of 101.

JOSEPH L. FISHER (1914-1992)
AND MARGARET W. FISHER (1921-):
PARTNERS IN LIVING RELIGION
FAITH IN ACTION

By George Kimmich Beach, Unitarian Universalist Minister

When he affiliated with the Unitarian Universalist faith, Albert Schweitzer characterized it as a way of "faith in action." Joseph and Margaret Fisher—Joe and Peggy (as we have always called them) —exemplify what Schweitzer had in mind. Their spiritual and moral convictions have undergirded a lifelong engagement in the civic, religious, and professional institutions of their community and world. Religion for them has always meant "faith in action."

Peggy Fisher first used the term "living religion" in her outline for a young people's course on Unitarian Universalist beliefs that she and Joe taught in their home congregation. For a living religion, she suggested, the Unitarian Universalist flaming chalice is an apt symbol: an inner light that inspires caring and active service.

Joe and Peggy Fisher have reflected deeply on the meaning of their activism. In their poetry and the essay-sermons, they have shaped their reflections into a vision of public and personal life. Peggy and Joe initially outlined the series and set to work. Their outline was enlarged to accommodate new themes as they emerged. The book, <u>Living Religion</u>, took more than fifteen years to complete.

Joseph Lyman Fisher was born in Pawtucket, Rhode Island, in 1914, one of two children in a Unitarian family. A trim athlete, he was a skillful boxer and an avid wilderness hiker and canoeist. He enrolled at Bowdoin College, in Brunswick, Maine, graduating in 1935, and began his career as an economist specializing in resource management. After the war, the Fishers moved to Cambridge, Massachusetts, where Joe continued graduate studies in economics, receiving a doctorate from Harvard University in 1947. The growing Fisher family then moved to the nation's capitol, living in Falls Church initially and in Arlington a little later. From 1947 to 1954 Joe was Executive Officer and Senior Economist of the President's Council of Economic Advisers. From 1954 to 1975 he worked for a private research and educational foundation, Resources for the Future, Inc., becoming its President in 1959.

Joe's greatest political triumph came in 1974. In the House of Representatives Joe soon established himself as a respected expert on economic policy. Looking back upon his public career, he took the greatest pride from his contributions to federal environmental policy and his successful role in creating the Bill of Rights for handicapped persons in Virginia.

During these and subsequent years Peggy and Joe were raising three daughters and four sons. With a husband so deeply involved in civic life, many of the burdens—and the joys, she adds—of raising the family fell to Peggy. (Joe "uncomfortably" recalls the answer one of their grade-school age daughters gave to a teacher's question to the children about what their fathers did for a living. She said, "My daddy goes to meetings.") Nevertheless, Peggy found time to establish her own career as an artist, an arts educator, and a poet.

Her own landscapes, figure paintings, and family portraits, in both oil and watercolor, are vibrant with color and feeling. Her poetry exhibits similar qualities: clear, forceful expression of perceptions and deeply felt values. She has received awards from the New York Poetry Forum and the National League of American Penwomen.

The partnership of Joe and Peggy Fisher has also been expressed through their religious community, the Unitarian Church of Arlington. Joe was elected to the Board of the Unitarian Universalist Association (UUA). When the position of UUA Moderator was suddenly vacated Joe was selected by his peers to fill the position. He was subsequently elected by the national membership to two more four-year terms.

The office of Moderator, normally held by a layperson, is the highest volunteer position in the UUA. Joe's twelve years of service, from 1964 to 1976, were marked by painfully divisive controversies in the denomination over the Vietnam War and "black empowerment." In conversation, years later, he recalled presiding at one particularly fractious UUA General Assembly, when a young woman in hippie garb approached him at the podium. What next? he wondered. She placed a string of "love-beads" around his neck, which he accepted with his broad smile. Suddenly the Assembly burst into applause, a tribute to his fair-minded and unflappable leadership under sorely trying circumstances. The tension of the moment was broken; the Assembly regained its confidence and unity.

In 1985 Joe's severe back pains were diagnosed as bone cancer. Through treatment he gained remission, enabling him to maintain the extraordinary activities that marked his entire adult life. Early in 1991 Joe's cancer returned.

His memorial service at the Unitarian church was attended by an overflow crowd, the largest number in its history. A few days earlier, family members and close friends gathered at Arlington National Cemetery to offer final appreciations—words, music, a brief dance. There his ashes were buried, next to the graves of two four-star generals. The marker reads: "Tech Sgt. Joseph L. Fisher, Member of Congress."

Abridged from Living Religion *by Joseph L. Fisher and Margaret W. Fisher (Arlington, VA: Clerestory Press, 1993)*

ARTHUR FOOTE II: CELEBRANT OF LIFE (1911-1999)

Harvard College 25th Anniversary Report
Courtesy of the Harvard University Archives

> **OCCUPATION:** Unitarian minister; minister of Unity Church since 1945.
>
> **OFFICES HELD:** Member, Governor's Advisory Council on Mental Health, 1948-53; president, St. Paul Council of Human Relations, 1949-50; vice-president, Minnesota Association for Mental Health, 1953-56, Minnesota Welfare Conference, since 1957; member board of directors, American Unitarian Association, 1954-57; co-chairman, Unitarian Universalist Hymnbook Commission, since 1956; president, Minnesota Council of Liberal Churches, since 1957.

When I decided, midway in my senior year, to enter our Unitarian Theological School in Chicago, I was not at all sure that the ministry would prove "my dish." More than one college-mate took me aside to assure me that with my stammer it was bound to be a mistake; and I guess only cussedness kept me from agreeing. During the summer I had other things (I mean another person) to think about: Becca and I were married August 6, 1933.

Once at Meadville, my inner doubts vanished. With a clear goal before me, I at last found studies that captured my total interest. We had many wonderful experiences during the next three years. To mention one, my student charge in Shelbyville, Illinois, whither we drove each Friday for a long weekend. The lay leader of this tiny parish was Winifred Douthit, an extraordinary and unforgettable character, a hunchback scarcely three feet tall and the best critic of sermons I've ever had the good fortune to meet. My Sunday afternoon course in Homiletics was worth any three at the school.

Graduating in March, 1936, Becca and I set sail for Europe, well loaded with letters of introduction to Unitarian leaders in Romania, Hungary, Czechoslovakia, Holland, England and Ireland. Traveling by car, we had five jam-packed exciting months.

Agreeing 100% with Horace Greeley's advice, on our return to the States in September, we headed for the West Coast. The assignment, to resuscitate two moribund churches. Sacramento had ceased operation three years earlier. Stockton, forty-five miles to the south, was in bad shape also. We stayed with this dual assignment nine years. When feelers came from one of the strongest of our middle-western churches, I found myself loth to leave. But I knew the two churches had grown to the point of needing a minister apiece, and that meant I'd worked myself out of a job.

In 1945 the Foote family packed up and trekked to St. Paul. That was twelve years ago. We have seen the church more than double in size, and add a fine new wing to its parish house.

If the foregoing sounds more than a mite pollyannish, my only defense is that it is written by a happy man, who has found the struggle to become a mature person challenging, the work of the ministry rewarding, and the role of husband and father both.

Harvard College 50th Anniversary Report

OFFICES HELD, HONORS AND AWARDS: Chairman of the Board of Trustees, Meadville/Lombard Theological School, 1960-1963; Chairman of the Hymnbook Commission, Unitarian Universalist Association.

PRINCIPAL WORKS: *Taking Down the Defenses*, Beacon Press, 1975; *Hymns for the Celebration of Life*, Beacon Press, 1964.

Finishing a twenty-five-year pastorate in Saint Paul in 1970, Rebecca and I decided to return to Southwest Harbor, her native and my adopted home, to enjoy our elective years. Our quarter-century in Minnesota was personally furfilling, but we were ready for a change of scene and occupation. A childhood visit to a famous old Italian pottery had left me with an itch to try my hand at turning lumps of clay into objects of usefulness and beauty. At the Saint Paul Art Center, I learned all I could about this craft, and now, for a dozen years, I have practiced this second career as a stoneware potter. It has proved immensely satisfying. First, we renovated my wife's ancestral home, one of our town's oldest, adding some modern conveniences and a studio wing. The house was built by her great-great-grandfather, Captain Nathan Clark, and looks out over our charming harbor.

Besides throwing pots, I keep as busy as I want to be with occasional preaching, growing vegetables, chopping wood for our three stoves, hiking, reading, trying to learn how to play the piano, and enjoying old (and not so old) friends who drop in on us—especially our children and grandchildren when they make it back to Maine. We travel a little, but not too much; it's too nice right here. Our proximity to Acadia National Park adds much to our enjoyment of life; and after many urban years we are glad for the slower, quiet life of a Maine village (slower and quiet, that is, except during the tourist season). Our blessings are many, and we enjoy counting them.

HENRY WILDER FOOTE: MINISTER, SCHOLAR, HYMNOLOGIST (1875-1964)

Harvard College 50th Anniversary Report
Courtesy of Harvard University Archives

Foote, the son of Henry Wilder Foote, '58, and Frances Anne Eliot, was born February 2, 1875, at Boston. He prepared at the Roxbury Latin School and at a private school. After receiving his Bachelor's degree with our class, he spent a year at the Graduate School of Arts and Sciences and was awarded an A.M in 1900. Two years later he was granted an S.T.B at the Harvard Divinity School. In 1929 a D.D. was conferred upon him by the Pacific Unitarian School for the Ministry in Berkeley, California, and in 1941 the Meadville Theological School bestowed on him the same honor.

In addition to many printed articles, sermons, and pamphlets I have written three books, *The Minister and His Parish*, 1924; *Robert Feke, Colonial Portrait Painter*, 1930; and *Three Centuries of American Hymnody*, 1940. I collaborated with H. F. Clarke in his life of Jeremiah Dummer. I also collaborated in editing two hymn books, *The New Hymn and Tune Book*, 1914 (as secretary of the Editorial Committee); and *Hymns of the Spirit*, 1937 (as chairman of the Editorial Committee); and with A. T. Davison in editing the *Concord Anthem Book* and the *Second Concord Anthem Book*.

Henry Wilder Foote, Hymnologist

by Arthur Foote II

Abridged from "Henry Wilder Foote, Hymnologist," in The Papers of the Hymn Society, *The Hymn Society of America, New York, NY.*

In 1927, the Directors of the American Unitarian Association appointed a Commission on Hymns and Services. My father was named chairman. Asked to serve with him were Dr. Curtis W. Reese, a leading representative of the humanist wing of the movement; Dr. Von Ogden Vogt, author of *Art and Religion*, 1921, and *Modern Worship*, 1927; and Rev. Edward P. Daniels, an accomplished musician. After the work was well under way, the Universalist General Convention also appointed a hymnbook commission. In 1931 it was decided "that the two Commissions should cooperate in editing jointly a book to be recommended to the two groups of Churches." *Hymns of the Spirit*, the result of their labors, thus became an important early milestone on the long road to merger of these two denominations in 1961.

For father, editing *Hymns of the Spirit* became much more than an avocation; it grew into what might be called "a second career" that added heavily to his duties as a parish minister at the First Church, Belmont, Massachusetts. Night after night, the light burned late in his third floor study; and the mornings of his summer vacations invariably found him working in his small study on the shore at Southwest Harbor, Maine. He was a scholar by nature, willing to work long hours and to take infinite pains to get things right.

If my father's interest in hymnology and the art of worship grew naturally from his childhood exposure in the family pew and in the parsonage of King's Chapel, so also came his life-long interest in Colonial and early American history. His forebears on both sides traced their ancestry back to the first days of the Massachusetts Bay Colony.

Naturally, my father derived considerable satisfaction that *Hymns of the Spirit* was so well received, both within and without the denominations for which it was prepared. But he also treasured one bitterly critical review in a Unitarian church bulletin, in which the minister called it "an atrocious collection, set to miserable, unsingable music," and ended with a plea to his congregation to "throw it out and secure a really good hymnal, like the Methodists'" (quoted from memory).

The year 1940, which saw the publication of *Three Centuries of American Hymnody*, also marked his formal retirement from the parish ministry, after sixteen years in the Belmont pulpit. He was a man of many intellectual interests, and he had in mind a number of books he now hoped to find time to write. America's entrance into the war, however, postponed his plans.

During the two years, 1943-45, my father served as the first minister of the newly formed Jefferson Unitarian Church in Charlottesville, Virginia, almost in sight of Monticello. Using the opportunity of being in Jefferson's home territory, he began the study that led to the only thorough survey of Jefferson's religion, published under the title *Thomas Jefferson: Champion of Religious Freedom; Advocate of Christian Morals.* An accompanying work, *Thomas Jefferson, Social*

Reformer, was also published the same year, and several years later he edited *The Life and Morals of Jesus of Nazareth, extracted from The Gospels by Thomas Jefferson.*

Father was goaded by his children into writing an essay for them. *The Religion of an Inquiring Mind*, published in his eightieth year, recounts the story of his own spiritual pilgrimage.

From the time of my father's early paper on "The Harvard School of Hymnody," his imagination played upon the fact that a small religious movement, commonly considered highbrow, should have created such a succession of beautiful religious lyrics, ranging from statements of a warm personal faith and gratitude to stirring calls to social justice and the service of mankind, over a period of approximately one hundred and fifty years.

Another long time concern was Negro education, and for more than half a century he served on the Board of Trustees of both Hampton Institute, and Penn School of Frogmore, South Carolina.

Such people as he do maintain the fabric of the world, and in the handiwork of their craft is their prayer.

STEPHEN H. FRITCHMAN: HERETIC (1902-1981)

By Carl Seaburg
Unitarian Universalist Association Directory, 1981-82

Stephen Hole Fritchman was born in Cleveland, Ohio on May 12, 1902 to Quaker parents of German-English descent. After a year at the Wharton School of Finance and Commerce, University of Pennsylvania, he attended Ohio Wesleyan University, receiving his BA degree in 1924. He remained there for a year as an instructor of English Bible.

From 1925 to 1927 he was religious news editor of the *New York Herald Tribune*. In 1928-29 he was associate editor of the *Methodist Church School Journal*. His formal connection with Methodism terminated in 1930 when he began a two year pastorate at the Unitarian Church in Petersham, Mass. He was ordained in 1930 into the Unitarian ministry. After Petersham, he spent six years at the Bangor Unitarian Church in Maine. From there he entered the educational and organizational work of the American Unitarian Association in Boston. He was youth director for the AUA from 1938 to 1947. In 1942 he also became editor of the AUA journal, *The Christian Register*.

He continued in his dual role until an eighteen-month controversy developed over his editorial policies and direction. Termed "the Fritchman Crisis," it sparked

charges and countercharges. Defenders held that he had taken a dull, denominational house organ and transformed it into a dynamic magazine, one that was timely, relevant, and controversial. Opponents agreed on the controversial part of that statement, but accused him of following a Communist line, of supporting Soviet policies in the denominational magazine. After a bitter ecclesiastical fight, he resigned in 1947.

The following year he became minister of the First Unitarian Church of Los Angeles, CA, and continued in that position until his retirement in 1969. Under his leadership the church became a center of resistance to the Cold War and entered creatively into the conflicts of those years. It vigorously supported liberal causes in the city and state. He himself was active in many organizations concerned with peace and civil liberties.

In his retirement he continued active in the causes which had enlisted his support all his life, as ever cheerful, energetic, and with a finely tuned sense of humor. In 1976 at Claremont, CA, he received the Annual Award of the UUA for Distinguished Service to the Cause of Liberal Religion. The Unitarian Universalist Service Committee, which he supported all his life, named its annual award after him in his honor.

His published works include *Men of Liberty*, "Unitarianism Today," *Young People in the Liberal Church*, and *Heretic: A Partisan Autobiography*.

He focused his intellect, talents, and energy on the great causes of our time—peace, disarmament, racism, the ongoing struggle against intolerance and hatred. He was nine years a denominational leader but twenty-eight years a parish minister. He was an excellent minister who always had a concerned ear, a caring heart.

As his UUA Award citation said, "there is little which has not felt your influence." And he himself said in his address to the UUSC, "If we truly believe that human beings are of supreme importance, we will not be neutral." Nobody ever claimed that Stephen Fritchman was neutral.

BUCKMINSTER FULLER: DESIGNER OF A NEW WORLD (1895-1983)

Richard Buckminster Fuller, who discovered the most economical way of being able to use space, was born in Milton, Massachusetts, in 1895. A Unitarian, he attended Milton Academy, Harvard College, and the U.S. Naval Academy in Annapolis. However, he found that formal education got in the way of his being able to educate himself to the full potentiality of the powers that were within him.

When one of the senior members of The Architects Collaborative in Harvard Square—an area which is noted for its architects—found out that Buckminster Fuller was going to be recorded for national public television and radio broadcast at the historic Meeting House of the First Parish in Cambridge, he said, "I think he is the Thomas Alva Edison of our time." Marshall McLuhan called Bucky "the 20th century Leonardo da Vinci."

Nonetheless, Buckminster Fuller was no mere technological inventor; his thought has profoundly affected our awareness of the amazing, emerging social and environmental potential of humanity.

It's important to note that in 1927 a drastic change took place in his life. He decided that he was not going to commit suicide but committed his life to the furtherance of humanity. He found ingenious ways of doing that repeatedly.

People began to say, "Oh Bucky, you're a thousand years ahead of your time!" A decade later, he noted, people were saying, "Oh, Mr. Fuller, you're a century ahead of your time." Now, he says that they said, "My, you certainly are up to date!"

SPOKEN AT CAMBRIDGE FORUM, HARVARD SQUARE, 1980

I was born here in 1895. I was the first generation of my family to go to Harvard, and I tell you that when I was young what was fundamental, what was reality, was everything you could see, smell, touch, and hear. The year I was born X-rays were discovered, but they didn't make any newspaper. Nobody knew that it was going to amount to anything—you couldn't see them anyway. When I was three, the electrons were discovered. That didn't make any newspapers. Nobody knew that was going to amount to anything. Marconi had invented theoretical wireless the year I was born; but didn't get the first SOS until I was twelve years of age.

I was eight years of age when the Wright brothers flew. I was seven when the first automobile came into Boston. Out of seven hundred in my class here at Harvard, entering in 1913, two had automobiles. One of them was Ray Stanley, whose father invented the Stanley Steamer, so that was logical. Automobiles were anything but for everybody. We didn't have any kind of roads except dust roads. Once in a while somebody was able to get through to a place like New York after getting mired and pulled out by horses.

Since that time in America and the world, the electron began to be of prominence, and we began to learn something about the invisible world. While you couldn't see it, the human mind and instruments began to open up a greater range of reality, ah, but invisible reality.

I was brought up here in this particular world— this Cambridge and Milton where I went to school— where my mother and all the schoolteachers said, "Darling, never mind what you think. Listen, we're trying to teach you." The working assumption of the older people was that the children's thinking was very unreliable.

Suddenly evolution does something absolutely amazing here, when the young discover that the grown-ups don't know what it's all about. So we

have the young world doing its own thinking; and without any experience, it had to make many mistakes. But it's getting now where it's not being politically exploited the way it was at first. I find the young everywhere around the world are completely intent in thinking about the total world. They're not impressed with local nations anymore. There's a young world coming along, each child born successively in the presence of less misinformation. Just think, until I was eight years of age, I had been told it's inherently impossible for man to fly. I've had undue, enormous amounts of misinformation. Each child, now, is being born in the presence of a great deal more reliable information.

I'm getting letters now—not very often, about five a year—from children who were born after humans got to the moon. How they find I'm someone they can write to I don't know, but they do, and they write incredibly beautiful letters, and the syntax couldn't be better. They say they are familiar with the critical path of all the things that had to be done before the blast-off to get humanity over to the moon and back safely. They say, "Humanity can do anything it needs to do; why don't we make this thing work?" So a young world is coming along which may very likely exercise that option.

MAX D. GAEBLER:
MINISTER IN MADISON AND BEYOND (1921-)

From Landmark in the Life of the First Unitarian Society of Madison, 1999.

Born in 1921 in Watertown, Wisconsin, midway between Madison and Milwaukee, Gaebler attended Harvard College and the Harvard Divinity School. Ordained by the historic First Parish in Cambridge, Massachusetts, in March, 1944, and installed as minister to students, he developed a focus on campus ministry which remained high among his priorities throughout his career.

Following three years as minister of the First Parish Church United, Westford, Massachusetts, and four years as minister of the Unitarian Church of Davenport, Iowa, Mr. Gaebler was called by the First Unitarian Society of Madison in 1952. He served as minister there for 35 years, retiring in 1987. As minister *emeritus* of that congregation he and his wife, the former Carolyn Farr, continue to live in Madison.

When Mr. Gaebler was invited to accept the Madison ministry, that congregation was still in the process of settling into its new meeting house, designed by its own member, the renowned architect Frank Lloyd Wright. Indeed Mr. Wright himself sprang from a Welsh Unitarian family, and his own parents had been among the organizers of the Madison congregation. His father, William Wright, had served as secretary of the congregation when it was organized in 1879.

The meeting house opened in 1951. By the summer of 1952, when the Gaeblers arrived, visitors were swarming in and around the building to an extent that made it difficult for the congregation to carry on the appointed functions. As the congregation grew into its world famous new meeting house, Mr. Gaebler notes that its location in a residential neighborhood near the campus drew many students and young families with children, while the architectural distinction of the building appealed to many because of its intrinsic aesthetic values. The congregation grew rapidly, and under the ministry of Mr. Gaebler's successor, the Rev. Michael Schuler, it has become one of the three or four largest churches in the denomination.

During the years of his Madison ministry Max played many important roles in the wider life of the denomination. He served at various times as president of the Unitarian Ministers Association, as secretary of the Joint Commission on Ministry at the time of Unitarian Universalist merger, and as first president of the Midwest Unitarian Universalist Conference. In this last named capacity he presided over the then controversial establishment of the UUA Districts which today represent congregations in the entire mid-continent area. Later he served seven years as a trustee of the Meadville Theological School in Chicago. Following his retirement he served as president of the then still quite new organization of Retired Unitarian Universalist Ministers and Partners.

Perhaps his most important denominational service, however, was his leadership in enlarging and structuring the relationships of the Unitarian Universalist Association with religious liberals all around the world. During a year's leave of absence from the Madison congregation, he joined the UUA staff in Boston, organizing a Department of Overseas and Interfaith Relations. As director of that office he accompanied UUA President Dana Greeley on visits to liberal religious groups in Japan, the Philippines, India, and Europe. Their visit to the Unitarian Union of the Khasi Hills in the northeastern Indian state of Meghalaya (then still part of Assam) led to the development of a close and very fruitful relationship with this indigenous liberal movement. Their visit to Tokyo included the very first contact between American Unitarian Universalists and the Rissho kosei-kai (Buddhist).

On that same trip Gaebler and Greeley spent a week in Rome as guests of the Vatican during the early days of the second session of the Vatican Council. Relationships forged during that visit led Gaebler to an enduring involvement in broad ecumenical efforts, an involvement he continues vigorously through his activity in the Greater Madison Interfaith Association. In the course of that year he also represented the UUA in working with the secretariat of the International Association for Religious Freedom (IARF) on plans for that organization's triennial Congress the following summer in the Netherlands.

Yet another area of denominational life in which Max Gaebler played a central role arose out of the conflict engendered by the outbreak of the Black Power movement in 1968. Confronted by a Unitarian Universalist Black Caucus at its General Assembly in Cleveland that June, that UUA gathering was thrown into turmoil by the Black Caucus and its white support group. Reeling under the pressures of this highly charged situation, opponents of the separatist approach among both black and white delegates organized a biracial group committed to sustaining the denomination's traditional commitment to integration. The organization which emerged was called Black and White Action (BAWA). Mr. Gaebler was chosen on the spot as cochair of BAWA, serving jointly with Dr. Glover Barnes, an African-American scientist who was at that time a professor at the University of Buffalo. This organization, which won recognition at the UUA General Assembly in Boston the following year, continued to carry a torch for racial justice in Unitarian Universalist circles for more than a decade. BAWA and the cause it represented became a central and defining element in Dr. Gaebler's denominational activity.

Max Gaebler has been honored by both Unitarian Universalist theological schools, having been awarded an S.T.D. degree by the Starr King School for the Ministry in Berkeley, California, in 1968 and a D.D. degree by Meadville/Lombard Theological School in Chicago in 1975.

FRANK GANNETT:
NEWSPAPER PUBLISHER (1876-1957)

The Gannett Company, founded by Frank Gannett in Rochester in 1906, is an international corporation with headquarters in McLean, Virginia. Its daily newspaper group circulation is more than 7 million and includes USA Today, *a highly popular, nationally distributed daily.*

A native of New York, Frank E. Gannett (1876-1957) worked his way through college at Cornell and purchased the Elmira Star-Gazette in 1906 after a brief newspaper stint in Ithaca and Pittsburgh. By the end of the 1920s, Gannett owned 15 dailies in medium-sized markets in New York as well as a few papers in New Jersey, Connecticut, and Illinois.

When Frank Gannett died, the Unitarian Register *published the following report in February 1958.*

Frank Gannett, 81, Rochester, N.Y., publisher and one of the nation's most eminent Unitarian laymen, died December 3, 1957, of complications resulting from a fall suffered the preceding April. Funeral services were conducted in the First Unitarian Church of Rochester by Dr. David Rhys Williams, who had been Mr. Gannett's minister for nearly 30 years.

Mr. Gannett was noted for the development of his publishing group of 22 newspapers in 18 cities. The Gannett Company also owns four radio and three television stations.

Mr. Gannett's other achievements and activities were numerous, and he was the recipient of many honors.

A Republican, he campaigned as an avowed presidential candidate in 1939 and 1940, and his name went before the convention at which Wendell Wilikie was nominated. He urged 25 years ago the inclusion of a Secretary of Peace in the President's cabinet.

Mr. Gannett also was noted for his philanthropic support of research, especially in the newspaper and aviation industries and in the fields of health and medicine. One of the projects he supported produced the Teletypesetter, a typesetting device which can be operated at long distances by electrical impulses. Another was a $500,000 grant by the Gannett Newspaper Foundation to build a student health clinic at Cornell University, Ithaca, N.Y. He also was keenly interested in the development of public recreation facilities.

Honors conferred upon Mr. Gannett included the Civic Medal of the Rochester Museum of Arts and Sciences, received jointly with his wife; honorary membership in Phi Beta Kappa; the Navy's Distinguished Public Service Award; an honorary degree of doctor of journalism from Bradley University and a long list of other honorary doctor's and master's degrees.

Mr. Gannett's newspaper ventures began with his purchase in 1906 of a half-interest in the Elmira, N. Y., *Gazette*. The *Gazette* absorbed competition in the Ithaca-Elmira area, and he bought in 1918 two Rochester newspapers, merging them into the *Times-Union*, and moved to Rochester.

There he looked up a distant cousin, Rev. William Gannett, who was minister of the Unitarian church. Mr. Gannett shortly became a Unitarian and remained throughout the ensuing years a leader in the church.

Noting that most of the persons attending the funeral were familiar with the story of Mr. Gannett's life, Dr. Williams said that "there is one phase of that story about which I may be presumed to speak with some measure of authority. I refer to his religious life.

"Frank Gannett took his religious duties seriously. He made a conscientious effort to be present in the church of his choice on as many Sunday mornings in the year as his health and other obligations would permit.

"I have many reasons to cherish the memory of this man, but I shall cherish it most of all because he faithfully supported not only the freedom of the press over the years, but also the freedom of this pulpit during a 30-year ministry which must often have tried his faith in such a freedom. He was one who could disagree completely with the content of any specific sermon and still find inspiration in the sincerity of its utterance.

"It has been a rare privilege and a challenging responsibility to serve as his minister, for his religion was bound by no narrow creed. It was to do justly, and to love mercy, and to walk humbly before God."

DANA MCLEAN GREELEY:
THE FIRST UNITARIAN UNIVERSALIST
PRESIDENT (1908-1986)

Jon M. Luopa, Minister, University Unitarian Church, Seattle, Washington

Few figures in our denominational history embody our unique tensions as a religious movement as well as Dana McLean Greeley. Groomed by the New England Unitarianism of Channing, Emerson and Parker, he became an internationally respected advocate for world peace and interfaith understanding. Being in the cross-fire of many denominational struggles of the mid-20th century, he remained optimistic about the future of Unitarian Universalism, and of the world, and lived without guile or bitterness among those who could not follow him. In the last years of his life when he struggled against a debilitating cancer, he remained hopeful and courageous. He devoted his life to an institution even as his primary religious inspiration was the unique worth and dignity of every person.

A fifth-generation Unitarian, Dana was born on July 5, 1908 at 11 o'clock on a Sunday morning, the time of the week he liked best. The Greeleys hailed from Portland, Maine where their family pew was one behind the Longfellow pew at the historic First Parish Church. Dana grew up in Lexington, Massachusetts. In high school he served as president of the Theodore Parker Guild of the Young People's Religious Union at the Lexington First Parish, and later during his college years he served as president of the continental YPRU. When he was a senior in high school, his younger sister, Rosamond, died of a ruptured appendix. This family tragedy was instrumental in his decision to enter the ministry. At Star Island he proposed to Deborah Webster, whom he had known since childhood, and they were married on December 27, 1931. He graduated from Harvard College in 1931 and from the Harvard Divinity School in 1933.

Dana served briefly two congregations—in Lincoln, Massachusetts and in Concord, New Hampshire—before being called to the Arlington Street Church in Boston in 1935. Dr. Samuel A. Eliot had served as minister there for eight years following his service as president of the American Unitarian Association for twenty-five years.

There had been only three presidents of the AUA since 1900: Samuel A. Eliot, Louis C. Cornish, and Frederick May Eliot. Dana announced his candidacy for the presidency in 1958. It was a contested election, the first in the 133 year history of the association. (The final tally was 823 votes for Dana and 720 for Dr. Ernest Kuebler, the candidate of the board of directors.) Dana noted, "I was a grass-roots candidate and a by-petition candidate, but I seemed nevertheless to be too Bostonian (which I was) and to represent the establishment." Nearly fifty years old when elected in 1958, he would be the last president of the American Unitarian Association. Part of his platform had been merger with the Universalist Church of America.

Befriending Dr. Martin Luther King, Jr. and involvement in the civil rights movement were of paramount importance to Dana. His efforts in trying to help the association accept its own institutional racism were less successful. This short sketch cannot do justice to that important ongoing challenge. Dana was an outspoken critic of American involvement in Southeast Asia and denounced nuclear proliferation. He was instrumental in the founding of the World Conference on Religion and Peace in 1962. He practiced a broad ecumenism long before his participation in the Second Vatican Council as a delegated observer.

He was a birthright Unitarian with a universalist persona. He was as comfortable being with President Gerald Ford standing on the bridge over the Concord River at our nation's bicentennial in 1976 as he was conversing with Dr. Albert Schweitzer in Lambarene. The Universalists of the Phillipines, the Unitarians in the Khasi Hills of India, and the Rissho Kosei Kai of Japan, were as much his congregation as the cherished folk of Lexington, Concord, and Boston.

After retiring as president of the UUA in 1969, he served the First Parish in Concord, Massachusetts, where he died June 13, 1986.

DONALD SZANTHO HARRINGTON: THE COMMUNITY CHURCH OF NEW YORK (1914-)

By Bruce Southworth, Senior Minister of the Community Church of New York

Donald Szantho Harrington has offered one of the most distinguished and far ranging ministries of the 20th century. His leadership as preacher, activist, pastor, institution-builder, and theologian, as well as his service to the denomination and wider community reflect his devotion to liberal religion and to social justice. From 1944 to 1982 and thereafter as Minister Emeritus of The Community Church of New York, he has built upon and expanded the visionary ministry of John Haynes Holmes. One of the foremost legacies of Don Harrington's ministry was the continued and expanding racial and economic diversity of The Community Church congregation with its vision to embody the Beloved Community and the Church Universal.

During his service at Community, he oversaw the completion of a new, modern church building and the acquisition of adjacent buildings with meeting spaces for an expanded Sunday school, adult religious educational offerings, and community programs and groups. In 1952, he was among the co-founders and first co-chairs with A. Philip Randolph of the American Committee

on Africa, whose support for the African National Congress and leadership with economic sanctions helped to make possible the election of Nelson Mandela as President of the Republic of South Africa in 1994. His social justice work has been far ranging and included leadership in the civil rights movement, early opposition to the Vietnam War, and progressive politics. The Unitarian Universalist Association recognized him with the Holmes-Weatherly Award in 1983. He was also a significant leader in the merger of the American Unitarian Association and the Universalist Church of America, and he prepared the service of union and offered the sermon in 1960 at Boston's Symphony Hall.

As a theologian, Harrington has promoted the thought of Henry Nelson Wieman, and was a co-founder of CASIRAS, the Center for the Advanced Study in Religion and Science. In addition to his own contributions in elaborating a scientific theology, beginning in the 1950's Harrington also pioneered in celebrations of the Church Universal as part of the worship year at Community Church. These interfaith services not only continue as part of that worship calendar, but also influenced worship life in UU congregations across the continent.

In 1949, the year following the dedication of the new building, Dr. Holmes retired, and the congregation called the Reverend Donald Harrington as its Senior Minister. Institutionally, the church continued to expand programs and began to purchase adjacent brownstones in order to have space for its activities. In addition to housing the American Committee on Africa (the earliest and most effective anti-apartheid organization in the United States), the church has provided offices and space for the African National Congress, the American Indian Community House, Theater Off Park (off-off Broadway), the African Services Committee, the Unitarian Universalist Service Committee, Rissho Kosei-Kai's Horin Center, a nightly shelter for homeless men, and The Community Art Gallery. In 1960 in a unique display of interfaith cooperation, the newly formed Metropolitan Synagogue began to meet at Community and continues to do so, forty years later.

Embracing a vision of the Church Universal, Harrington began special worship celebrations to honor the insights, spirit and wisdom of various major religions. These included a High Holy Day Sunday (during the Jewish Days of Awe) plus a Seder with universal Haggadah; a Good Friday Tenebrae service adapted from Christian traditions; Hinduism's Divali Festival of Lights; and Buddhism's Wesak that commemorates the birth, enlightenment, and death of the Buddha. The Community News, the church's newsletter, and the Community Pulpit sermon series helped to promote these as they went to a wide mailing list of congregations and ministers.

Beginning in the 1960s, Harrington's preaching reached tens of thousands of New Yorkers through the live broadcast of Community Church worship services over WQXR, the radio station of the *New York Times*. Harrington also served as a columnist for and as a member of the Board of the *Saturday Review/World*, a magazine edited by Norman Cousins. He was also the author of numerous articles in various journals and periodicals.

During his ministry, Harrington helped to bring the congregation into greater contact and collaboration with the American Unitarian Association. Dr. Holmes, who had resigned his ministerial fellowship in 1918, resumed his Unitarian affiliation in 1952. The congregation once again sent delegates to the annual meetings and became active with the AUA. It also began providing building loans to UU congregations in the 1960s, provided scholarships to UU theological students, and endowed the Sophia Lyon Fahs Center for Religious Education at Meadville Lombard Theological School.

Denominationally, Harrington served on the last Board of Trustees of the American Unitarian Association and the first Board of the Unitarian Universalist Association. His sermon, "Unitarian Universalism—Yesterday, Today, and Tomorrow," at the service of merger in 1960, articulated an inclusive vision of the Church Universal.

In 1968, with co-leadership of his Black Chairman of the Board of Trustees of The Community Church and others across the continent, Harrington helped to found BAWA, (Black and White Action), to support those in the association who wished to have racially integrated programming and activities. The Community Church had been racially inclusive during the ministry of John Haynes Holmes, and upholding the value and vision of racial integration was deep-seated within the congregation. Notwithstanding that history, guest speakers included diverse points of view, such as the debate between Malcolm X and Bayard Rustin in 1962.

Harrington was active in politics from the beginning of his ministry. He became a member of the Liberal Party when he moved to New York and rose to the position of State Chairman serving in that capacity for twenty years.

Dr. Harrington retired as Senior Minister of The Community Church in 1982 and became Minister Emeritus. His wife of 43 years, the Reverend Vilma Szantho Harrington, whose ministry included exceptional service with him on the ministerial staff of Community Church, died that October.

In 1984, he married Aniko Szantho, the niece of Vilma. With her completion of theological studies and ordination in 1990 to the Unitarian Universalist ministry, she began service to several village congregations in Transylvania, and Dr. Harrington embarked on innovative economic development projects to assist the rural Unitarian villagers. In addition, he has arranged numerous pilgrimage tours for North American Unitarian Universalists and expanded awareness of the historic connections to these liberal religious forebears. Under Rev. Aniko's leadership, they have developed an extensive religious publication program in English and Hungarian languages.

VILMA SZANTHO HARRINGTON: WOMAN MINISTER (1913 - 1982)

By Donald Szantho Harrington, Minister Emeritus of The Community Church of New York

Vilma was born in the tiny Transylvanian village of Aldoboly, Hungary on January 15, 1913. She remembered vividly the vicissitudes of World War I, when there was little food and no sugar.

In 1926, when she was thirteen years old, Vilma went to the gymnasium to prepare for entrance to the University. Her four older brothers were often asking her what she wanted to be when she grew up, to which her answer always was, "A Minister!" Her father and mother shook their heads. When girls graduated from high school, they got married and settled down to have families. There was no provision in church law for a woman to study for or to be ordained as a minister. No woman had ever been admitted to any of the theological schools in the capitol city of Kolozsvar. But Vilma was persistent, and asked her father to intercede with the authorities at the Unitarian headquarters. He finally agreed to do so, though muttering that he couldn't understand why she couldn't become a doctor or a lawyer if she had to have a higher education.

In 1931 Vilma was admitted to the almost four hundred year old Unitarian Seminary in Kolozsvar. She considered her decision to be not just a divine calling, but an imperative human calling. As she put it in one of her memoirs: "I wanted to work with people from the cradle to the grave, with young and old, whether rich or poor, whether happy or sad, and I felt that the only profession that offered such an opportunity was the ministry."

When the day arrived, not only the villagers, but reporters from nearby Torda and Kolozsvar were present. One old man had some doubts. He put it this way: "It is all very well, Miss Reverend, but I am wondering where you will be minister, who will be the minister's wife?"

In 1936, at the age of twenty three, Vilma was recommended by church authorities for a year's study at Manchester College, Oxford. Later, she made her way to Meadville on the shores of Chicago's Lake Michigan. I often asked her to go walking with me. One evening I proposed.

Our joint ministry began at the Peoples Liberal Church of Chicago. In 1944, we responded to the call to come to New York City as Junior Colleague and ultimate successor to the famous John Haynes Holmes, who was one of our heroes. Here in New York we ministered together, she in one capacity or another, for almost forty years.

CHARLES HARTSHORNE:
THE EINSTEIN OF RELIGIOUS THOUGHT
(1897-2000)

By John B. Cobb, Courtesy of the Center for Process Studies, Claremont, California

Charles Hartshorne was born in Kittanning, Pennsylvania, the son of Marguerite Haughton and Francis Cope Hartshorne, clergyman. He entered Haverford College in 1915, leaving to join the Army Medical Corps for two years. He completed his college work at Harvard and took the Ph.D. in philosophy there. Among his teachers were R. B. Perry, W. E. Hocking, C.I. Lewis, H. M. Sheffer, and J. H. Woods. His dissertation was on "The Unity of All Things."

Hartshorne studied for two years in Europe. On his return to Harvard, he spent three years as Instructor and Research Fellow. He and Paul Weiss edited the papers of Charles Sanders Peirce in six volumes (*Collected Papers of Charles Sanders Peirce.* Cambridge and Harvard University Press, 1931-1935). He found in Peirce a highly congenial spirit, and he appropriated many of Peirce's concepts and arguments.

During one of these years he was assistant to Alfred North Whitehead, whose thought was also highly congenial to the vision he had been shaping on his own. He learned much from Whitehead, and one major contribution he made throughout his career was introducing students to Whitehead and expounding his ideas.

In 1928, Hartshorne accepted a position in the Department of Philosophy of the University of Chicago, where, except for a Fulbright appointment in Australia, he taught until 1955. Soon after moving to Chicago he married Dorothy Cooper. Dorothy Hartshorne played an important role as editor and bibliographer of his writings. They had one child, Emily.

His ideas were set forth in a series of books: *Beyond Humanism: Essays in the New Philosophy of Nature* (Chicago: Willet, Clark & Company, 1937), *Man's Vision of God and the Logic of Theism* (Chicago: Willet, Clark & Company, 1941), *The Divine Relativity: A Social Conception of God* (New Haven: Yale University Press, 1948), and *Reality as a Social Process: Studies in Metaphysics and Religion* (Glencoe: The Free Press and Boston: Beacon Press, 1953). These books established Hartshorne as a major challenge to the dominant currents in both philosophy and theology and as the center of a small but vigorous movement.

Partly because of tensions in the Department of Philosophy at Chicago, Hartshorne accepted an invitation to teach philosophy at Emory University. As he approached Emory's mandatory retirement age, he moved to the University of Texas, whose retirement policy was more flexible. He taught there until 1978.

During these years he continued to be a prolific writer. *Creative Synthesis and*

Scientific Method (LaSalle: Open Court, 1970) concentrates less on his doctrine of God and thus offers a more balanced view of his position on a wide range of issues. His productivity has continued even past his retirement at Texas, including extensive assessment of the great thinkers of the past. *Insights and Oversights of Great Thinkers: An Evaluation of Western Philosophy* (Albany: State University of New York Press, 1983) is especially significant in this regard.

Volume One of the Library of Living Philosophers *is devoted to Einstein and volume twenty to Hartshorne.*

JOHN F. HAYWARD: PHILOSOPHER OF RELIGION AND THE ARTS (1918-)

By Kenneth A. Olliff, Editor of The Journal of Liberal Religion

John Frank Hayward, growing up in Wellesley, Massachusetts, in the 1920s and 1930s, cites as a primary influence an appreciation for music and religion intertwined in singing with his mother while she played an upright piano in their home. She was also responsible for teaching him to pray. He remembers his father as an early artistic and quasi-religious influence also, in spite of the fact that he was an atheist. A jewelry designer who commuted to his own business in downtown Boston, his father gave him a love of story. "Every Saturday night he spun long stories made up on the spot about a Swedish farm couple somewhere in America and their little town and neighbors."

The family was Congregationalist until John advocated for a change while he was in Sunday school: "In my early childhood I remember chafing under the inexpert teaching and ill disciplined classes of a Congregational Sunday school until I was driven into open rebellion."

The minister while Hayward was in high school was James Luther Adams, a man who would become a lifelong friend, mentor, and second father. Adams emphasized that all parts of culture interfaced with and must come under the lens of religion, including and especially political life. Hayward reports: "Mr. Adams initiated me into the drama of politics and the necessity for citizen participation in social action. While the congregation grumbled about his politics, they greatly honored him for his wisdom, his kindness, his intellect, and his pastoral warmth." In addition to influencing Hayward's emerging social ethical views, Adams was instrumental in shaping his love for the arts. "Adams invited me to sing in his church choir. He could not have known then that he set in motion, by recordings and song, my life long devotion to classical music." Adams also introduced Hayward to literature, reading Shakespeare and Dante with him, and helping him to begin to make the connection between the arts and religion.

Despite the disillusionment that he felt with religion during his philosophy major at Harvard, Hayward did agree to go to Meadville, although he says he had little intention of becoming a minister. Nevertheless, he moved to Chicago to attend Meadville Theological School and the University of Chicago Divinity School after receiving his A.B. at Harvard in 1940.

During Hayward's first years of study at Meadville, Muriel Sternglanz came to Chicago, enrolling at the University of Chicago School of Social Service Administration. Their romance ripened, and they were married in Chicago: "My last year at Meadville I was in love with Muriel. Jim and Margaret Adams loved her, too, and welcomed her into their home. They attended our wedding along with Muriel's parents and mine. They comforted us and ministered to us when, a month later, Muriel's brother was killed in the war. When I received my Bachelor of Divinity degree from Meadville, I decided to enter the war as a Navy chaplain."

After Iwo Jima, Hayward's regiment went to the Hawaiian Islands. While they were in mid voyage President Roosevelt died. Hayward was requested by the captain of the ship to hold a memorial service for Roosevelt.

In November 1945 Hayward left the Navy and finished his Ph.D. in theology, writing a dissertation using Tillich and Whitehead as primary sources for *The Theology and Philosophy of Mythical Symbolism*.

Upon graduating in 1949, he accepted a call to become the minister of the First Unitarian Church of Columbus, Ohio. After three years in Columbus, however, he received an unsolicited phone the University of Chicago Divinity School, asking him to consider a teaching position in religion and the arts. Hayward taught courses in the visual arts, myth theory, and theology.

One of his guest preaching excursions was to the Unitarian Fellowship in Carbondale, Illinois. An old friend, Milton McLean, visited in the congregation. Southern Illinois University in Carbondale had asked McLean to start a religious studies program. He told Hayward that the university was looking for a director for the program.

Hayward was engaged in founding the religious studies department and was professor of philosophy. A major influence of his years in Carbondale was the Carbondale Unitarian Fellowship. Jack and Muriel joined the fellowship soon after arriving in Carbondale and both were involved for many years until her death in 2001. He was named "honorary minister" for his long involvement and part-time ministerial assistance. He has preached there many times over the last thirty years, and the experience has kept him grounded in congregational life after leaving theological education for university teaching. This long-term ministry has given him an opportunity to utilize in a congregational setting many of the ideas he developed earlier in his career.

CLARA COOK HELVIE:
UNITARIAN MINISTRY PIONEER (1876-1969)

By Catherine F. Hitchings, author of Universalist and Unitarian Women Ministers

Clara Cook Helvie was ordained in a period when there was decided prejudice against women as Unitarian ministers.

She was born in Chaumont, New York January 24, 1876 to James H. and Marge (Beckwith) Cook. She was descended from eleven Mayflower pilgrims and was a cousin of William Howard Taft. Her mother died when she was very young, and her father became a recluse in the Adirondack Mountains.

Clara Cook lived with relatives who renamed her Clara Bailey, she attended public schools in Buffalo, New York and Sunday School at the First Unitarian Church. Despite many difficulties, she obtained a good education, graduating from Canton's Business College in Buffalo and attending Emerson College of Oratory in Boston in 1901.

Widowed by 1916, she attended Meadville Theological School and graduated in 1917. For five summers she returned for postgraduate study and attended Harvard Summer School of Theology for one summer. When she applied for ordination to the Unitarian ministry, she found that no woman had been ordained into the denomination since Rowena Morse Mann in 1906, and many men were adverse to women ministers despite the fact that thirty-nine women had been ordained since 1871. She was told, essentially, that women hadn't contributed any worthwhile work except Margaret Bowers Barnard. This highly conservative opinion discounted the important work of the Iowa sisterhood in establishing societies in the midwest and untold other contributions made by women over the previous forty-six years.

Several churches offered to ordain her. She accepted the offer of the Wheeling, West Virginia Unitarian church and was ordained there at the age of forty-one. She was minister for the parishes of Wheeling, West Virginia 1917-1921, Moline, Indiana 1921-1926, Westboro 1927, Middleboro, Massachusetts 1930-1936, and Milford, New Hampshire 1938-1942. She retired April 1, 1942.

Clara pursued her interest in women ministers in the 1920's by compiling a manuscript titled "Unitarian Women Ministers" which was never published. Thirty years later she collected short biographies of Universalist women ministers. She was the only woman minister to take part in the dedication service of the Unitarian Headquarters at 25 Beacon Street and of the First Church in Washington, D.C.

She bequeathed most of her estate to the American Unitarian Association, the income of which was to assist needy ministers. She died in her eighty-third year, July 22, 1969.

LOTTA HITSCHMANOVA: FOUNDER, UNITARIAN SERVICE COMMITTEE OF CANADA (1909 - 1990)

Courtesy of the First Unitarian Congregation of Ottawa, Canada

Dr. Lotta (as she is known) was a refugee from Czechoslovakia during World War II, fleeing to Belgium, southern France and Portugal, before finally coming to Canada. She began to work on behalf of refugees with the Unitarian Service Committee in Boston. Three years after arriving in Canada, she founded the Unitarian Service Committee of Canada with the help of the people in the Ottawa Unitarian Congregation. In recognition of her work, she has received awards from various governments, and Canada has made her a Companion of the Order of Canada, the nation's highest award.

Members of the Unitarian Congregation of Ottawa are proud to have helped at the beginning and now to have her bust as a reminder of our present obligation to help those in need. Don Saxon, then President of the Congregation, learned that Harold Pfeiffer had his original sculpture of Dr. Lotta in his basement. After a visit to Dr. Pfeiffer's, a bronze was commissioned and presented as a gift to the church.

Dr. Lotta was rewarded for her work many times, including the designation Companion of the Order of Canada, the Rotary International Award for World Understanding, and national awards from Lesotho, Korea, India, Greece, and France. Dr. Hitschmanova proudly accepted these awards for the USC and wore them on her self-designed uniform, five rows of ribbons.

Lotta Hitschmanova was from Czechoslovakia, born in 1909 in Prague, the daughter of a prosperous family. She entered the University of Prague in 1929, studying languages, and spent two of those four years in Paris at the Sorbonne. Lotta managed to be a correspondent for several papers until the signing of the Munich Pact in 1938. Her views were definitely anti-Nazi, so she was persuaded to leave Czechoslovakia for her safety. In 1941, she was in Marseilles, trying to get a visa to go to the United States. The migration service she appealed to was not able to help, but they did need a secretary and interpreter fluent in French, English, German, Spanish and Czech! She was able to forget her own pain by helping others. However, her diet of beets and carrots led to a collapse on the street from fatigue and hunger. She was taken to a clinic run by the Unitarian Service Committee, an outreach of the American Unitarian Association in Boston.

Thus began Lotta Hitschmanova's introduction to the Unitarian Service Committee. She had originally wished to emigrate to the US, but the visa that came through was from Canada. She caught the last boat from Lisbon to New York, and then went on to Montreal. She settled in Ottawa and joined the Unitarian church there.

By 1945, the idea of a Canadian Unitarian Service Committee had become a possibility. Representatives from the six Canadian Unitarian churches—from Ottawa, Montreal, Toronto, Hamilton, Winnipeg and Vancouver—met and eventually approved the notion. At first, the organization was limited to raising funds from Unitarians only, but that didn't last long. Unitarians were, however, the core support for many years.

JOHN HOLMES:
POET AND FRIEND OF POETRY (1904-1962)

By Doris Holmes Eyges, widow of the poet

John Holmes, member of the First Parish in Cambridge, Harvard Square, was a poet. The record is there in the published volumes of his work. After Along the Row, based on his undergraduate days at Tufts, Holmes' first major publication was Address to the Living, which came out in 1937 with the only blurb Robert Frost ever wrote. Much of Holmes' humorous and light verse appeared in The New Yorker and was collected in Fair Warning in 1939. Map of My Country, from 1943, when the U.S. was at war, was adopted by the Navy for inclusion in the libraries of its ships and stations. Copies that survive in second-hand bookstores or personal libraries often have water stains or pages rippled by dampness. Unitarian Universalists familiar with Hymns for the Celebration of Life can find four hymns whose words are poems of John Holmes. The Double Root, 1950, The Symbols, 1955, and The Fortune Teller, a National Book Award nomination 1961, were all books of his own poems. He also produced textbooks, anthologies, and books of literary criticism.

Holmes was a charismatic man, tall, quiet, pipe-smoking, tweedy, serious. In the larger world of literature, he was a powerful encourager of poets. John Ciardi, Anne Sexton, Maxine Kumin, George Starbuck, Philip Booth are some of those who record their gratitude to him. Uniquely free of competitiveness, John Holmes simply loved to have poetry happen. In the Boston area he was unmatched as an enabler of poetry in the mid-twentieth century.

John Holmes, the poet, used the simple form of his name. After graduation from Tufts in 1929, Holmes studied at Harvard and then taught at Lafayette College in Easton, Pennsylvania where one of his colleagues, a contemporary and friend, was the poet Theodore Roethke. There, too, he met his first wife, Sarah Frances Ludlow. A job opened at Tufts and the young couple moved back to Massachusetts in 1934.

These were busy years for the teacher/poet. He wrote every day. His habit was to start with letters, and then proceed to the real thing, the poem of the moment, as a four finger typist. Invitations came to give lectures, and to review books.

For eight years Holmes served as poetry editor of the *Boston Evening Transcript*. A particular chum there was Howard Mumford Jones, Harvard English professor specializing in American Literature. During a spell when Holmes had a scarcity of books of verse to review, he and Jones decided to make up a poet. They took the middle names of two secretaries and concocted Preston Gurney. Holmes would refer to him in a column, or compare the fictional Gurney with some actual versifier being reviewed. One day Holmes was in Goodspeed's book shop under the Old South Church. A clerk took a book down off the shelf and handed it to him saying, "You write so much about this poet I figured I should set this aside for you." Holmes thought Jones was going to an awful lot of trouble to play this joke on him. But, no, it was a slim volume published about 1900 by Preston Gurney.

Sarah Holmes died in 1947. A year later John Holmes married Doris Vivian Kirk, a young colleague in his department. Evan Kirk Holmes was born in 1950 and Margaret Nash Holmes in 1954. A rich, full season for the poet came during what was to be this last decade of his life.

More intense than the public associations were two poetry workshops that grew up around John Holmes. The first began in 1949. Its regulars were John Ciardi, Richard Eberhart, May Sarton, and Richard Wilbur. They met in each other's homes to read, analyze, and criticize their current poems.

In 1999 Tufts University put on a splendid day of celebration of the opening of the John Holmes collection in the Tisch Library.

JOHN HAYNES HOLMES:
THE COMMUNITY CHURCH OF NEW YORK
(1879-1964)

By Donald Szantho Harrington, Minister Emeritus, The Community Church of New York

John Haynes Holmes—the prophetic founder and minister of The Community Church of New York, located at the very heart of the inner city—and I worked together as colleagues during the last twenty years of his life. Our apartments were across the hall from each other in the same building next to the Church, so I saw him every day. Every Monday morning we sat together in his study, evaluating the week past and planning the weeks to come. Every Saturday evening we met with our wives to review our preparations for Sunday morning. There were no questions we could not or did not discuss. He was my mentor and model for ministry; I was his choice for colleague and successor to carry forward the work he had begun. For seventeen years we sat together in the pulpit of the Community Church; for the first five he preached three times a month, I once; for the next twelve years I preached three Sundays, and he one. We shared all other churchly duties, I picking them up gradually as he had to relinquish them because of the ravages of Parkinson's physical assault upon his body.

Holmes served The Community Church as Jr. Colleague, Senior Minister and Minister Emeritus for a total of fifty-seven years.

I have said many times that I believe John Haynes Holmes was the greatest all-around minister of religion of the 20th Century: pacifist, orator, churchman, social service organizer, racial and social justice pioneer, pastor, adult educator, political participant and leader, poet and philosopher, all at once!

Holmes may have been best known for his stalwart pacifism and early recognition of the greatness of Mahatma Gandhi. It was in 1921, when Gandhi was almost unknown, that Holmes preached a sermon entitled *The Greatest Man Alive in the World Today*—not Wilson, Lloyd George, Lenin, Stalin, not Trotzky; not Clemenceau, Churchill or Tolstoy, but Mohandas K. Gandhi of India, the apostle of non-violence! On April 3, 1917 he preached on *A Statement to my People on the Eve of War*, declaring: "So long as I am your minister, this Church will answer no military summons. Holmes offered the church people his resignation, which they promptly refused.

Holmes had an extended visit with Gandhi in India shortly before Gandhi's assassination. He told me that he had found Gandhi deeply discouraged by the communal violence and partitioning of India and Pakistan. Gandhi said, "Holmes, I have failed, totally failed. They will worship me, but they will not follow me!" I tried to reassure him, but he would not be comforted.

In an age of oratory, Holmes was among the greatest. He spoke with a passion that carried everything before it.

Working with Paul Blanshard and Norman Thomas, Holmes and Rabbi Wise founded and co-chaired the New York City Affairs Committee which investigated the questionable Mayoralty of Jimmie Walker and ultimately helped replace him with reformist Fiorello La Guardia.

Holmes was among the founders of several of the most important organizations for social justice: the National Association for the Advancement of Colored People, with W.E.B. Du Bois; The American Civil Liberties Union, with Roger Baldwin; The League for Industrial Democracy, with Harry Laidler; The Planned Parenthood Movement, with Margaret Sanger. A few of the others are The Fellowship of Reconciliation, The War Resisters League, and The India League of America. Holmes was a regular speaker on Town Hall Tonight, radio's great first public forum.

The Congregation sponsored several counseling Services in the Church itself: the first church-sponsored Marriage Counseling Center with Drs. Abraham and Hannah Stone, associates of Margaret Sanger; an individual Psychological Counseling Center with Dr. Alfred Adler; a Legal Counsel Service with retired Judge Ralph C. Roper; and a Social Service Advisor with Irene Roggeveen, open to one and all needing help.

Holmes's Community Forum drew hundreds of New Yorkers every Sunday evening to hear outstanding personalities in the news. A Multiple Round Table Discussion Group gave everyone a voice on Sunday afternoons.

In constant demand as a University Chapel preacher in all parts of the country, Holmes carried his message of international and interracial humanhood far and wide, reaching—with his message, his eloquence and the example of his life— hundreds of thousands of young people, students and ministers.

Not least was his Ministry of the Mails. He answered every letter immediately, sometimes dictating fifty or sixty letters a day. He was able to get his whole passionate soul into a few sentences. He early advised me to use the mails. "Phone calls are over and quickly gone," he said, "but a beautiful and true letter can be returned to again and again."

One hundred years ago the black poet of the Harlem Renaissance, Countee Cullen, whose widow, Ida Cullen, was for many years a leader of the Community Church, wrote a special poem to John Haynes Holmes, testifying to his enduring influence:

MILLENNIUM

Once in a thousand years a call may ring
Divested so of every cumbering lie,
A man espousing it may fight and sing,
And count it but a little thing to die.
Once in a thousand years a star may come,
Six pointed, tipped with such an astral flow,
Its singing sisters must bow hushed in dumb,
Half mutinous, yet half-adoring show.
Once in as many years a man may rise
So cosmopolitan of thought or speech,
Humanity reflected in his eyes,
His heart a haven every race can reach,
That doubters shall receive a mortal thrust,
And own, "This man proves flesh exalts its dust."

DUNCAN HOWLETT:
MINISTER, AUTHOR, AND FORESTER (1906 -)

By Clifton Davis Librarian Emeritus, Bangor Theological Seminary, Maine

Duncan Howlett was born May 15, 1906, in Newton, Massachusetts. He received the SB. degree from Harvard in 1928, the LLB. Degree in 1931, and in the same year he was admitted to the Massachusetts Bar. Following the practice of law for two years, in 1933 he yielded to a lifelong interest in religion and returned to Harvard where he was awarded the STB degree with honors in 1936, while serving as Minister of the Second Church, Unitarian, in Salem, Massachusetts. Dr. Howlett was ordained to the Unitarian ministry in Salem, Massachusetts, November 17,1935. Howlett was at that church from 1933 to 1938. From there he went to the First Unitarian Church, New Bedford, Massachusetts (1938-1946). In September of 1946 he became Minister of the First Church in Boston, Unitarian, a position he held for the next twelve years. In 1958, he was called to All Souls Church, Unitarian, in Washington, D.C., the position from which he retired in 1968.

In addition to his concern with public affairs during the entire range of his ministry, Howlett played an active role in Unitarian denominational affairs. Among the various committees and boards on which he served were those of the Beacon Press, the Historical Library, and the *Christian Register*. He was President of the Unitarian Historical Society, Chairman of Commission I, "The Church and Its Leadership"; Chairman of the Washington Advisory Committee of the Unitarian Universalist Association Department of Social Responsibility; member of Harvard University Overseer's Committee to visit the Divinity School (1940-62); Chairman, D.C. Advisory Committee to the U.S. Commission on Civil Rights; and member of the D.C. Commissioners' Crime Council; Executive Committee of the Washington Home Rule Commission; and the Washington Urban Institute.

Duncan Howlett has written the following titles: *Man Against the Church*; *The Struggle Between Religion and Ecclesiasticism* (1954); *The Essenes and Christianity; An Interpretation of the Dead Sea Scrolls* (1957); *The Fourth American Faith* (1964); *No Greater Love: The James Reeb Story* (1966); *The Critical Way in Religion* (1980); and *The Fatal Flaw at the Heart of Religious Liberalism* (1995).

On retiring from the active parish ministry in 1968, Howlett became deeply involved in the environmental movement, particularly in the area of forestry. In Maine he organized and was the first President of the Small Woodland Owners Association, popularly known as SWOAM. The conservation of natural resources emphasizing the responsible management of woodland on the part of citizen forest owners became for him a "second career." The continuing search for "truth" has motivated Dr. Howlett throughout his life, truth that is lived out in human experience. Moulton Library is indeed fortunate to receive his gift of books and papers.

HOMER A. JACK:
SOCIAL ACTIVIST (1916-1993)

By Alex Jack, his son, educator on health and diet

As the clouds of war gathered over Europe in 1937, Homer A. Jack, a young Cornell graduate student, found himself teaching at a small college in Athens. He was completing his Ph.D. in biology and visited Europe to finish his thesis on the biological field stations of the world. On a tour of the continent at the end of the following school year, he visited Stalin's Russia, Hitler's Germany, and Mussolini's Italy. In Moscow, the authorities confiscated his camera, in Germany and Austria he witnessed overt anti-Semitism, and in Italy he observed ominous signs of spreading fascism. The lessons he learned about totalitarianism far outweighed the knowledge he acquired of the local flora and fauna.

Returning home to upstate New York, Homer threw himself into peace activities to prevent America from being drawn into a second world war. He edited the *Rochester No-War News* and helped organize a rally that attracted 3000 people. Homer's grandparents had immigrated from Central and Eastern Europe to avoid poverty and oppression. His parents, Alexander and Cecelia Jacobowitz (later shortened to Jack) had been active socialists and freethinkers. In Rochester they had known and marched with Susan B. Anthony, the leader of the suffragist movement. As an only child, Homer shared his parents' radicalism, distrust of organized religion, and worship of nature. Tom Paine's lyrical refrain, "The world is my church and my religion is to do good," summed up the Jack family's theological outlook.

At Monroe High School in the early 1930s, Homer met Esther Rhys Williams, the daughter of the local Unitarian minister and lead actress in many school plays. At Cornell, Homer kept in touch with the radiant sociology major at Oberlin College, and in 1939 the young couple were wed. The radical roots of Esther's family matched the Jacks, extending from descendents of Samuel Adams, the Revolutionary War mastermind, on her mother's side to the Kremlin where Esther's uncle, journalist Albert Rhys Williams, was a biographer and confidant of Lenin during the Russian Revolution. Over the years, Esther's father, Rev. David Rhys Williams, had earned his own reputation as a fiery orator and champion of labor, civil rights, and pacifism. As the drums of war started beating, he was one of the few Rochester clergymen to support Homer's anti-war activities.

As these political and personal forces converged in his life, Homer abandoned a career in science for the ministry. "I was much more interested in men than mice," he later quipped. With his father-in-law's encouragement, he enrolled at Meadville Theological School in Chicago and prepared for the Unitarian pulpit.

After graduating from Meadville, Homer accepted the pulpit of the Unitarian Church in Lawrence, Kansas. Despite being the site of abolitionist crusader John Brown's "Free Kansas" movement, Lawrence was violently anti-Negro and antilabor. Black people were not allowed to sing in the University of Kansas choir because "their voices are different," the university football team would not accept black players, and the local hotel refused to serve Negroes, even at a private breakfast for the ministerial council. Homer spoke out against racism and war, especially the strategic bombing of civilians by both sides and other atrocities.

Returning to Chicago from Lawrence, Homer accepted the position as executive secretary of the Chicago Council Against Racial and Religious Discrimination and for nearly five years worked tirelessly for racial justice, not only for Negroes but also for Mexican-Americans, Japanese-Americans (resettling in the Midwest from relocation camps), and other minorities.

In 1948, Homer accepted a call to the Unitarian Church of Evanston and his family, now including two small children, moved to the North Shore. Staunchly conservative, Evanston was the home of the Women's Christian Temperance Union (WCTU), Northwestern University, and, in 1954, the international assembly of the World Council of Churches (which Homer attended as a journalist since Unitarians were barred from membership). From his pulpit, in Chicago area committees, and with the local ministers' association, Homer waged a steady campaign to desegregate Evanston and the North Shore (including Northwestern, the local hospital, and the YMCA) and introduce revolutionary ideas of freedom and independence for Africans and Asians. During his tenure church membership rose from 175 to 600, and so many people came that Homer had to hold two services on Sunday mornings until a new sanctuary could be built.

In 1959 Homer resigned from the Evanston Unitarian Church at the height of his popularity and moved to New York. He served as executive director of the National Committee for a Sane Nuclear Policy.

In 1965 Homer moved to Boston to become director of the Social Responsibility Department of the Unitarian Universalist Association during an era marked by unparalleled interfaith cooperation and internal denominational conflict. Under the helm of President Dana McLean Greeley and Homer, the UUA assumed leadership on a wide variety of civil rights and peace issues. However, the rise of the black power movement following King's assassination split the denomination into bitter factions. As one who had devoted and risked his life for racial justice, Homer suddenly found himself under attack by black militants.

As the UUA closed ranks, a new conservative administration took power and Homer was fired. Homer accepted the position of Secretary-General of the newly founded World Conference on Religion and Peace (WCRP) in New York. In 1984 Homer received the Niwano Peace Prize from Rissho Kosei-Kai, a Buddhist sect in Japan.

In the late 1980s, he moved to Swarthmore, Pennsylvania to work on his autobiography, be near his collected papers at the Swarthmore College Peace Collection, and spend more time with his children and grandchildren.

Upon returning from a trip, Homer was diagnosed with pancreatic cancer. Memorial services were held at the United Nations, Swarthmore, and Evanston, and in Boston the Unitarian Universalist Association established the Homer A. Jack Office of International Affairs in honor of his contributions to peace and freedom.

CHARLES RHIND JOY:
INTERNATIONAL HUMANITARIAN (1885-1978)

By Charles Rhind Joy. From the 25th anniversary record of the Harvard College Class of 1908, published in 1933.

BORN: Boston, Mass., Dec. 5, 1885. 1885. Robert Joy, Arabella Sophia Parke.

YEARS IN COLLEGE: 1904-1908.

DEGREES: A.B., 1908; S.T.B., 1911

OCCUPATION: Minister.

I majored in English literature at Harvard College, and from the College entered the Divinity School. It was my ambition to combine theology and literature in one career. That ambition has never been realized, and never will be realized now. The ministry, I have found, is too exacting a profession in these modern days to look with favor upon such divided loyalties. For a few years I did serve as Literary Editor of *The Christian Register*, but this is the nearest approach I have ever made to the realization of the old ambition, which is now dismissed, I am sure, for good.

I was married in the Chapel of the Divinity School the day after Commencement to Lucy Alice Wanzer, Dean Fenn officiating. In the fall of that year I was settled in the First Parish of Portland, Maine, which had had none but Harvard men as its ministers from the time of its organization more than two hundred years before. Among them was Thomas Hill, predecessor of Charles W. Eliot as President of Harvard College.

My resignation from the Portland church was precipitated by the outbreak of the World War. I was opposed to the war. My preaching became unacceptable. I resigned. I sought service overseas with the Y.M.C.A.

Returning to America I resumed my work in the ministry. In 1922 I was called to be minister of the First Church in Dedham. I became Literary Editor of *The Christian Register*, and Secretary of the Unitarian Ministerial Union.

In January 1927 I became minister of All Souls Church in Lowell. I became Secretary of the Committee on the Supply of Pulpits for the Unitarian Ministerial Union. This work led directly to a call from the American Unitarian Association to become an Administrative Vice President.

THE 50ᵀᴴ ANNIVERSARY
HARVARD COLLEGE CLASS BOOK REPORTS:

From 1940 to 1954 I was engaged in international relief work. This work took me all over the world in such posts as executive director of the Unitarian Service Committee, European director and associate director of the Save the Children Federation, international representative, chief of the Korean Mission, and executive consultant for African affairs for C.A.R.E. In the course of these first two periods of my life I found time to write, translate, or edit a dozen books: *Topical Concordance of the Bible*, three books on labor and political conditions in the Soviet Union, and eight books on one of the truly great men of all time, Albert Schweitzer. The third period of my life began in 1954, since when I have been devoting my whole time to speaking and writing.

Charles Joy has received the following honors: S.T.D., Pacific Unitarian School for the Ministry, 1933; Cruz Vermelha de Dedicacao, Cruz Vermelha de Merito, Cruz Vermelha de Benemerencia (all Portugal); Medaille Commemorative de la Grande Guerre, Palme Academique (both France); honorary life member, Portuguese Red Cross; Officer of the French Academy. His publications include: *Topical Concordance of the Bible*; *One Great Prison; Police State Methods in the Soviet Union*; *Coercion of the Worker in the Soviet Union*; *Albert Schweitzer—An Anthology*; *The Africa of Albert Schweitzer*; *Wit and Wisdom of Albert Schweitzer*; *A Psychiatric Study of Jesus* (translation); *Goethe—Two Addresses*; *Goethe—Four Studies* (translation); *Animal World of Albert Schweitzer*; *Music in the World of Albert Schweitzer*.

GYORGY KEPES:
EXEMPLAR OF THE VISUAL ARTS (1906-2001)

By Edgar J. Driscoll Jr., Boston Globe *Correspondent and Scott S. Greenberger,* Boston Globe *Staff*

Gyorgy Kepes founded MIT's Center for Advanced Visual Studies to break down the barriers between art and technology, but the internationally known painter, sculptor, and photographer never learned to drive a car or even ride a bicycle. His Wellfleet summer home didn't have running water.

Nevertheless, Mr. Kepes was "always interested in finding the connection between science and art," said his son, Imre of Pelham. "He probably felt there was no separation."

Mr. Kepes, who died Dec. 29, 2001, in Cambridge at age 95, lamented that many people fail to see the connections among diverse disciplines. The result, he said, is a feeling of isolation and rootlessness in a cold, contemporary world.

"Essentially what I feel is that the public—artist and scientist, too—have lost the ability to communicate with each other," he said in an interview in 1965. 'What I'm interested in is how we reestablish communication of ideas."

He spent much of his career at the Massachusetts Institute of Technology, where he was a professor of visual design from 1946 until retiring in 1974. He founded the Center for Advanced Visual Studies in 1964 and was its head until

1974.

The Hungarian native was often described as a renaissance man. He was the author of "Language of Vision" and "The New Landscape," and was widely known for his abstract paintings. His work was shown in one-man exhibits around the world. He produced symphonies of color and mood in his paintings, which were often sand-textured (he painted many of them in Wellfleet). Mr. Kepes's son and daughter say he was fascinated by the geometry and symmetry in nature.

He was born in Selyp, Hungary, in 1906. After graduating from the Royal Academy of Fine Arts in Budapest, he joined the Germany studio of Laszlo Moholy-Nagy, a famous Hungarian artist who experimented with many materials.

Mr. Kepes met his wife, the late artist Juliet Appleby Kepes, on a London street in 1936. In a Globe interview in 1989, Mr. Kepes said that on the autumn day they met he was a "restless" soul who had wandered the capitals of Europe.

He spied 17-year-old Juliet walking with her mother up and down Shaftesbury Avenue, looking for the studio of a photographer who was supposed to take Juliet's picture.Mr. Kepes was smitten. "My life is saved," he recalled thinking. They began meeting and fell in love, and when Mr. Kepes got an offer to teach at the Chicago Institute of Design in 1937, he asked her to go with him.

At MIT, the shy, soft-spoken Mr. Kepes discovered that "scientists have a clearer and richer horizon than most artists have." "So I started a series of seminars to find meeting areas for scientists and artists in understanding the world," he recalled. The Center for Advanced Visual Studies, which he described as his "dream project," was born.

Asked why Mr. Kepes, a man who spent much of his life trying to bring artists and scientists together, rejected some popular technological inventions, his daughter, Juliet Stone, said he was "a man of many contradictions."

Stone recalls that the family didn't have a television. "He felt strongly we should use our imaginations and read and draw," said Stone, of Watertown.

In addition to his son and daughter, Mr. Kepes leaves six grandchildren and a great-grand-child.

UNITARIAN NOTE

Gyorgy and Juliet Kepes were members of the First Parish in Cambridge, Unitarian Universalist.

JAMES R. KILLIAN, JR.: PRESIDENT OF THE MASSACHUSETTS INSTITUTE OF TECHNOLOGY (1904-1988)

By Paul E. Gray, President of M.I.T., & David S. Saxon, Chairman of the Corporation

Through more than half a century of exemplary dedication to Massachusetts Institute of Technology, Jim Killian demonstrated rare qualities of mind and spirit. In the most critical times his perspective was invaluable in understanding and strengthening the role of technology in modern society. He initiated the postwar evolution of M.I.T. to what he called "a university polarized around science, engineering, and the arts," a vision that gave a humanistic sensitivity to its role as a foremost institution of science and technology.

Throughout an association spanning more than sixty years, Dr. Killian's contributions to M.I.T. were enormous. His deep understanding of its goals and his wise judgment have left a mark upon the Institute that will never be forgotten. A man of enviable erudition, Jim Killian possessed as well a natural eloquence and charm, a warm and gracious manner, and a gentle, wry humor that was never unkind. All these gifts he put to use in the service of M.I.T.

Dr. Killian's commitment to public service was equally impressive. During the 1950's he served President Eisenhower in evaluating national technological and intelligence capabilities, and, as Presidential Science Adviser from 1957 to 1959, Dr. Killian put into place strong mechanisms for providing U. S. presidents with the best scientific advice the nation had to offer. Although he was not a scientist himself, Jim Killian always had a rare and special understanding of what it means to be a scientist and it was because of this valuable insight that he was such a great leader of scientists.

It was also during these Washington years that Dr. Killian brought into being official national concern for arms control and disarmament, soundly grounded on realistic scientific principles and knowledge.

In the 1960's Dr. Killian was chairman of the Carnegie Corporation's study of educational television in the United States and was the principal author of its report. That report led to the establishment by Congress, at Dr. Killian's urging, of the publicly financed Corporation for Public Broadcasting, which he served as a director for six years, including one year as chairman. He later received two George Foster Peabody Awards for his substantial achievements on behalf of public broadcasting.

Jim Killian was a skilled and talented writer, and we are fortunate that his legacy to us includes two excellent personal memoirs, *Sputnik, Scientists, and Eisenhower* and *The Education of a College President*, and many memorable speeches.

FOR FAITH AND FREEDOM

In expressing his free faith through cooperative action, James Killian served as chairman of the Standing Committee of the Unitarian Church in Wellesley MA, member of the Board of Directors and Moderator of the American Unitarian Association, and honorary cochair of Cambridge Forum national radio and television public affairs broadcasts. In affirming his faith he declared:

"I find in Unitarianism the freedom and stimulus to seek a lofty sense of the meaning of life. The important thing is to build a faith in a divine power or principle larger and beyond oneself. For me, Unitarianism contributes most effectively toward this objective."

GEORGE ELBERT KIMBALL: OPERATIONS RESEARCH INNOVATOR (1906-1967)

By Philip M. Morse

Abridged from Biographical Memoirs, National Academy of Sciences. Vol. 43 *(New York: Columbia University Press, 1973).*

George Kimball was a generalist, capable of achieving outstanding recognition in two fields of science and of leaving his mark on other fields of human endeavor. Perhaps his greatest contribution was the education and inspiration he gave to many younger men, now working in various fields of science and technology.

He was born in Chicago in 1906 and grew up in New Britain, Connecticut. After a year at Exeter Academy, he went on to Princeton. His thesis for the doctoral degree, granted in 1932, was on the quantum mechanics of the recombination of hydrogen atoms. He applied for a National Research Fellowship in chemistry and won, going to MIT for the two years 1933-1935. In 1965 he wrote of those times: "The great Depression was at its height (my first job after I earned my Ph.D. paid the magnificent salary of $900 a year). As a result, the group of graduate students and postdoctoral fellows with whom I worked shared office space. We spent our evenings as well as our days there, but not always at our work. There was a ping-pong table, and someone discovered that the long, long corridors of M.I.T. made a wonderful place to roller skate. Every afternoon we had tea, served by Alice Hunter, student in chemistry, who has since done me the honor of becoming my wife. Those teas became a sort of discussion group, led by Norbert Wiener, who would argue violently on any subject."

In 1942, when I was asked by the Navy to organize a group to analyze antisubmarine tactics, Kimball was one of the first persons I recruited. Within the year

he became Deputy Director of the group, called the Operations Research Group (ORG) during the war, later called the Operations Evaluation Group, U.S.N.

In the midst of all this, Kimball's work with Henry Eyring and John Walter, started ten years earlier, was completed and the book *Quantum Chemistry* was published in 1944.

After this, Kimball went to the Chemistry Department at Columbia, to resume his research and teaching in theoretical chemistry. Professor of Chemistry as of 1947, he received the Presidential Citation of Merit for his war work; and he was elected to the National Academy of Sciences in 1954.

Even during the war Kimball had become convinced that operations research could be effectively applied in industry and in the public sector. He was interested in enlarging public awareness of its potentialities and was active in organizing the Operations Research Society of America, which was founded in 1952, with Kimball as a member of the society's first council. By 1964, when he was elected the society's president, the society had about 5,000 members.

In the 1950s Kimball came full time to A. D. Little, first as Science Advisor and then, in 1961, as Vice President.

Kimball also did his part as citizen and parent. John B. Lathrop, a neighbor and colleague at A. D. Little, reports: "George had a strong sense of responsibility to the community and gave it as much time as he could. He spent many years as officer, committeeman, or consultant for church, Boy Scouts, and community."

For his last several years, Kimball suffered from serious cardiac illness. He died on December 6, 1967.

UNITARIAN NOTE

Dr. Kimball's activities included service as president of the Unitarian congregation in Hackensack, New Jersey.

W. M. KIPLINGER: PUBLISHER OF THE KIPLINGER LETTERS (1891-1967)

By Austin H. Kiplinger, President of the Kiplinger Editors

W. M. Kiplinger's association with Unitarianism began during his college years at Ohio State University in 1908-1912. As a standard product of Midwestern Methodism, he had attended Sunday school as a boy and learned the customary catechism of the times. In later life, he delighted in regaling listeners with the words of old hymns like "Brighten the Corner Where You Are" and "Washed in the Blood of the Lamb."

His own views began to form in the atmosphere of educational liberalism in which many young

students found themselves during the Woodrow Wilson political era. These were given a framework by his association with a fellow student, Irene Austin, who later became Mrs. W. M. Kiplinger. Her father, Judge James Austin of Toledo, Ohio, was an active member of the First Unitarian Church of Toledo.

After moving to Washington in 1916, Mr. and Mrs. Kiplinger attended All Souls Unitarian Church (which, by the way, was also the home congregation of the Chief Justice, former President William Howard Taft). In the early 1950s, when a new congregation was being formed in Bethesda, Md., the Kiplingers became friends with John Baker, minister of the new group and together with others in the community, became founding members of the Cedar Lane Unitarian Church, which now occupies an important role in the neighborhood adjoining the National Institutes of Health and Naval Medical Center in Bethesda. Through Mr. Kiplinger's interest in gardening, the new church created a surround of azaleas on the adjoining grounds. The Kiplingers remained members of Cedar Lane until W. M. Kiplinger's death in 1967.

In 2001, W. M. Kiplinger's son, Austin Kiplinger, honored his father's memory with an endowment grant for a program in ethics at the Cedar Lane Church.

OBITUARY

From The Washington Post, August 7, 1967

W. M. Kiplinger, 76, founder of the *Kiplinger Letters* and *Changing Times* magazine, died of a heart attack yesterday at his home, 6609 River Rd., Bethesda. Long a force in Washington journalism, Kip—as he was known to friends and associates — prided himself upon being "a reporter's reporter. "Twenty years ago, the *Saturday Evening Post* estimated that he was "the best paid and most influential reporter in the world; also the most independent." An aggressively unostentatious man who shunned Washington society life, Mr. Kiplinger covered the Nation's Capital for about 50 years as an Associated Press reporter, a business correspondent and an editor. But the distinguishing mark of his career was his penchant for writing Washington news in a breezy, staccato style that the folks back home understood.

Mr. Kiplinger left AP in 1919 to become correspondent for the National Bank of Commerce of New York. As such, he established a query service to answer questions of clients about what was happening in Washington. One evening in September, 1923, he decided to send all his clients a letter, a supplemental summary of Washington news. This was the first *Kiplinger Washington Letter*, which has since remained in continuous weekly publication. Like the other letters he eventually published, such as the *Kiplinger Tax Letter* and the *Kiplinger Agriculture Letter*, the *Washington Letter* is colloquial in style, with "flag words" underscored and a controversial amount of prophetic opinion. It was Mr. Kiplinger's experience that "men in public life would often give you the straight story in private, then reverse their field in their pro forma public statements."

In 1947 he inaugurated the monthly magazine, *Changing Times* [now entitled *Kiplinger's Personal Finance Magazine*], which now has well over one million in circulation.

WALTER DONALD KRING: MINISTER AND POTTER (1917 - 1999)

Autobiographical Reflection

Walter Donald Kring was born in Lakewood, Ohio on March 10, 1916. The family moved to California just in time to face the Great Depression and the Long Beach earthquake, the second worst earthquake in modern times.

Walter Donald went to Occidental College. In college, Walter was very much interested in philosophy and religion, and Occidental College offered two scholarships for juniors at the University of Hawaii and Lingnan University in Canton, China. Walter applied for and was accepted for the exchange scholarship to Hawaii.

Thus, he spent his junior year at the University of Hawaii, studying Oriental religion, philosophy, and anthropology through the exchange program. The greatest event of that year was his meeting and studying with a great Quaker, Thomas R. Kelly. Walter was Kelly's only major student, and under him, Walter studied ethics, Western philosophy, as well as Chinese, Japanese, and Indian religion and philosophy. Most of all he was impressed with Kelly's Quaker views in religion, especially the belief in man as a being who could go to God directly without intermediaries.

Walter Kring went to Harvard Divinity School in the Fall of 1937 and graduated in the Divinity School Class of 1940.

Although from his Quaker teachers he had strong feelings against the war, he volunteered for the Naval Chaplaincy. With the Naval Chaplaincy program, Walter preached to large congregations of approximately 1500 men. Chapel was compulsory, and he enjoyed his work with the bright young sailors.

While decommissioning in South Boston, Walter Kring made contacts with the First Church in Boston. He preached several times at the Second Church, and they wanted to extend a call to him. But the last time he preached there, he discovered—to his surprise—that there was a pulpit committee from the First Unitarian Church in Worcester, Massachusetts. They wanted him to visit Worcester. He began his ministry in Worcester in September 1946. After nine years of ministry he was called to All Souls Church in New York City.

No account of Walter Kring's ministry would be complete without some mention of his work as a potter. After settling in Worcester, Mr. Kring built a high-temperature kiln. He displayed many of his pots in American museums while minister at the Worcester church. Kring was able to continue his hobby all through his ministry at All Souls.

Adapted from Safely Onward: The History of the Unitarian Church of All Souls, New York City, *by Walter Donald Kring, Volume 3: 1882-1978 (New York: The Unitarian Church of All Souls, 1991).*

NOTE

Walter Donald Kring died suddenly on January 15, 1999

Active in denominational affairs, he served as secretary of the American Unitarian Association, a trustee of the Unitarian Universalist Service Committee, and president of the Board of Trustees of Beacon Press.

A dedicated historian and author, Mr. Kring published *Liberals Among the Orthodox: Unitarian Beginnings in New York City, 1819 - 1839* in 1974, *Henry Whitney Bellows* in 1979, and *Herman Melville's Religious Journey* in 1997.

From the Unitarian Universalist Association, 1999-2000 Directory.

ARTHUR BECKET LAMB:
CHEMIST, EDITOR, EDUCATOR (1880-1952)

By Allen D. Bliss
From the Journal of the American Chemical Society Volume 77, Nov. 20, 1955

There are many old New England names in the roster of distinguished American scientific men, and Arthur Becket Lamb earned a place among them at an early age. His family migrated in 1630 from near London to Roxbury, Massachusetts. Arthur B. was born on February 25, 1880.

Arthur Lamb was a "biology major" in college. When his undergraduate work was completed, he chose chemistry for graduate work. Chemistry had been chosen now for a career. He registered at Harvard Graduate School. Lamb had organized his Tufts College graduate research into a thesis, taken the examinations, and received the Ph.D. degree from Tufts prior to the Harvard graduation. The Harvard Faculty learned of this and decided that it was proper to grant him the Harvard Ph.D. also, since the two theses embodied completely different work. Harvard appointed him as instructor in electrochemistry.

The War Department, upon the entrance of the United States into the World War in 1917, turned to the Harvard department for help. Lamb was made Chief of the Defense Chemical Research Section. As Chief, he continued to practice chemistry, but he became an accomplished executive. His natural, kindly and approachable manner and disposition were of the greatest value in cementing friendships, and making new ones.

By the end of 1920 Lamb was faced with the decision between either remaining in Washington and resigning from the Faculty at Harvard, or returning to the University. He chose the latter alternative and in September of 1921 was once again active in University teaching and research.

The American Chemical Society chose Arthur B. Lamb as its President for the year 1933.

During the late 1930's Lamb served as deacon in the First Unitarian Parish of Brookline, as a member of the Board of Trustees of the Brookline Public Library and of the Winsor School.

Arthur B. Lamb was promoted to Professor in 1920, and in 1940 he was made Dean of the Graduate School of Arts and Sciences. He retired from the Directorship of the Harvard Chemical Laboratory in 1946 and from undergraduate teaching two years later. The University allowed him to retain his office and laboratory suite for *Journal of the American Chemical Society* work and several continuing research problems. The American Chemical Society presented him with its highest honor, the Priestley Medal, at the 116th Meeting in Atlantic City in September of 1949.

As teacher, research director, editor, consultant and citizen, his services extended over half a century. His personality and teaching reached and permeated all of chemistry, and his contributions to and influence on chemistry will long outlive all of us who knew, admired and loved him.

UNITARIAN NOTE

The presentation of the Joseph Priestley Medal of the American Chemical Society symbolizes the creative union of the natural sciences and the Unitarian celebration of the world. Priestley was not only the discoverer of the element oxygen but a Unitarian minister who served in Birmingham, England and Northumberland, Pennsylvania. Benjamin Franklin was one of his hearers and admirers. Priestley's gift to Thomas Jefferson of his harmony of the synoptic gospels of the New Testament inspired President Jefferson to prepare his own *Harmony with the New Testament,* which is repeatedly issued now as *The Jefferson Bible.*

WILLIAM L. LANGER:
HISTORIAN OF DIPLOMACY (1896-1977)

Memorial Minute adopted by the Faculty of Arts and Sciences, Harvard University

Born in South Boston on March 16, 1896, Bill was three years old when his father died suddenly. Mrs. Langer, pregnant with their third son and without money, supported and cared for the three boys, taking boarders and working as a dressmaker to make ends meet. Langer affectionately recalls a Spartan but happy childhood: good food, demanding household chores, and — from the age of nine onward — a series of part-time jobs. And always there was school. The third-grade teacher with the rattan cane that hurt his hand nonetheless interested Langer

133

in history, geography, and spelling. Afterwards came the Boston Latin School, an arduous three-mile walk, and then Harvard.

Receiving his A.B. in 1915, Langer taught German for two years at Worcester Academy. With the first World War underway, intensely curious about its origins, and already Wilsonian in his thinking, he simultaneously studied international relations at Clark University. In December 1917, he enlisted, serving in France in a chemical warfare unit, whose history he wrote immediately after the Armistice: his first book. Then he returned to Harvard as a graduate student in history —"a Subject" he says, "every aspect of which aroused my interest and engaged my thought." Archibald Cary Coolidge, the first scholar in America to see the importance of studying Russian, Near Eastern, and Asian history, became his mentor and close personal friend.

He received the Ph.D. degree in 1923. When Professor Coolidge died early in 1928, Langer succeeded to his course on the Ottoman Empire and its many subject peoples. He became, in 1936, the first incumbent of the Coolidge chair, founded by his beloved teacher's own bequest.

In his autobiography, Langer later described the sudden attacks of "stage-fright," beginning in 1938, that beset him while lecturing, and turned each class into a nightmare for him. Such was his iron control, however, and so unaffected was his actual performance that this revelation astounded even colleagues who had taught courses jointly with him and attended all his lectures.

Langer's writings had the same magisterial quality as his teaching. *The Diplomacy of Imperialism* in two volumes (1935) carried the subject down to 1902, into an era when friction was replacing equilibrium. Langer performed a prodigious amount of research, using all the appropriate languages, and then achieved a splendidly organized, clearly written, and almost preternaturally objective, even detached, treatment of the complex material. Unlike any other historical studies of their scope, these books have remained standard for more than forty years.

As World War II moved into its most threatening phases, President Roosevelt in the summer of 1941 appointed Colonel William J. Donovan as chief of the first United States coordinated foreign intelligence service in our history. Langer became Deputy Chief and then Chief of the Research and Analysis Branch of this agency, by 1942 known as the Office of Strategic Services. The R and A branch became as large as a university faculty, with its own offices overseas and its members attached to offices of other OSS branches.

In 1950, Langer obtained an additional year of leave to organize the office of National Estimates in the newly established Central Intelligence Agency. But except for membership after 1961 on the President's Foreign Intelligence Advisory Board, the year 1952 marked the end of Langer's government service. He was awarded the Medal for Merit by President Truman in 1945. It would be

hard to think of any productive scholar-historian who ever made so extensive a contribution to government in war and peace.

Back at Harvard in the early fifties, Langer became intimately connected with the Regional Studies Programs and their affiliated research centers, established for Russia and East Asia after the war. In 1954 he was instrumental in founding the new center for Middle Eastern Studies, and in 1955 became Director of the Russian Research Center and chairman of the entire Regional Studies effort. These enterprises still flourish and owe him a debt of gratitude.

Honors naturally poured in upon Langer. He cherished his membership in the American Philosophical Society. Harvard and Yale awarded him LL.D. degrees, Harvard in 1945, at the Commencement just after the end of World War II. The University of Hamburg followed in 1955, its gown including a starched white ruff that turned Langer into a living portrait by Holbein.

William Langer and his wife, Rowena, were regular Unitarian congregants at The First Parish in Cambridge, MA; during his years of government service in Washington DC, they attended All Souls Church and especially appreciated the prophetic ministry of A. Powell Davies.

JOHN HOWLAND LATHROP: BROOKLYN'S WORLD MINISTER (1880-1967)

By Olive Hoogenboom
This selection is abridged from The Unitarian Church of Brooklyn: One Hundred Fifty Years, *1987:*

A POST-WORLD WAR II MINISTRY

From 1946 to 1949, annual visits to Czechoslovakia by Lathrop, accompanied by his wife, strengthened the bonds between the First Church in Brooklyn and that war-devastated country. While World War II raged, Czechoslovakia was used by the Germans as a dumping ground for orphans from nearby countries. By the war's end, it had nearly a million destitute children, many of them mere babies. In some areas nearly all of the children suffered from tuberculosis. The Unitarian Service Committee grew out of the denomination's relief efforts in Czechoslovakia and became an official agency of the World Health Organization.

From June to December 1946, John and Lita Lathrop directed a five-pronged program launched by the Service Committee to help these children and assist Czechoslovakia. The Lathrops were ideally suited to their mission. They were linked with Thomas Masaryk, revered as the father of Czechoslovakia, through his wife's connection with the Brooklyn church. Also, because of the Service Committee's work, the word Unitarian brought instant recognition. The denomination was known not only in Czechoslovakia, but throughout Europe and "identified with all that is most truly human—sympathy, understanding, sharing, eagerness to serve."

The most important part of the Unitarian Service Committee's efforts for Czechoslovakia was a medical mission chaired by Dr. Paul Dudley White of Harvard Medical School.

Traveling throughout the country with a medical school on wheels, these American doctors performed demonstration operations, held conferences and lectures, and bolstered medical care by inspecting and improving hospitals.

In 1946, Lathrop became the president of the International Association for Liberal Christianity and Religious Freedom (IARF). This organization was founded in Boston in 1900 and later was used to gather up the churches excluded from the World Council of Churches in 1938 (the year after Lathrop and other liberal churchmen had participated in its founding). Besides the United States, England, and the Brahmo Samaj of India, fourteen or fifteen European countries were usually represented in the IARF, whose delegates frequently held summer conferences and committee meetings in Europe.

Lathrop actively participated in many worthy causes. Although sharing so much of his time with other organizations was sometimes hard on his church, through him the First Church helped shape important organizations and policies. Lathrop served in the national government's Department of Research and Education; he worked in the early birth-control movement and advertised its first worldwide campaign in his church's Calendar, and he was closely associated with Florence Kelley in the National Consumers' League, of which he became president.

For many years, he was president of the Brooklyn Urban League, which grew out of a 1916 meeting in his study. He was also president of the Brooklyn Council for Social Planning and the Brooklyn Health Council.

John Howland Lathrop died on 20 August 1967.

A PRESENTATION

In 1957, the American Unitarian Association presented the Eighth Annual Unitarian Award in recognition of Distinguished Service to the Cause of Liberal Religion to

John Howland Lathrop:

John Howland Lathrop, ordained Minister in the Unitarian denomination for fifty years, member for six years of the Board of Directors of the American Unitarian Association, world figure in the field of Liberal Religion, past president of the International Association for Liberal Christianity and Religious Freedom, delegate from the American Unitarian Association to the Brahmo-Samaj Cente-

136

nary, India.

John Lathrop has lived a rich and busy life devoted to the welfare of his fellowmen at home and abroad. In his youth a student of social problems, he has throughout his life applied his knowledge and wisdom in many fields.

Whether as ardent defender of civil liberties or in other fields, he has never hesitated to express his convictions regardless of their popularity. This he has done in the pulpit and out with an incisiveness and clarity peculiarly his own, and hence remarkably persuasive.

Possessing, together with his other attributes, a deeply religious outlook on life and an intellectualism that has freed him to search out and share the truth, John Howland Lathrop represents the best in Unitarianism.

MARGARET LAURENCE:
THE FIRST LADY OF CANADIAN LITERATURE
(1926 - 1983)

From the First Unitarian Church of Ottawa

Jean Margaret (Peggy) Wemyss was born in Neepawa, Manitoba, on July 18, 1926. After graduating from high school in 1944, Margaret attended the University of Winnipeg, and in 1947 and married John Fergus Laurence. In 1950, after living for a year in England, Margaret and her husband, a civil engineer, moved to British Somaliland. While there, she wrote a translation of a Somali book of prose and poetry, *A Tree for Poverty*. Mrs. Laurence said that it was at that time that she "began seriously to write." A travel book, *The Prophet's Camel Bell*, written some years later, describes the Laurences' experience in Somaliland.

They moved to Accra, Ghana in 1952, with their 2-month-old daughter, Jocelyn, who was born in England. During their subsequent five years in Africa, Margaret produced her first novel, *This Side Jordan*, which won the 1961 Beta Sigma Phi Award for best first novel by a Canadian. A collection of short stories, *The Tomorrow Tamer*, written a few years later, is also set in West Africa. Out of her African years came an interest in contemporary literature by Africans, which resulted in her study of Nigerian fiction and drama, *Long Drums and Cannons*. The Laurences' son, David, was born in Ghana in 1955.

After leaving Africa, the family lived for five years in Vancouver, and during this time, Margaret wrote *The Christmas Birthday Story*.

After Vancouver, there followed seven years in England. In the ten-year period, 1964-1974, the Manawaka books were published:

> *The Stone Angel* (1964)
>
> > *A Jest of God* (1966), for which she received the 1967 Governor

General's Award,

    and which was the basis for a movie entitled "Rachel, Rachel," starring Joanne Woodward

The Fire Dwellers (1969)

A Bird in the House (1970)

The Diviners (1974), 1975 Governor General's Award winner

A collection of her essays, *Heart of a Stranger*, was published in 1976. An hour-long documentary film, *Margaret Laurence: First Lady of Manawaka*, was produced by the National Film Board of Canada and premiered in Winnipeg on May 7, 1979. Adaptations of many of her works have been made for radio and television. Many of her books have been translated into other languages.

The last decade of her life focused on promoting causes she passionately sup-
ported -- peace, social justice, the equality of women, environmental protection -- through letters, lectures, essays and fundraising campaigns.

Margaret Laurence died on January 5, 1987, and, at her request, her ashes were brought by her children, Jocelyn and David, to be interred in Riverside Cemetery, Neepawa, on June 23, the day before the official opening of The Margaret Laurence Home, the former Simpson house where she, "the first lady of Canadian Literature," had lived in her youth.

ALFRED MCCLUNG LEE (1907-1992) AND ELIZABETH BRIANT LEE (1908-1999): FRONTLINE SOCIOLOGISTS

By John F. Galliher and James M. Galliher, University of Missouri

The Lees' professional careers are best captured, according to Betty Lee, by the Italian phrase, *tutti e due insieme*, or both together in everything.

Al was born August 23, 1906, and Betty, September 9, 1908. They first met on a so-called "blind" date at the home of friends in Oakmont, Pennsylvania, in 1926. They then wandered around in the quiet of a local cemetery. A year later, after Betty had finished her sophomore year of college and Al had graduated, they were married.

Al's father was a Pittsburgh attorney who was known in the area for his defense of African Americans, immigrants, and other powerless people. Al recalled that on one occasion his father learned that the local Ku Klux Klan planned a raid on a local black church during the Sunday evening services. His father asked the minister if he could be the featured guest speaker that evening. When the KKK arrived, his father confronted them in the center isle of the church and pulled off

the leader's mask, thus identifying him. Perhaps as a result of this surprise they left without a word. Later, however, reflecting the KKK's special brand of cowardice, a cross was burned in the front yard of the family's home.

In 1945 Al and Betty left the Episcopal church over the issue of racism in the church, after Al's having been a vestry member in a Detroit congregation. Al recalled that "the clergy did not like a talk I gave at a church meeting on racism in the church. We gradually left and put our kids in a Unitarian Sunday School." After that time the Lees remained active Unitarians and also participated in Friends' Meetings. Al served as president of the American Unitarian Fellowship for Social Justice.

Betty Lee completed her dissertation in 1937, the second woman to complete graduate training in sociology at Yale. The dissertation, titled *Eminent Women: A Cultural Study*, is squarely placed in a feminist tradition.

Unlike Betty's dissertation, Al's dissertation, *The Daily Newspaper in America*, was published as a book in 1937.

Their *Fine Art of Propaganda*, published originally in 1939, was based on an analysis of Father Charles Coughlin's speeches, which were filled with anti-Semitic utterances. In retrospect it seems unlikely that two very junior sociologists, with so few sociological role models to follow, would have attacked a figure who at the time had great prominence through his nationally syndicated radio program.

The audience for this book by the Lees was primarily the general public. The Lees felt it necessary to challenge Coughlin among the general public, for this is where he had attracted considerable support. The enduring quality of this book, which explains why it was still in print in the late 20th century, is that it is as relevant as it was during the 1930s.

In 1941, Al was elected executive director of the Institute for Propaganda Analysis which had published the book. Aside from publishing Betty and Al's book on propaganda, the institute had other activities: "One million children in 3,000 public and private high schools of this country are being taught to develop critical, questioning attitudes of what they read in the newspapers, hear on the radio or see in the motion pictures through monthly bulletins, teaching guides and other materials prepared for classroom use by the Institute for Propaganda Analysis."

Race Riot by the Lees and Norman Daymond Humphrey is an analysis and a detailed chronology of events leading to and including the Detroit race riots of June 1943. The book noted how fascism and American demagogues such as Father Charles Coughlin, Huey Long, and the Rev. Gerald L.K. Smith were similar to Hitler and Mussolini.

Fraternities without Brotherhood is another example of clinical sociology. *Fraternities without Brotherhood* could have been written yesterday as a description of the racial and class discrimination of fraternities and sororities.

Sociology for People: Toward a Caring Profession, published in 1988, asks how sociology can aid the "rank-and-file people" and help emancipate them from the manipulation by elites.

For some time sociologists have been intrigued by the nature of human commitment to both ideas and to a course of action. What is beyond dispute is that the Lees displayed an early and continuing commitment to each other, to their sons, and to a sociology that could serve the community.

Abridged from Marginality and Dissent in Twentieth Century American Sociology, *State University of New York Press, 1995*

ARTHUR LISMER:
PAINTER & EDUCATOR (1885-1969)

By Gregory Halpern, photographer and author of Harvard Works Because We Do

Born into a working-class Unitarian family amidst the fog and factory smoke of Sheffield, England, Arthur Lismer was eventually to find fame as a young, impressionist painter of the Canadian countryside. Considered by many a place of industrial ugliness, Sheffield may have inspired in Lismer the desire to celebrate what bastions of untouched nature remained in the world. As a boy, he took lonely hikes through the English countryside, on shorelines of sharp cliffs and on the borders of bellowing seas and narrow fjords. On these trips Arthur took his sketching books and his paints, recording day by day the limitless incantations of the moody and weather-filled seascapes.

As a boy, Lismer drew casual cartoons, animals, woodlands, Boer War heroes and caricatures, drawing discreetly even during weekly Unitarian services (much to his mother's dismay).

At the time, many British artists were immigrating to Canada where, it was said, prospects for an active career in the commercial arts were increasing. As friend after friend emigrated and wrote back of successes, Lismer found he could bear Sheffield no longer, and in 1911 chopped up his former office desk, made a traveling trunk of it and boarded ship for Canada. He had left his fiance and family in England, though in a year's time, after having established himself in Toronto, he would return to England, marry Esther in the local Unitarian church, and return to Canada with his new bride.

In Toronto, Lismer had found work with Grip, perhaps Canada's most prominent commercial art firm. There, he befriended the firm's crew of talented artists, who, with Lismer, began traveling to the Canadian countryside for painting trips. The group of friends would come to form what is today known as the "Group of Seven." Collectively, the Group deeply altered the Canadian art scene. In 1914, after a three week trip with co-worker Tom Thomson, Lismer wrote the following: "The first night spent in the North and the thrilling days after were turning points in my life. . . the bush, the trails, lakes, waterfalls . . . moving camp from one wonderful lake to another portage and tent-pitching, fishing and sketching, and above all, the companionship of a great individual, a wonder with canoe, axe and fish line."

Until now, the natural beauty of Canada had not been painted successfully in its own style, represented for its own character and spirit, or celebrated by Canadian artists for its unique beauty. The concept of doing so, in fact, had seemed a foreign one. "It is necessary," Lismer wrote, "that as Canadians we should believe we are capable of producing great art as we believe we are capable of doing great deeds."

In what would prove a coming of age for all Canada, Lismer and the Group of Seven memorialized the Canadian landscape in one painting after another, describing the land with brilliant impressionist colors, coarse brush strokes, and a romantic sense of form and natural rhythm.

In 1929 Lismer was offered the position of Educational Supervisor at the Art Gallery of Toronto. It was there that Lismer flourished as a teacher and as an educational leader.

In a lengthy booklet about the school published by the Art Gallery of Toronto, Lismer eloquently and persuasively describes the school's purpose and value:

The aim of the Art Centre is not to train artists, or teach art, or instruct in drawing, but to lead out from the child, encouraging every spark of feeling and originality and to aid in the extension and co-ordination of hand, eye and mind toward the development of a more emotionally active and alive little personality.

Each Saturday morning Lismer seemed to accomplish the impossible: he drew hundreds of people into the Art Gallery, filling its rooms and crowding its halls so that only standing room remained. It seems that each day his classes provided something of a famous event. Relatively careless of his clothes and appearance, Lismer was known to move happily through the Gallery, disheveled and energized, observing and encouraging his children, guiding their hands as they drew, his own coat pockets bulging with pencils, crayons, pipe, paper and notebooks.

DUNCAN LITTLEFAIR:
A UNITARIAN PREACHING NATURALISTIC
RELIGION (1912- 2004)

Three years after Duncan Littlefair received a Ph.D. degree from the University of Chicago, he was for thirty-five years the minister of what became the dominant church in Grand Rapids, Michigan: the Fountain Street Church. For more than a half a century he has been in Unitarian ministerial fellowship, known as a radical critic of organized religion. For a decade minister colleagues were gathered as a group by the Rev. Roy Phillips to visit for three days each year with Dr. Littlefair for a seminar on ministry. A Grand Rapids congregation of 1,000 to 1,700 assembled on Sundays. The church was a center for performing arts events by Duke Ellington, Ella Fitzgerald, Dave Brubeck, and E. Power Briggs. The church forum featured educational occasions with astronomer Harlow Shapley and anthropologist Margaret Mead, as well as speakers including Paul Blanshard, Paul Tillich, Alan Watts, and Henry Nelson Wieman. Among the other featured visitors to the Fountain Street Church were Eleanor Roosevelt, Ralph Bunche, Linus Pauling, Hans Morganthau, Arnold Toynbee, and Robert Frost. The cogregation and minister were noted for liberal religious community action in such fields as drug rehabilitation, a Planned Parenthood clinic, the Council on World Affairs, and the American Civil Liberties Union.

PREFACE

By Duncan E. Littlefair

I was born and brought up in Toronto. My father was variously an "atheist" or "Free Thinker." He was not interested in religion. Neither of my parents completed grade school. Only one of my six brothers attended high school. I was blessed by being the seventh son and thus free from the obligation of family support. Basically, I had only myself to look after.

My mother introduced all of her sons to the Presbyterian Church. It "took" only with me. I am grateful for the exposure. I memorized the shorter Catechism and hundreds and hundreds of Bible verses. This experience has been valuable to me. I love to quote the Bible to some of my conservative friends who have lost sight of the variety and richness of religious insight expressed in that great book.

At the age of 12 or 13 I left the Presbyterian Church for a Baptist Church. I was deeply intrigued with a religious group organized on a totally democratic basis. In later years they abandoned this principle to pursue the rewards of order, unity and success. I still advance the notion that religiously we are all on our own. No one has the answers. No one speaks for another. No one controls another. No one speaks

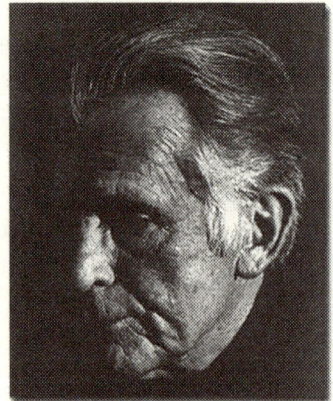

for God. I think that the Unitarians, like the Baptists, have fallen into the trap of the efficiency of a "United Voice," central organization and rules of conduct and procedure, not to mention financial success.

I got my Bachelor and Theological degrees from McMaster University, Hamilton, Ontario. Grant Butler and his wife, Calla, and I were fellow students. Night after night Calla and I waged a relentless battle with Grant to break him free from his fundamentalism. Those of you who remember his work in the Extension Program are aware of how blessed was our effort.

In the spring of '36 I was about to graduate and realized acutely then, as I had been somewhat aware for a time, that there was no place for me in any church in Canada! A miracle occurred. I read a book called The Wrestle of Religion with Truth, by a man named Henry Nelson Wieman. It was a "Damascus Road" experience. For the first time I found a man who was speaking my language, expounding a religion that demanded my attention. The way was open!

I came to the University of Chicago in the fall of '36 and have been totally involved in preaching a Naturalistic Religion since that time. The religion I preached is the religion of my culture—Christianity. I have never preached a sermon without a biblical text. I have never, even slightly, encouraged any supernatural idea or belief. I have never taken refuge in any absolute. I have never pretended to speak for "God." I use the term "God" poetically. My quest is to find the spirit, to find the meaning and worth of Life. The function of the church is to find a way to encourage people in the quest.

"Here's to the wonder, miracle, glory and joy of life."

Littlefair: Texts and Photographs by Michael William Grass

DOROTHY LIVESAY:
CANADIAN CREATOR OF LITERARY CULTURE
(1909-1996)

By Phillip Hewett, Emeritus Minister, Unitarian Church of Vancouver, BC, Canada

Dorothy Livesay, it is generally agreed, was one of the foremost Canadian poets of her generation. She was born in Winnipeg on 12 October 1909, during the first snowstorm of the season—a fact that she herself considered symbolic of her identity: Reared on snow she was manacled on ice and it was strangely fitting that she died also, on 29 December 1996, during one of the rare snowstorms in Victoria, B.C.

Her parents, J.F.B. Livesay and Florence Hamilton Randal, were both writers, having met while working for the *Winnipeg Telegram*. They fostered Dorothy's literary interests from an early age, although it was not until much later that she discovered that her mother had written published poems. It was her mother who came upon a poem Dorothy had written at the age of 13 and took it upon herself to submit it to a newspaper for publication. Dorothy's anger at having what she considered private material thus invaded was tempered by the cheque for two dollars that she received in payment.

At the age of 19 her first volume of poetry, a slim collection entitled *Green Pitcher*, was published. But it was during her year of graduate work at the Sorbonne in Paris (1931-32) that the economic effects of the Depression and the rise of Fascism affected Dorothy so strongly that she became a theoretical Marxist and then an active Communist.

Dorothy carried this political commitment back with her to Toronto, where she enrolled in the School of Social Work as a means of carrying her activism into practice. For the fieldwork that comprised the second year of her course, she was accepted by the Family Service Bureau in Montreal, where she was directly exposed to the poverty and misery of the unemployed in a city experiencing the worst effects of the Depression. Her concern for the plight of women, in particular, spurred the development of the strongly feminist emphasis that became a feature of her writing. But her literary output during this period was strongly ideological, which perceptibly affected its quality.

It was during the mid-forties that Duncan and Dorothy discovered the Unitarian Church. Dorothy's religious upbringing had been conventional. As she herself described it in a sermon delivered in the Unitarian Church of Vancouver in 1956:

I was brought up in an orthodox religious atmosphere. My mother's Church of England views dominated my early years. I paid little attention to the fact that my father was a heretic and sceptic—himself an escapee from the Plymouth Brethren. However, after steadfast attendance at church and Sunday school, at 15 years old I startled my teacher by questioning certain articles of Anglican dogma... Later, at university I found a very free spirit of enquiry into the historical origins of Judaism and Christianity. Perhaps this made it all the easier for me to repudiate orthodox religion, and eventually to accept as a substitute the deterministic, Marxist view of the origin of man. The paradox continued however, for at the same time that I was embracing economic determinism and naturalism, I was also taking delight in a study of the seventeenth-century poets—all of whom were writing not in praise of man, but for the greater glory of God!

Dorothy and Duncan continued to live in Vancouver until 1958. She did some school and university teaching during this time, but her literary output remained fairly slight. Then, as her children grew older, she felt free to apply for a Canada Council fellowship to study the teaching of English at London University's School of Education. This turned out to mark a new point of departure in her life. The following February she received the news that Duncan had died of a massive stroke, and returned briefly to Vancouver. But she was soon back in London, then for brief period in Paris, working for UNESCO. Later the same year she succeeded in obtaining a position on the staff of a teachers' training college in what was then Northern Rhodesia but became the independent nation of Zambia while she was

there. Her political and social concern involved the mistreatment of children and also the need for improved health and dietary standards. "I can do very little about all this, although I can put some of it into poems."

In 1975 she once again was instrumental in founding a poetry magazine, *CV/ II*, the title harking back to the *Contemporary Verse* of the 1940s. It became an important addition to the Canadian literary scene.

The honours which came Dorothy Livesay's way in later life culminated in her being named an officer of the Order of Canada in 1987.

ARTHUR LOVEJOY: FOUNDER OF THE HISTORY OF IDEAS MOVEMENT (1873 - 1962)
Tussling with the Idea Man

By Dale Keiger
Abridged by courtesy of Johns Hopkins Magazine, *April 2000.*

Lovejoy was an idea man. Ideas were his stock in trade, specifically ideas about ideas. Intellectual concepts have histories, and this is what fascinated him: how the great ideas developed and mutated and combined and recombined and coursed from century to century. He was an archaeologist of the intellect, digging for the foundations of Western thought. A physicist of philosophy (though his preferred analogy to science was as analytic chemist), seeking to reduce systems, creeds, and -isms to their fundamental particles.

Arthur Lovejoy was born in 1873 in Berlin, Germany, where his father was conducting medical research. When Lovejoy was 18 months old, his mother killed herself by an overdose of pills. Her husband responded by abandoning medicine and becoming a minister. He wanted his son to take a clerical collar as well, but Arthur was more interested in a rational basis for theology, what he termed "a quest for intelligibility," so he studied philosophy and comparative religions at the University of California and applied the techniques of a historian to his intellectual pursuits. He was hired by Stanford in 1899 but quit two years later when the president dismissed Lovejoy's colleague because the latter's politics had offended a trustee. Harvard's philosophy department wanted him, but President A. Lawrence Lowell blackballed him as a troublemaker. (Lovejoy would later co-found the American Association of University Professors, perhaps confirming Lowell's worst fears.) Johns Hopkins University, apparently not so easily scared, hired him for its philosophy department in 1910.

Lovejoy was a philosophy professor but didn't like what he considered artificial disciplinary lines. So he founded his own Hopkins interdiscipline, the history of ideas.

In his most famous book, *The Great Chain of Being*, he examined the idea, derived by the Neoplatonist philosopher Plotinus from Aristotle and Plato, that all of creation forms a chain. The chain includes all that could possibly exist, starting with God, in an infinite series of forms, each of which shares at least one attribute with its neighbor in the chain. Lovejoy traced this idea through 2,000 years of intellectual history, demonstrating its influence on thought in the West. He follows parts of the Great Chain conception through Augustine, Thomas Aquinas, Roger Bacon, Liebniz, and Spinoza, pausing along the way to discuss Copernican astronomy and Kepler.

An important aspect of Lovejoy's work was his examination of how the meanings of words changed over time, and the effect those changes had on ideas. He'd take "nature" or "romanticism" and demonstrate how people used these terms without being fully cognizant of the ambiguities caused by shifting definitions. Lovejoy once subjected himself to interrogation by the Maryland Senate, when he'd been nominated for the state's educational board of regents. A legislator asked Lovejoy if he believed in God. George Boas recalled, "I am reliably informed that in reply Lovejoy developed at length 33 definitions of the word God, consuming 15 cigarettes meanwhile, refusing to be interrupted or ruffled, and ended by asking the committee member which of these meanings he had in mind when putting the question." As the story goes, no one felt inclined to ask him another question, and Lovejoy was confirmed. Unanimously.

In 1923, he and colleagues founded the Hopkins History of Ideas Club. Meetings were open to anyone. You needn't be a Hopkins professor. You needn't be a professor at all. Graduate and undergraduate students were welcome. Six times a year, participants would assemble. The meetings drew writers, historians, philosophers, biologists, political theorists...anyone who thrived on scholarly dialogue.

Arthur Lovejoy died in 1962.

ARTHUR ONCKEN LOVEJOY CHAIR IN HISTORY

Professor Lovejoy was the first chairman of the Maryland chapter of the American Civil Liberties Union, and his opinions often appeared in the editorial pages of the Baltimore *Sun*. He also was a founder of the American Association of University Professors and a strong proponent of the right of faculty members to teach unencumbered by ideological restrictions. He allied himself with the Unitarian movement.

UNITARIAN NOTE

Perhaps the most impressive demonstration of the history of ideas movement is the publication of *Philosophers Speak of God*, by Charles Hartshorne and William L. Reese, published by the University of Chicago Press in 1953. The book grew from a course entitled "Ideas of God in the Great Systems" taught by Lovejoy's fellow Unitarian, Charles Hartshorne, to students including William L. Reese, who elicited his professor's interest in coauthoring the book. This history of ideas not only includes a systematic classification of ideas of God but a presentation and critique of theistic and atheistic ideas throughout history in both the East and West.

FLORENCE HOPE LUSCOMB:
A RADICAL FOREMOTHER (1887-1985)

From "Special Projects" report of the Massachusetts Foundation for the Humanities

Florence Hope Luscomb grew up in the 1890s and died in the 1980s. During her long life, she embraced and advanced a range of causes from woman suffrage to civil liberties. She was 33 years old when the Nineteenth Amendment finally enfranchised women; she was still active when American women rediscovered feminism in the 1960s and 1970s.

Born in Lowell in 1887, she moved to Boston with her mother two years later when her parents separated. Her mother was an ardent and active supporter of suffrage and other radical causes, and Florence followed in her footsteps. She remembered going with her mother at the age of five to hear Susan B. Anthony speak, and she spent many Saturday mornings in the 1910s selling the suffrage paper, *The Woman's Journal*, outside the Park Street Station.

Florence Luscomb was among the first women to graduate from M.I.T. with a degree in architecture. From 1909 to 1917, she was a partner in a woman-owned firm in Boston, but her true love was the suffrage cause. She helped organize rallies, trolley tours and street meetings; in 1915, she logged more than 220 speeches in 14 weeks during the campaign for an amendment to the state constitution. When World War I caused a building slump, she left architecture to become executive secretary of the Boston Equal Suffrage Association. She helped organize and was president of a Boston local of the United Office and Professional Workers of America. She held paid positions with the Boston League of Women Voters, the Massachusetts branch of the Women's International League for Peace and Freedom, and organizations concerned with prison reform and factory safety. Beginning in the 1920s, she served on the board of civil rights, civil liberties, and other liberal organizations, including the NAACP and the Massachusetts Civil Liberties Union. After her mother's death in 1933 gave her financial independence, she became a full-time social and political activist.

Florence Luscomb ran for public office four times, including a race for Boston City Council in 1922 which she lost by less than one percent. Her campaigns for the U.S. House of Representatives in 1936 and again in 1950 were meant to educate voters and expand the two-party system. In 1952, she ran for Governor of Massachusetts on the Progressive Party ticket, a third party that opposed the anti-Communist policies of the Truman administration.

She fought McCarthyism and was called upon to defend herself before a committee of the Massachusetts legislature. In her pamphlet *Blacklisting the Constitution*, she condemned the anti-Communist investigations as un-American attempts to suppress dissent. In the early 1960s, she wrote the first anti-Vietnam War leaflet distributed in Boston, and visited both China and Cuba. When 1970s feminists turned to her as a "foremother," she encouraged the new movement to be inclusive. Just as she had once urged labor unions to include women, in the 1970s she reminded feminists to reach out to poor women and women of color. A lifelong radical, at age ninety she was living in a Cambridge commune. She died in 1985 at age 98.

ROWENA MORSE MANN: FIRST WOMAN DOCTOR OF PHILOSOPHY (1870-1958)

By Catherine F. Hitchings
Courtesy of the Universalist Historical Society

Rowena Morse Mann was a famous orator, scholar, and the first woman to receive a Ph.D. from the University of Jena, Germany. She was born in Ithaca, New York in 1870, the daughter of Sarah (Fitchette) and Benjamin Morse, and

was extremely well-educated. She graduated from the University of Iowa in 1891 and taught science in the Omaha High School in Nebraska before deciding to prepare for the Unitarian ministry. She attended the Divinity School at the University of Chicago throughout the late 1890s. Winning a traveling scholarship for 1901 to 1904, Rowena traveled to Germany where the studied at the University of Berlin, only to discover the authorities would not grant a woman a degree. In 1904, after a hard struggle to gain recognition for her studies, she received a Ph.D. from the University of Jena. Hers was a test case, and when she graduated summa cum laude, the university changed its admissions policy to include women. A tablet was placed at the university in 1933, commemorating this event.

Upon her return from Europe, Rowena Morse preached one year in Geneva, Illinois and here was ordained to the Unitarian ministry March 29, 1906. She was minister for the Unitarian parishes in Keokuk, Iowa from 1906 to 1910, Kenosha, Wisconsin for one year, and the Third Unitarian Church in Chicago from 1911 to 1922. From 1914 to 1917 she served as a director of the Western Unitarian Conference. In the summer of 1921, she brought her pioneering spirit to Harvard University, conducting a service at Harvard Divinity School's Andover Chapel.

Anita Trueman Pickett, meeting Dr. Mann on this occasion, remembered her as "a delightful companion, humorous as well as inspiring."

In 1912 she married the Rev. Newton Mann (1836-1926) of Omaha, Nebraska whom she had met while teaching in the Omaha High School early in her career. She had given a sermon one Sunday in the Unitarian church there, and soon afterwards she gave up her first teaching job to study for the ministry. Newton Mann's first wife, Eliza J. (Smith), had died in 1908, leaving him to care for their son and daughter.

When her husband died in 1926, Rowena Morse Mann retired from the ministry and began lecturing extensively. Her scholarly and practical background, as well as her "informed, unbiased and vigorous" mind made her lectures on sociology, politics, ethics and art extremely interesting. In 1919 she was asked to fill out the commitments of Rev. Anna Howard Shaw, an ordained Protestant Methodist minister, who had contracted pneumonia and would die later that year. Thus Rowena Morse Mann became a lecturer for the Association for the League of Nations. With notable Americans such as ex-President William Howard Taft and A. Lawrence Lowell of Harvard University, she toured the country seeking to increase support for the League of Nations and President Woodrow Wilson's planned peace treaty.

She translated *Theories of Knowledge* (1904) and *Moral Education and the Scientific Method* (1925). When she lectured on philosophy at the Weimar-Jena Summer School in 1933, she became the first woman to lecture on that subject in any German university. She was a director of the Chicago branch of the American Association of University Women, a member of the American Psychological Association and of the American Philosophy Association, and an honorary member of the Chicago Woman's Club.

Well-loved, especially as a minister, Rowena Morse Mann died March 3, 1958.

JOHN P. MARQUAND:
AUTHOR (1893-1960)

These paragraphs introduce the John P. Marquand Collection at Yale University, a rare and extensive gathering in 51 boxes of materials open for research:

John Phillips Marquand, leading American writer of the twentieth century, was born on November 10, 1893, to Philip and Margaret Fuller Marquand, both descendants of old New England families. Although he was born in Wilmington, Delaware, and lived in Rye, New York, until he was fourteen, Marquand considered himself a New Englander. He was educated at the Newburyport (Massachusetts) High School and at Harvard University, from which he was graduated in 1915. From 1915 to 1917, he was assistant magazine editor of the Boston *Transcript*. After a brief period as advertising copywriter in 1920 and 1921, he became a novelist and published *The Unspeakable Gentleman* (1922). Marquand was a frequent contributor of short stories to several popular magazines of the day, most notably *The Saturday Evening Post, Cosmopolitan, Collier's*, and *Good Housekeeping*. Many of his novels were also serialized in shortened form in these magazines.

A recurring theme in many of Marquand's works concerns the life and times of the middle and upper classes in twentieth-century New England--particularly Boston—as illustrated in *The Late George Apley* (1937), *Wickford Point* (1939), and *H. M. Pulham, Esquire* (1941). Marquand also wrote several mysteries featuring the Oriental detective Mr. Moto. Film versions of the Mr. Moto mysteries enjoyed great popularity. Marquand's writings were widely received and sold well. In addition, many of his works were successfully adapted for stage and screen.

In 1922, Marquand married Christina Sedgwick. From this marriage, which lasted thirteen years, a son and a daughter were born. In 1936, Marquand married Adelaide Hooker. Two sons and a daughter were born of this union, which also ended in divorce in 1958.

John P. Marquand died in his sleep of a heart attack on July 16, 1960 in Newburyport, Massachusetts.

THE SPIRE ABOVE YANKEE CITY
by John P. Marquand

What follows is from an article published by the American Unitarian Association in the Christian Register, *November, 1949.*

Newburyport, on Massachusett's North Shore, has been immortalized by Sociologist W. Lloyd Warner as "Yankee City" in the scholarly series of the same name. Also, it is the locale (under the name "Clyde") of the latest book, Point of No Return, *by Newburyport's best known citizen, John P. Marquand. What does the First Parish church mean to this venerable seaport? What does its spire symbolize to its citizens? In this sermon, delivered at the beginning of the campaign to raise funds for the rebuilding of the spire, Pulitzer Prize winner Author Marquand gives his answers. He was chairman of the Steeple Committee, and is active in the affairs of the Unitarian Church.*

I have heard it said that this spire should not be raised again. I have heard it said that the debt incurred by its restoration is too dangerous, that it would be better at most to build a simpler, cheaper spire. I have heard it said that it is only an elaboration, that it perform no useful function, and answers no social need. This is only common sense. It would be much cheaper, much easier, not to rebuild this spire. The workmen who are now engaged in restoring it could readily be employed in more useful work. But then so, too, could have the stonecutters who adorned the Cathedral at Chartres and so, too, could Michelangelo whose paintings in the Sistine Chapel do nothing to support its ceiling. Art very seldom performs a practical function, but the man through all the ages has never lived by bread alone. The people of Newburyport throughout this town's long history have never been motivated solely by the dialectics of materialism. Because they never have been and I hope they never will be, they are rebuilding this church steeple now so that it will.

EDWARD S. MASON:
POLITICAL ECONOMIST (1899-1992)

Edward Sagendorph Mason was a member of the First Parish Unitarian Church in Harvard Square who exemplified liberal religion in both thought and action. In addition to his notable contributions to the science of government, he served as chairman of the Sloan Commission on Cable Communication which issued recommendations for the future, On The Cable. *He was a consultant to the Center for International Affairs, a member of Resources for the Future and a director of the Asian Development Corporation. His lifelong sustained, perva-*

sive role in the field of higher education is fondly remembered by colleagues in the words of the Harvard faculty memorial minute which follow.

Edward Sagendorph Mason was a great scholar and a distinguished public servant. Warmly esteemed by all who knew him, he was a devoted member of the Harvard community, whose contributions to this university still shape many of its activities a quarter century after his formal retirement.

Through the first decades of his career, Ed Mason's academic work dealt mainly with the relationship between government and business. In the 1930s his seminar on industrial structure, monopoly and price rigidity was a centerpiece in this field. In this earlier period and in the 1950s Ed initiated the modern field of Industrial Organization. He created the dominant paradigm of the industry study, exploring the relationship between industry structure, the conduct of firms in the industry, and the economic performance that resulted. Mason's collaborators and students dominated the field and remain important to this day; they include many lawyers as well as economists.

In 1941 Ed and his colleague and old friend, William Langer, went to Washington to help organize the research and analysis branch of what originally was the Office of the Coordinator of Information, later the Office of Strategic Services. To this office Ed attracted some of the ablest economists of that generation. Throughout his career, the respect and affection that so many of Ed's colleagues felt toward him enabled Ed to attract an extraordinary group of scholars to one major endeavor after another.

Ed Mason's services to Harvard, in addition to his primary lifetime activities of teaching and research, were numerous and diverse. In the troubled environment of 1969, on the eve of his retirement, Ed was called on to serve as acting Dean of the Faculty of Arts and Sciences. Prior to that, from 1947 to 1958, he was Dean of what is now the Kennedy School of Government. It was during this earlier deanship that Ed began his involvement with developing countries, an interest that was to occupy much of the last three decades of his career.

Among his many accomplishments, Ed regarded the mid-career program for government officials from developing countries, now called the Mason Fellow Program, as his crowning achievement.

BERNARD MAYBECK: CALIFORNIA ARCHITECT (1862-1957)

By M. H. White and Professor Charles Gilman Hyde

Born in New York City on February 7, 1862 to German immigrants who had come to America slightly more than a decade earlier, Bernard Ralph Maybeck (1862-1957) grew up in a family circle that encouraged him to draw and paint. He studied at the Deutsche-Americanische Schule and the Benjamin Franklin School in New York, learning both French and German before entering the college of the City of New York.

Bernard Maybeck was 19 when he arrived in Paris. The École des Beaux-Arts was near the studio, and Maybeck decided to become an architect. Although his training seemed inadequate, his high scores on the entrance examination gained him admission in 1882 in the atelier of Jules André, elected as one of the forty members of the Institut

de France.

Finding opportunities limited in Kansas City, Maybeck left for San Francisco, returning to Kansas City late in October, 1890, to marry Annie White with whom he returned to California to make his lifelong home. Eventually he found work in the office of A. Page Brown, whose commissions included the California building at the Chicago World's Fair of 1893. Maybeck supervised its construction and had an opportunity to see the Fair's other buildings and its formal layout, which he admired. The Maybecks moved to Berkeley in 1892.

In 1895 Phoebe Apperson Hearst indicated her desire to donate funds to the university for a mining building that would commemorate her husband, who had made his fortune in that occupation. To Maybeck, the sole architect employed by the university, fell the task of preparing a sketch for the building, a rendering that Mrs. Hearst approved. This led Maybeck to urge that the university prepare a campus development plan. The Board of Regent's initial negative reaction gave way before Mrs. Hearst's endorsement of the idea. She asked that Maybeck be given a two-year leave to act as professional advisor for an international competition to select the best design, the prizes to be donated by her. In 1896 Maybeck published a sketch of his own to illustrate the kind of approach that might be followed, although, as advisor he could not become a competitor.

Maybeck established his architectural office in San Francisco and began a practice that concentrated on the design of private homes, churches, and club buildings. Most of his over two hundred commissions demonstrate Maybeck's originality and his refusal to follow conventional ideas of how a building should appear. His later experiences in large-scale design were for college campus plans, first for Mills College in 1918 and then for Principia College.

Among various indications of the living art of Bernard Maybeck we find the three-dozen cherished residences in the Berkeley hills. His simple shingled design of the Unitarian Church of Palo Alto has been celebrated for the mystical atmosphere he achieved. When the Unitarian Church of Berkeley was forced to move from the University of California campus, he not only recommended the large site with a Bay view but gave a generous gift to make its purchase possible.

Most honored now among his achievements as a California architect is the Palace of Fine Arts in San Francisco which houses the Exploratorium, a unique educational center which features exhibits of science, art, and human perception.

VASHTI CROMWELL MCCOLLUM: ADVOCATE FOR CHURCH/STATE SEPARATION (1916-)

By James T. McCollum, President of the Arkansas Chapter Americans United for Separation of Church and State

Vashti Ruth Cromwell, named for the queen of Ahasuerus in the first book of Esther who was one of the few biblical women to stand up for women's rights, was born in Lyons, New York on 6 November 1912 to Arthur G. and Ruth C. Cromwell. She was raised in Rochester, New York and after graduation from a public high school, attended Cornell University on a full tuition scholarship until the market crash of '29. Transferring to the University of Illinois, she eventually obtained her AB in the College of Liberal Arts and Sciences in 1944 and MS in Mass Communications in 1957, after interruptions for marriage and children.

After arriving in Champaign-Urbana to attend the U of I, she met Dr. John P. MCCollum, a staff member, whom she married in 1933. Their three sons all graduated from college with at least one degree. James Terry, the oldest, went on to obtain a JD from the U of I College of Law and practiced law in Rochester, New York for nearly 34 years until his retirement in 1994. Dannel obtained an MS in History from the U of I and was the longest serving mayor of Champaign, Illinois, serving three terms. Errol Cromwell, after obtaining his BS in Mechanical Engineering from Southern Illinois University, eventually established a chain of bicycle stores along with a partner and was actively engaged in that enterprise until his retirement in 1996. All three remain active in other pursuits.

Vashti was to live up to her namesake when she and her oldest son, Jim, were confronted with pressure to enroll him in a Christian Sunday school type class that was being offered in the public schools of Champaign during school hours. Resisting the pressure at first, she and her husband eventually relented and allowed Jim to attend the classes the balance his 4th grade year. However, the following year, the MCCollums, feeling that such a program was totally inappropriate in the public schools, refused further participation. This, of course, resulted in Jim taking heat from his peers and suffering some indignities at the hands of his unenlightened 5th grade teacher.

After unrequited attempts to have the program discontinued administratively and after much soul searching, with the aid and support of the Rev. Phillip Schug, the Unitarian minister in town, and with financial assistance from a group of Jewish businessmen in Chicago, she filed a writ of mandamus in the Champaign County Circuit Court in the late summer of 1945. At this point things really became rough for the MCCollums, ranging from physical confrontations between Jim and his peers, to vandalism of their home, to attempts at terminating Prof. MCCollum's employment at the university. Fortunately, for Dr. MCCollum, his tenured status secured his position with the university. However, Vashti's employment as an adjunct instructor in the women's physical education program, was terminated.

The three judge panel, sitting to hear the case in the Circuit Court, decided that, in spite of the clear language in the Illinois constitution to the contrary, the practice violated neither it nor the establishment of religion clause of the 1st Amendment of the U. S. Constitution. The Illinois Supreme Court agreed with the lower court and the case was appealed to the U.S. Supreme Court, which granted certiorari in the fall of 1947. 50 years ago, on 9 March 1948, the US Supreme Court handed down its landmark decision in the Peo. of the State of Illinois, ex rel MCCollum -v- Board of Education, 333 US 203 (1948), in a decision, written by Justice Hugo L. Black, that was to become a landmark case in U.S. constitutional law. The significance of the decision was that it was the first case of impression that held the several states accountable to the strictures of the establishment of religion clause of the 1st Amendment of the U.S. Constitution under the aegis of the due process clause of the 14th Amendment. All cases, involving school prayers, aid to parochial schools, sectarian religious displays on public property and other such incursions into Jefferson's wall of "separation of church and state" by the states and their municipalities, descend from this case.

As in any such case and particularly in this one, because of the MCCarthyistic mood of the late 40's and 50's, when Communism was considered the scourge of humanity and atheists were considered by many as either Communists or fellow travelers, this case took its toll on Mrs. MCCollum and her family. However, she was resolute, as was her namesake in the Bible, and persisted, despite disappointing losses in the lower courts, until she finally triumphed with her decisive 8 to 1 victory in the high court. For the results of this case alone, if not for her courage and perseverance, she deserves recognition in the annals of U.S. constitutional law.

Among the awards and recognition accorded her in subsequent years were the prestigious John Haynes Holmes Award (now the Holmes-Weatherly Award) from the Unitarian Fellowship for Social Justice, the second person to be so honored. Other recipients were Whitney Young, Roger Baldwin and the Rev. Martin Luther King, Jr. She also has received recognition from the Illinois ACLU, the Champaign County Chapter of the Illinois ACLU, the Roger Baldwin Foundation of the Illinois ACLU, Americans United for the Separation of Church and State, the Rochester, New York Chapter of Americans United, the Freedom From Religion Foundation and the American Humanist Association.

Vashti MCCollum, this gutsy lady who wouldn't let sectarian special interests take over the public schools, finally passed on to her rewards on 20 August 2006, 7 weeks prior to her 94th Birthday. The legacy she left behind in the field of U S constitutional law will not soon be forgotten.

A book, written by Mrs. MCCollum about the circumstances of the case, entitled "One Woman's Fight", has been reprinted by the Freedom From Religion Foundation and can be obtained from them.

WADE MCCREE, JR.:
SOLICITOR GENERAL OF THE UNITED STATES
(1920-1987)

By Kin Foley MacKinnow
Text and photos courtesy of The Bulletin, *Boston Latin School Association*

Almost as a matter of course, many Boston Latin graduates go on to illustrious and rewarding careers. What is not at all usual is to be so respected and revered that your name is inscribed in gold on the upper frieze of the Boston Latin School auditorium. There is room for only 38 names on that list and the final spot was given to Wade Hampton McCree Jr. '37, who passed away in 1987. He joins such luminaries as John Hancock, Joseph Kennedy and Leonard Bernstein.

Well-respected for his impressive career and his integrity, McCree has always been known as a groundbreaker. He was a member of Phi Beta Kappa and graduated summa cum laude from Fisk University in 1941. After a four-year stint in the Army during World War II, he graduated from Harvard Law School in 1948. At a time when some lunch counters wouldn't serve black people, McCree became the first African-American judge appointed to the U.S. Court of Appeals for the 6th Circuit and the second African-American solicitor general in the history of the United States. McCree came from a long line of people determined to have an education despite all difficulties. His grandmother, Martha Hale McCree, a widow of a Union soldier with 13 children to support, worked in food services at Fisk University in Tennessee and encouraged her children to attend college. McCree's father was one of her three children to attend Fisk, working as a butler to pay for school.

After graduating 12th in his class from Harvard Law School in 1948 and passing the bar exam, McCree and his wife, Dores, a Simmons graduate, moved to her hometown of Detroit. There, McCree entered into private practice at the legendary black law firm of Bledsoe & Taylor. In 1953 he was appointed to the Workman's Compensation Commission by Governor G. Mennen Williams. Two years later he became the first African-American to be named a judge of the Circuit Court for Wayne County, Michigan.

President John F. Kennedy appointed him to the U.S. District Court for the Eastern District of Michigan in 1961, another first for an African-American. In 1966 President Lyndon B. Johnson appointed him to the U.S. Court of Appeals for the 6th Circuit. He served there until 1977, when he left to become solicitor general of the United States, the second African-American to hold that office - Supreme Court Justice Thurgood Marshall was the first. President Jimmy Carter, who nominated McCree to the post, said at his memorial service that McCree was "a true American hero."

Called the "10th Justice," McCree served as solicitor general for four years.

McCree personally argued 25 cases in the U.S. Supreme Court, including the Richard Nixon presidential tapes case and the Bakke "reverse discrimination" case.

THE PLAQUE ON BEACON HILL

At the headquarters of the American Unitarian Association in Boston, the Dining Room of Eliot House features a plaque whose inscription includes these lines:

Wade and Dores were devoted members of Detroit's First Unitarian Universalist Church and Wade served as vice moderator of the UUA in 1965-66.

SIDNEY E. MEAD: HISTORIAN OF RELIGION IN AMERICA (1904-1999)

By Martin Marty, The Fairfax M. Cone Distinguished Professor, Emeritus, at the Divinity School of the University of Chicago

Mead's youthful background found him a convert in what may well be described as the Fundamentalism that was taking shape in the 1920s, where Minnesota was an arena for its encounters with Modernism and Liberalism. He had "walked down the sawdust trail" of a revival, become part of a form of Methodism that he saw as subliterate, and become familiar with the world of "bible schools." As he came to maturity, Mead—who married rather young to Mildred LaDue, an artist and soul-mate through all his years—made his way to California and was accepted at the University of Redlands, which had American Baptist affiliations. The University of Chicago, to which he came for doctoral work and to begin his teaching career in 1941, had been founded by such Baptists who—especially in its Divinity School—were associated with the modernist wing. Mead found this approach congenial and could have been best described as a liberal Baptist in the 1940s.

From 1943 to 1960 he taught in the cooperative experiment called the Federated Theological Faculty. It was based in the University's Divinity School but had close bonds with the Chicago Theological Seminary, Disciples Divinity House, and the Meadville Theological School, a Unitarian seminary of which Mead became president in 1956.

During his late Chicago years Mead joined the First Unitarian Church of Chicago.

The entry "Unitarianism" is not to be found in the indices to Mead's books. One has to track down Unitarian motifs through his discussions of national founders like Thomas Jefferson, who had prophesied that in due course all the churches would turn Unitarian, and especially of Ralph Waldo Emerson, whom Mead found so congenial. A careful reading of Mead would find him instinctively aligning himself with what some have called "the Romantic Enlightenment" more than the purely rationalist version. Emerson and the Transcendentalists spoke to Mead's soul as Jefferson and Franklin spoke to his mind.

Mead's masterpiece, *The Lively Experiment: The Shaping of Christianity in America* published in 1963, is a collection of carefully crafted essays that he first published in journal form and then edited to form a coherent work. Incidentally, "Christianity" in Mead's book did not include Roman Catholicism, which received slight mention. He wrote just before the breakthroughs on the ecumenical front and before the new accents on "women's history" or "ethnic" (as in Afro-American, Hispanic, etc.) history came to question the focus on Ahlstrom and Mead's "mainstream." (Those who studied with him at the University of Iowa and Claremont Theological School testify that he was extremely open to the worlds of women and "multi-cultural" students even if he did not take these into the center of his own inquiries.)

Mead's concentration in *The Lively Experiment* had to do with the grand Jeffersonian and Madisonian moves toward religious freedom and individualism—"from coercion to persuasion." But he devoted attention as well to Abraham Lincoln, whom he regarded as the most profound theologian of the American experience. The fact that Lincoln was the only American president never to have joined a church was a feature that Mead, uneasy with denominationalism, enjoyed pointing out.

The *Nation with the Soul of a Church* (1975), was a more polemical collection of essays. In it he began to define what became a trademark Meadian theme, "Religion of the Republic." Robert N. Bellah, in a famed essay in 1967, spoke of this as "Civil Religion." For Mead, this religion's rootage was in what historian Crane Brinton had spoken of as religion that was "simply Enlightenment, with a capital E." Conrad Wright and other historians of Unitarianism have shown the congruence between this "founding fathers" faith and the Arminian theological stirrings in New England that took shape in the Unitarian denomination in the 19th century.

The *Religion of the Republic* vied with institutional religion. Mead noted, "I came from outside "the church" as institutionalized, and although I have found very congenial companionship with some professional churchmen, I now realize that I never felt comfortable and seldom felt completely welcome inside their temples." Perhaps, he thought, he should be seen as a member of the "Alumni Association" of church institutions. That stance would hardly qualify Mead or anyone for candidacy for excommunication from the Unitarian Universalist Association!

Finally, in more papers collected by students, *Love and Learning*, he is most autobiographical and "ecclesiastical," worrying as he does in some of the essays about the low quality of learning among seminarians and ministers. As so often, one finds here a kind of "lover's quarrel" with the manifestations of religion by an historian with a kind of Transcendenalist's soul and, therefore, one expressive of uneasiness about the very institutions—university, theological school, religious body, and nation—that he served.

His work on religion in America was strengthened by his having received unusually strong appreciation by both secular historians and teachers in the field of American Studies. A symbol of this fact is the rare distinction of his having been honored at a joint session of the American Church History Association and the American Historical Association.

DANIEL MELCHER: PUBLISHING EXECUTIVE (1912 - 1985)

By Chandler B. Grannis

Daniel Melcher, North American publishing executive, contributed to library service as an innovator in developing professional publications, reference services, and methods for improving book production and distribution.

Melcher was born July 10, 1912, at Newton Center, Massachusetts, the son of Marguerite Fellows Melcher and Frederic Gershom Melcher (later President of R. R. Bowker Company). Daniel Melcher graduated from Harvard College (A.B.) in 1934. In 1934 and 1935 Melcher was a publicity assistant at the London publishing house of George Allen and Unwin, and an assistant and student of publishing methods at other houses in London and Leipzig, Germany. In 1946 he was Director of the National Committee on Atomic Information, also in Washington.

When he joined the R. R. Bowker Company, New York, in 1947, Melcher was appointed Publisher of the firm's *Library Journal*. He quickly began developing the 70-year-old magazine into a major publication dealing with every aspect of the library profession, and in 1954 he founded, as an adjunct, *Junior Libraries* (*School Library Journal*, beginning 1961).

At the same time, Melcher had been working on the idea of a series of current in-print directories of American books. He devised the procedures by which the directories could be edited and produced, and in 1948 the firm launched the annual *Books in Print*, with author and title indexes. There followed, also under Melcher's vigorous direction, *Paperbound Books in Print* (1956), *Subject Guide to Books in Print* (1957), *Forthcoming Books* (advance listings), and *American Book Publishing Record* (catalogue listings, current and cumulative, in Dewey cataloguing sequence, 1961).

Meanwhile, Melcher was writing articles on library questions for *LJ* and on book distribution and book manufacturing for *Publishers' Weekly*. He contributed to the automated "belt press" concept of book manufacturing. His concern for distribution made him a major force in the mid-1960s in establishing the International Standard Book Numbering System.

He was Board Chairman of Gale Research Corporation, 1971-73, and thereafter an independent consultant. He was a member of the ALA Council, 1972-74, and from 1969 a board member of Institutes for Achievement of Human Potentials, with a special interest in the ways by which very young children can learn to read.

UNITARIAN NOTE

Daniel Melcher of Unity Church (Unitarian), Montclair, N.J., to honor his father, made possible the annual Melcher Book Award presented by the Unitarian Universalist Association for a work judged the most significant contribution to religious liberalism.

FREDERIC G. MELCHER: DEAN OF AMERICAN PUBLISHING (1879-1963)

The esteemed dean of American publishing served as a member of the Board of Directors of the American Unitarian Association and was an active supporter of its Beacon Press. He was also a member of the Commission on Planning and Review which published Unitarians Face a New Age *(1936). What follows is from an article penned by his son, David Melcher, published in the January 1967 issue of the American Library Association's* ALA Journal.

FRED MELCHER AS I KNEW HIM

By Daniel Melcher

When I was six years old and entering the first grade, the teacher asked each of us to tell what kind of work our father did. When it came my turn, I said, "Well, he doesn't work exactly, he just sits at his desk and talks to people."

Perhaps it was on the basis of that observation that I decided quite early that I also wanted to be a publisher. As a matter of fact, I had already produced my first book, poems, composed by myself, hand lettered by myself, and dummied up in folio form complete with an instruction to "put picture here" and a colophon. I didn't bother to identify the author on the title page, but I took great pains to identify the printer in the colophon.

Needless to say, our house was always full of books, some of which became mine, but some of which were birds of passage which I had to read rapidly before

they were taken back to the office. My father avidly collected Frost and Lindsay and examples of fine book design by such men as Updike, the Grabhorns, Bruce Rogers, and so forth. But he did not necessarily prefer the rare or limited edition. For the most part, he favored, instead, the most readable edition of his favorite books. He did have one specimen, though, from the greatest book of them all, namely the Gutenberg Bible, a reminder of the part FGM played in getting the U.S. Congress to purchase a perfect Gutenberg Bible for the Library of Congress.

Other books flowed through our house. When my father thought I was of an age to be interested, a series of books began to appear on what every boy should know about sex, and I received them in the spirit in which they were offered and also lent them around the neighborhood.

Once, a good many years later, I suggested that my father spend a bit more on clothes. He thought about it, and then said: "I am sorry, but I can't get interested in it. There are so many things that interest me more."

There were a great many things that interested him more, and he gave them both money and time. One was the Unitarian Church in which he took a very active part, culminating in another medal, this time a medal for the most distinguished contribution to the literature of liberal religion. After his death it was named for him, the Frederic G. Melcher Award.

He took an interest in the Montclair schools, serving on the Board of Education, in the Montclair Public Library, and in the Montclair Art Museum. He took an interest in the civic affairs of Wellfleet, Cape Cod, where he vacationed each July.

Those Julys on Cape Cod were what we children remember best about him. The rest of the year he would be constantly on the go, but in July he went where there was no telephone and made a complete change of pace. The cottage at Wellfleet looks out from the top of a bluff, past two headlands, across twenty miles of bay. We didn't belong to any yacht clubs, but we took time to read, and sail, and walk the dunes, and go clamming at low tide, and pick blueberries, and go for the mail and the daily newspaper. My father loved that spot so much he specified that his ashes were to be scattered there when he died. And so it was done.

From the *Library Journal*, April 1, 1963

Mr. Melcher lived in Montclair, N.J., for 45 years and was active in local civic and church affairs. He served on the Montclair board of education for 13 years and was a trustee of the Montclair Art Museum. Active in the Unitarian Church of Montclair, he was at various times superintendent of its Sunday school and president of its board of trustees. The contributions of Mr. and Mrs. Melcher to the life of the church were marked last year when the church dedicated a children's library room in their name.

ROBERT MILLIKAN: SCIENTIST (1883-1953)

By Daniel J. Kevles, Stanley Woodward Professor of History, Yale University.Abridged from Scientific American, *1979.*

Robert A. Millikan was the most famous American scientist of his day. In 1923 he became the second American (A. A. Michelson had been the first, in 1907) to win the Nobel prize in physics. Millikan is best known to physicists for measuring the charge of the electron with his oil-drop experiment; in the span of a remarkably productive career he also made significant contributions to the study of the photoelectric effect, hot-spark spectra and, above all, cosmic rays. He was more than a research scientist; between the wars he headed the new California Institute of Technology, advised industrial corporations and philanthropic foundations, and played a key part in the development of federal policy for academic science.

The son of a Congregational minister and the former dean of women of a small college, Millikan was born in 1868 in Illinois and was raised from the 1870's in Maquoketa, Iowa (population 3,000). He showed no particular scientific inclinations, and neither his family or school nor the agrarian environment stimulated him to move in a technical direction. At Oberlin College (where his mother had gone before him) he pursued a standard classical curriculum; his move toward physics came when his professor of Greek, impressed with Millikan's abilities, invited him to teach an introductory physics course in the preparatory school run by the college. (When Millikan protested that he knew nothing about the subject, the professor replied, "Anyone who can do well in my Greek can teach physics.")

After Oberlin he went to Columbia University, where he was the only graduate student in physics. One summer he worked under Michelson at the University of Chicago. Having earned his doctorate in physics at Columbia, Millikan spent a postdoctoral year in Europe, where his teachers included Max Planck, Walther Nernst and Henri Poincare; he acquired what was on the whole a better than average training for an aspiring American physicist at the turn of the century.

Joining the University of Chicago faculty in 1896, Millikan poured his considerable energies into developing the physics curriculum. At that time American students in both high school and college relied on foreign textbooks. Millikan wrote or co-authored a variety of books and laboratory manuals that became classroom standards. (*A First Course in Physics*, written with Henry G. Gale, sold more than 1.6 million copies between 1906 and 1952.)

World War I interrupted Millikan's research career. By now one of the nation's leading physicists, he was increasingly active in the professional affairs of his discipline and in the National Academy of Sciences. He was also a pioneer in developing links between industry and academic physics: he became a consultant to the research department of Western Electric, primarily to advise the company on vacuum-tube problems, and he pointed a number of his students toward careers in industry. Early in 1917, to help mobilize science for defense, Millikan went to Washington as a vice-chairman and the director of research of the newly established National Research Council in the National Academy of Sciences. Like many scientists engaged in defense research during World War I, Millikan soon entered the armed services. As a lieutenant colonel in the Army Signal Corps, he directed work in meteorology, aeronautical instruments and communications, and in his National Research Council capacity, he played an important role in initiating and advancing a major project to develop devices for the detection of submarines.

Millikan's success in the wartime mobilization was no mean achievement. The National Research Council, a private organization like its parent the National Academy, had no Federal appropriation; it had limited private resources and no authority in governmental affairs. During the war, as a friend recalled, Millikan learned how to "sell science" to a wide variety of people, military and civilian alike.

Millikan's work in the wartime National Research Council particularly impressed the astrophysicist George Ellery Hale and the physical chemist Arthur A. Noyes, who were inaugurating a venture in education and research in southern California. In 1921, at their urging, Millikan moved to Pasadena to become head of the new and munificently financed Cal Tech and director of its physics laboratory. With a knack for making wealthy southern Californians think it a privilege to be invited to contribute to the institute, he enlarged the Cal Tech endowment and physical plant. Millikan's traits, fused with Hale's vision, Noyes's wisdom and all that money, made Cal Tech virtually an overnight success.

Between the wars Millikan was an influential member of the National Academy and of the National Research Council and its fellowship board, which he helped to administer so as to improve the quality of American physics, particularly in theoretical studies. During World War II he turned over an increasing fraction of his administrative responsibilities at Cal Tech to younger staff members who were running various defense projects. Relinquishing his chief executive's position to Lee A. DuBridge in 1946, Millikan remained at the institute until his death in 1953. Throughout the Cal Tech years, in spite of his administrative commitments, he taught a course in atomic physics and took a keen interest in graduate students. He also maintained an active research program almost to the end.

UNITARIAN NOTE

Robert A. Millikan served as president of the congregation now known as the Neighborhood Unitarian Universalist Church of Pasadena.

ASHLEY MONTAGU:
ANTHROPOLOGIST AND SOCIAL BIOLOGIST
(1905-1999)

By Steven Harnad, Professor of Cognitive Science, University of Southhampton, United Kingdom

Ashley Montagu, born Israel Ehrenberg in East London in 1905, was one of those rare men of learning who succeeded in making substantive scholarly contributions to their academic disciplines while at the same time maintaining contact with the educated layman, indeed contributing substantively to the latter's learning. In addition, he was a dedicated and articulate social critic, concerned with bringing to bear the findings of the social and biological sciences toward the betterment of man's lot, while subjecting some of those very findings to critical social scrutiny. His accomplishments in these three domains, the scientific, the public-educational, and the socioethical, will be treated as a unity in what follows, in accordance with what is evidently the spirit of the program that has guided his life's work.

Although Montagu's contributions span a variety of fields in the social and biological sciences, his principal legacy will indisputably consist of his critical analysis of the concept of race.

The problem of race preoccupied Montagu from the beginning of his intellectual career, more than a quarter century before the 1954 U.S. Supreme Court desegregation decision in Brown v Board of Education of Topeka, which heralded the civil rights activism that has since followed in America. Montagu's work played a role in that Supreme Court decision, as well as in shaping the social consciousness that ushered it in and has attended it ever since. If some of his ideas, as they are discussed below, appear to be relatively uncontroversial and a matter of common knowledge and assent, let it not be forgotten that that very knowledge and assent is in some measure due to the work and efforts of Montagu, and that he was also forcefully expounding those ideas at an earlier time, when they were far from accepted, and indeed being brutally violated on a scale unparallelled in human history.

Montagu's papers on race in the late 1930s, culminating in his book *Man's Most*

Dangerous Myth: The Fallacy of Race and followed by a series of works, had the effect of upsetting the traditional concept of race accepted by most anthropologists in that it challenged the reality of anything corresponding to that notion. Montagu emphasized that gene-frequency analysis of traits would tell us more about the evolution of human populations, arguing that the omelet conception of racial mixing was totally artificial and did nothing to explain the origins and consequences of the differences between populations. Since men were all originally gatherer-hunters, wherever they were, the environmental challenges faced by different populations tended to be very similar; hence, one would not expect mental differences. This theory, as set forth in an article coauthored with the geneticist Theodosius Dobzhansky, subsequently became generally accepted by anthropologists. Montagu was also asked to draw up the United Nations Educational, Scientific and Cultural Organization's Statement on Race in 1950.

UNITARIAN NOTE

Dr. Montagu was a member of the Princeton Unitarian Fellowship in New Jersey. He affirmed *The Natural Superiority of Women.*

MARY CARR MOORE:
COMPOSER, TEACHER, FAR WESTERN
ACTIVIST FOR AMERICAN MUSIC (1873-1957)

By Catherine Parsons Smith Associate Professor of Music, University of Nevada, Reno

Mary Carr Moore's formal connection with Unitarianism came through her mother, Sarah Pratt Carr, a minister who in the 1890s organized several new Unitarian congregations in the Fresno area of California's Central Valley. Mary Moore's life was centered around music from an early age. Although she was born in Memphis and passed her early years in Louisville, by the age of ten she had relocated with her family to the west coast, where she remained, living successively in Napa, San Francisco (where she received her formal training as a singer and composer), rural Lemoore (CA), Seattle, San Francisco again, and finally (from the mid-1920s) in Los Angeles.

Moore was initially trained as a singer, but soon turned toward composition. While most American composers, especially the women among them, primarily wrote songs and piano pieces for their students, Moore concentrated on operas, composing a total of eight over a period of more than forty years. The first, really an operetta—composed to her own libretto at the age of nineteen—was performed by a group of young people in San Francisco; she sang the lead role. After a pause of almost fifteen years, in which she abandoned composition for a time in favor of child rearing and teaching in Lemoore and then Seattle, she set to work on her four-act grand opera based on the story of the Whitman Massacre of 1847 at a time when survivors of the massacre were still living and controversy still swirled around both the missionaries and the murders. The idea of using an opera to tell something approximating recent regional history was a novel one. She commissioned a libretto from her minister-suffragist-novelist mother. Their determination to tell the story without superimposing a romantic triangle and to represent Native American participants as individuals made their project unique. *Narcissa: Or, The Cost of Empire*, had its premier in Seattle in 1912. Several of the principals were imported from New York for the occasion, but no experienced conductor was willing to risk conducting an opera by a woman composer; therefore Moore herself became a conductor. (She conducted revivals in San Francisco in 1925 and Los Angeles in 1945 as well.)

One hallmark of Mary Carr Moore's teaching was her ability to persuade even the most inhibited of her students to compose freely. In the 1930s and 40s, their work was often performed at a manuscript club, whose goal suggests the breadth of Moore's vision: "It has been the wish of the founder, Mary Carr Moore, that, in this club, the one tie would be that of the Universal Language, MUSIC, and that all division of religion, politics, or custom might be forgotten, and all work together in the cause of HARMONY."

ARTHUR E. MORGAN:
HUMAN ENGINEER AND COLLEGE PRESIDENT
(1878-1975)

By Donald Szantho Harrington, Minister Emeritus of the Community Church of New York

Arthur Morgan, President of Antioch College. I first met Arthur Morgan when I was sixteen years old. He was speaking in Boston about Antioch College and his dream of a new and better kind of education. I said to my mother, "I must go to Antioch!" I applied the next day.

The Fall of 1931 found me in the entering Freshman class at Yellow Springs. I found Arthur Morgan very much at the heart of things at Antioch. When he was on campus he frequently went walking early on Sunday mornings in beautiful, thousand acre Glen Helen at the campus' edge. He let it be known that students would be welcome to walk with him. He carried the makings of breakfast in a knapsack on his back, and somewhere along the way would stop, build a fire and cook breakfast to undergird the discussion. It meant getting up early, around five thirty a.m., but I walked often with him. Sometimes there were just the two of us.

Arthur Morgan was born near Cincinnati, Ohio, but his family soon moved to St. Cloud, Minnesota, where he grew up. His father was an engineer, and his own interests leaned in that direction. Very early in his life he seems to have had a concern for social improvement for when he was just ten years old he was publishing great quotations for human uplift on a regular basis in one of the St. Cloud newspapers. In 1895, at the age of seventeen, he experienced a vivid vision of an

ideal community while walking home through the woods. The Utopian dream of an ideal society was thereafter to direct his steps for the rest of his life.

After graduating from high school he left home, at the age of nineteen and spent the next three years doing many kinds of outdoor work, mostly in Colorado, finding that there was a real dearth of understanding of hydraulic engineering.

At the age of thirty-two, he founded his own engineering company, and three years later, after a disastrous flood had practically wiped out the city of Dayton, Ohio, he was called to take full charge of the Miami River Flood Control Project, involving the building of several huge dams. This work he did so well as to be set on the road to worldwide engineering fame.

In 1919 Arthur Morgan was appointed to the Board of Antioch College, a dying institution in Yellow Springs, Ohio, a moribund village some eighteen miles from Dayton. He saw Antioch and Yellow Springs as a kind of double opportunity to test out his higher educational ideas and his concepts for community development. He was made President, and there began a thrilling experiment in innovative higher education. The college slogan inherited from Horace Mann, the first President, was, *"Be ashamed to die until you have won some victory for humanity!"*

In fifteen years Arthur Morgan built up Antioch College to where it was ranked among the top three colleges of the nation in a study by the Carnegie Corporation. Perhaps the most notable of his innovations was the work-study method in which students would study for ten weeks, and then go off campus to work on a job out in the real world. He believed that such an alternation would keep curriculum alive and help the student to apply and assimilate what he was learning in the classroom.

In 1933, Arthur Morgan was called by President Franklin D. Roosevelt to initiate and head the vast development project known as the Tennessee Valley Authority, at that time the greatest effort at regional development of natural resources and human beings ever attempted in the history of the world.

Morgan told the story of how Roosevelt had told him that he had a free hand, but not twenty steps from Roosevelt's office, he was met by Jim Farley with a long list of people to be employed. Arthur Morgan, with typical forthrightness, turned sharply about, took Farley by the arm and took him right back into the President's office, showed the President the list, and asked if he was or was not to have a free hand. Laughing the President took the list, and reassured him that he and no one else would make the decisions.

When Arthur Morgan came home to Yellow Springs, a crowd of a thousand persons had gathered at the station to say "welcome home! we love you! He turned his thought and energy to the problem of revitalizing America's small communities, the "Seedbed of Society" and the garden in which human character is grown. It was a return to an old love, for he had already built model villages in Ohio and Tennessee and sparked a successful "intentional" community in North Carolina. He had been the moving force transforming the village of Yellow Springs from a moribund little hamlet to an exciting and vibrant ideal community in which people wanted to live. He succeeded beyond his own modest hopes, and Yellow Springs today is a monument to his vision and idealism.

THE MORISON BROTHERS:
A UNITARIAN HERITAGE

By 1720 the Scotch ancestors of the Morison brothers whom we celebrate crossed the Atlantic to settle in New Hampshire. There they found a greater measure of political and religious freedom which allowed them to pursue their search for that better way of life they were determined to achieve.

John H. Morison, born in Peterborough, New Hampshire in 1808, was a graduate of Harvard College and Divinity School whose distinguished service as a Unitarian minister led to his being honored by Harvard University with the degree of Doctor of Divinity in 1858. Among the later descendants of this long notable family are three twentieth century brothers: Robert, Elting, and John. Each has made a contribution in separate fields of science, technology, and society in relation to practical affairs.

MIT has celebrated their contributions to life as follows:

Robert Swain Morison:Research Scientist and Administrator 1906-1986

Robert, after graduation from Harvard and the Harvard Medical School in 1934 became a research scientist and then joined the Rockefeller Foundation where he became Director of Medical and Natural Sciences. He then moved to Cornell University where he established and headed their first Life Sciences Division, from which he retired to join the Program of Science, Technology and Society (STS) at MIT. While he was a distinguished college administrator, one of his principal interests was the study and discussion of the medical and scientific problems of the day such as public health, medical ethics, aging and death. He was, among other things, one of the founders of the Hastings Institute for Society, Ethics and the Life Sciences, a Trustee of the National Science Foundation and a member of the first General Motors Science Advisory Committee. As a scientist and teacher, he had an unusual capacity for absorbing complex technical and philosophical facts and ideas on a wide variety of subjects and then combining and translating them into essays or lectures that left his students excited and his colleagues fascinated by the depth of his knowledge and the clarity of his expression.

Elting Elmore Morison: Father of Contemporary History of Technology: 1909-1995

Elting (Harvard, 1932), after leaving the US. Navy at the end of World War II, became a member of the MIT faculty where he edited all the letters and papers of Theodore Roosevelt while teaching at the Sloan School of Management. His special field dealt with the relations between technology and society, out of which came two of his widely read books: *Men, Machines, and Modern Times* and *From Know-How to Nowhere*. He was a member of the MIT faculty for most of his teaching career, a member of the Lewis Commission in the late 1940's and was instrumental in the formation of STS (Science Technology and Society. In the words of one of his contemporaries, he became 'the father of contemporary history of technology.' He connected machinery and technological invention to social change, to individual imagination, and to politics in a way that has permanently redefined the field.

Johns Hopkins Morison: Industrial Executive. 1913-

John (Harvard 1935) once jokingly described himself as "the youngest brother who stayed home to make money so my older brothers could think lofty thoughts." But in fact, John Morison has been one of the more creative entrepreneurs and technological innovators in modern American life. After spending several years in Brazil and in the U.S. Navy in World War II he returned to New Hampshire to take over, with his father, an insolvent foundry in an effort to restore the industrial economy of that state after years of suffering in the depression and World War II. In the course of his lifetime, he transformed the Hitchiner Manufacturing Company into a multinational corporation, known as a "best practice" firm because of the sophistication of its technologies and its extensive worker education and participation programs. While their basic process is still the "lost wax,' technology described in the Old Testament, they do admit that they have added a "few new wrinkles with the help of our friends at MIT."

"The Morison Family," The Program in Science, Technology, and Society, MIT, 2000.

Robert S. Morison   Elting E. Morison   John H. Morison III

UNITARIAN NOTE

The ongoing faith in life exhibited by generations of the Morison family is symbolized by
their religious home in New Hampshire, the Peterborough Unitarian Church.
photos: three portraits from first page

MARGARET MOSELEY: MOUNTAIN-MOVING CIVIL RIGHTS ACTIVIST (1901-1997)

From the Margaret Moseley Papers, Schlesinger Library, Radcliffe Institute

A community peace and civil rights activist, Moseley was born in Dedham, Massachusetts in 1901, and graduated from high school in Dorchester in 1919. Unable to pursue a career in nursing or business because of racial discrimination, Moseley was a founding member of a consumers' cooperative in Boston in the 1940s, served on the board of the Civil Liberties Union of Massachusetts and Freedom House in Roxbury. She was president of the Community Church in Boston, and Massachusetts legislative chair for the Women's International League for Peace and Freedom, which established the Margaret Moseley Memorial Peace Education Fund in her honor in 1989. After moving to Cape Cod in 1961, she helped form local chapters of the National Association for the Advancement of Colored People and WILPF. She was a founding member of the Community Action Committee of Cape Cod, and the Fair Housing Committee on Cape Cod. She was also active in the Unitarian Church of Barnstable, becoming a founding member of the Social Responsibility Committee, and the first woman to chair the Prudential Committee; the governing body of the church. She was also on the boards of the Cape Cod Section, Mass. Society for the Prevention of Cruelty to Children, and Elder Services of Cape Cod and the Islands. Moseley died in 1997.

MEMOIRS

There were about 3,200 students in Dorchester High School when I was there. (I graduated in 1919.) The year I entered, one black fellow had graduated in June and there was one other black girl in my class. So for three years, she and I were the only two. I had lots of friends in school but when there was a party, such as a birthday party, when the other girls in the group would be invited and I was not invited, it made me come to the realization that I was not socially accepted in their families.

Finally, in my last year, the other young woman—the one who was the only other person of color—and I thought it would be nice if we were to do something together such as studying nursing. So we determined that as soon as we graduated, we would study nursing. In those days you didn't have to go to college, you could do three years of training and be a qualified R.N. I saw no way to get the money to go to college. I thought nursing would be something I could do.

My friend Ruth and I tried Massachusetts General and other hospitals in Boston to be accepted for training. There wasn't a hospital in Boston that would take us. They told us very candidly that they did not accept colored people for training. Ruth's people were from the Washington D.C. area, so there wasn't too much of a problem with her. Her mother said, "If they won't take you in Boston, you don't have to feel bad. You can work at a Freedman's Hospital in Washington. You'll get just as good training and you won't have to be putting up with discrimination."

I asked my parents if I could go, too, but they wouldn't let me. To them I might as well say I was going to Mississippi, Alabama, Georgia, anywhere in the Deep South. They had such a horror of life in the South that my mother said, "Indeed, we will not let you go down there."

MAURINE NEUBERGER : UNITED STATES SENATOR (1907-2000)

By Jeff Mapes Courtesy of The Oregonian, *Portland, February 23, 2000*

Maurine Neuberger, whose pioneering political career ranged from a legendary margarine-mixing demonstration in the Oregon House to election to the U.S. Senate, died of a bone marrow disorder at a Portland nursing home. She was 94.

Elected in 1960 to fill the Senate seat left vacant by the death of her husband, Richard, she championed consumer protection, was an early opponent of the tobacco industry and in her long retirement years came to be the venerated elder stateswoman of Oregon Democrats.

A former high school English teacher in Portland, she was the third woman elected to the U.S. Senate and the only one to serve in the legislative body from Oregon. The Neubergers gained notice in 1951 as the first married couple in U.S. history to serve together in a legislature, he in the Oregon Senate and she in the House.

It was Maurine Neuberger, however, who earned the bigger headlines that year when she battled the state's then-powerful dairy industry over a law forbidding the sale of yellow margarine in Oregon. Donning a striped apron, she pulled out a mixing bowl in the House and showed her colleagues -- all of them men -- just how much work it took to mix food coloring into the lard-white butter substitute.

The ban was lifted, and her culinary demonstration became part of Oregon political lore. Friends remembered her as a candid, personable and occasionally tough politician who helped shape the model for how women could successfully serve in public office.

Maurine Brown was born on Jan. 9, 1906, in the Tillamook County town of Cloverdale. Her father was a physician and her mother a dairy farmer -- an irony noted after her margarine-mixing episode.

She graduated from the University of Oregon in 1929 and became a teacher in Portland in 1932. She taught physical education and then became an English teacher, the kind with impeccable grammar, at Lincoln High School. Years later, after her Senate career, she served on a committee that advised the American Heritage Dictionary on proper usage.

In 1945 she married Richard Neuberger. He won a seat in the state Senate in 1948 and she won her House seat in 1950. Both were elected again in 1952, with Maurine winning more votes.

Her husband's Senate career was cut short by a series of health problems that began with testicular cancer and ended in his death from a cerebral hemorrhage on March 10, 1960, at the age of 47.

She quickly decided to run on her own in the November election. She didn't have a lot of role models. Sen. Margaret Chase Smith, R-Maine, was the only other woman in the Senate (the first woman elected to the post was Hattie Caraway of Arkansas, in 1932).

In office, Mrs. Neuberger followed her husband's political liberalism while focusing many of her efforts on consumer issues. A reformed pack-a-day smoker, she sponsored one of the first bills to require warning labels on cigarette packaging and even wrote a book attacking the tobacco industry.

She took on meat packers for artificially adding water to hams, bedding manufacturers for selling blankets that weren't flame-resistant and cosmetics firms for their packaging practices. She also called for pollution controls on autos, years before they became a reality. "No industry I know of has ever been able to regulate itself to the interest of the consumer public," she once declared.

POLITICS: WOMEN'S NEW FRONTIER

Maureen Neuberger, a member of the First Unitarian Society of Portland, Oregon, wrote an article published in The Christian Register *issue of May 1955, from which these lines come:*

My direct interest in politics developed when my husband ran for office and was elected to the State Senate. I found it exciting to plan campaign procedure, to attend meetings and talk with voters about legislation. Needless to say, I learned more about my state, its constitution, and its legislative procedure, than I could have hoped to know through any other educational program.

Not every woman has the freedom from home and family that I have; therefore she cannot participate by running for public office. But there are women who can and who do make a great contribution to themselves and their community.

My husband and I have found it a great asset to work as a team in our political life, as well as in our professional life as a writer and photographer pair.

We women in active politics and you women at home cannot live in this "changing world" without having a desire and a duty to let your thoughts be known. You have never before had such opportunities to be informed and stirred by the events of each day. Besides the usual methods of communication of world events, your minister now discusses the topics of the day and ventures to express an opinion in the field of politics. This is a far cry from the days of Jonathan Edwards and the ministration of fire and brimstone.

It is a woman's world as well as a man's world, and I see from the evidence around me that women are not going to shirk their part.

MAX OTTO:
UNITARIAN HUMANIST (1876-1968)
A BIOGRAPHICAL NOTE

By G. C. Sellery Dean, Emeritus, *College of Letters and Sciences, University of Wisconsin*

Professor Max Carl Otto was born in the historic town of Zwickau, Saxony, in 1876, and was brought to America by his immigrant parents in his fifth year. He went to school, through the sixth grade, in Wheeling, West Virginia, where his father kept a restaurant. He studied the Lutheran catechism diligently under a stern, old-fashioned pastor, and also learned to concentrate so thoroughly on what he heard in church that he could repeat the essentials of the sermon to his Lutheran parents. The resulting development of the power of concentration has stood him in good stead ever since.

He was admitted to the state university at Madison, where he majored in history under the great Frederick Jackson Turner. He up graduate studies in philosophy, and won his Ph.D. in 1911.

Otto also produced three books with significant titles: *Things and Ideals*, *Natural Laws and Human Hopes*, and *The Human Enterprise*. His share in the controversial *Is There a God?* debate in *The Christian Century* with H. N. Wieman and D. C. Macintosh as his antagonists, reveals with clarity the antithetic position he reached.

Mr. Otto's service as a teacher of philosophy, and as chairman of the department of philosophy at Wisconsin since 1936, came to an end in 1947, when he became a professor *emeritus*. He has been honored with the presidency of the Western branch of the American Philosophical Association.

The philosophy which Max Otto has at heart, pragmatism, is essentially an American product, rooted in the common problems and common sense of men and women, at work in business, agriculture, politics, economics, science, or religion. The underlying purpose of this philosophy is the enhancement of human life for all

Max Otto's philosophy was conceived—and born—in Wisconsin. Of course his native endowment of mind and heart, his experiences of life, and his struggles for clarity of purpose underlie the vision he caught at the university. One may also safely assert that the elder La Follette's program for social betterment had a part in Max Otto's philosophy, and that it was nurtured, enriched, and confirmed by the teachings of William James and John Dewey—especially of John Dewey, his good and great friend.

Within the broad reaches of his philosophy, Max Otto, a man of genuine religious temper, places stress on the need of our age for a nontheistic faith.

UNITARIAN HUMANIST WHO FEARED A CREED

Edwin H. Wilson, a primary author of the first "Humanist Manifesto" and a lifelong advocate of Unitarian humanism, desribed Max Otto's refusal to sign the manifesto.

Prior to 1933, Max Otto (professor of philosophy), Horace M. Kallen, and V. T. Thayer (a signer of the manifesto) were all young men on the faculty at the University of Wisconsin at Madison. V. T. Thayer was an educator and editor who wrote extensively on church-state separation. At one time, Max Otto and Horace Kallen roomed with the Thayers. According to Dr. Thayer, there was an occasion when the three young men were the lone dissenters on an issue before the campus. This position would not be unusual for anyone whose thinking was generally categorized as radical, as was the case with this group.

Unfortunately, the manifesto editors did not contact Dr. Kallen in 1933 to seek his signature and advice. However, because he was continuously important to humanism, I have included him in this history. When asked in 1973 why he had not been invited to sign "A Humanist Manifesto" in 1933, Kallen wrote to me that John Dewey had once asked him to sign the document. He explained that he had responded to Dewey by saying that he had had stronger objections (left unspecified) to signing the 1933 document than "Humanist Manifesto II" in 1973.

Max Carl Otto, although he declined to sign "A Humanist Manifesto," never wavered in his humanism and was the author of a series of important books and reference material on church-state and educational issues. In response to the request for his signature on the manifesto, Dr. Otto replied on April 4, 1933:

I cannot believe that publishing the "Humanist Manifesto" will in the slightest degree "clarify the public mind" or "constitute a constructive work" in any significant sense. It will, on the contrary, I fear, be one of those theoretical gestures which leave with some persons a feeling that something has really been done when all that has been done is that something has been said. I am of the opinion that Humanism, as I understand the philosophy of it, cannot be "sold" to men and women; it must be attained by them, and that means slow, painstaking work. Much as I regret to say, No, to your request that I join you in a general announcement of ideas and aims, I do so with real conviction. Why must we, too, advertise?

It is not surprising that Otto refused to sign, given his view on humanism. In his 1949 book, *Science and the Moral Law*, he said: "All Humanisms have one thing in common. It is the ideal of realizing man's completest development. From here on they diverge."

Dr. Otto was a lifelong member of the First Unitarian Society of Madison, Wisconsin

WINFRED OVERHOLSER: PSYCHIATRIST (1892-1964)

By Edric Lescouflair, Harvard College '03

Dr. Overholser was born on April 21, 1892, in Worcester, Massachusetts, to Edwin Moses and Mary Jane Overholser. After graduating from nearby Wellesley High School, he enrolled in Harvard College, pursuing a degree in economics. Overholser received his A. B. *cum laude* in 1912. Subsequently he studied law and medicine at Boston University and was awarded an M.B. in 1915 and an M.D. degree in 1916.

In 1917 Overholser began the type of work that would occupy most of his life when he accepted a position at the Westboro State Hospital in Massachusetts. The advent of the First World War created a need for the study of psychiatric ailments affecting soldiers, and he received military leave to go to France to work in the neuropsychiatric section of the U.S. Army Medical Corps. The work in France qualified him to become the assistant superintendent of Gardner State Hospital in Massachusetts in the early 1920s.

In 1937 Overholser received the appointment that defined his life of medical service. He was nominated by the American Psychiatric Association to be the superintendent of St. Elizabeth's Hospital, a government run institution in Washington, D.C. He held that post until 1962.

Once in Washington, Overholser continued in his tradition of caring for the mentally ill and treating patients with compassion, realizing that a mental illness should not be ideologically differentiated from a physical ailment. He was an active Unitarian who was a trustee of All Souls Church in Washington, D.C. Religion played a major part in his life, and he often examined the relationship between religion and mental disorders. On this topic, he wrote, "Religious conflicts are not, of course, necessarily related to mental disorder; they are, in fact, a part of everyday life. There are certain conflicts, however, that are the outgrowth of mental disorder and a manifestation of it." He was an active member of the Unitarian Service Committee, and he served as the moderator of the American Unitarian Association from 1946-1948. Overholser achieved some renown as a proponent of liberal religion. He served as the president of the American Psychiatric Association (1947-1948).

Winfred Overholser died in Washington, D.C. on October 6, 1964. His work includes two books, *The Handbook of Psychiatry* (1947), and *Psychiatry and the Law* (1953).

UNITARIAN NOTE
Why I Believe in Advancing Unitarianism

By Winfred Overholser

If there ever was a time that cried aloud for freedom of the spirit and the mind, recognition of the rights of man, a practical putting into effect of the basic principles of the Golden Rule—in short, a true religious liberalism—that time is now.

We have won a long and costly war that was forced upon us by totalitarian despots. It is not enough, however, to sit back and assume that automatically the forces of democracy will now reassert themselves and that all will be well. There never was anything automatic about the rise or maintenance of freedom; it must always be fought for vigilantly and vigorously. Hitler and Mussolini are fortunately dead, but the evil forces of autocracy, the negation of the rights of the individual, greed and oppression still live.

What has this to do with Unitarianism? Just this: Beyond all creedal churches, it emphasizes the fundamental worth of man, and the truth that he can best show his devotion to god by trust and faith in his fellow man and by the spirit of Christian brotherhood. Unbound by formal creeds, it seeks improved human relations as the most realistic approach to the Kingdom of God on earth.

From *The Christian Register*, May 1946

MARY WHITE OVINGTON: FOUNDER OF THE NAACP (1865-1951)

By Carolyn Wedin Professor of English, Emeritus, *University of Wisconsin-Whitewater*

It is hard to overestimate the influence of Unitarianism on Mary White Ovington, who was born at the time of the assassination of President Lincoln and at the end of the Civil War; and died long after World War II in 1951. It is doubly difficult to overestimate the influence of Mary White Ovington on Unitarianism.

Her childhood Brooklyn church, the Second Unitarian, had been in the forefront in the Abolitionist battle against American slavery. But all that was forgotten, the work assumed done, by the time Ovington began to question the roles of women, of Blacks, of "good people" in the racially hostile atmosphere of the turn of the 19th century.

Since I can say what I think here, I will tell you after so very many years of "living" with this remarkable woman through researching and writing her biography (*Inheritors of the Spirit:*

Mary White Ovington and the Founding of the NAACP), I believe that not only was Mary White Ovington THE founder of the NAACP in 1909, but that she almost single-handedly pulled in and kept together the radicals, the socialists, the journalists, the writers, the newspaper owners, the Blacks and the Whites, the Jews and Unitarians into the 20th century cause of justice, freedom, and sanctuary from lynching of Black Americans.

You don't have to take my word; you shouldn't. You should go to her own story, and the story of this cause, told so readably in her 1947 book, *The Walls Came Tumbling Down*. And now, too, you have access to her serial autobiographical narrative first published in the *Baltimore Afro-American* in 1932-33, in a 1995 republication by the *Feminist Press*, called *Black and White Sat Down Together: The Reminiscences of an NAACP Founder*.

Ovington's early Unitarian training to think and question, question and think, emerged strongly in her late published and unpublished writing as it did throughout her life.

Her completion of the manuscript for *The Walls Came Tumbling Down* is in itself a great, inspiring story of aging and dedication. Over several years of first great enthusiasm, then through strokes, loss of eyesight, hospitalization, and shock treatments, she struggled on.

Finally she had it ready to send to readers, including first and foremost, John Haynes Holmes. He was delighted with it: "What surprised and excited me was the fact that what you have written is far more than a mere history of the NAACP. It is an autobiography in the true sense of the word and a fascinating one. . . . The whole thing has a fine literary quality, and a frankness of confession . . . which is wholly consistent with modesty and with restrained feeling. But all through what you have written, there is the passion of your conviction and high idealism, and this gives the book an absorbing quality which is remarkable."

Some of Mary White Ovington's last, shaky, handwritten letters were to Holmes, her friend and minister, who faithfully visited her and wrote her in the hospital (The Institute for Living in Hartford). In 1948 she regretted not being with him for a Community Church dedication and concluded. "These are difficult days but there is always hope. Yours, Lovingly, Mary W. Ovington."

KENNETH LEO PATTON:
A RELIGION FOR ONE WORLD (1911-1994)

by Maryell Cleary, Unitarian Universalist Minister

Born in Three Oaks, a small town in western Michigan, Patton lived his early years there with his mother, brother and maternal grandparents. He never knew his father. His family belonged to a strict Methodist church. He attended two church services on Sundays, morning and evening, and in between the adults allowed no secular amusements. He recalled hearing cheers and shouts from the neighboring baseball field on Sunday afternoons, wanting to join in but not allowed to go.

When he was eight or nine Patton moved with his mother and brother to a working-class suburb of Chicago. There he graduated from high school, the first in the family to do so. He went on to junior college, working at night to finance art lessons on Saturdays. Thus began his lifelong passion for the visual arts. At the age of 20 he began writing poetry. He completed his college work at Eureka College, from which he received a B.A. in 1937.

Though he would have liked a career in art, Patton chose ministry as a way to support his family and make use of his talent in writing and speaking. While serving several Disciples of Christ churches in small mid-Illinois towns, he developed a talent for beautiful extemporaneous prayer. At the same time he commuted to the University of Chicago to work on a degree in theology. There he studied with such outstanding teachers and humanists as Edward Scribner Ames, Henry Nelson Wieman and A. Eustace Haydon. Haydon, who spoke in poetic language with a beautifully-modulated voice, influenced Patton greatly. He showed the younger man that religion could be much more than a set of dogmas, that it could include all the arts as well. Patton received an M.A. in 1939 and a B.D. in 1940.

In 1942 Haydon suggested that Patton, now a confirmed humanist, apply for the open pulpit of the First Unitarian Society of Madison, Wisconsin. Patton did so, was called, and served until January, 1949. He helped the Society obtain the services of famed architect Frank Lloyd Wright for the design of its new building. While in Madison, he published his first three books: *Strange Seed*, 1946, a slim volume of lyric poetry; *Beyond Doubt*, 1946, a collection of radio talks; and *Hello, Man*, 1945, poetry and poetic prose which celebrated humanism and naturalism in religion. The latter established him as a major spokesperson for this still new approach to religion.

In 1949 Patton was invited to become minister of the Charles Street Meeting House, an experimental church in Boston created by Clinton Lee Scott and the Massachusetts Universalist Convention to revitalize Universalism and to reinstate a Universalist presence in Boston. Since Universalists' traditional message, that a loving God would not condemn anyone to hell, had been accepted by other denominations, Universalists needed a new focus and a wider scope. Patton's fifteen-year ministry redefined the meaning of the word "Universalism" by bringing the arts of all religions and cultures into "a religion for one world."

While at the Meeting House Patton wrote a prodigious amount of worship material. He also arranged as hymns and readings, words from great poets like Walt Whitman, and selections from the world's scriptures. Using a mimeograph machine and a printing press in the church basement, Patton published pamphlets, books and sermons as well as weekly supplements for the looseleaf hymnals. Two volumes of *Hymns of Humanity* came from the mimeograph machine, while *Man's Hidden Search*, 1954, a classic statement of naturalistic mysticism, and Clarence Skinner's *Worship and the Well-Ordered Life* rolled off the printing press. Patton's most ambitious project, *A Religion for One World*, 1964, published in conjunction with Beacon Press, gave an in-depth account of this experiment in universal religion, lavishly illustrated with photographs. When the newly-merged Unitarian Universalist Association needed a new hymnal, Patton was an obvious choice for a place on the Hymnbook Commission. Many of the hymns and readings used in the Meeting House became part of *Hymns for the Celebration of Life*, 1964. Old hymn tunes came to new life with his words, as in "We are the earth upright and proud," set to "Eine Feste Burg," and "Brief our days but long for singing," set to the melody of "Jesu, Joy of Man's Desiring."

In 1964 the Unitarian Society of Ridgewood, New Jersey invited Patton to become its minister. At this time he felt the need of a larger and more secure income and a home for his family outside the center city.

As a minister, Patton was an iconoclast. He disdained any special treatment as a clergyman. He would not call himself "Reverend," saying that he was no more to be revered than anyone else. He never used the honorific, "Doctor," though entitled to do so by an honorary degree. He refused to wear a pulpit robe, even at his own installation service. He did not preach sermons, he gave addresses, and not in a church sanctuary but in a meeting house.

He retired in 1986 and died of congestive heart failure in his Ridgewood home on Christmas Day, 1994.

LINUS PAULING:
NOBEL LAUREATE FOR PEACE AND
CHEMISTRY (1901-1994)

by Thomas Blair, Harvard College '03

The biography of two-time Nobel laureate Linus Pauling may be just as extraordinary for its twists as for its peaks. Why did a boy who studied advanced mathematics at twelve years old nearly decide not to attend college? Why was he called unpatriotic and ousted from his job at Cal Tech while he led the struggle for the Nuclear Test Ban Treaty?

Pauling grew up in a German immigrant family in Portland, Oregon; the son of a pharmacist, he gained early scientific experience watching his father behind the counter. Pauling's father recognized and encouraged his son's extraordinary curiosity, as evidenced by a letter he wrote to the Portland Oregonian when his son was nine years old. The elder Pauling, seeking reading suggestions for Linus, wrote, "don't say the Bible and Darwin's 'Origin of the Species,' because he has already read them." An eager and independent student, Pauling remembered being fascinated with entomology at 11, geology at 12, and chemistry at 13.

His father died when Linus was nine years old, leaving Mrs. Pauling with a larger family than she could support. Linus therefore worked as soon as he was old enough to do so, but he found time throughout his childhood and youth to study science—and any number of other things—on his own.

In 1954 Pauling was awarded the Nobel Prize for Chemistry. Choosing among many smaller achievements, the Nobel Committee cited his "research on the nature of the chemical bond holding molecules together and its use in understanding the structure of complex substances such as protein and antibodies."

Pauling frequently credits his wife as the catalyst of his professional success. He also credits his wife for helping to inspire his initial involvement in nuclear disarmament -- she not only encouraged his activism, but also exhorted him to study economics and social theory, so that he could understand the issues he was trying to address and defend the positions he took. Characteristically, Pauling recalls his activism in terms at once simple and grand: "I was working toward the goal of a world without war."

Pauling was awarded the Nobel Prize for Peace on October 10, 1963, the day the Nuclear Test Ban Treaty went into effect. The chairman of the Nobel Committee declared that without a petition like Pauling's, there surely would not have been such swift action for a ban on nuclear weapons testing -- and perhaps there would have been no treaty at all.

Linus Pauling was diagnosed with cancer in 1991, and died August 19, 1994, at his ranch in Big Sur, California. In addition to work that has permanently improved the fields of chemistry, biochemistry, and peace activism, he leaves a simple statement of resounding encouragement to his admirers: "You can contribute, and you can't be sure how great your contribution is, but you can contribute, so do it."

Pauling and his wife, Ava, were members of the First Unitarian Church of Los Angeles.

CECILIA PAYNE-GAPOSCHKIN: ASTRONOMER AND ASTROPHYSICIST (1900-1980)

by Herbert F. Vetter
From UU World, *January-February 2003*

She was the first woman to receive tenure and the first to chair a department in the faculty of arts and sciences at Harvard. Her dissertation was hailed as "the most brilliant Ph.D. thesis ever written in astronomy." Yet few have heard of Cecilia Payne-Gaposchkin (1900–1979), an English-American astronomer—and Unitarian—who discovered the true physical constitution of the universe.

"Payne-Gaposchkin's most dramatic scientific contribution was the discovery that hydrogen is millions of times more abundant than any other element in the universe," said Jeremy Knowles, dean of the faculty of arts and sciences, as Harvard celebrated her accomplishments in February 2002 by adding her portrait to the Faculty Room in University Hall, where only one other woman is depicted. He quoted an undergraduate's wry assessment: "Every high school student knows that Newton discovered gravity, that Darwin discovered evolution, even that Einstein discovered relativity. But when it comes to the composition of our universe, the textbooks simply say that the most prevalent element in the universe is hydrogen. And no one ever wonders how we know."

In her 1925 dissertation Cecilia Payne showed that stars are "all essentially of the same composition," according to astronomer Owen Gingerich. At the time, however, she distrusted her discovery that stars are made almost entirely of hydrogen and helium. Princeton astronomer Henry Norris Russell wrote to her that "it is clearly impossible that hydrogen should be a million times more abundant than the metals," but he later discovered that she was right—and took credit for explaining the phenomenon.

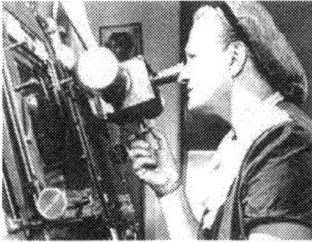

Born and educated in England, she came to the United States to study in 1923 at the encouragement of the director of the Harvard Observatory. At the time, the chair of Harvard's physics department would not accept a female graduate student, so the faculty committee that awarded her Ph.D. effectively created a department of astronomy. After receiving her degree, "she lectured in the astronomy department, but her lectures were not listed in the course catalogue," Knowles said. "She directed graduate research without status; she had no research leaves; and her small salary was categorized by the department under 'equipment.' And yet she survived and flourished. 'It was a case,' she said, 'not of survival of the fittest, but of the most doggedly persistent.'"

In 1933 she visited Germany and met the Russian astronomer and political exile Sergei Gaposchkin. She arranged a place for him at the Harvard Observatory. They married two years later. In 1938, Harvard officially appointed her to the faculty of astronomy, and in 1956, she was the first woman promoted to a full professorship.

She and her husband were members of the First Parish in Lexington, where she taught nine- to twelve-year-olds in the Sunday school. Her daughter Katherine Haramundanis tells a story about her mother donning heavy woolen slacks and walking more than three miles to teach Sunday school one bitterly cold winter morning when the family car would not start. The story reveals a great deal about her character. In her autobiography she described her attitude in the face of slow promotions and low pay: "I simply went on plodding, rewarded by the beauty of the scenery, towards an unexpected goal."

LESLIE T. PENNINGTON:
MINISTER OF LIVING DEMOCRACY (1899-1974)

by James Luther Adams Address at the First Parish in Cambridge, Massachusetts

At the celebration in 1866 of the 250th anniversary of the organization of the First Church (Unitarian) in Cambridge, Mass., Oliver Wendell Holmes, Jr., at that time a justice of the Supreme Judicial Court of Massachusetts, said: "The founders of this parish. . . and their fellows planted a congregational church, from which grew a democratic state. They planted something mightier than institutions.... Whether they knew it or not, they planted the democratic spirit in the heart of man. It is to them we owe the deepest cause we have to love our country—that instinct, that spark, that makes the American unable to meet his fellowman otherwise than simply as a man, eye to eye, hand to hand, and foot to foot, wrestling on naked sand."

Leslie Talbot Pennington, born in 1899 in Spiceland, Indiana, was of this heritage, though he sprang also from Quaker loins, bearing the name of a venerable Quaker family. Accordingly, he attended and graduated from Earlham College. He was a worthy scion of the democratic tradition so forcefully described by Mr. Justice Holmes. Both the Puritan spirit and the dissenting spirit of the Friends are to be discerned in the many-faceted life and in many a sermon of Leslie Pennington.

Leslie served Massachusetts parishes in Lincoln and Braintree, and from New England he went to Ithaca, New York, then back to Cambridge and on to Chicago, and finally back to West Newton. His participation in the life of the community and of the denomination is remembered wherever he has lived and worked. From the earliest days of his ministry he was a member of civic associations as well as of ecumenical enterprises.

Leslie Pennington's concern for a living democracy became most conspicuous in the city of Chicago through his leadership in an enterprise that gained national repute, the Hyde Park-Kenwood Community Conference. This conference, like the First Church itself, under-took well over twenty years ago the slow and painful task of bringing about desegregation and of developing a peaceful pluralistic community. Leslie as the outstanding leader gave to this ecumenical enterprise the best energies of his life, and with marked success. The Conference continues to be the creative, integrating power in that community. Indeed, today the section of Chicago called Oak Park (on the West Side), like certain other communities in the nation, has taken this Community Conference as a model. For these and similar manifestations of Christian leadership Leslie received numerous awards, including three honorary doctorates.

As Leslie was ever aware, the ideal of a democratic congregation promoting the priesthood and prophethood of all believers cannot be pursued without raising a dust. I recall that in the midst of the desegregation effort in the Chicago parish Leslie at one juncture felt obliged to bring about the resignation from the church

of two prominent laymen who in principle rejected the goal of integration. When the issues and the differences became crystal clear he said privately to these two laymen, "Either you two leave this church, or I do. Your leaving will indicate goodwill that you are professing for this church. I think that each of you had best depart." ... They did.

When I first knew Leslie as a theological student in Cambridge, he was known among his fellow students as a poet. One of his oldest friends and colleagues, the Rev. Miles Hanson, Jr., of Weston, Massachusetts said: "Leslie was gifted with an interest in every aspect of life. He loved his farm in Moretown, and the green hills of Vermont. His retirement years were spent working in his garden among the flowers he loved. and watching the birds crowd his feeders. Leslie lived in covenant not only with God and men but also with nature."

WILLIAM PICKERING: SPACE EXPLORER (1910-2004)

From The New Zealand Edge

Rocket Man

The launch of Sputnik in 1957 forced the United States into the space race. Fighting in the Cold War the Americans needed to show the world that they too could launch a rocket into space—and they had to do it quickly. Less than three months later Explorer 1 was launched from Cape Canaveral, Florida. The man behind it: William Pickering from Wellington, New Zealand.

In the next ten years Pickering went on to be a central figure in the American space race. Once he and his team conquered the earth's orbit, the sky was, literally, the limit. He worked at marrying the possibilities of technology with humanity's wonderment at outer space and, by sending spacecraft to the far edges of the solar system, made us more aware of the galaxy we live in.

William Hayward Pickering was born in Roxburgh Street, Mount Victoria, Wellington in 1910. His mother died when he was six and he was sent to live with his grandparents in Havelock, in the Marlborough Sounds at the northern tip of the South Island. Here Pickering attended Havelock Primary School, the first school of the greatest New Zealand scientist, Ernest Rutherford.

In 1923 he started boarding at Wellington College. His father, a pharmacist, had left New Zealand to work in the tropics, an environment he didn't believe was a healthy one for his sons. He completed a bachelor's degree in electrical engineering in 1932, and returned to New Zealand after receiving his Ph.D. in Physics in 1936, hoping to work as an engineer. Unable to find satisfactory employment he returned to education and to California, and joined the Caltech faculty. During

World War II Pickering had also become involved in the Jet Propulsion Laboratory. Jet technology was comparatively new to Caltech. By 1954 he was the Lab's Director.

On October 4,1957 the Soviet Union launched Sputnik. After 10 years of Cold War the Soviets had beaten the Americans into space. Circling the globe every 90 minutes, Sputnik contained a beeping transmitter that could be received by any short wave radio on earth. The American public knew it was there. Pickering said: "It was only the beeping reality of Sputnik that suddenly made the threat of intercontinental atomic warfare with ballistic rockets more than a science fiction story."

Explorer 1 was launched from Cape Canaveral, Florida on January 31, 1958, less than four months after Sputnik. A photo of the men holding a model of Explorer 1 represents both the entry of America in the space race and William Pickering's proudest moment.

In 1993 the president of Calthech, Thomas E. Everhart, said: "More than any other individual, Bill Pickering was responsible for America's success in exploring the planets—an endeavour that demanded vision, courage, dedication, expertise and the ability to inspire two generations of scientists and engineers at the Jet Propulsion Laboratory."

Dr. Pickering's affiliation was with the Throop Memorial Church of Pasadena, a congregation allied with the Unitarian Universalist movement.

DANIEL PINKHAM: COMPOSER (1923-)

by Kee deBoer and John B. Ahouse

The oldest of three boys, Daniel Rogers Pinkham had come into the world on June 5, 1923, in Lynn, Massachusetts, bearing a surname that was nationally as well as locally famous. Three generations earlier the Vegetable Compound and other patent remedies of Lydia E. Pinkham had become household standbys, and though the founder of the firm realized only limited wealth, her children and grandchildren had made "Lydia Pinkham" into an eminently profitable industry. Daniel's father, who was to rise to the presidency of the company in the 1960s, was in a position to provide his sons with a private education, which for Daniel meant continuing a family tradition by attending Phillips Academy in Andover. Pinkham recalls his father's view that wrestling and exposure to Old Testament narratives were the most meaningful parts of an Andover education; for Daniel however, it was to be music, though not without a similar exposure to the cadences of Scripture.

At Harvard Pinkham pursued choral composition with Archibald "Doc" Davison (1883-1961), a man he remembers as an inspired organist and conductor. Beginning in his second year he studied composition with Walter Piston, who emphasized consistency of style and filled the younger musician with practical ideas on "what works and what won't" in actual performance.

Throughout his Harvard years Pinkham was continuing to prepare himself as a performer on the harpsichord and organ. He studied the former with Wanda Landowska and her pupil Putnam Aldrich (1904-1975). His organ teacher was E. Power Biggs, with whom he learned repertory and developed a working collaboration, replacing Biggs on occasional broadcast concerts from the Germanic (now Busch-Reisinger) Museum at Harvard. It was Biggs who gave the first professional performance of a Pinkham work, presenting his Sonata No. 1 for organ and strings (with Arthur Fiedler) in 1944.

Teaching at the New England Conservatory has been his mainstay, absorbing nearly all his teaching activity since then. With the arrival of Gunther Schuller as director in 1967, Pinkham petitioned for a restructuring of the curriculum to enable him to create and chair his own Department of Early Music Performance, a highly congenial arrangement.

In the fall of 1958, Pinkham had also been alerted to an imminent opening to succeed Elwood Gaskill as organist and choir director at King's Chapel, Boston's most venerable musical institution. The decision to seek this position was to be decisive for shaping the balance of his career. Founded in 1686 (the present building was completed in 1758), King's Chapel had housed the first pipe organ in an American church (1713), and was the scene of the first known music festival (1786) in the new United States. Today the diminutive Chapel remains a landmark in downtown Boston, where a slender iron fence still protects it from the highrise resealing of the city center. Prominent among earlier organists and conductors at the historic site were William Selly in the 18th, B. J. Lang in the late 19th, and, for a brief period, Virgil Thomson in the present century.

In twenty-five years of ignoring his doctor's advice to "slow down," Pinkham has criss-crossed the country for countless premieres and honors, and for appearances at increasingly frequent "Pinkham Festivals." By virtue of putting down his professional roots early in his career, however, and leaving them undisturbed, he has remained closely identified with the region where his musical life began. Boston, in the meantime, has become the early music capital of the country, not least through the efforts of Pinkham himself; and no place could be a more suitable home for the musician and his music.

VAN RENSSELAER POTTER:
GLOBAL BIOETHICS (1911-2001)

In 1970 Van Potter coined the word "bioethics" and defined this comprehensive field of thought and action. The contribution of the remarkable life work of this member of the Unitarian Society of Madison, Wisconsin to the environment of humankind is described by colleagues of the McArdle Laboratory for Cancer Research at the University of Wisconsin, Madison.

Dr. Potter was born on August 27, 1911 on the farm his paternal grandparents had homesteaded in northeastern South Dakota. He graduated from Pierpont High School in 1928 in a class of 12. In the fall he entered South Dakota State College, with a total of eight hundred dollars contributed by his two grandmothers. From his sophomore year on he earned all his expenses and received special recognition from his professors and his employer, the Head of Experiment Station Chemistry, Dr. Kurt Walter Franke. Although beginning by washing rat cages and making up rat diets, he was soon feeding and weighing the animals and dissecting them when they died after consuming grain later shown to contain trace amounts of the element selenium. He was allowed to design and carry out experiments lasting several months, and to co-author several papers in the *Journal of Nutrition* on work done as an undergraduate. He received his B.S. degree with High Honors in 1933, majoring in chemistry and biology. He received a Ph.D. in Biochemistry with a minor in Medical Physiology in 1938.

After specializing in cancer research for 20 years, Dr. Potter entered the local political scene in 1960 on the side of those who were activists in the struggle to gain support for the Frank Lloyd Wright vision of a building on the shores of Lake Monona, in Madison.

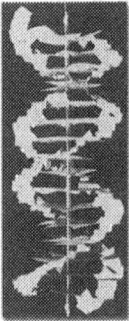

At the national level, Dr. Potter was elected President of the American Society for Cell Biology in 1964, and President of the American Association for Cancer Research in 1974. He was elected to membership in the American Academy of Arts and Sciences and the National Academy of Sciences, and as a Fellow of the American Association for the Advancement of Science. Throughout his career, he served on committees and panels for the American Cancer Society and the National Cancer Institute.

At the international level, Dr. Potter presented lectures on his research. In addition, he coined the word "bioethics" in 1970. In 1971 he dedicated his first book on the subject to Aldo Leopold, a well-known Wisconsin professor who had much earlier called for a "land ethic". He retired in 1982 and in 1988 published the book, *Global Bioethics, Building on the Leopold Legacy*. Until his death, Dr. Potter published a series of articles on his vision of bioethics as a bridge between the sciences and the humanities in the service of world-wide human health, and a protected environment.

ROBERT JULES RAIBLE: UNITARIANISM IN DALLAS (1899 - 1968)

by Wayne Gard

The Rev. Robert Jules Raible preached his first sermon as Dallas minister in 1942. He had been born in Louisville, Kentucky, and had been brought up as a Unitarian. After graduation from Louisville Boys' High School in 1917 and the University of Kentucky in 1921, he started to become a farmer; but, on suffering from an attack of poison ivy so severe that his mouth was swollen shut and he had to be fed through a tube, he gave up that plan.

He worked for a Louisville bank for two years, then entered the Harvard Divinity School, from which he received his Bachelor of Divinity degree. In 1929 he received the degree of master of education from the Harvard Graduate School of Education. In June, 1924, Raible married Mildred Galt; and in 1925 he was ordained. For the next three years he was assistant minister at the First Parish in Cambridge, Massachusetts, serving under Dr. Samuel McCord Crothers and spending much of his time in work with Harvard and Radcliffe students. Then, for four years, 1928-32, he was minister of the First Parish at Peterborough, New Hampshire. In 1932 he accepted a call to become minister of All Soul's Unitarian Church in Greenfield, Massachusetts. In Greenfield, where he served for a decade before leaving for Dallas, he engaged in many types of community work, including that of an air-raid warden.

In 1944, after two Negroes began attending services at the church, the board of trustees voted to welcome two Negroes to church membership. In 1946 the church, which then had 160 active members, engaged an architect to draw up plans for a church auditorium that would seat about 250 persons and for auxiliary buildings. The church adopted a new constitution and bylaws, the former stating that "the purpose of this church shall be to maintain services for worship and to foster the ideals of liberal religion in this community." The minister pointed out some accomplishments of the Unitarian Church: "It has made clear that science is not an opponent but is a handmaid and servant of religion. The Unitarian Church fought the battle for evolution and that for acceptance of what was called the higher criticism of the Bible." In 1948 the church had 371 members.

In 1952 the church engaged an architect for an educational building. In 1953 the church expanded its library, and the Laymen's League sponsored the formation of a Boy Scout troop. The World Federalists and the Americans for Democratic Action made use of the church buildings, as did the Society of Friends.

Outside organizations using some of the church facilities included the National Association for the Advancement of Colored People, the Jewish Welfare Federation, and the Republican Women's Club. In the spring of 1956 the church was permitting the use of its facilities by many outside organizations, including the Dallas School for Blind Children, Great Books, General Semantics, a Bahai group, a Brownie troop, Girl Scout leaders, the Junior League, the YMCA, the Cancer Society, a State Fair 4H group, Hadassah, B'nai B'rith, the League of Women Voters, and sponsors of various piano recitals.

"The Unitarian Church is the expression of the democratic position and principle as applied to religion. It is a free faith for free men. The Unitarian Church says that free men can discover truth for themselves if open inquiry is allowed. " In 1961 a Unitarian-Universalist fellowship was formed in the Oak Cliff section of Dallas.

When the new auditorium was formally dedicated, the minister proudly was joined for this occasion by his two sons, the Rev. Peter S. Raible and the Rev. Christopher G. Raible. Dr. Dana M. Greeley, president of the Unitarian Universalist Association, spoke.

At an evening meeting in the new auditorium, members bade farewell to Dr. Raible, who was retiring after twenty-two years as minister.

Melissa Rice recalled the hobby of Dr. Raible in experimental tomato growing and told of his yearly disappointment when, on returning from summer vacation, he found that the tomato vines he had planted in the spring, watered carefully, and tied to stakes had wilted and died. In one August, she related, she and Fern Harper decided to play a trick on the minister, who was due home that evening after dark. The two women bought big, ripe tomatoes at a grocery store and tied them to the stakes and dry vines in the driveway strip of the Raible home. That night when the minister and his wife drove in and saw the red tomatoes, his eyes bugged out as if he were seeing a miracle.

Dr. and Mrs. Raible left soon for the retirement home they had bought at Marlboro, Vermont. The governor of Kentucky, the native state of Dr. Raible, commissioned him as an honorary Kentucky colonel.

MARY JANE RATHBUN: MARINE ZOOLOGIST (1860-1943)

By Lucile McCain, U.S. National Museum

Born in Buffalo on June 11, 1860 Miss Rathbun was educated in the schools of that city and thereafter devoted a long life of service to the Smithsonian Institution and the U.S. National Museum. In 1884 she obtained a position as clerk in the Fish Commission, which she held until 1887, when she was appointed by Secretary Spencer F. Baird, of the Smithsonian Institution, to a position as copyist in the Division of Marine Invertebrates of the National Museum. Later she became aide, then assistant curator of this division. After her resignation in 1914, she was appointed honorary associate in zoology, which title she held until her death.

Miss Rathbun worked for many years alone and unaided to build up the Division of Marine Invertebrates to its present high standard of excellence. She instituted a record system upon which others have never been able to improve. It not only is in use in the division to this day, but has been studied and adopted by other divisions of the museum. She also established a systematic catalogue of the thousands of specimens of marine invertebrates handled by the division, whose files contain hundreds of catalogue cards made out by her in longhand during the many years before a typist was available for this work. The division, as it is constituted and operated today, continues to rest upon the solid foundation that she built for it.

Because of her enterprise, the collections and correspondence of the division grew to such proportions that it became imperative for her to have assistance in handling them. When she asked for such an assistant, however, she was told that the museum funds would not permit the appointment of another person. It was then that she made the decision which forever after endeared her to her colleagues, and particularly to the man who benefited by her action. Without hesitation, on December 31, 1914, she resigned her position, in order that her salary could be used for paying an assistant. The assistant for whom she thus made place was Dr. Waldo L. Schmitt, who later became curator of the division. He declares that but for this act of sacrifice he might never have embarked upon the career to which he devoted his life and which has only recently led to his designation as head curator of the Department of Biology at the museum.

Though now resigned from the museum payroll, Miss Rathbun went to work as usual, and continued to serve full time for twenty-five years thereafter. Thus her Government service ended as it began—with devotion to science and without compensation.

UNITARIAN NOTE

An American National Biography article states: "A Unitarian, she devoted her life to science."

CURTIS W. REESE:
STATESMAN OF RELIGIOUS HUMANISM (1887-1961)

by Mason Olds, Unitarian Universalist Minister

Curtis Williford Reese was born September 3, 1887, on a farm in Madison County, North Carolina which is in the western part of the state in the Blue Ridge Mountains. The Reeses were very devout Southern Baptists and many of them had been ministers. Reese once said: "One of my paternal great-grandfathers was a Baptist preacher, one of my paternal grandfathers and two of my paternal uncles were Baptist preachers, my father is a Baptist deacon, two of my brothers are Baptist preachers, and a sister married a Baptist preacher."

Later Reese decided to enter the ministry, which meant that he thought that God had given him the "call." He entered the Baptist College at Mar's Hill, North Carolina, and graduated in May 1908. He was ordained to the Baptist ministry. It was during his seminary studies that Reese first began to have any doubts about his religious faith. Since he felt that the Bible was divinely inspired, it came as quite a shock to encounter "higher criticism" even in a conservative Southern Baptist context. Also, Reese had a friend, Ralph E. Bailey, who later made the transition from the Baptist ministry to the Unitarian. Bailey has remarked: "In 1908, he and I were students at the Baptist seminary in Louisville, where I soon shocked him to his knees by my heresy. Much of his time was devoted, I think, to prayer that I be corrected in my outspoken apostasy from Baptist truth."

Moreover, it was in Louisville that Reese first came into contact with Unitarianism. In fact, he took some Baptist tracts over to the Unitarian church and picked up some of the Unitarian materials. One pamphlet especially appealed to him; it was entitled, "Salvation by Character," and it was probably this experience that later contributed to Reese's move into Unitarianism.

Reese wrote the minister of the Unitarian Church in Toledo, Ohio, and set up a meeting with him. At this meeting Reese presented a statement of his faith which consisted of the following: "(1) a Universal Father, God, (2) a Universal Brotherhood, mankind, (3) a Universal right, freedom, (4) a Universal motive, love, and (5) a Universal aim, progress." When Reese inquired if his faith were consistent with Unitarianism, the minister assured him that it was. He decided to transfer from the Baptist church to the Unitarian. He said: "My mother said very sincerely that she would rather have seen me dead. She was sure when I died, I would burn in hellfire and brimstone forever and ever."

It was during this period that Reese was elected to the Board of Directors of the Meadville Theological School, which at that time was located at Meadville, Pennsylvania. Reese wanted the school to be relocated in Chicago; he therefore contacted Morton D. Hull, a wealthy businessman and an active Unitarian, and secured a pledge from him of $100,000 if the school should come to Chicago. At the next meeting of the Board of Directors in February, 1926, Reese told of the pledge and it was decided that Meadville would relocate in Chicago. Reese also worked out with Shailer Mathews "an associated relationship" between Meadville and the University of Chicago, as well as negotiating the purchase of the President's House and Channing House.

In January, 1930, Reese gave up his position as Western Conference secretary and accepted the position as dean at the Abraham Lincoln Centre in Chicago. The Centre was founded in 1905 by the Unitarian minister, Jenkin Lloyd Jones. Reese lived in an apartment in the Centre designed by the famous architect, Frank Lloyd Wright. The programs for the Centre were many and varied; it had a Friday morning forum, where outstanding speakers with all varieties of opinion were provided a platform from which to be heard. Also, the Centre published a journal, *Unity*. The Centre had a counseling center and ran a clinic for "optional parenthood." It sponsored "study classes, social service, a boys' and girls' camp, a public library, domestic science classes, instruction in music with glee clubs and an orchestra, various special activities for boys and girls, and dramatics." Non-Jews, Jews, and Negroes were on the staff, and Reese maintained in the early days a fifty percent balance of whites and blacks in all programs; later as the neighborhood changed they ministered to an even larger percentage of blacks.

In 1926 he published his first book, *Humanism*, followed in 1931 with *Humanist Religion* and in 1945 with *The Meaning of Humanism*. He also edited in 1927 *Humanist Sermons*, and in 1931 he edited a book entitled, *Friedrich Nietzsche*, which was the lectures of the late George Burman Foster, professor of comparative religion at the University of Chicago.

Retiring as dean of the Abraham Lincoln Centre in 1957, Reese and his wife moved to Kissimmee, Florida. On May 22, 1959, he was presented the Holmes-Weatherly Award for service to liberal religion by the American Unitarian Association. On June 5, 1961, while attending a Board of Directors' meeting of the Meadville Theological School and the commencement exercises, Reese died of a coronary attack; and with his passing another pioneer of religious humanism faded from the religious scene.

Reese was one of the founders and was president of the American Humanist Association for fourteen years. Reese objected to the theists referring to humanists as atheists. He said: "Most of the Humanists hold some one of the several non-Theistic theories of God."

In his book entitled, *Humanism*, he said: "The liberal recognizes and zealously proclaims the fact that purposive and powerful cosmic processes are operative, and that increasingly man is able to cooperate with them and in a measure control them. What these processes be styled is of but little importance. Some call them cosmic processes, others call them God."

Abridged from *Religious Humanism in America*; Mason Olds, Editor (University Press of America, 1978)

AURELIA HENRY REINHARDT:
PRESIDENT OF MILLS COLLEGE (1877-1948)

by Clare B. Fischer Aurelia Henry Reinhardt Professor of Religion and Culture, Starr King School for the Ministry

Born in California, one of six children, Aurelia Isabel Henry began to excel in her studies while attending Boy's High in San Francisco. She pursued a degree in English literature at the University of California, Berkeley, graduating in 1898. After several years of teaching in Idaho, she returned to her studies of literature and completed a Ph.D. at Yale University in 1905. During this period, Aurelia Henry not only wrote a dissertation (on Ben Johnson's work *Epicoene*) but also translated Dante's essay "De Monarchia" from Italian into English. Both studies were published, attesting to her strong scholarship and fine writing style. Aurelia Henry's literary pursuits in higher education were an indication of the determination that would mark all of her achievements in later life. She was, significantly, among a small group of women who undertook graduate education in the early 1900s and an even smaller number of women who would demonstrate leadership in educational administration, religious life, and civic engagement.

Aurelia Henry married Dr. George Reinhardt in 1906. Just six years later, she found herself a widow and the single parent of two small sons. She was able to secure a teaching position through the University of California's extension program. Then, in 1916, her life and that of a small, struggling women's college irreversibly changed when she assumed the presidency of Mills College in Oakland. She remained as its head for twenty-seven years, retiring in 1943 after a successful program of student and faculty expansion. Among the universities granting her honorary degrees were the University of California, the University of Southern California, and Oberlin College.

In addition to her work as an educator, Aurelia Reinhardt worked tirelessly for peace. As early as 1919, she publicly declared herself an advocate for world peace. Although a Republican Party activist, she broke ranks to stand behind President Woodrow Wilson's plan for the League of Nations. A member of more than a dozen peace organizations for the next three decades, she served as a delegate to the founding meetings of the United Nations in San Francisco in 1945. She spoke to dozens of church and community groups about the imperative of peace and the importance of international collaboration, including the value of cultural and educational exchange exemplified by UNESCO.

Aurelia Reinhardt also took a leadership role as president of the American Association of University Women. She spoke for women's equal access to education and professional recognition throughout her life.

The importance of Unitarian religious identity for Aurelia Reinhardt cannot be overstated. Married in the First Unitarian Church of Berkeley, she was later to join the church to which her family had belonged, the Oakland Unitarian Church. She joined a select group of religious leaders in the movement to prepare the report of the Commission on Appraisal, *Unitarians Face a New Age*. She wrote the chapter on worship, which remains a singular contribution to Unitarian understanding of liturgy and worship. In the same period, she served on the Board of Trustees of the Starr King School for Ministry in Berkeley. She stated this goal for professional religious leadership: "Let us not forget that the future includes more women in the ministry than we have ever known before."

MALVINA REYNOLDS:
SONGWRITER / SINGER / ACTIVIST (1900-1978)

by Nancy Schimmel

Born Malvina Milder of Jewish socialist immigrant parents in San Francisco, Malvina was refused her diploma by Lowell High School because her parents were opposed to the U.S. participation in World War I. She entered UC Berkeley anyway, and received her B.A. and M.A. in English. She married William Reynolds, a carpenter and organizer, in 1934 and had one child, Nancy, in 1935. She completed her dissertation and was awarded her Doctorate in 1936. It was the middle of the Depression, she was Jewish, socialist, and a woman. She could not find a job teaching at the college level. She became a social worker and a columnist for the *People's World* and, when World War II started, an assembly line worker at a bomb factory. When her father died, she and her husband took over her parents' naval tailor shop in Long Beach, California. There in the late forties she met Earl Robinson, Pete Seeger and other folk singers and songwriters and began writing songs.

She returned to Berkeley, and to the University, where she took music theory classes in the early fifties. She gained recognition as a songwriter when Harry Belafonte sang her "Turn Around." Her songs were recorded by Joan Baez, Judy Collins, The Seekers, Pete Seeger, and the Limeliters, among others. She wrote songs for Women for Peace, the Nestle Boycott, the sit-ins in San Francisco on auto row and at the Sheraton-Palace, the fight against putting a freeway through Golden Gate Park and other causes. She toured Scandinavia, England and Japan. A film biography, "Love It Like a Fool," was made a few years before she died in 1978. Ellen Stekert is writing a biography and would like information about Malvina's pre-1945 activities.

EDITOR'S NOTE

When Ellen Stekert's biography is written, it will be fascinating to examine her view of Malvina's religion. Already at hand are three interpretations.

First, when addressing the centennial celebration of the First Unitarian Church in Sioux City, Iowa, in 1985 Dr. John Brigham quoted the second stanza o the ballad "God Bless the Grass" made famous by Pete Seger and written by a person he identified as Malvina Reynolds:

"God bless the truth that fights toward the sun,
They roll the lies over it and think that it is done
It moves through the ground and reaches for air,
And after a while it is growing everywhere,
And God bless the truth."

A second interpretation is offered by Dr. Richard Boeke, Minister Emeritus of the First Unitarian Church of Berkeley in Kensington, California, who recently wrote:

"Malvina Reynolds was a member of the UU Church of Berkeley, CA. She sang at our church services about ten times while I was minister there...She lived on Parker Street, named for Unitarian Minister, Theodore Parker (near Channing Way and a mile from the Longfellow School)."

A third interpretation is expressed in these lines by her daughter, Nancy Schimmel:

"To say Malvina Reynolds was a Unitarian might be stretching it a tiny bit. She and my father were married in the Unitarian Church in Santa Cruz. However, both my parents were raised atheist and never wavered from that mindset (nor have I). You could possibly describe my mother as a 'Steve Fritchman Unitarian' My parents drove from Long Beach sporadically to attend his church in Los Angeles during the McCarthy era.

"Malvina was happy to give singing sermons at UU churches around the country."

From my point of view, these interpretations are reminders that the same Unitarian can be an atheist with respect to a supernatural God while, as a theist, affirming the sacred power of the world and all therein.

In her jubilant, liberal rejection of traditional other-worldly religion, Malvina wrote and sang "This World":

"I'd rather go to the corner store
Than sing 'Hosanna' on that golden shore
I'd rather live on Parker Street
Than fly around where the angels meet."

ELLIOT LEE RICHARDSON: LAWYER AND PUBLIC SERVANT (1920-1999)

The Massachusestts Historical Society Annual Report for 2000 published "Memoirs" by John Sears, which are here abridged.

Four Cabinet appointments! And two ambassadorships, and two constitutional offices in a major state, and a slew of other public offices of consequence. As we review his extraordinary life and unique achievements, from start to finish, there was Richardson the Lawyer.

President of the *Harvard Law Review*, and clerk to Judge Learned Hand—who is seen by many American scholars as the greatest of our jurisconsults, on a par with Elliot's hero Justice Holmes. Later clerk to Justice Felix Frankfurter. Associated with, and soon a partner of, the highly respected Boston law firm now known as Ropes and Gray, and a lecturer in law at the Harvard Law School.

His legislative skill drew Richardson into his first national public service, appointed by President Eisenhower in 1957 as Assistant Secretary for Legislation in the U.S. Department of Health, Education, and Welfare. His lawyerly skills led the same president to appoint him U.S. attorney for the District of Massachusetts in 1959, where he began a brilliant prosecutorial career by tackling major influence peddlers in Boston and brought down a White House intimate, Bernard Goldfine, for tax evasion.

These lawyerlike qualities made him one of Massachusetts's more successful attorneys general, and then—as the world knows all too well—the United States attorney general who refused to accommodate the corruption of the Nixon White House and forced a vice president out of office. Those same skills served him—and his country—later when he patiently negotiated a superb international treaty on the Law of the Sea, having been appointed by President Carter, who recognized talent across the aisle.

Starting with service as a town meeting member and library trustee in Brookline in 1950, followed by service on the staffs of Sen. Leverett Saltonstall (1953-1955) and Gov. Christian Herter (1955-1956), he showed lifelong fidelity to a type of progressive (now called "moderate") Republicanism: problem-solving with conscientious attention to consequences, management with considerable care for those whose money was being spent, public service with complete integrity.

In the term that followed, Richardson did a masterful job reorganizing the delivery of welfare services in the Commonwealth, against heavy odds and entrenched interests. He provided manful and meaningful aid when the governor perceived that the time had come to support public services and systems in Massachusetts with a sales tax—a battle won despite heated opposition from legislative leadership. (How different from the attitudes of a later day!)

Much has been made of his extraordinary courage in refusing to fire special Watergate prosecutor Archibald Cox and of his resignation in the face of presidential pressure. In 1969, Massachusetts Attorney General Richardson was appointed by President Nixon as Under Secretary of State.

The State Department appointment initiated Richardson's astonishing career in the upper levels of federal service. In those years he chaired a sub-cabinet committee that worked to reduce U.S. establishments abroad and to modernize the diplomatic corps. In mid-1970, he became secretary of the troubled Department of Health, Education and Welfare, supervising 107,000 civil servants. In the ensuing three years he restored the morale of the agency, energized the Head Start program, decentralized services, and helped to articulate the Nixon-Brooke "guaranteed annual income" scheme. He worked on some of the earliest desegregation busing proposals and was hard at work on other reforms when the president asked him to become Secretary of Defense in 1973. Just as he was mastering this enormous agency and reordering its priorities, after three months he was moved once again, this time to become Attorney General of the United States.

From 1973 to 1978, he made perhaps his grandest contribution to the problem-solving of the republic—and also experienced his most notable hour in public service in the Watergate affair.

As the Watergate troubles unfolded, he kept for a time the storm-tossed ship in navigable waters. But when the president's men demanded that Archibald Cox, as special prosecutor, agree not to subpoena further data from the White House, Richardson made clear his objections. Then, when Nixon stuck to his position and asked Richardson to fire Cox, as the world well knows Elliot decided he had to depart himself, telling the president that he considered his resignation to be "in the public interest."

Fortunately, President Ford, newly installed, stepped in and Elliot found himself at Winfield House in London, as a highly successful American ambassador to the Court of St. James's. As in all his public service, his success here owed much to his charming and accomplished wife Anne, who had been captivated, according to family accounts, not by his intelligence so much as by his skill as a ballroom dancer. But the ambassadorship also ended prematurely, when the president—setting Elliot on a track for the highest offices—appointed him Secretary of Commerce in 1976. There he took a lively and effective interest in job creation and explored the possibilities of corporate democracy and flextime.

His public service did not end at the Commerce Department. President Carter asked him to negotiate a treaty on the Law of the Sea, which he did with extraordinary skill and considerable disappointment when the United States failed to sign. Later he monitored elections in Namibia and Nicaragua. President Clinton awarded him the Presidential Medal of Freedom in 1998.

What Elliot Richardson was, in the end, was a polymath, an intellectual, a public servant *par excellence*, a keen observer, and a truly great manager. He was also—as his family and friends would emphasize—a superb human being.

UNITARIAN NOTE

Elliot Richardson was a lifelong member of the First and Second Church in Boston. This Unitarian Universalist congregation, the oldest church in Boston, was founded in 1630. The covenant then signed in the course of the two days is still the basis of membership in the church.

IRMA ROMBAUER:
THE JOY OF COOKING (1877-1962)

by Marion Rombauer Becker

This is the tale of an acorn—a few recipes circulated by my mother, Irma von Starkloff Rombauer, for a class she was asked to hold in the early 1920's for the benefit of a Unitarian church in St. Louis— that grew into a great oak. How she loved the group which made up the Women's Alliance!

Mother's early housekeeping days, after her marriage to Edgar Rombauer in 1898, gave little evidence of culinary prowess. "Will it encourage you," she asked in one of *Joy*'s prefaces, "to know that I was once as ignorant, helpless and awkward a bride as was ever foisted on an impecunious young lawyer? Together we placed many a burnt offering upon the altar of matrimony."

The minutes of the First Unitarian Women's Alliance are misplaced and the memories of its surviving members somewhat hazy about just when between 1922 and 1924 Irma Rombauer got together a sheaf of seventy-three mimeographed recipes as a foundation for their cooking course.

Mother was over fifty when we persuaded her to compile a more comprehensive cookbook. Privately printed in 1931, the 3,000 copies could boast 500 tested recipes from which "inexperienced cooks cannot fail to make successful souffles, pies, cakes, soups, gravies, if they follow the clear instructions given on these subjects. The Zeitgeist is reflected in the chapter on Leftovers and in many practical suggestions." The Zeitgeist, now so painful to recall, was the Great Depression.

Mother's friends made sales lively, but not brisk enough to suit her. A pilgrimage to consult Mr. Kroch, of Kroch's International Bookstore, Chicago, brought forth his startled comment: "Two thousand copies privately sold in two years, woman—and you come to me?"

An American Institution

by Molly Finn

The Joy of Cooking is an American institution. It was the only cookbook chosen by the New York Public Library during its centennial celebration in 1995 as one of the 150 most influential books of the century. Since it was first published in 1931 it has provided encouragement, information, and remedies for kitchen emergencies to countless uncertain brides, college students, experienced cooks, innocents, and snobs. With its excellent index and well–tested recipes, it has

been the reference book of choice for those interested in traditional American food.

The best thing about *The Joy of Cooking*, however, is the voice of its author, Irma Rombauer. She engages in a constant dialogue with her readers, telling stories about herself and her family, sprinkling the text with genuine witticisms and excruciatingly corny puns, and making sure everybody knows that cooking is not an occult science or esoteric art, but part of the everyday work of the vast majority of women (and a few men) that can be turned into fun with her help.

The *Joy of Cooking* has always been a family enterprise, and through all the revisions of the work as it changed and expanded from 1931 through 1975 it has been recognizable as essentially the same book. In 1951, for the third revision, Irma's daughter Marion Becker joined her mother as coauthor, and after Irma's death in 1962 Marion continued as author through the book's fifth revision, published in 1975 shortly after Marion's death. That edition sold about 100,000 copies per year between 1975 and 1997, by which time fourteen million copies of *Joy* had been sold.

LEVERETT SALTONSTALL: UNITED STATES SENATOR (1892-1979)

by Thomas Blair, Harvard College '03

"SALTY"

Thoroughly Bostonian and thoroughly patrician, Leverett Saltonstall was born in Middlesex County, Massachusetts to a family deemed the wealthiest in the state.

He was educated at Noble and Greenough School and Harvard University, where he earned a bachelor's degree in 1914 and a law degree three years later. The gubernatorial opponent who accused Saltonstall of being "born with a diamond-studded spoon in his mouth" was hardly exaggerating; "Salty" was a tenth-generation Harvard graduate. He was also the descendant of no fewer than eight governors of Massachusetts, including a leader of the Massachusetts Bay Colony, as well as one Lord Mayor of London from the reign of Elizabeth I. As Governor and U.S. Senator of Massachusetts, however, Saltonstall distinguished himself in his own right, fulfilling the old ideal of the gentlemanly "Boston brahmin."

Always sociable and active, Saltonstall rowed and played hockey while at school and built a reputation—as he would as Speaker of the House in Massachusetts, as Governor, and as a senior U.S. Senator—for extraordinary personality. Upon graduating from law school he joined the army as a lieutenant, serving in France but, as he later recalled, seeing "no actual conflict except those following strenuous evenings in Bordeaux and elsewhere." Saltonstall returned to the United States in 1918 and began to practice law in the following year.

He soon moved ever deeper into politics, winning the election for Alderman of Newton, the town in which he was born, in 1920. Three years later he won a race for Massachusetts State Representative, and his political career took off from there. "Salty," as he was known in Massachusetts politics, became Speaker of the House in 1926, serving until shortly after a 1936 unsuccessful run for Lieutenant Governor. Saltonstall was President of the Unitarian Club of Boston, a trustee of Massachusetts Eye and Ear Infirmary, and Director of Perkins School for the Blind.

In 1938 Saltonstall accomplished a feat that has always been difficult for Republicans: he defeated a Democrat in the Massachusetts gubernatorial election. His opponent, Boston Mayor James Curley, had seen fit to call Salty "a man with a Harvard accent and a South Boston face." The label appealed to Massachusetts voters, and Salty's image of aristocracy coupled with identification with the average Bostonian helped him win reelection in 1940 and 1942. He had a distinguished career as Governor; in his six years in office he lowered the state's deficit by 92%, mediated a massive teamster strike, and built a reputation for an ability to work well with Democrats and Republicans alike.

His social concern remained strong, as well; proof of Irish ancestry gained him admission to the Charitable Irish Society, and he used his power as Governor to establish an interfaith committee to combat discrimination, particularly anti-Semitism. Described as a "liberal Republican," he was even popular enough to win nomination as chair of a national conference of Governors in 1943..

When Henry Cabot Lodge resigned from the Senate in 1944, Salty decided to make a bid for Washington. He pulled off what one contemporary journalist called the "political miracle" of winning Boston (and the rest of the district), thus beginning a long and distinguished career in the United States Senate.

Seen as a moderate by both parties, he also tended to take the typically Democratic positions of favoring foreign aid and international cooperation, and advocated such policies as disarmament, increasing civil liberties, and supporting a minimum wage. He served on seven committees—Appropriations, Defense, Legislative, Armed Services, Preparedness, Small Business, and Government Procurement—and helped to pass such legislation as the National Act against Discrimination in Employment, the Cape Cod National Park, and a bill for improving children's access to health care. By all accounts universally popular—or at least not disliked—in the Senate, Salty served as Republican whip, remaining, as one biographer recalled, on speaking terms with all the members of the Senate.

Saltonstall retired from the Senate in 1966; he commented that he "wanted to quit when he was still doing the job rather than just fade away in the Senate." He returned to his Dover, Massachusetts farm—his old retreat from his days in the State House—with his wife, Mary, whom he'd met in dancing school as a teenager. The farm had always been a sanctuary for the Saltonstalls and their six children, and Salty had always been an avid rider and farmer, reportedly selling 1600 eggs in his penultimate year as Governor.

Known to his death as "New England's favorite son," Saltonstall remained active and sociable. His political legacy of compromise and personality have helped him remain known as "a senator's senator," a man who did his job with duty and grace.

UNITARIAN NOTE

Leverett Saltonstall, descendant of Sir Richard Saltonstall of Colonial Days, was a member of the Unitarian Church in Chestnut Hill as well as of the Dover, Massachusetts Unitarian Church and president of the Unitarian Club of Boston.

LILIAN STEICHEN SANDBURG: WOMAN OF A MILLION NAMES (1883-1977)

"To My Wife and Pal, Lilian Steichen Sandburg" was the dedication line in Carl Sandburg's first published book, Chicago Poems." *Carl and Lilian's very souls were dedicated to each other in lifelong creative union. One symbol of this fact is the Sandburg Hall of the flourishing Unitarian Universalist Church of Ashville, North Carolina, where she was a generous contributor.*

The following narrative of this romance is abridged from an unpublished presentation to the Madison Literary Club in Wisconsin on November 13, 2000.

By Faith B. Miracle, independent editor

On December 29, 1907, Carl Sandburg, then calling himself Charles, checked in at 344 N. Sixth Street in Milwaukee to report for work as an organizer for the Wisconsin Social-Democratic Party. On that same day, party member Lilian Steichen, younger sister of Edward Steichen, was ending her Christmas visit with her parents near Menomonee Falls and returning to her teaching position in Princeton, Illinois. She stopped in at party headquarters to say good-bye to her socialist friends and met, by chance, the new party organizer. They talked for a while. She gave him her address in Princeton, and he promised to send her some samples of his writing. Six months later they were married in Milwaukee after a spirited exchange of remarkable letters.

At the time of their first meeting, Carl had received his formal education at Lombard College in his hometown, Galesburg, Illinois. He had held a number of odd jobs, beginning at age 11 when he worked as a janitor in a real estate office each morning before school, for which he was paid 25 cents a week. He delivered papers each day after school, earning $1 a week. When he was 14, his father's work hours were cut in half. Carl had to quit school, and he hired out to a dairy farmer. That was on the eve of the Panic of 1893, a period of hard times in the nation. Later Carl traveled the country in boxcars, finding work where he could, and served with the Illinois volunteers in the Spanish American War. It was because of his military service that Lombard College offered him admittance and free tuition for his freshman year, in spite of the fact that he was 20 years old and did not have a high school diploma. He was considered a "special student."

Lilian became a dedicated worker in the Wisconsin Social-Democratic Party. She translated socialist pamphlets and articles from German to English, English to German. In later years, thinking back to that day in December 1907 when they met, Carl Sandburg would describe a young woman "with midnight black hair" who, he suspected was smarter than he was.

And so we come to the letters. The first is from Lilian, postmarked Princeton, Illinois. As promised, Carl had sent her some samples of his writing, and on January 17, 1908, she wrote: "Dear Mr. Sandburg, . . . I have your leaflets "Labor and Politics" and "A Little Sermon." Do tell me how you contrive to be a moral philosopher and a political agitator at one and the same time—and especially how you contrive to write such Poet's English one minute and the plain vernacular the next. The combination is baffling. Artist, poet-prophet on the one hand; man of action on the other. Yours Cordially, Lilian Steichen"

That was the beginning. Carl had met his match. Helga tells us, "He was gone, my father, after that, caught in the web of love . . . "

By February 24, Lilian had had the opportunity to read some of Carl's poems, and she had changed her mind about poetry. "The poems—the poems you sent are wonderful. To think I wrote so despairingly of poetry to you . . . . You discover to me the only poetry that has ever satisfied me since I learned to think 20th century thoughts."

The letters increased in length and number, sometimes two or more a day, with postscript added to postscript. They discussed literature. Lilian read the German writers—Heine, Hauptmann, Sudermann. Carl's mentor was Walt Whitman.

"Dear Charles Sandburg, . . . I have been conscious in rare poignant moments in my life of something very beautiful deep deep within . . . so finely attuned was that heart of yours, you caught the fine vibrant note from the depths and gave it strength and quality. But for you the sweet small hush yearning upward toward light and utterance would have subsided back to the dark depths and so died forever. So glad thanks to you—for Voice, for Life. This is the Wonder and the Hope."

Carl visited the farm the end of March. Lilian met him with horse and buggy at the Brookfield station, and on the way home they were caught in a wild thunderstorm. For the rest of their lives they referred to it as their "great ride," "the Baptismal rain." The intensity of the wind and lightning matched the intensity of their feelings, and they responded to the storm with abandon and celebration. They were together at the farm for a week, and Edward, home from Paris for his birthday, spent some time there with them. Carl and Lilian romped in the woods like children, took long walks, and planned their future together. It was during this time that she began calling him Carl, his given name, and he began calling her Paula, derived from an affectionate nickname used by her family. After that, Helga tells us, all his love poems would have the same title: "Paula."

"Paula"

Woman of a million names and a thousand faces,

I looked for you over the earth and under the sky.
I sought you in passing processions
On old multitudinous highways
Where mask and phantom and life go by.
In roaming and roving, from prairie to sea,
From city to wilderness, fighting and praying,
I looked.
Dusty and wayward, I was the soldier,
Long-sentinelled, pacing the night,
Who heard your voice in the breeze nocturnal,
Who saw in the pine shadows your hair,
Who touched in the flicker of vibrant stars
Your soul!
***

When I saw you, I knew you as you knew me.
We had known far back in the eons
When hills were dust and the sea a mist.
And toil is a trifle and struggle a glory
With You, and ruin and death but fancies,
Woman of a million names and a thousand faces.

MAY SARTON:
A POET (1912-1995)

By Lenora P. Blouin
Courtesy of the Celebration of Women Writers: http://digital.library.upenn.edu/women

May Sarton, the only child of George and Mabel Elwes Sarton, was born in Wondelgem, Belgium in 1912. In that same year George Sarton, a historian of science, founded the journal *Isis.* From her father May learned about discipline and a fierce dedication to work and from her mother, an artist and designer, she learned about dedication and creativity, whether applied to gardening or to life. In 1916 the Sartons arrived in the United States after fleeing Belgium and the advancing Germans, settling in Cambridge, Massachusetts where George Sarton took up a post at Harvard as a part-time instructor and, with financial assistance from the Carnegie Institute, as a full time scholar, devoting his life to the study of the history of science. May enrolled in the "progressive" Shady Hill School and here, through the influence of Agnes Hocking, founder and poetry teacher, developed her life long love for and interest in poetry. May Sarton later wrote eloquently of these years in her memoir *I Knew a Phoenix.*

May Sarton graduated from the Cambridge High and Latin School in Cambridge in 1929. Although winning a scholarship to Vassar, she had been smitten, much to the chagrin of her father, by the theater after seeing Eva Le Gallienne perform in *The Cradle Song*. From that moment forward she was determined, upon graduation, to join Le Gallienne's Civic Repertory Theatre in New York. Even while spending a year as an apprentice, honing her speaking voice, learning the basics of theater, and devoting herself to the study of acting, Sarton wrote poetry. At the age of seventeen a series of sonnets was published in the December, 1930 issue of *Poetry* magazine, some of which were included in her first published volume, *Encounter,* in 1937.

The end of the 1930s was a rich, creative time for Sarton as her second volume of poetry, *Inner Landscape* (1939) appeared and the novel, *Fire in the Mirror,* was completed, although never published. In 1940 Sarton undertook what was to become an annual poetry reading/lecture tour of colleges throughout the United States, beginning in Santa Fe, New Mexico. During the first half of the 1940s she worked at Pearl Buck's East and West Society in New York, writing documentary scripts for the United States War Information Office, all while continuing to produce poetry and novels. Finally, in 1946, her novel *The Bridge of Years* was published, followed two years later by the volume of poetry, *The Lion and the Rose*. Sarton continued to meet many prominent artists and writers, including H.D. (Hilda Doolittle), and Bryher (Annie Winifred Ellerman McPherson), Stephen Spender, W. H. Auden and the Sitwells: Dame Edith and her brothers, Osbert and Sacheverell.

The 1950s, although filled with accomplishments, brought many tragedies, beginning with the death of her mother in 1950 and of her beloved Marie Closset in 1952. The losses, though great, would be tempered by meeting Judith Matlack, the woman with whom she would live for fifteen years, and to whom she would remain devoted until Matlack's death in 1982. In these years, she published her third and fourth novels, *Shadow of a Man* (1950), and *Shower of Summer Days* (1952), as well as a volume of poetry, *The Land of Silence* (1953) which won the Reynolds Lyric Award. In 1954 Sarton wrote her first memoir, *I Knew a Phoenix*, excerpts of which first appeared in the New Yorker. This genre became an important one for Sarton and brought her a tremendous audience of readers and correspondents. Her next novel, *Faithful Are the Wounds* was published in 1955 and eventually led, in 1958, to a dual nomination, together with her volume of poetry, *In Time Like Air*, for a National Book Award. Although neither won the award, *In Time Like Air* is considered by some critics, including poet and scholar Constance Hunting to be one of Sarton's best books of poetry.

By this time Sarton's father had died and in 1958 she sold her parent's home in Cambridge, Massachusetts and bought an old house in Nelson, New Hampshire, the subject of which became the basis of her next memoir, *Plant Dreaming Deep* (1968).

Three volumes of poetry appeared during these years: *Cloud, Stone, Sun, Vine* (1961), *A Private Mythology* (1966) and *As Does New Hampshire* (1967). *A Private Mythology* contained her first published free verse.

In 1973 a new chapter in Sarton's life began with the sale of her house in Nelson, New Hampshire and with her move to Wild Knoll, the house in York, Maine. It is clear that the end of the 1970s marked an increasingly fertile period for May Sarton in which she honed the journal style and produced her third memoir, *A World of Light: Portraits and Celebrations*. As in the first two memoirs, Sarton delineated memorable portraits of the people who had most influenced and inhabited her life.

The decade of the seventies ended with the production of the film," World of Light." *A Portrait of May Sarton*, produced by Martha Wheelock and Marita Simpson. Filmed in her house by the sea, described so eloquently in the 1977 journal by the same name, Sarton talks about her vision of life, her work and the muses who influenced her. Familiar themes such as solitude, poetry, the natural world, and love in its many forms are all here. Unbeknownst to its producers though, at the time this film was being made, Sarton was facing a mastectomy which was performed shortly after the film's completion. This surgery ushered in the beginning of serious physical challenges, which intensified during the next decade.

By 1984 Sarton could publish her journal, *At Seventy,* with a sense of renewal. She had recovered from the mastectomy and was again looking to the future. In the face of growing older and experiencing the limitations of illness, she wrote, "I am more myself than I have ever been." Poems came again and were published in the volume, *Letters From Maine*.

During her lifetime Sarton rued the fact that for most of her writing life, the major critics and the literary establishment had ignored or dismissed her work. The massive number of letters she received each week from her "fans" could not assuage the hurt over this neglect and yet even now after her death, more than forty of Sarton's books are still in print; *Journal of a Solitude* has never gone out of print since it was first published in 1973. Critical recognition, having come late in her life, has grown and will continue to grow into the future, positioning May Sarton in her rightful place in literary history.

ARTHUR MEIER SCHLESINGER, JR.: UNREPENTANT LIBERAL HISTORIAN (1917-2007)

Abridged from his 25th Anniversary Harvard College Report:

I spent my first year after graduation at Cambridge University. I then returned to Harvard as a member of the Society of Fellows. After Pearl Harbor, I went to Washington, first in the Office of War Information and subsequently in the Office of Strategic Services. I went overseas in 1944 and served in England, France, and Germany. I entered the Army along the way and emerged with the rank of corporal. After my discharge at the end of 1945, I lived in Washington as a freelance writer. In the autumn of 1947 I joined the Harvard History Department and for the next dozen years or so lectured in American intellectual history. I became interested in politics, headed the research staffs in Adlai Stevenson's two campaigns and, after the happy events of November, 1960, went back to Washington as Special Assistant to John F. Kennedy, '40. In 1962 I resigned my Harvard professorship. I have written eight books and am now midway into a multi-volume study of *The Age of Roosevelt.*

Abridged from his 50th Anniversary Harvard College Report:

How can half a century have passed so quickly? But what a half-century it has been!

In 1961, John F. Kennedy '40 asked me to come to the White House as one of his special assistants. For a historian, the opportunity to watch history in the making from so intimate a vantage point was irresistible. Working for John Kennedy was a most exhilarating experience, so tragically concluded in 1963. I had resigned my Harvard professorship earlier that year in deference to the rule restricting leaves of absence to two years. The history department did not fill the vacancy, and, in 1964, Harvard invited me back. My debt to Harvard was incalculable; but, I had lived nearly forty years of my life in Cambridge, and, as Thoreau said when he left Walden, I felt that I had several more lives to live and could spare no more time for this one.

I spent a semester at the Institute for Advanced Study at Princeton and then accepted a Schweitzer professorship at the City University of New York, where I teach today. Politics has remained an avocation. I worked hard for Robert Kennedy in 1968 and George McGovern in 1972, but could not bring myself to vote for Carter either in 1976 or 1980. He was a little conservative and pious for my taste. After a while I began to feel like Senator David B. Hill who, when asked whether he was still a Democrat, replied, "Yes—very still." But, if my father's cyclical theory holds up (and it has held up pretty well this century), the Reaganite 1980's, like the Eisenhower 1950's and the Harding-Coolidge-Hoover 1920's, will soon fade into historical memory. (For a further explanation, see my book *The Cycles of American History*) The 1990's, like the 1960's, the 1930's, and the first decade of the century, ought to be a time of idealism and reform in the style of the Roosevelts and the Kennedys. I cannot wait.

My first wife and I divorced in 1970. We had four children, three of whom went to Harvard and Radcliffe. They all grew up in the turbulent 1960's but emerged unscathed, and I am close to them all today. In 1971, I married Alexandra Emmet (Radcliffe '58). Our Harvard Classmate Teddy White lived across the street. How much Teddy would have enjoyed our Fiftieth! How greatly he will be missed!

Looking back over the half-century, I cannot resist the conclusion that most things have gotten worse. I do not think it is an optical illusion to see the leaders of our youth as giants—giants for good

(Roosevelt and Churchill), giants for evil (Hitler and Stalin). Ronald Reagan as President of the United States? Ollie North as presidentially designated "national hero?" The Contrast as presidentially certified "moral equivalents of the Founding Fathers?" Henry Adams, '58 (1858) wrote, "The progress of evolution from President Washington to President Grant, was alone evidence enough to upset Darwin." What would Henry Adams have made of Ronald Reagan?

UNITARIAN NOTE

Arthur M. Schlesinger, Jr., is a publicly self-identified Unitarian.

A Life in the Twentieth Century by Arthur Schlesinger, Jr. (Boston: Houghton-Mifflin).

RICHARD SCHULTES: EXPLORER OF THE AMAZON JUNGLE (1915-2001)

ONE MAN, ONE RIVER: A STORY OF AMAZON EXPLORATION

By Hugh Synge, Director of Plant Talk

Born into an East Boston immigrant family fallen onto hard times, Richard Schultes was the first of his family to go to University. As a student at Harvard, he came under the influence of Oakes Ames, the distinguished orchidologist and director of the Harvard Botanical Museum. In Ames's class on Plants and Human Affairs, the young Schultes came to study peyote (*Lophophora spp.*), fascinated by stories of hallucinogenic effects. A small cactus from New Mexico, this plant had at that time spread to almost 80 tribes in the USA, who used it as a medicine and ritual sacrament. As part of his studies, Schultes spent six weeks in 1936 living among the Kiowa in the midwest. He was, in Wade Davis's words, "one of the last generation scholars to actually know the Kiowa men and women who had lived the culture of the Plains." Taking peyote with the Kiowa, attending their night-long ceremonies and sweat lodges, Schultes listened to the stories of the Kiowa and came to understand the place of peyote in their lives. His career as an ethnobotanist had begun.

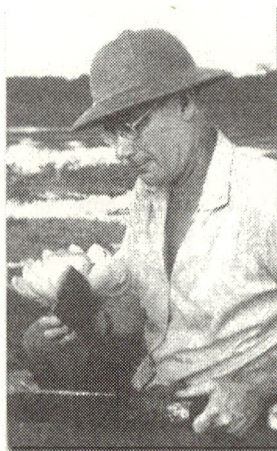

His next quest was the long-lost identity of *teonanacatl* and *ololiuqui*, the most revered hallucinogenic plants of the Aztecs. An American botanist had argued that teonanacatl was simply the Aztec name for peyote, and not the sacred mushroom reported by the Spaniards. Schultes traveled to Oaxaca, Mexico, to find it. Soon he and his companion, local botanist Blas Pable Reko, located a group of Mazatec people who used the mushroom in nocturnal ceremonies, where native healers invoked the medicinal power of mushroom through prayer. They called the mushroom "the little holy ones." Schultes was not the first to attend a *teonanacatl* ceremony, but he was the first botanist to collect and identify the mushrooms, now known as *Panaeolus sphinctrinus*. This extraordinary discovery led to the birth of the psychedelic era, and the term (not coined by Schultes) "magic mushrooms". A year later, Schultes was able to identify the even more sacred and potent *ololiuqui* as the morning glory *Turbina corymbosa*. It was later found to contain chemicals very close to LSD.

As World War II started, Schultes returned to Harvard and accepted a fellowship to study arrow poisons in the NW Amazon, which was to be the area of his greatest travels. He arrived in Colombia in 1941, where on his first day, on the outskirts of Bogotá, he discovered a new species of orchid no more than an inch high. He pressed it in his passport and sent it to Oakes Ames, who named it *Pachyphyllum schultesii*, the first of many plants named in Schultes' honour.

From 1941 to 1953 Schultes traveled extensively in the Colombian Amazon, a land he termed *Where the Gods Reign*, the title of a book of photographs from the region. In these years, he collected over 24,000 specimens and made numerous ethnobotanical discoveries. A particular interest was the source of the arrow and dart poisons know as curare. Finding a reliable source of supply was vital to Western medicine, where it is a muscle relaxant used in surgery.

Enduring the dangers of rapids, bouts of disease such as malaria and beri-beri, loss of equipment and plant materials, Schultes stayed as long as 14 months in the forest without a break, mainly traveling by canoe along the rivers. Once, sick and ill, he had to paddle for 40 days to Manaus to seek medical help. Another time, he had to wait at a remote airstrip for two months for a flight out. With no contact to the outside world, life in perhaps the remotest tropical area on earth was harsh and unpredictable. Schultes was driven by his passion for plants, his appreciation of the way of life of the indigenous people and his fascination about how the plants were used.

After 1953, the focus of Schultes's work returned to Harvard. He devoted much of his time to his students. With chemist Alfred Hofman, he wrote the leading book on hallucinogenic plants and published a volume of his evocative black-and-white pictures from his travels. He continued to visit Colombia, where he helped establish vast national parks in the Amazon. He was awarded Colombia's highest honor as well as WWF's Gold Medal.

He died in Boston on April 10, 2001, at the age of 86.

ALBERT SCHWEITZER:
EXEMPLAR OF LIFE (1875-1965)

By J. S. Bixler, President of Colby College From the Christian Register, April 1942

Albert Schweitzer once remarked in conversation, "I think that the most important trait in a religious worker is complete devotion to the truth." The remark summarized the characteristic quality of Schweitzer's own life. When he was a popular teacher and theological professor in Strassbourg, he wrote books on New Testament criticism which reflected his complete responsiveness to the demands of scholarship and his unwillingness to allow personal feelings or hopes to interfere with his passion for the facts. As a writer on Bach and editor of his organ works, he has emphasized the objectivity needed for the correct interpretation of Bach. To hear Schweitzer play is to forget Schweitzer the performer and even Bach the composer, as the eternal musical forms which Bach caught and set down on paper flow into the mind of the listener. Furthermore, Schweitzer's life as a medical missionary in equatorial Africa testifies to his supreme concern for the abstract ideal of justice and his unwillingness to let private ambitions stand in its way. When asked why he went to Africa when a brilliant career in Europe was open to him, he replied very simply that the black man had been exploited by the white long enough and that it was time to try to even the scales. Now that the white man has developed the science of medicine it is only decent that he should share it. If I believe this, he added, I should go myself and not leave the job to others.

In his books on ethics he comes to the conclusion that "reverence for life" is the supreme moral rule. In one sense this puts him in the class of Lebensphilosophen or thinkers like Nietzsche who find in the will to live the clue to what is most real and important. But for Schweitzer the will to live does not lead to the will to power. "I am life that wills to live," he says. "and as I examine this will in myself I become aware of its presence in others." For him the will to live thus becomes the will to love. In this way Schweitzer has effected a remarkable personal synthesis of the two main tendencies in German philosophy, one with its emphasis on spirit, form, and reason, the other with its stress on living instincts, and has shown also how they can be set to work for society.

In Schweitzer's life it is true not only that various interests combine to form a harmony but also that they separate again to produce a most extraordinary variety of accomplishments. Is it not fair to say that he is the most versatile genius of our time? He is a skilled concert organist, whose records are well known in this country, and an authority on organ construction. His "Life of Bach" is still definitive in its field, as is his edition of Bach's organ works. He has published books on ethics, on New Testament criticism (where his ideas still have to be reckoned with by all writers on Jesus' apocalyptic teaching), and on the history of religions with special reference to India. He has not only taken an M.D. degree and become a practicing medical missionary, but has set up a research center in Africa where his associates have isolated the germ of one of the dreaded tropical diseases.

During the First World War Schweitzer was interned in Africa and his hospital practically fell to pieces. After the war he toured Europe, giving lectures and recitals which brought enough money to start anew and on a sounder basis. In a day of complete political anarchy he gives us a picture of the kind of international unity that the spirit of love can bring about when it works with devotion and intelligence. A German Alsatian in a French Protestant mission in equatorial Africa, he is supported by money raised in England, Sweden, Norway, Denmark, Switzerland, Spain, Canada, and the United States. Is he not a prophet and teacher with a message for us as truly as for the Africans to whom he ministers? *Albert Schweitzer: The Man and his Mind* by George Seaver (London: Charles Black, 1955).

UNITARIAN NOTE
Albert Schweitzer was an honorary member of the Unitarian Church of the Larger Fellowship.

PETE SEEGER:
FOLK SINGER AND SONGWRITER (1919-)

By Thomas Blair, Harvard College '03

A member of the Community Church of New York, Pete Seeger was born to a musicologist and a music teacher, both faculty members of the Juilliard School in New York, NY; as a *Philadelphia Inquirer* reporter later wrote, it was a family "whose chromosomes fairly burst with music." Music and activism blended naturally for Seeger, who at sixteen saw a performance that has since directed his life.

As Seeger recalled: "In 1935 I was sixteen years old, playing tenor banjo in the school jazz band. I was uninterested in the classical music which my parents taught at Juilliard. That summer I visited a square dance festival in Asheville, North Carolina, and fell in love with the old-fashioned five-string banjo, rippling out a rhythm to one fascinating song after another." Whereas most popular music seemed sappy or trivial to Seeger, these songs seemed frank, straightforward, honest. Folk music's new convert was to become its greatest proselyte.

"I liked the rhythms," Seeger said. "I liked the melodies, time tested by generations of singers. Above all, I liked the words."

Seeger returned to boarding school at Avon Old Farms in Avon, Connecticut, where he dabbled in Marxism, music, and journalism, doing well enough in his studies to matriculate at Harvard in 1936. Harvard's sociology department proved a weaker attraction than the life of a traveling musician; Seeger left college in the middle of his sophomore year, setting out to absorb American folk music straight from its roots in communities across the country. He later explained that he got too interested in extracurricular activities to remain in school, commenting that if he were at Harvard, he would study languages, anthropology, and geography.

However, like Edwin Land and Bill Gates, Seeger did quite well with just half of a Harvard College education. Swapping watercolor paintings for food and shelter, Seeger traveled all around the United States, learning "a little something from everybody" as he sought to master the five-string banjo and internalize the folk traditions he'd come to love. On the road Seeger met Woody Guthrie and Huddie Ledbetter, who both became strong influences and collaborators in Seeger's early career.

In addition to churches, migrant camps, and everything between, Seeger made his way to the Library of Congress, where he fortified his background in folk music as an assistant in the Archive of American Folk Song.

Seeger, Guthrie, and others formed Seeger's first group, the Almanac Singers, in 1940. Seeger and Guthrie traveled throughout the United States and Mexico as singer-activists, bolstering labor movements with song as they blended activism and folk music. In 1942, Seeger joined the Army, where he continued to play and sing, performing for his fellow soldiers and picking up "soldier songs" as he could.

Discharged a corporal in 1945, Seeger founded People's Songs, Inc., a musicians' union through which he hoped to bind labor movements and folk music in a relationship that would advance both. People's Songs eventually grew to 3,000 members, and Seeger remained involved in politics, campaigning for 1948 Progressive candidate Henry A. Wallace and helping to establish the musical side of labor organizing.

In 1948 Seeger co-founded The Weavers, a folksinging quartet with which he recorded such classics as "If I Had a Hammer," "Kisses Sweeter than Wine," and "On Top of Old Smoky." Seeger also toured extensively on his own, helping to establish the Newport (Rhode Island) Folk Festival and selling out such venues as Carnegie Hall.

His position in mainstream music was stifled by blacklisting, however, as controversy surrounding his ties to the Communist Party led major television networks to keep him off the air. The House Committee on Un-American Activities called Seeger to hearings in 1955; instead of citing the Fifth Amendment as grounds for silence, Seeger cited the First, a move for which he was sentenced to a year in

jail for contempt of court. Citing his uncondi-
tional willingness to share his music regardless
of supposed political alliances—Seeger even
offered to play a song for the court. Needless
to say, the committee declined. Although his
sentence for contempt was soon overturned,
Seeger remained blacklisted by many organizations—briefly including even his alma mater,
which finally invited him to Cambridge when
students protested this prohibition. Nonetheless,
he remained firm in his love of sharing music.
"I'd sing for the John Birch Society or the
American Legion, if they asked," he said. "So
far they haven't."

Seeger continued playing in spite of political controversy, recording such hits
as "Where Have All the Flowers Gone?" and "Turn, Turn, Turn." His clear and
catchy singing and his mastery of the five-string banjo—as well as steel drums
and several other instruments -- have won him tremendous popularity. As Seeger
wrote to his Harvard classmates in 1990: "Have been a traveling, performing
singer and songwriter for fifty years, in every state of the union and thirty-five
foreign countries. Fortunate to have a family that stuck by me, even when I
traveled too much, or got into political hot water." "Life has been easier on me
than any lazy person like myself has the right to expect."

The musician's work has since extended to environmentalism and folklorist
studies of America's music. Among other projects, Seeger has helped to organize
the Hudson River Sloop Restoration, Inc., for which he raised over $60,000 to
build a genuine Hudson River sloop, *Clearwater*. *Clearwater* now spearheads
"sloop festivals," at which residents of the Hudson's banks collaborate to address
pollution in the River and elsewhere. Whether in songwriting, musicology, or
activism, Seeger has enjoyed a life dedicated to music and to humanity, winning
thousands of admirers and greatly influencing folk music and activism alike. He
currently lives on the Hudson River with his wife of nearly sixty years, in a cabin
the couple and some friends constructed decades ago, enjoying his surroundings
and still performing from time to time.

ROY WOOD SELLARS:
PHILOSOPHER OF RELIGIOUS HUMANISM
(1883-1973)

By W. Preston Warren of Bucknell University

Originator of critical realism, emergent evolutionist anteceding Lloyd Morgan
and Samuel Alexander, proponent of a double knowledge and identity theory of
the brain-mind relationship, and original American writer on religious humanism
and drafter of the Humanist Manifesto, Roy Wood Sellars was born in Seaforth,

Ontario, in 1880.

Although he had friends in the village and countryside, he had no intellectual competitors. He went to the village school; and on completion of the eight grades at Pinnebog, he was sent to the Ferris Institute at Big Rapids to prepare him for the university. "There, he said, "I began to stand out and gained the friendship of both Mr. and Mrs. Ferris." W. D. Henderson, his teacher in physics and chemistry, once visited Sellars's home and saw his father's library. "Now I know," he said, "why Sellars has stood out."

A year at the Ferris Institute prepared him for the university, but he taught in a rural one-room school for a year—all eight grades—and had more pupils than usual pass the county examinations. He himself passed an examination for a first-class lifetime teaching certificate. Earning twenty-eight dollars a month, he saved most of it.

Roy entered the University of Michigan in 1899. He washed dishes for his board during his first year, and then, with his brother, cooked his own meals. He states that he was not well prepared for the university, yet his selection of courses threw him in with the class ahead of him. Still, he says, he "made a go of it," so much so indeed that on graduation his class voted him one of the two most scholarly of its members. This opinion was evidently shared by Professor Wenley of the philosophy department, who recommended him for a fellowship at the University of Wisconsin, and then invited him back to teach at Michigan while he himself was on sabbatical leave. In 1904 he was offered a teaching fellowship in philosophy at the University of Wisconsin.

In 1918 Sellars published *The Next Step in Religion*. The next step in religion was an outright humanism. According to Sellars, religious thought historically has been prescientic and hence mythopoetic. The time had arrived for a religion which comes to terms with the world disclosed through science. The universe of science shows no evidence of being deiform, but it does hold human values which should be cherished by both the individual and society; and it does present the option of living from the viewpoint of the whole and the long run, and this is what constitutes religion. Let men therefore live as citizens of a world to be made the most of.

In 1922, Sellars published his *Evolutionary Naturalism*. The major content of this book went back to his doctoral thesis. It was an epochal publication. Both Lloyd Morgan's *Emergent Evolution* and Samuel Alexander's first statement of emergent evolution were published a year later. Morgan added an appendix to his volume distinguishing his position from that of Sellars. "Mine," said the latter, "was more systematically empirical and naturalistic." There was no introduction or a mysterious nisus or or extra-natural control. Material organization was the key concept. Morgan told Sellars that to his knowledge, he (Sellars) was the first to publish on emergent evolution. Sellars retired in 1950 from his teaching

activities.

In 1928 Sellars published *Religion Coming of Age* and was soon afterwards selected to draft the *Humanist Manifesto*. Published in the *New Humanist* (1933), the *Manifesto* was signed by some thirty humanists. Sellars both preceded and followed the publication of the Manifesto with a number of brief articles in clarification of humanism as a religion. Then, in the 1940's, he was invited to contribute chapters to *Religious Liberals Reply* and *Religion in the Twentieth Century*. The outcome was two papers: "Accept the Universe as a Going Concern" (1947) and "Naturalistic Humanism" (1948). A significant addition to these writings came in the late 1960's in a chapter on "Religious Existentialism" in *Reflections on American Philosophy from Within*. Other unpublished papers have been compiled by Professor Sellars himself for a final rounding out of his thought.

Sellers' philosophy taken overall is a philosophy of the human scene in its cosmic context. He writes: "I see this little planet spinning in space and marvel at its history. This is not a story-book tale but one of struggle and tragedy and accomplishment. Stubbornness mixed with kindliness will achieve much but intelligence must be added. Out of these ingredients should come wisdom. Thus I triangulate and extrapolate. It is obvious that I am concerned with participative democracy in the masses, and with the growth of international institutions. Patriotism is not enough. There must be resolutions of conflicts. And this is made possible by some openness of mind and by some recognition that it is tactically wise to agree to disagree, and wait on time."

UNITARIAN NOTE

The liberal religious confluence of two philosophies is suggested by the conclusion of the essay by Sellars, a Unitarian, in his chapter of *The Philosophy of Alfred North Whitehead*.

"No other writer of recent times has so forced me to ask second questions as has Professor Whitehead."

ROD SERLING:
AMERICAN MASTER (1924-1975)

A long-term member of the Unitarian Universalist Community Church of Santa Monica, California—where his wife, Carolyn, is still a member—Rod Serling is celebrated online in this biography by the Public Broadcasting Service: American Masters.

Known primarily for his role as the host of television's *The Twilight Zone*, Rod Serling had one of the most exceptional and varied careers in television. As a writer, a producer, and for many years a teacher, Serling challenged the medium of television to reach for loftier artistic goals. The winner of more Emmy

Awards for dramatic writing than anyone in history, Serling expressed a deep social conscience in nearly everything he did.

Born in Syracuse, New York in 1924, Rod Serling grew up in the small upstate city of Binghamton. The son of a butcher, he joined the army after graduating from high school in 1942. His experiences of the working-class life of New York, and the horrors of World War II enlivened in him a profound concern for a moral society. After returning from the service, Serling enrolled as a physical education student at Antioch College, but before long realized that he was destined for more creative endeavors.

Changing his major to English literature and drama, Serling began to try his hand at writing. As a senior, after marrying his college sweetheart, Carolyn Kramer, he won an award for a television script he had written. Encouraged by the award, Serling started writing for radio and television. Beginning in Cincinnati, he soon found a home for his unique style of realistic psychological dramas at CBS. By the early 1950s he was writing full-time and had moved his family closer to Manhattan.

Serling had his first big break with a television drama for NBC, called *Patterns*. Dealing with the fast-paced lives and ruthless people within the business world, *Patterns* was so popular it became the first television show to ever be broadcast a second time due to popularity. Throughout the 1950s he continued to write probing investigative dramas about serious issues. He was often hounded by the conservative censors for his uncompromising attention to issues such as lynching, union organizing, and racism. Television dramas including *Requiem for a Heavyweight* and *A Town Has Turned to Dust* are still considered some of the best writing ever done for television.

The opening shot from *Night Gallery* with Serling as host. The series was Serling's follow-up to *The Twilight Zone*. Serling weekly unvelied disturbing portraiture on *Night Gallery* as preface to a diverse anthology of horror, fantasy, and science fiction.

Fed up with the difficulties of writing about serious issues on the conservative networks, Serling turned to science fiction and fantasy. Self-producing a series of vignettes that placed average people in extraordinary situations, Serling could investigate the moral and political questions of his time. He found that he could address controversial subjects if they were cloaked in a veil of fantasy, saying "I found that it was all right to have Martians saying things Democrats and Republicans could never say."

The series was called *The Twilight Zone* and was incredibly popular, winning Serling three Emmy Awards. As the host and narrator of the show, he became a household name and his voice seemed always a creepy reminder of a world beyond our control.

In June of 1975, he died of a heart attack. Today Serling's legacy continues to grow. With over 200 produced teleplays to his credit, Rod Serling was perhaps the most prolific writer in television history.

HERBERT A. SIMON: ARTIFICIAL INTELLIGENCE PIONEER (1916-2001)

This Nobel Laureate in Economics known "for his pioneering research in the decision-making process within economic organizations," was a member of the First Unitarian Church of Pittsburg, PA beginning in 1955. The following autobiography was issued by the Nobel Foundation.

I was born in Milwaukee, Wisconsin, on June 15, 1916. My father, an electrical engineer, had come to the United States in 1903 after earning his engineering diploma at the Technische Hochschule of Darmstadt, Germany. He was an inventor and designer of electrical control gear, later also a patent attorney. An active leader in professional and civic affairs, he received an honorary doctorate from Marquette University for his many activities in the community. My mother, an accomplished pianist, was a third generation American, her forebears having been '48ers who immigrated from Prague and Köln. Among my European ancestors were piano builders, goldsmiths, and vintners but to the best of my knowledge, no professionals of any kind. The Merkels in Köln were Lutherans, the Goldschmidts in Prague and the Simons in Ebersheim, Jews.

By the time I was ready to enter the University of Chicago, in 1933, I had a general sense of direction. The social sciences, I thought, needed the same kind of rigor and the same mathematical underpinnings that had made the "hard" sciences so brilliantly successful. I would prepare myself to become a mathematical social scientist. By a combination of formal training and self study, the latter continuing systematically well into the 1940s, I was able to gain a broad base of knowledge in economics and political science, together with reasonable skills in advanced mathematics, symbolic logic, and mathematical statistics. My most important mentor at Chicago was the econometrician and mathematical economist, Henry Schultz, but I studied too with Rudolf Carnap in logic, Nicholas Rashevsky in mathematical biophysics, and Harold Lasswell and Charles Merriam in political science.

In 1949, Carnegie Institute of Technology received an endowment to establish a Graduate School of Industrial Administration. I left Chicago for Pittsburgh to participate with G. L. Bach, William W. Cooper, and others in developing the new school. Our goal was to place business education on a foundation of fundamental studies in economics and behavioral science. We were fortunate to pick a time for launching this venture when the new management science techniques were just appearing on the horizon, together with the electronic computer. As one part of the effort, I engaged with Charles Holt, and later with Franco Modigliani and John Muth, in developing dynamic programming techniques-- the so-called "linear decision rules"--for aggregate inventory control and production smoothing. Holt and I derived the rules for optimal decision under certainty, then proved a certainty-equivalence theorem that permitted our technique to be applied under conditions of uncertainty. Modigliani and Muth went on to construct efficient computational algorithms. At this same time, Tinbergen and Theil were independently developing very similar techniques for national planning in the Netherlands.

Meanwhile, however, the descriptive study of organizational decision-making continued as my main occupation. Gradually, computer simulation of human cognition became my central research interest, an interest that has continued to be absorbing up to the present time.

In this sketch, I have said less about my work on decision-making than about my other research in economics because the former is discussed at greater length in my Nobel lecture. I have also left out of this account those very important parts of my life that have been occupied with my family and with non-scientific pursuits. One of my few important decisions, and the best, was to persuade Dorothea Pye to marry me on Christmas Day, 1937. We have been blessed in being able to share a wide range of our experiences, even to publishing together in two widely separate fields: public administration and cognitive psychology. We have shared also the pleasures and responsibilities of raising three children, none of whom seem imitative of their parents' professional directions, but all of whom have shaped for themselves interesting and challenging lives.

My interests in organizations and administration have extended to participation as well as observation. In addition to three stints as a university department chairman, I have had several modest public assignments. One involved playing a role, in 1948, in the creation of the Economic Cooperation Administration, the agency that administered Marshall Plan aid for the U.S. Government. Another, more frustrating, was service on the President's Science Advisory Committee during the last year of the Johnson administration and the first three years of the Nixon administration. While serving on PSAC, and during another committee assignment with the National Academy of Sciences, I have had opportunities to take part in studies of environmental protection policies. In all of this work, I have tried—I know not with what success—to apply my scientific knowledge of organizations and decision-making, and, conversely, to use these practical experiences to gain new research ideas and insights.

In the "politics" of science, which these and other activities have entailed, I have had two guiding principles—to work for the "hardening" of the social sciences so that they will be better equipped with the tools they need for their difficult research tasks; and to work for close relations between natural scientists and social scientists so that they can jointly contribute their special knowledge and skills to those many complex questions of public policy that call for both kinds of wisdom.

DOROTHY T. SPOERL:
MINISTER, EDUCATOR, EDITOR (1906-1999)

By Dorothy T. Spoerl Abridged from an interview with Margaret Gooding and Helen Zidowecki

Dorothy Mary Tilden was born on March 20, 1906 in Brooklyn, N.Y. to Joseph Mayo and Gertrude Estelle (Bennett) Tilden.

I am a native New York State Universalist. Brought up as I was, I could hardly escape a "career" either in the church or academia. From the age of ten, I lived in Galesburg, Illinois, on the campus of Lombard College. Galesburg is on both the Sante Fe and the Chicago, Burlington and Quincy railroads, both of which were then the major transcontinental trains. My father was not only the president of Lombard, but through many of the years on either the state or national Universalist boards or committees, and a "popular" speaker at many events. Anyone who was going anywhere on denominational business went through Galesburg and was apt to be invited to stop off and speak at the college chapel. Therefore, a lot of dinner talk was of denominational affairs, and I met many of the "important" people of Universalism, but also of Unitarianism, because the Western Conference, centered in Chicago, was not unknown in our academic halls. Furthermore, we children went with our folks to many affairs, conventions, and what not, and got a good "dose" of enthusiasm.

I went to work for Roger Etz in Charlestown, including some preaching, discovering some thirty years later that Charlestown was Starr King's father's church and later his (Starr King's). But my introduction to Unitarianism came in summer conferences, which included 'those dreadful Unitarians,' as our Galesburg people said. I met Curtis Reese, whom I adored with all the zeal of a high school girl and who "made a liberal out of me," as to religion. He, along with Waitstill Sharp (head or the Religious Education Department at American Unitarian Association and later with the Unitarian Service Committee) and Robert Dexter, took time to talk to an aspiring young church worker. Going into the church was inevitable.

At mid-year of that year at Boston University, we had a Ferry Beach reunion, and I met again the "young minister from Vermont." That summer I went to Ferry Beach as a celebration of having my M.A. in Religious Education and left at the end of the week engaged (on the pier at Old Orchard Beach) to the "young minister" [Howard Spoerl].

My husband, Howard, and I were at the church in Orono, Maine. Prowling in the excellent University of Maine Library, I ran into the twenty or so volumes (or was it twelve) of Frazier's *The Golden Bough* (first published in 1890) and read it through with mounting excitement. I began to devise a course on mythology for the Orono church school. I wrote it up for the Christian Leader. The editor wanted to know if I was sure that I wanted him to print it, as he was afraid that it would "close many doors in the denomination" to me and Howard. I said "yes" anyway. Sophia Fahs read it, was already of the same mind, and invited me to come and talk with her about working with her on *Beginnings of Life and Death*.

Two years as a minister's wife and we decided that Howard was more academic than ministerial, so we threw in the sponge and moved to Boston so he could get his Ph.D. in Psychology and Philosophy at Harvard (and thereafter we shifted between preaching and teaching for the balance of our lives). What you can do with and for young people in one is the same as the other, but there are different approaches and a wider area of trust sometimes from the young for teachers than for preachers.

Dorothy worked for the Benevolent Fraternity in Boston, which included Bulfinch Place Unitarian Church under Christopher Eliot, father of Frederick May Eliot, then Chester Drummond. She worked with children in the North End Union one day a week. Abigail Eliot (Frederick's sister and cousin to T. S. Eliot) also taught in the church school. She was one of the leaders in nursery school education.

So Howard could go to Harvard (we had, of course, saved nothing on our munificent $2000 salary, par for those days), I wrote to Waitstill Sharp, who was then head of Religious Education of the American Unitarian Association and asked if he could get me a full time job in the Boston area. I was sent to an interview with the Benevolent Fraternity of Unitarian Churches. This was the strangest interview of my life. It went like this, "You want to be RE Director?" Me: "Yes." He: "Where did you go to school?" Me: "Lombard and BU." He (a high official in the Boston Edison, I think it was): "I never interviewed anyone before. What else should I ask you?" Me: "Why don't you ask me if I want the job?" He: "Do you?" Me: "Yes, very much." And he hired me. When I went there, it had had three ministers in the past 150 years.

1942-1944 when the American International College got a new and liberal president, Howard and Dorothy returned to Springfield, where he remained the rest of his life. Dorothy returned as minister of Second Universalist Church and Professor of Philosophy at AIC. She attended Smith part time, then Clark full time, receiving her Ph.D. in Psychology from Clark in 1942, with major work in child development and a thesis on the impact of a bilingual childhood at college age.

Around 1946 Dorothy represented the Universalists on the Joint Curriculum Committee. Dorothy was appointed in 1954 as one of four Curriculum Editors for the Council of Liberal Churches (CLC), with Edith Fisher Hunter, Lucile Lindberg, and Robert Miller under Ernest Kuebler. The CLC included Unitarians, Universalists, American Council for Judaism, and the Ethical Society. She was a speaker at numerous institutes, such as at Ferry Beach in 1948.

1960-1964 Dorothy was curriculum editor of the Unitarian Universalist Asso-ciation. This included editing the Beacon Science Series.

I got a phone call from Ernest Kuebler. By then I had been on the curriculum committee of the Council of Liberal Churches for many years, and had been for a time one of four part time editors for the Council of Liberal Churches. He wanted to know if I would like to come to Boston to do research in religious education and be curriculum editor. I said, "yes" and went. He told me later (half in jest) that I was "the only person he could hire (it was the year of merger) because the Uni-tarians all thought I was Unitarian and the Universalists knew I had been brought up a Universalist, therefore I wasn't controversial at that point in history."

In 1987, she received UUA Distinguished Service Award. In 1994, she received the Angus MacLean Award in Religious Education.

In 1973, I was awarded the degree of Doctor of Sacred Theology from Starr King School of Ministry. In 1979, I was presented a Doctor of Divinity by Mead-ville/Lombard Theological School.

VILHJALMUR STEFANSSON: ARCTIC EXPLORER (1879-1962)

By Edric Lescouflair, Harvard College '03

Vilhjalmur Stefansson was born on November 3, 1879, in Ames, Manitoba to Johann Stefans-son and Ingibjorg Johannesdottir, who were both Icelandic immigrants in America. Christened William, he would eventually change his name to its Icelandic variation. The Stefanssons lived in a tiny log cabin about a hundred miles north of Manitoba in an area known as New Iceland because of its immigrant population. The family moved to North Dakota in 1881 following an 1880 flood in Manitoba. From the beginning, Stefansson was a rugged character who felt at home in the wild. Although he went largely without a formal primary education, he often practiced reading the Bible and local publications. His father died while he was but a youth, and he decided to ease the hardships of his mother by moving in with his sister, and creating a meager income by helping his brother herd cattle and sell horses.

Stefansson was introduced to secondary education in 1898 at the University of North Dakota's Preparatory Department, from which he was forced out in 1902 for supposedly inciting a protest within the student body. He then enrolled at the University of Iowa, from which he received his B.A. in 1903.

Before leaving North Dakota, Stefansson had met William Wallace Fenn and Samuel Eliot, both of whom had seen potential in the young man to become a Unitarian minister. They offered to fund his studies at Harvard Divinity School.

Stefansson's passion, however, lay beyond the realm of conventional studies. After aborting his theological studies upon the completion of one year, he entered the world of anthropology. In 1906, Stefansson left the divinity school to join the Anglo-American Polar Expedition, and traveled to the Arctic. Ever the adventurer, he neglected to make contact with his colleagues and spent the winter months among the native Inuit of Tuktoyyaktut, learning from the people how to hunt and fish.

The second expedition included Rudolph Anderson, a classmate of Stefansson's from the University of Iowa. This journey took the men to northern Alaska, where Stefansson continued his study of the natives. For the next two years he explored the area on his way to Victoria Island to study an isolated group of Inuit who still used primitive tools and had strong Caucasian features, and whom some believed were descended from Vikings. Surviving this trip was far from easy. He notes that just after the outset, "the group was short of three things: ammunition, which we all knew was a necessity, and tea and tobacco, which the Eskimos believed were necessities. When we reached the mouth of the Horton on our way back to camp, we divided our party in two... Our troubles began. It took us thirteen days to get to camp. We were delayed by blizzards, and found the hunting poor along the way. There was not enough food for the six of us. We ate what we could, including the tongue of a beached bowhead whale. Four years dead, the carcass would have been hidden in the snow except that foxes had been digging into it... The pieces we ate were more like rubber than flesh."

The study of this group transformed Stefansson's livelihood into more of an academic pursuit as he published his findings from this unique group of Inuit in *Scientific American* and the *Literary Digest*. The culmination of this study was the book *My Life With the Eskimo*.

Stefansson essentially wanted to emphasize the fact that the arctic was not the desolate, windswept land that it was largely believed to be. The two books that he wrote to this effect were *The Story of Five Years in Polar Regions* and *The Northward Course of Empire*.

Stefansson's accomplishments are widely recognized. He was the last explorer to discover new lands in the Arctic, and above all, he recognized the unique beauty of a culture other than his own and introduced society to the reality of the Arctic sans the myths and rumors.

On April 10, 1941 Stefansson married Evelyn Schwartz Baird. He subsequently moved from New York to Vermont, and then to Hanover, NH, where he and his wife were active in the Unitarian Fellowship and "Stef" pursued his research, writing, and public speaking at Dartmouth College. Vilhjalmur Stefansson died in Hanover, N.H. on Aug. 26, 1962.

ADLAI E. STEVENSON:
A VOICE OF CONSCIENCE (1900-1965)
The Legacy of Adlai Stevenson An Exhibition at the Princeton University Library, February 6 - April 9, 2000

Adlai Ewing Stevenson, governor of Illinois (1949-1953), Democratic candidate for President in 1952 and 1956, and United States Ambassador to the United Nations (1961-1965), was born in Los Angeles, California on February 5, 1900, the son of Lewis G. Stevenson and Helen Davis Stevenson. He grew up in Bloomington, Illinois, where his ancestors had been influential in local and national politics since the nineteenth century. Jesse Fell, his maternal great-grandfather, a prominent Republican and an early Lincoln supporter, founded *The Daily Pantograph*, a Bloomington newspaper. His paternal grandfather, Adlai E. Stevenson, served as Grover Cleveland's Vice President during his second term, was nominated for the office with William Jennings Bryan in 1900, and ran unsuccessfully for Illinois governor in 1908.

In the early 1930s, Stevenson began his involvement in government service. In July 1933, he became special attorney and assistant to Jerome Frank, general counsel of the Agricultural Adjustment Administration (AAA) in Washington, D. C. In 1934, after the repeal of Prohibition, Stevenson joined the staff of the Federal Alcohol Control Administration (FACA) as chief attorney. A subsidiary of the AAA, FACA regulated the activities of the alcohol industry. He returned to Chicago and the practice of law in 1935.

In 1945, he accepted an appointment as special assistant to the Secretary of State to work with Assistant Secretary of State Archibald MacLeish on a proposed world organization. In 1947, Louis A. Kohn, a Chicago attorney, suggested to Stevenson that he consider running for political office. Stevenson, who had toyed with the idea of entering politics for several years, entered the Illinois gubernatorial race and defeated incumbent Dwight H. Green in a landslide.

Early in 1952, while Stevenson was still governor of Illinois, President Harry S. Truman proposed that he seek the Democratic nomination for president. Despite his protestations, the delegates drafted him, and he accepted the nomination at the Democratic National Convention in Chicago with a speech that according to contemporaries, "electrified the nation

Prior to the 1960 Democratic National Convention, Stevenson announced that he was not seeking the Democratic nomination for president, but would accept another draft. Because he still hoped to be a candidate, Stevenson refused to give the nominating address for relative newcomer John F. Kennedy, a cause for future strained relations between the two politicians. Once Kennedy won the nomination, Stevenson—always an enormously popular public speaker—campaigned actively for him. Kennedy offered Stevenson the position of United States Ambassador to the United Nations. Stevenson accepted the U.N. ambassadorship.

In October 1962, Stevenson demonstrated his seasoned statesmanship during the Cuban Missile Crisis. After the United States discovered offensive nuclear weapons in Cuba, Stevenson confronted Soviet Ambassador Valerian Zorin in an emergency meeting of the Security Council, challenging him to admit that the offensive weapons had been placed in Cuba and declaring that he was prepared to wait "until Hell freezes over" for Zorin's answer.

In 1964, increasingly disillusioned by his inability to participate in the formulation of policy at the United Nations, Stevenson considered running for the U.

S. Senate from New York, and was also regarded as a possible running mate for President Lyndon B. Johnson.

Stevenson addressed the Economic and Social Council in Geneva in July 1965. During a stop in London, Stevenson died suddenly on July 14, 1965. Following memorial services in Washington, D.C; Springfield; and Bloomington, Illinois, Stevenson was interred in the family plot in Evergreen Cemetery, Bloomington, Illinois.

REMARKS OF THE PRESIDENT OF THE UNITED STATES, LYNDON BAINES JOHNSON, ON THE DEATH OF ADLAI EWING STEVENSON
The White House July 14, 1965
The President's Remarks

The flame which illuminated the dreams and expectations of an entire world is now extinguished. Adlai Stevenson of Illinois is dead.

His great hero, Abraham Lincoln, said at the beginning of his political career, "I have no other ambition so great as that of being truly esteemed of my fellow men, by rendering myself worthy of their esteem."

Like Lincoln he was a great emancipator. It was his gift to help emancipate men from narrowness of mind and the shackles which selfishness and ignorance place upon the human adventure.

Like Lincoln he will be remembered more for what he stood for than for the offices he held, more for the ideals he embodied than the positions in which he served. For history honors men more for what they were than who they were. And by this standard, Adlai Stevenson holds a permanent place on that tiny roster of those who will be remembered as long as mankind is strong enough to honor greatness.

JESSIE TAFT:
PYSCHOLOGIST, SOCIOLOGIST, EDUCATOR
(1882-1960)

By Mary Jo Deegan
Abridged from Women in Sociology *(Greenwood Press, New York, 1991).*

Jessie Taft was a brilliant symbolic interactionist who studied women, their view of the world, and the application of their values in various situations. A feminist, a scholar with limited academic ties to sociology, and a noted social worker, Taft worked in a professional world distinct from that of mainstream, academic men in sociology. Her incisive work has been ignored by sociologists.

Taft was born on June 24, 1882, when women were agitating for the right to higher education. Her parents, Amanda May Farwell and Charles Chester Taft moved from Vermont to rural Iowa where she was born and raised. Her father ran a prosperous wholesale business selling fruit, making this "old" American family, financially comfortable, but not affluent. Jessie was the eldest of three daughters, and her mother was a traditional homemaker who suffered from progressive deafness. This disability led to increasing isolation from her children. Virginia Robinson, Taft's biographer, euphemistically explained this distance between mother and daughter: "Her mother was too competent a cook herself to want the children bothering her in the kitchen."

In addition to her father, Taft was profoundly affected by two men, George H. Mead and Otto Rank. (1982), But as great as the imprint left by men, Taft's life was surrounded by women: their ideas, issues, friendships, life-styles, and institutions. Her life with Robinson, her friendship with Ethel Sturgess Dummer, her feminist epistemology, and her female clients and colleagues are all indicators of her woman-centered life.

By 1905 Taft had moved to Chicago and earned a bachelor of philosophy degree from the University of Chicago. Although Taft was enrolled as an undergraduate, all her coursework was done at the graduate level.

The summer of 1908 became a turning point in her life. She studied with W. I. Thomas, who was developing a number of radical ideas on women's dress, standards of behavior, right to vote, and occupations She also met Virginia Robinson: together they explored ideas, friendship, and professional commitments. Both women returned to their respective teaching positions at the end of the summer, but longed to do more invigorating and substantial work. When the University of Chicago offered Taft a fellowship in 1909, she eagerly accepted it.

Taft returned to Chicago and, in 1913, completed her doctorate on "The Woman Movement from the Standpoint of Social Consciousness." She wanted to become a professor, but the academic barriers to women were nearly insurmountable. Her first jobs, were located in an Eastern network of female social workers with different training, ideals, goals, and practices.

Her first position after graduation was as assistant superintendent of the New York State Reformatory for Women.

Women's extreme difficulty in finding academic employment in sociology in this era is reflected in Taft's life.

Despite her erratic employment in a field for which she was untrained, Taft soon became a leader in social work, first in Philadelphia and then nationally. In many ways—too numerous and complex to explore here—Taft shifted her theory, practice, and network after her charismatic encounter with Otto Rank in 1926. Taft became the director of the School of Social Work at the University of Pennsylvania in 1934, and she filled this position until her retirement in 1950. Taft died rather suddenly in 1961, eleven years after her retirement.

UNITARIAN NOTE

Upon graduating from West Des Moines High School, Jessie Taft independently chose to become a Unitarian.

ROBERT ULICH:
EDUCATOR OF EDUCATORS (1890-1977)

By Heather Miller, editor and author

Robert Ulich was a professor of the history and philosophy of education at Harvard University from 1935 until 1960. During those years, he published ten books whose subjects ranged from comparative education to the history of educational thought to his own philosophy of self-transcendence outlined in his best known book, *The Human Career*.

Born in Bavaria to a family with a long tradition of religious and contemplative thinkers, Ulich entered the Humanistisches Gymnasium at the age of 9. Over the course of the following decade, he was educated in the Classics as well as English, French and Hebrew. Ulich's classical studies provided him with a long and profound sense of Western history which proved critical to his academic career.

Ulich's commitment to education expressed itself professionally in his 1917 appointment as assistant director of Leipzig Public Libraries. In 1921 Ulich became the assistant counselor in charge of adult education at the Ministry of Education of Saxony. Two years later, he was made counselor in charge of Saxon University, a position he would hold for ten years. Ulich's professional endeavors as an educational administrator were informed by his sense of history and sociology, just as these experiences enriched his later philosophical work. Between the years 1928-1933, Ulich also taught philosophy at the Dresden Institute of Technology.

In 1929 he married Elsa Brandstroem, daughter of the Swedish ambassador to Russia. As a Swedish Red Cross nurse, she had acted on behalf of German prisoners of war by visiting heartrending camp after camp all over Siberia, and thereafter became known as the Swedish Angel of Siberia.

In 1933, in response to a group firing of colleagues at the Dresden Institute of Technology who were described as "racially and politically undesirable, " Ulich resigned both his professorship there and his position with the Ministry of Education of Saxony. Ulich was offered a one year position as lecturer in comparative education at the Harvard Graduate School of Education. After one year, Ulich was appointed Professor of the History and Philosophy of Education and was soon naturalized as a U.S. citizen.

There is little question that the tragic rise of the Nazi party in Germany, whose ultimate aims Ulich foresaw with uncommon clarity, shaped his approach to educational philosophy. Ulich wrote, "Nothing is more dangerous to mankind than the divine gift of faith uncontrolled by the equally divine gift of reason."

Just as he argued for an overarching vision for education in the U.S., Ulich argued it is the school's responsibility to aid an individual in discovering a purpose in life—without which maturity is impossible. "If our schools fail to help a person discover his purpose," Ulich cautioned, "they fail in almost everything that really matters."

Education, wrote Ulich, was a long enduring process of cultural self-evolution in which we must discover ourselves as part of a reality that is creative and whose power compels a cosmic reverence. His thinking reflected a secular religiousness. As Ulich explained, "The most radical and comprehensive thinking leads a person beyond the boundaries of the merely empirical and rational into the sphere of the mysterious."

Ulich's religiousness was a spirituality and a belief in belonging to a cosmic totality and an aversion to every dogmatism. This belief may have been nourished by his friendship with Paul Tillich, whom he first met at the Dresden Institute of Technology and knew later when both men were at Harvard University. His philosophy of self-transcendence conformed with the Unitarian faith to which he and one of his favorite educational philosophers, Thomas Jefferson, belonged.

Arts education, suggested Ulich, both in practice and in appreciation, was one of the best means of achieving self-transcendence. Indeed Ulich himself, throughout his busy academic career, found time to become a poet. He published three books of poetry over the course of his lifetime.

As a scholar of comparative education, Ulich analyzed the American school system. In his 1951 book, *Crisis and Hope in American Education*, published by the Beacon Press of the American Unitarian Association, Ulich outlined the weaknesses of the current system, mentioning as key factors in its failure "the lack of a coherent curriculum in schools and undergraduate studies."

In 1954, Ulich's prolific contributions to the fields of the history of education, philosophy of education, and comparative education were recognized with his appointment to the first James Bryant Conant Professorship at Harvard University. He retired from teaching in 1960 and returned to Germany in 1970.

CAROLINE VEATCH: PHILANTHROPIST (1870-1953)

Caroline Veatch left a Unitarian legacy of greatness, a rare resource for the advancement of Unitarian Universalist faith in action: the Veatch Program of the Unitarian Universalist Congregation of Shelter Rock in Manhasset, NY. That

Long Island congregation grants several million dollars every year not only to strengthen activities of the Unitarian Universalist Association of Congregations, but also to foster worldwide aid by means of the Unitarian Universalist Service Committee, and to provide grants to both UU and non-UU organizations. They provide:

1. *Grants to strengthen UU institutions and community life.*
2. *Grants to projects that increase UU involvement in social responsibility.*
3. *Grants to strengthen Unitarian/Universalist or indigenous religions institutions*

worldwide.

4. *Grants to nonprofit organizations addressing issues of social and economic justice.*

CAROLINE VEATCH: A MINISTER'S APPRECIATION

By Gerald F. Weary

When Carrie Veatch was suffering from spinal arthritis and confined to a wheelchair, I called on her regularly from 1945 to the year of her death in 1953. It is well that people know the story of her growing interest in The North Shore Unitarian Society, including the story of Carrie's life and that of her husband, Dr. Arthur C. Veatch, the noted geologist who left a legacy of royalty rights by which the Shelter Rock Society receives a percentage of the proceeds from the production of oil and natural gas in the North German Plain. I had asked Carrie Veatch whether she should be willing to leave her royalty rights to the church upon her death, and on receiving her agreement, got her notarized signature to a legal instrument that embodied the agreement.

After I had been calling on Carrie for nearly three years, she told me she was in need of a lawyer, and she asked me whether I knew one I could recommend to her. I recommended a member of my congregation, James E. Nickerson, a trial and appellant court attorney who was a member of a prestigious Wall Street law firm. Carrie wanted a lawyer to rewrite her will and to sort out and evaluate her estate papers and those of her deceased husband. In performing these legal services for Carrie, Mr. Nickerson had many conversations with her, and so came to know her as a person.

On one of my visits in the seventh year of my calling on her, she told me royalties had begun to accumulate in Germany from the start of production of oil on a concession her husband had acquired, and if I were willing to try and get them out of Germany, and I succeeded, she would give one half of them to the church. She fulfilled her promise, and on the second remittance of royalties from Germany, she again gave one half of them to the church.

Since I knew Carrie owned the overriding royalty rights of the OEG Concession in Germany, the thought occurred to me that I should ask her whether she would be willing to continue sharing her remittances of royalties with the church while she lived, and leave her royalty

rights to the church upon her death. I called on Mr. Nickerson and asked him what he thought of my idea. He replied that I was the only person who could put the question to Mrs. Veatch. He said he knew Mrs. Veatch respected and trusted me.

I acted, and Carrie agreed. When I told Mr. Nickerson this, he at once prepared a legal instrument, a trust, that embodied Carrie's agreement, and gave it to me. I got Carrie's notarized signature to it, and then Mr. Nickerson put his notarized signature to it. As trustee, Mr. Nickerson was of course obliged to turn over the royalty rights to the church upon Mrs. Veatch's death.

Over the next twenty years, the church had been receiving millions and millions of dollars in royalties. The church had granted millions of dollars to the Unitarian Universalist Association.

Late in the summer of 1993, the Shelter Rock church in Manhasset dedicated a building on its property to Caroline E. Veatch, and asked an artist to paint a portrait of Caroline Veatch.

A UNITARIAN UNIVERSALIST ASSOCIATION CITATION
THE ASSOCIATION PRESENTS A CONGREGATION ANNUAL
AWARD
FOR DISTINGUISHED SERVICE TO THE CAUSE OF UNITARIAN
UNIVERSALISM
TO THE CONGREGATION OF THE NORTH SHORE UNITARIAN
UNIVERSALIST SOCIETY OF PLANDOME, NEW YORK
June 21, 1985

This award is presented to the Congregation of the North Shore Unitarian Universalist Society for their outstanding and unique contribution to liberal religion and specifically to the Unitarian Universalist movement.

For the past two and one-half decades, since receiving the generous bequest from Caroline E. Veatch, you have planned effectively to use that trust to advance intelligently and responsibility the values we share.

You have done this by strengthening the institutions of our denomination: the Unitarian Universalist Association, our theological schools, the Unitarian Universalist Service Committee, and untold numbers of individual congregations of our religious fellowship. Indeed, it is difficult to think of any aspect of our work that has not benefited from the benign influence of your support.

You have advanced the values of liberal religion by giving support to secular movements and organizations which stand for equality, justice and peace. Many programs working to improve the human condition and to alleviate suffering would not have seen the light of day without your tangible support.

You have done this with an impressive degree of modesty.

We, your colleagues of the Unitarian Universalist Association, salute you:
- for your example of wise philanthropy
- for your disciplined effort to aid in the search for religious truth
- for your social conscience

It is no exaggeration to state that the original bequest of Caroline E. Veatch and your subsequent contribution to our movement has been one of the major events in our history.

VON OGDEN VOGT:
EXEMPLAR OF RELIGION AND ART (1879-1964)

By John F. Hayward, Professor of Philosophy, Emeritus, Southern Illinois University

This master liturgist, who excelled at celebrating Life in the liberal tradition, was born in Altamont, Illinois. Following his years of education at Beloit College, Yale Divinity School, and Harvard Divinity School, he served as a Congregational minister from 1911 to 1925 and then became a Unitarian minister. Here Professor John F. Hayward speaks personally of the Rev. Von Ogden Vogt, his mentor in religion and the arts before Hayward began his teaching career at the University of Chicago and the University of Southern Illinois.

How did I come to know Dr. Vogt? He was minister of Chicago's First Unitarian Church from 1925 until his retirement in 1944. In 1940, the year I entered Meadville Theological School in Chicago. In my senior year (1943) I became Vogt's assistant in two capacities: I did services for the children in Hull Chapel, 9:30-10:30, and then helped Vogt do the main church service at 11:00. He had a heart weakness and his doctor had ordered him to do nothing in the Sunday service besides the pastoral prayer and the sermon. I handled the rest of the liturgy.

Vogt's liturgical style left an indelible imprint upon me. He wore a robe, processed behind the vested choir while we all sang the opening hymn, and made all his movements in that large chancel without hurry and with a kind of statuesque dignity. His voice was clearly articulated and carried to the far end of the nave without mechanical amplification, without strain, and with no lack of clarity. He preached largely extemporaneously in a firm, slow, thoughtful pace, fidgeting with his eye-glasses over the edge of the high pulpit. The eye-glass twitch always intrigued and unsettled me: would he ever drop them? He never did. He would as often address the ceiling as the people, a kind of high, lofty presentation which put him in the ranks of an earlier style of oratory. For all of his dignity and ceremonial precision, he had a few humane lapses which may have been secretly deliberate. While giving the announcements he would walk down from the chancel to floor level and, as it were, chat with the people. The announcements were always followed by a hymn which he would announce. Sometimes he would forget the hymn number and peer slowly toward the hymn board, pausing while reading the number. Also, if his wife, Ellen, felt he had left anything out of the announcements, she would call out loud and clear, "Von, don't forget, - - - etc." Thus I learned that a liberal church could copy a kind of high church dignity without being stuffy.

His greatest work was the First Unitarian Church building itself. When he first came to their ministry the church was simply that small building which we now call "Hull Chapel." The new building needing to be built would be an addition to Hull Chapel. As one who had traveled widely in Europe, he had a special love for the majesty of Gothic architecture, a love, also, for reasons other than gothic grandeur and solemnity. He knew that the medieval church was used for all kinds of community meetings, including commerce. It was also designed to be a microcosm of the Christian's universe, lofty as honoring God, long and narrow as expressive of each life journey, with a bright and attractive altar and reredos representative of the City of God toward which all pilgrims move. He wanted to decorate his church with symbolic cartouches of major natural and cultural activities. On the reredos back of the altar were placed symbols for life and death, stars and planets, and the range of living species. In the string course above the arches of the nave were placed a number of marble cartouches representing various human professions and trades. His idea was to use the microcosm-macrocosm stretch to establish a sacred space which is at once a refuge from the world and a replica of it, corresponding to the inward and outward facets of religious faith and action. The gothic flavor connects the people with their historic past. The symbolism and the liturgies were designed to match the ongoing developments of modern civilization. Over the entrance he had engraved the phrase: "Up from the world of the Many to the Overworld of the One." And on the exit lintel of the same doors was the answering phrase: "Back to the world of the Many to fulfill the life of the One."

Vogt's theory of worship, as expressed in his book *Modern Worship*, begins with praise. No matter what actual or threatened troubles, dangers, problems exist, one cannot pray until one acknowledges with hallelujahs the sacred gift of life itself and all that supports and goes with life. The next element is contrition: the recognition that our human efforts seldom if ever match the bounty of divine benefit. The third element is analysis and resolution of particular ways in which personal and communal life may be improved and strengthened, ending again on a note of praise. He was fond of quoting the famous passage in Isaiah 6 where the prophet's vision of the glory of God in the temple terrifies him because he regards himself as "a man of unclean lips" dwelling with a "people of unclean lips." The angel purges Isaiah's contrition with a coal from the altar and Isaiah is then ready for God's command to go forth on his prophetic journey. Another feature of the church of which Vogt was proud is the crypt where there is a columbarium of niches in the wall for the placement of the ashes of deceased persons with their names and identities inscribed on the little marble slabs covering each niche. He liked the idea that the church is founded not only upon the grand foundations of Western history but also on the flesh and blood labors of persons whose remains are present in its actual foundation. This is not ancestor worship, but it is ancestor respect. Finally, here is the wording of the plaque in Chicago's First Unitarian Church. I was invited to supply the words, and Denison Hull, the church's architect, designed it and had it cut into a marble slab which he mounted on the wall of the north aisle, at the middle point of the nave.

CAROLINE FARRAR WARE:
HISTORIAN AND SOCIAL ACTIVIST (1899-1990)

By Ellen Fitzpatrick, Professor of History of the University of New Hampshire
Abridged from American Quarterly, *Volume 43, Issue 2 (June1991)*

Caroline F. Ware, a professor of history at American University and a New Deal activist edited *The Cultural Approach to History*, featuring an array of distinguished historians including Merle Curti, Ray Allen Billington, Constance Green, Ralph Gabriel, and Ware herself.

The cultural approach Ware advocated attempted to shift the focus of historical analysis from institutions and elites to social realities among Americans often lost in the story of the nation's past. It placed heavy emphasis on social and economic context, explicitly recognizing the diminishing roles of individuals in the modern industrial world. And it stressed the interdependence of social, economic, and cultural forces. Only by delineating the "total structure of society" would historians be able to assess the significance of individuals, ideas, and events.

Yet for Caroline Ware, *The Cultural Approach to History* was less an inspiration to pursue new areas of study than an affirmation of her own historical research. For nearly fifteen years, Ware had been struggling to broaden the focus of historical analysis by incorporating industrialism and the experiences of the working class. From her doctoral dissertation on "The Industrial Revolution in the New England Cotton Industry," prepared in 1925 and published as *The Early New England Cotton Manufacture*, to her innovative study of Greenwich Village published in 1935, Ware worked to advance historical understanding of the "inarticulate." The forces that shaped their lives had stood at the center of Ware's intellectual agenda long before the American Historical Association formally unveiled the "cultural approach to history" in 1939.

The Early New England Cotton Manufacture was one of the most important historical studies of industrialization written in the early twentieth century. Ware's study of Greenwich Village explored in an ethnically diverse urban community what Helen and Robert Lynd pursued in their classic portrait of Muncie, Indiana—*Middletown.*

The origins of Ware's innovative intellectual concerns reached back to the early years of her life. Born on August 14, 1899, in Brookline, Massachusetts, Caroline was the first child of Henry and Louisa Ware. The Wares were an old and distinguished New England family with enduring ties to Harvard University. Caroline's "great-great-grandfather" had served as a professor at the Harvard University Divinity School; her father was a lawyer and municipal judge who had attended Harvard College and Harvard Law School. There was a long tradition of civic activism in the family history, and it was carried on by both of Caroline's parents throughout her early life.

Although her own family was comfortably situated, Ware perceived the divisions of social class from an early age. Brookline, she recalled, was a community divided between those who resided at "the top of the hill" and those who lived at "the bottom of the hill."

The top of the hill was where the professional people lived, the business people; the bottom of the hill was where artisans and the laboring people lived. The top of the hill was Republican, Protestant, with very few exceptions; the bottom of the hill was Irish and Catholic, with very few exceptions.

Ware's history of *The Early New England Cotton Manufacture* brought together the various ideas that had informed her intellectual apprenticeship in an extraordinary way.

The comprehensive scope of *The Early New England Cotton Manufacture* alone set a high standard in American social history. Ware offered her book not simply as an economic history of a local industry but as a regional study that illuminated a process that would transform the United States. Unlike traditional institutional history, it combined analysis of large-scale economic trends with careful assessment of the human and social costs of industrial growth. The motives and methods of entrepreneurs stood side by side with the struggles and strategies of the workers they employed. This was an important departure from many other industry-centered economic histories. It also presaged the interest of future labor historians in class formation and the culture of industrial work.

Her research on *The Early New England Cotton Manufacture* earned Caroline Ware her doctoral degree and great respect in the historical profession. Her years of work on the cotton manufacture also led Ware to the most meaningful personal attachment of her life—her relationship with her future husband, Gardiner Means. Enrolled in business courses at the university, Means lived in the same apartment building as Ware, across the street from Widener Library. A pilot during World War I (he had the top bunk above Adolf Berle in basic training camp), Means had worked in a small textile business in Lowell before coming to Harvard. The couple married in 1927, but Ware decided to keep her own name. Not long after earning her doctoral degree, Ware secured an academic position at Vassar College.

In 1931 a community study of Greenwich Village was: *Greenwich Village 1920-1930: A Comment on American Civilization in the Post War Years.* In the late 1950s, Ware devoted great energy to coauthoring and editing a volume of the United Nation's *History of the Cultural and Scientific Development of Mankind.*

Honored at a Smith College conference devoted to the history of New England's working class in 1979 Caroline Ware expected to "feel old bat, a voice out of the past." Instead as she listened to the "path-breaking" scholarship being done in labor history she was struck by "how completely at home [she] felt." It is little wonder that Ware felt a sense of belonging among practitioners of the new labor and social history. The paradigm for cultural history she created anticipated many of the concerns animating contemporary historical work. Many historians, however, have tended to overlook that fact.

UNITARIAN NOTE

Caroline Farrar Ware came from a prominent Unitarian family with an activist tradition.

ALFRED NORTH WHITEHEAD: NEW WORLD PHILOSOPHER (1861-1947)

By A. H. Johnson

Alfred North Whitehead was born on February 15, 1861, at Ramsgate England. Many environmental factors contributed to his personality. He grew up in a family which was concerned with education, religion, and local administration. His father and grandfather both had directed a private school. Later his father became a clergyman of the Established Church, holding among other offices that of Honorary Canon of Canterbury. The importance of human initiative was impressed on Whitehead at an early age. Leaders in Church and State visited his home. National and local affairs were frequently discussed in his hearing. His father, as Vicar of St. Peter's Parish, exerted a very powerful influence in the surrounding districts. His home was located in an area of England studded with historic remains— Roman forts and Norman churches. Here were the beaches where the Saxons had landed. Here St. Augustine had preached his first sermon in England. Here, too, was the great cathedral of Canterbury. Thus, an awareness of the past was ever present in his youthful consciousness. From these various sources Whitehead developed, early in life, a profound and lasting interest in history, religion, education and social problems.

In 1880 Whitehead went up to Cambridge University and remained there as a student and a Fellow until 1910. During student days he was most fortunate in his academic and social contacts. He took lectures only in mathematics, but as a member of various student-faculty groups he profited from vigorous "socratic discussions" involving experts in politics, religion, philosophy, and literature. One of the more formal of these groups, called "The Apostles," met in the rooms of members "from 10 P.M. Saturday to any time next morning.... The active members were eight or ten undergraduates or young B.A.'s, but older members who had 'taken wings' often attended. In this stimulating environment Whitehead was impelled to do what he calls "a large amount of miscellaneous reading." His later references to Kant are based on work undertaken in this period when he "nearly knew by heart large parts of Kant's *Critique of Pure Reason*." (He remarks: "I was early disenchanted"). The rather humorous confessions of ignorance concerning Hegel which Whitehead was accustomed to make in his Harvard classroom, were due apparently to his first contacts with that gentleman. "I have never been able to read Hegel: I initiated my attempt by studying some remarks of his on mathematics which struck me as complete nonsense."

In 1910 Whitehead moved to London and was soon immersed in numerous academic duties at the University of London. He became aware of, and grappled with, problems relating to higher education in modern industrial civilization. As teacher (Professor at the Imperial College of Science) and as administrator (Dean of the Faculty of Science, Chairman of the Academic Council which manages the internal affairs concerned with London education) he enlarged his apprehension of the relevant data which he used so skillfully later, when he at last had an opportunity to deal with pressing philosophical problems. During the years in London he lived through World War I, saw his two sons and one daughter devote themselves to the service of their country. In 1919 he dedicated *The Principles of Natural Knowledge* to "Eric Alfred Whitehead, Royal Flying Corps: Killed in action over the Foret de Gobain, March 13, 1918.

The last stage in Whitehead's academic career began when he accepted an invitation to become Professor of Philosophy at Harvard in 1924. This appointment was transformed into that of Professor Emeritus in 1937. At Harvard Whitehead found time to publish the results of his mature philosophical speculations—thoughts based on years of serious meditation. In the course of private discussion he once remarked: "From twenty on I was interested in philosophy, religion, logic, and history. Harvard gave me a chance to express myself."

This brief outline of some of the important episodes in Whitehead's life constitutes a woefully inadequate indication of the variety and depth of experiences which provided the foundation for his outstanding achievements. Yet it should be clear that here is a man uniquely fitted to undertake the great task which he set himself in his later years—the formulation of a philosophy which would do justice to all the rich and varied data of the twentieth-century world. Here, obviously, is a mind profoundly aware of the vast range of problems which confront the modern man. It is a keen and disciplined mind, appreciative of the wisdom of the past but not a victim of blind idolatry. The past provides data for use in the present and the future, but at each moment there is creative activity guided by ideals. Above all, this great man is not an arm-chair philosopher. Like Plato's "philosopher king" he has mixed theory and practice. The result is unique efficiency in thought and action.

Whitehead's great and ever-increasing influence flows through two channels: his numerous books and articles, and his direct personal associations with colleagues and students in the university environment.

From the *Wit and Wisdom of Alfred North Whitehead*, Beacon Press 1947

UNITARIAN NOTE
Whitehead's formative series of Lowell Lectures, *Science and the Modern World* and *Religion in the Making*, were delivered at King's Chapel, the very

earliest Unitarian Church in the United States. Unitarian Philosopher Charles Hartshorne was a major interpreter of his thought.

Whitehead was a notable friend of Unitarians who said, "Unitarians come the nearest to having found a way to adapt the Christian ideas to the world we live in."

WILLIS RODNEY WHITNEY: THE "FATHER OF BASIC RESEARCH IN INDUSTRY" (1887-1958)

By Guy Suits, Director of the General Electric Research Laboratory

Willis Rodney Whitney once compared scientific research to a bridge being constructed by a builder who was fascinated by the construction of the problems involved. Basic research, he suggested, is such a bridge built wherever it strikes the builder's fancy—wherever the construction problems seem to him to be most challenging. Applied research, on the other hand, is a bridge built where people are waiting to get across the river. The challenge to the builder's ingenuity and skill, Whitney pointed out, can be as great in one case as the other.

The metaphor could be applied to Whitney's own career. There surely was never a builder more stimulated by the problems of his craft. As the "father of basic research in industry," Whitney was living proof of the fact that the essential qualities that mark the great builders are the same wherever "bridges" may happen to be built.

In one sense, the whole endeavor that we know as modern industrial research—with its heavy emphasis on basic science—is a bridge that was largely built by Whitney at a time when there was precious little demand for it. The people at the

water's edge, by and large, could hardly see the river, much less any necessity for crossing it. To Whitney, however, the need was clear.

He returned to the faculty of M.I.T. where he soon established a reputation by his work in electrochemistry, proposing the now universally accepted electrochemical theory of corrosion. At this time, working with Professor A. A. Noyes, he also contributed to the development of the modern theory of solution. Academic life, with its combination of research and teaching, was so congenial to Whitney that he once declared that he would rather teach than be president. It was to this thirty-two-year-old teacher and experimenter that the General Electric Company turned in 1900 in search of a man who could establish and direct the first laboratory in American industry to be devoted primarily to basic research.

As Whitney remarked later, his decision to make research in industry his career was prompted by "a desire to take part in more extensive research than could be accomplished by my personal efforts alone. I would have been glad to have been one of a large group of cooperators in colloid research [in academic life] but the greater rate of possible accomplishment in industry decided the case for me."

The Research Laboratory under Whitney addressed itself vigorously to the problem of producing new knowledge, whether "basic" or "applied," and it did so with notable success. During the time Whitney headed General Electric research, a great many important scientific and practical achievements were attained. Fundamental studies of vacuum phenomena and incandescent solids provided important foundation stones for improved electric lighting and for the important new field of electronics. The same basic science made possible Coolidge's development of the modern x-ray tube, and much later, Langmuir's concept of atomic hydrogen welding. Whitney himself developed high-frequency heating for therapy, embodied in the device known as the Inductotherm, and was very active in the laboratory-wide submarine detection project of the First World War that led to the famous "C"-tube detector. It can be truthfully said that the many important accomplishments of Whitney and his associates in industrial scientific research have had a profound and beneficial effect on the lives of nearly all civilized people.

Abridged from the *Biographical Memoir* of the National Academy of Sciences

UNITARIAN NOTE
Why I Believe in Advancing Unitariansim

By Willis R. Whitney

The religious seeker is for human welfare. The scientific spirit is the organized search for truth. Scientists from Newton to Galileo on have been subjected to all kinds of criticism by authoritarian religion. The dogmatic barriers to church affiliation that have kept innumerable men of science out of the churches are not found in the five bases of Unitarian Advance.

The free church is a plausible instrument of moral progress worthy of the support of scientists. It allows for growth and change; scientists are changing all the time. I'm for experiment. An experiment is a thing you do when you don't know the answer.

Such work as the Unitarian Service Committee is doing has got to be done in order for us to reach the One World we want. It paves the way for good will! The liberal church can further the one great problem that we all face, that of establishing international peace. It will come slowly and by experimentation. How are we going to bring about international peace with people behaving the way we do? It must come about by thought that is based on human equality and that is international in scope. It will require education. The adults in the churches will cause trouble; adults are conservative. Religious training is another word for good will on a universal scale. There is no more important work than this. Experimental and co-operative good will, active in the promotion of world peace, is the principal thing now.

From *The Christian Register,* May 1946

HENRY NELSON WIEMAN: PHILOSOPHER OF NATURAL RELIGION (1884-1975)

By Ralph Burhoe Founding Editor of Zygon, The Journal of Religion and Science
From the Unitarian Universalist Directory, Boston, 1976

Born in Rich Hill, Missouri, on 19 August 1884, Wieman has often been cited, along with the Jesuit paleontologist, P. Teilllard de Chardin, and the mathematician-philosopher Alfred North Whitehead, as one of the three great pioneers during the first half of the twentieth century who began to forge an interpretation of Western religion that would constructively relate it to contemporary scientific views of the nature of things. All three wrote some of their most creative ideas in the twenties and thirties. Wieman was greatly influenced by Whitehead and also by John Dewey, who were a generation older. But, in his 1917 Ph.D. thesis at Harvard, Wieman was also wrestling with how to interpret human values in the light of contemporary descriptions of man by such scientists as psychologist Edward L. Thorndike and biologist C. J. Herrick. Wieman's pioneer book was *Religious Experience and Scientific Method* (Macmillan, 1926), where he firmly held that man's assertions about religious or God questions must and can be as objectively grounded as are scientific assertions in general. In the Preface he wrote: "The chief purpose of this book is to show that religious experience is experience of an object, however undefined, which is as truly external to the individual as is any tree or stone he may experience." Wieman tenaciously continued to work out this rationale for religion into his 91st year.

Mrs. Wieman told me that two days before his death he was at a meeting presenting his views and responding to critical questions with his usual carefully reasoned enthusiasm. In his Preface to a 1971 reprinting of his first book he wrote: "This book was my first attempt to solve the problem which has engaged the last forty-five years of my life . . .: How can we interpret what operates in human existence to create, sustain, save and transform toward the greatest good, so that scientific research and scientific technology can be applied to searching out and providing the conditions—physical, biological, psychological and social—which must be present for its most effective operation? This operative presence in human existence can be called God ...."

Wieman was professor of philosophy at Occidental College from 1917 to 1927; he became professor of philosophy of religion at the University of Chicago Divinity School in 1927, during the heyday of that school's modernist prominence, and served until 1947, and he was professor of philosophy at the University of Southern Illinois from 1956 to 1966. He was ordained to the Presbyterian ministry in 1912, and while teaching at the University of Oregon in 1949 was asked by a Unitarian clergyman who had been his student why was he not a Unitarian, whereupon Wieman became a member of the church in Eugene. He was fellowshiped as a Unitarian minister in 1950 and was active in the

Unitarian fellowship at Carbondale, Illinois, during his residence there from l956 to 1966. He was the author of many books and journal articles on various aspects of his lifetime efforts to interpret the reality of the "Source of Human Good" in the light of modern knowledge. He was a visiting professor at Meadville/Lombard Theological School in 1967 and the Starr King School for the Ministry in 1968. He was one of the developers of *Zygon, Journal of Religion and Science*, which grew out of the Isles of Shoals conferences and began publication with the support of Meadville/ Lombard Theological School in 1966.

EARL MORSE WILBUR:
HISTORIAN OF UNITARIANISM (1886-1956)

By Henry Wilder Foote, author of Three Centuries of American Hymnody
From the Unitarian Yearbook 1957-58

Earl Morse Wilbur was born in Jericho, Vermont, on April 26, 1866, and he died in Berkeley, California, on January 8, 1956. His father was a lawyer who came from hardy Vermont pioneering stock and Earl was reared in the austere life of the

place and period. His intellectual promise developed early and opened his way to the University of Vermont, from which he graduated in 1886, the youngest member of his class. The summer of that year, while taking further studies with a view to teaching, he met W. W. Fenn, then a student in the Harvard Divinity School who became his life-long friend. It was on Fenn's advice that, after a year of school teaching, he entered the Divinity School, from which he graduated in 1890 with the degrees of A..M. and S.T.B.

His family connection had been with the

orthodox Congregational church in Jericho, and he had intended to enter the orthodox ministry until he discovered that he had reached theological beliefs unacceptable to that fellowship. So after graduation he accepted an invitation to become an assistant to Rev. Thomas L. Eliot of the Unitarian Church in Portland, Oregon. In 1892 he was ordained, and later succeeded Dr. Eliot as minister of the church. In 1898 he married Dr. Eliot's daughter Dorothea, and, after a year of study in Europe, moved to Meadville, Pennsylvania, to become minister of the Independent Congregational Church of that city where he also did some teaching in the Meadville Theological School.

In 1904 funds were donated to establish the Pacific Unitarian School for the Ministry, and Wilbur was asked to become its Dean and to plan its development. He served the School in this capacity (with the title of President after 1911) until 1931. The task proved to be difficult and arduous, but with self-sacrificing devotion he succeeded in creating a small but efficient seminary primarily intended to serve Unitarian churches on the Pacific Coast.

Soon after the School was opened he gave a course of lectures on the rise and evolution of Unitarian doctrines. He soon discovered the lack of any adequate historical research in this field, and thus was led into the studies which have given him his great reputation as the foremost authority in the development of liberal religion. He saw the rise of Unitarianism in England and America as only the later aspects of a much earlier widespread movement in Hungary, Poland and other countries on the Continent of Europe, and he proceeded to equip himself to investigate that largely unexplored field. The long-forgotten and fragmentary records were buried in remote and seldom visited libraries and called for a working knowledge of nine different languages, ancient and modern. Fortunately, after his resignation as President of the Pacific Unitarian School for the Ministry (now called the Starr King School for the Ministry), he was enabled by a grant from the Guggenheim Foundation, followed by another from the Hibbert Trustees in England, to spend three years (1931-1934) in Europe, searching every locality where evidence could be found and gathering a great collection of books and copies of manuscript documents, most of them hitherto quite unknown to, or unobtainable by scholars in the Western world.

At any time this would have been a notable contribution to historical research but its importance was greatly enhanced when, during and after World War II, many of the libraries which he had explored in Poland and Hungary were destroyed or their contents scattered, and the information which he had gathered would, but for him, have been forever lost. These records, many of them unique, are now in the library of the Starr King School, which has the world's richest collection of Unitariana.

In 1925, Dr. Wilbur published his first book on the subject, *Our Unitarian Heritage*, a preliminary study, which was followed in 1945 by the first volume of his far more comprehensive *History of Unitarianism: Socinianism and its Antecedents*; the second volume, *History of Unitarianism: in Transylvania, England, and America* (down to 1900), appearing in 1952. These massive books tell the story in clear and lucid English with the authority of a great scholar and have lasting value, for no future writer will have access to all the resources of which Dr. Wilbur was able to avail himself before World War II. Their reliability is underwritten by his Bibliography, published in Rome (Italy) in 1950, which runs to more than 60 pages and is a monument of scholarly completeness and accuracy. Few scholars have been able to produce works so likely to be accepted as the final authority on the subjects with which they deal.

Earl Wilbur's ability was recognized by his alma mater, the University of Vermont, as early as 1910, when it conferred on him the honorary degree of Doctor of Divinity, and the Starr King School gave him an honorary S.T.D. near the end of his career. But though recognition of his outstanding scholarship was widespread, he remained the most modest and unassuming of men, pleasing in manner, gentle and lovable, though firm in his convictions. From his youth he was a lover of the mountains, a mountain-climber and camper until late middle age. He made frequent trips to the Atlantic seaboard and generally contrived to revisit Jericho. His last visit was that of April, 1955, when, on the 89th anniversary of his birth, he read a delightful paper of personal reminiscence at the Visitation Day meeting of the Alumni of the Harvard Divinity School, who turned their dinner into a birthday party in his honor. His death in his 90th year leaves all who knew him with heartfelt gratitude for a character so honorable and a life so rich in fruition.

SAMUEL WILLISTON: DEAN OF AMERICA'S LEGAL PROFESSION (1861-1963)

This first recipient of the American Bar Association's gold medal for "conspicuous service to American Jurisprudence" was cited for his "monumental work in restating the law of contracts."

In 1953 a Jubilee gathering of Williston's former Harvard Law School students declared, "You, one of the Olympians, have contributed more than anyone that our generation knows to a great fountain of learning. Your sucess as a teacher has been returned in our universal love for you."

When, early in his career, Professor Williston was incapacitated by mental illness for several years and received salary while on leave, he not only expressed his profound thanks, but later contributed to the university an amount greater than his unearned salary.

He was an innovator throughout his subject, but by steps, and in response to an intellectual detachment which stifled overwhelming loyalties or the afflatus of revelation. Such men certainly never figure among the Luthers of this world, and no doubt the world owes much to its Luthers; abuses get deeply rooted and entwine so much that to tear them out will fetch along much that is good. The eruptive energy necessary can apparently be nurtured only upon burning concepts, arrived at intuitively, coming with the impact of absolute certainty. But whatever their services, revolutionaries obstruct the path to truth; the qualities which clear it are wholly inconsistent with theirs: skepticism, tolerance, discrimination, urbanity, some—but not too much— reserve towards change, insistence upon proportion, and, above all, humility before the vast unknown.

In the author of this book these qualities were happily fused, as he who reads it will learn. He will find the picture of one who had neither vanity, nor its counterpart, self-depreciation; neither pedantry, nor intellectual slackness; neither worship for the past, nor a heart open to each new-comer; it will not be hard to see why the serene spirit—even under its frequent load of illness—should have ended by making its possessor one of the great figures of his calling, final authority when he speaks. But one thing he will not find, for it is reserved to us who were his pupils; he will not come to know him as a teacher. For that, one should have sat under that unperturbed young man; one should have felt the impact of the apparently effortless self-possession, which, though it never imposed itself, always won. For, while this Socrates of ours never coerced our assent, like his prototype he did not let us alone until we had peered into the corners of our minds, and had in some measure discovered the litter they contained. Such self-revelation was indeed often painful—is painful still—but out of it came a gratitude which has endured; still endures after the initial difference in years has been foreshortened almost to the vanishing point. We would give up much to keep this memory; we do not shame ourselves in acknowledging that we have never shaken free from the dominance, then secured; it has been a happy subjection, dishonoring neither side. And this book in which he tells us of himself is for all of us a fortunate occasion: once more it gives us an opportunity to salute our master.

From *Life and Law* by Samuel Williston (Boston: Little, Brown, and Co., 1940).

UNITARIAN NOTE
Samuel Williston was a member of the Unitarian Church in Harvard Square, Cambridge, MA.

EDWIN H. WILSON:
UNITARIAN HUMANIST LEADER (1899-1993)
By Teresa Maciocha, editor and social activist

Edwin Henry Wilson was born on August 23, 1898, in Woodhaven, New York. He was raised in Concord, Massachusetts, where he attended the First Parish Church, a Unitarian fellowship. Wilson's father had no use for the church; it was his mother who introduced him to Unitarianism, albeit of the conservative variety.

During World War I, Wilson served in the Army Signal Corps. In 1922, he

received a bachelor's degree in business administration from Boston University. After a brief
period as a sales manager, he returned to school
in 1924 to attend the Meadville Theological
School, at that time located in Meadville, Pennsylvania, and exclusively Unitarian. (The school
moved to Chicago in 1928. Meadville had a long-
standing relationship with Universalist Lombard
College—a relationship which was formalized in
1964 when the name was altered to the current
Meadville Theological School of Lombard
College.) Wilson graduated from Meadville in
1926 with degrees as a graduate of divinity and
doctor of divinity, after which he spent a year
abroad as a Cruft Fellow, studying at the Sorbonne in Paris.

Following his ordination in 1928, Wilson became a practicing Unitarian
minister in Dayton, Ohio. Over the next sixty-five years, he had pulpits in Sche-
nectady, New York; Chicago, Illinois; Yellow Springs, Ohio; Salt Lake City, Utah;
and Cocoa Beach, Florida.

Throughout his life, Wilson maintained a dedication to learning, but it was
during the period when he was a matriculated student that he became exposed
to and convinced of the validity of the humanist outlook. His conviction that
"humanism has time, science, and human need on its side" proved to be lifelong.

Ed Wilson's humanist career began in 1929 when he became a regular contributor to *The New Humanist*, then a mimeographed newsletter published by the
Humanist Fellowship in Chicago. Primarily composed of students from a number
of universities and colleges in the Chicago area—in particular, the University of
Chicago—the fellowship was a forerunner of such humanist organizations as the
American Humanist Association. By 1930, Ed Wilson was the managing editor
of the publication (no longer mimeographed but printed) as well as one of the
co-owners.

Nineteen hundred thirty-three was a milestone year for Wilson. It marked both
the publication of "A Humanist Manifesto" in *The New Humanist* and the beginning of his fifty-two year marriage to Janet Wilson. The Wilsons had two sons,
John and Dana.

When *The New Humanist* ceased publication in 1936 due to lack of funds,
Wilson continued to spread the humanist message with his own modestly
produced Humanist Bulletin. In 1941, that was succeeded by *The Humanist*, still
in publication today. Wilson served as editor of *The Humanist* for sixteen years
(consecutively from 1941 to 1956 and then as interim editor for a period between
1963 and 1964). In addition to editing and contributing to *The Humanist*, he was
also one of the founders of the American Humanist Association, incorporated in
1941, and served as its executive director from 1949 to 1970. Subsequently, he
was a member of its board of directors and was named the association's official

historian.

In 1952, Wilson participated in the founding and naming of the International Humanist and Ethical Union (based in the Netherlands), uniting the humanist movement worldwide. He remained an active member for forty years.

Wilson's dedication to humanism earned him much respect and many honors. In 1955, he was awarded the American Humanist Association's Humanist Merit Award. In 1978, he received the Distinguished Service Award, the Unitarian Universalist Association's most prestigious honor to the cause of liberal religion. And in 1979, he was named the AHA's Humanist of the Year.

Early in his career, Dr. Wilson contributed to the body of humanist liturgy by collecting hymns and services, even writing a hymn called "Where Is Our Holy Church?" During a 1987 interview with Beverley M. Earles (currently an officer of the American Humanist Association, but at that time a doctoral student of religious studies), Earles asked Wilson how he thought he'd be remembered. Wilson laughingly replied that most likely it would be as the composer of that hymn.

Dr. Wilson was a primary author of both *Humanist Manifesto I* (originally published in 1933 as "A Humanist Manifesto") and *Humanist Manifesto II* (1973). He knew that both the consensus process of creating the first manifesto and its publication were significant events worthy of recording in this book, which he wrote over the course of many years during the 1970s and 1980s.

Wilson remained a fierce advocate of religious humanism his whole life. In the interview with Earles, she reported to Wilson that she had heard said of humanists: "They're atheists who can't quit the habit of going to church." To this somewhat lighthearted challenge, Wilson responded that he thought churchgoing "was a good habit. It organizes one's life. It's where your friends are. I find a great deal of stimulation in the institution of continuing education." In fact, Wilson always equated the humanists' quest for greater knowledge while striving toward the ideal of a "good life" as a form of continuing education.

A productive and vigorous man all his life, Ed Wilson died in Salt Lake City, Utah, on March 26, 1993, at the age of ninety-four.

From *Modern Documents: Edwin H. Wilson: Genesis of a Humanist Manifesto,* Humanist Press, American Humanist Association.

DAVID RHYS WILLIAMS:
A PROPHET IN ROCHESTER (1890-1970)

By Nancy J. Salzer
From A History of the First Congregational Society of Rochester, New York

In 1928 David Rhys Williams left the Third Unitarian Church of Chicago to answer the call of our church. His thirty-year ministry was the longest in our history. He retired in 1958, but served as Minister *Emeritus* until his death in 1970. David Williams's ministry here spanned three tumultuous decades of American history—economic depression, world war, cold war, and internal suspicions. Through it all, he was steadfast in his principles, and our church grew under his leadership.

When David Williams was called by our church, he told the trustees: "If there is anything you don't want me to talk about in the pulpit, let me know about it now, so I can decline the call of this church." He was not restricted, and he did not hesitate to put into action as our minister his deep belief that social questions were truly religious questions. He once said that a vital function of religion is to "challenge the complacency and inertia of the rest of mankind."

He had not been in Rochester long before he plunged into controversy. In 1932 he protested from his pulpit the arrest in Rochester of several women who had been distributing pacifist literature. In the same year he protested when the city council, citing depression related financial problems, cut back on appropriations for libraries, schools and museums. Our church gave planned parenthood its first home in Rochester, and David Williams was the first local clergyman to support planned parenthood publicly.

David Williams was twice the target of right-wingers seeking to brand him a Communist. In 1938 he was labeled a Communist by a small group of Rochesterians calling themselves the Rochester Social Justice Club. In this period Williams had been criticizing Father Charles Coughlin's pro-fascist, anti-Semitic radio talks. Williams answered the charge with a sermon outlining his belief in democracy, parliamentary government, minority rights, and civil liberties.

During the McCarthy period (the late 1940s and early 1950s), Williams again came under fire. Around this time, thirteen members of the church accused Williams of being "soft on Communism," and sought to oust him from our pulpit. Beyond the political issue, there were factors of just plain church politics involved. This faction attempted to sway the opinions of others in the congregation, but when the affair was brought to a vote in a congregational meeting, only the original thirteen voted against Williams. The thirteen subsequently left the church. This incident could have become very difficult, but during that period the board of trustees had excellent leadership which worked hard to maintain church unity.

In 1957 several members organized the Rochester Memorial Society, advocating simple, dignified memorial services rather than the traditional elaborate and ostentatious funeral practices. The Society has grown to a membership of over a thousand families, now a majority from outside our congregation.

David Williams retired on November 2, 1958. On March 28,1970 Minister *Emeritus* David Rhys Williams died at the age of eighty.

GEORGE HUNTSTON WILLIAMS: HISTORIAN OF THE CHRISTIAN CHURCH (1914-2000)

By Forrest Church Senior Minister, Unitarian Church of All Souls in New York City

George Huntston Williams spent his early years in the rural village of Huntsburg, Ohio. This accounts for his coinage of the middle name, "Huntston," and with this, a lifetime of frustration at the many of us who persisted in spelling it incorrectly. Highly sensitive as a child (a sensitivity that continued throughout his life), George could not abide the teasing his given middle name, Pease, prompted, so he changed it to reflect the town of his youth. His maternal grandparents, with whom he lived for a time, each embodied an aspect of his character and later interests. George W. Pease was active in all civic aspects of the community, from the Congregational Church to the local academy. A leading citizen, revered by all, his personal struggle with perfection nonetheless forbade him to receive communion to the very end of his days. In sharp contrast, George's grandmother was of a mystical nature, in James Luther Adams's words, "prone to absorption in an ecstasy of peace, particularly during the celebration of the Lord's Supper." By his own admission, George's temperament, together with his lifelong fascination for atonement and the sacraments were rooted in Huntsburg.

George's parents cast an even brighter light and longer shadow over his life and career. His mother, Lucy, was a gentle, sensitive soul, ecumenical by nature, universalist in spirit, her lifelong dedication to social justice powered by compassion. Many of these same characteristics, together with loving patience, effuse the nature of George's wife, Marjorie. His father, David Rhys Williams, was a powerhouse of a man. A dedicated pacifist, socialist and champion of women's rights, David was among the most outspoken Unitarian ministers of his day. Severe by nature, powered more by anger and a sense of justice than by compassion, David would not permit his children to speak above a whisper at home on Saturdays when he was writing his sermon. During his later youth in Rochester, New York, where his father served as minister of the First Unitarian Church, George would sneak downstairs after bedtime and listen through the balustrade to Eugene V. Debs or W. E. B. Dubois engage in passionate late night discussion. The night after Sacco and Vanzetti were executed, George vividly remembered his father's shaking his fists at the heavens and shouting, "God damn!"

His family connections with both Congregationalism and Unitarianism, further instructed by his mother's and grandmother's ecumenical faith, led George toward ordination in both communions. His college years at St. Lawrence, a Universalist school, initiated an abiding interest in Universalist history as well. During his seminary year abroad from Meadville, he studied the trinity at L'Institute Catholique in Paris. He began his teaching career at Starr King School for the Ministry in Berkeley, California and then, in 1949, was named a professor and then Acting Dean of the Unitarian founded Harvard Divinity School. His greatest legacy was the ecumenical expansion of a tiny, and relatively small faculty. For most of his teaching career, he served as Hollis Professor of Divinity at Harvard, the oldest established Harvard University chair (and the only professor who was permitted to graze his cow on the Common).

One of George Williams's mentors, John T. McNeill, told him that he should speak from his own community of faith, ever aware of its needs. That he did so, and eloquently, is evident from hundreds of articles and sermons published over the years, and most notably from several of his major works: *The Radical Reformation* (1962); *American Universalism* (1971); and *The Polish Brethren* (1978). Yet, Professor Williams was anything but sectarian in his faith or predictable in his beliefs or interests. As a Trinitarian Unitarian and sacramental protestant, George displayed a capacious mind, investing his studies of church history with remarkable empathy and critical balance. Both are on full display in dozens of his works, most notably in *Anselm: Communion and Atonement* (1960).

If, from the time of his Meadville Theological School B.D. thesis on Paul Tillich (1940), George Williams subscribed fully to Tillich's "Protestant Principle" (that the first word of religion should be spoken against religion), throughout his life he remained faithful to the Constantinian church. Even his best-known book, *The Radical Reformation* (1962), displays the creative tension between his dedication to individual conscience, especially with respect to the separation of church and state, and his devotion to the church universal, in its responsibility for the character of society as a whole. This devotion was never more evident than during his participation as an observer at the Vatican II Council in 1962 (eloquently expressed in the sermon he delivered in the Cathedral Church of St. John in Boston following Pope John XXIIIs death in 1963. Williams had the unique distinction of having been the only person in the United States to predict the election of Pope John Paul II. He wrote a book on *The Mind of John Paul II* and was knighted by the pope in a special celebration in St. Paul Church, Cambridge, Massachusetts.

Engaging the issues of his own time, George Huntston Williams sounded the same themes he pondered in his historical studies. His statement on McCarthyism, "The Reluctance to Inform" (1957), helped shape the national debate. In 1967, he joined William Sloane Coffin, to perform the "sacrament" of burning Vietnam era draft cards at Arlington Street Church in Boston. And, yet, he was as avid and public in promoting a "pro-life" position on abortion, promoting his views throughout the early 70s in several articles and opinion pieces.

Another academic and existential concern throughout George Williams's life finds its fullest expression in *Wilderness and Paradise in Christian Thought* (1962). Typical of his typological approach to church history, here he juxtaposes the theology of nature with the idea of the university. Expressed here as vividly as anywhere in his writings, George passion for the environment and his devotion to the academy lead to a conceptual breakthrough in which each (as with body and mind) is completed by a devout attention to the other. As in the case of his typologies of sacrament and prophecy and of conscience and community, Williams's historical embrace of Mother Nature and academic nurture encompasses polar opposites, his expansive sympathies illuminating both.

A like array of antinomies informed George Williams's life. Sensitive to others yet hypersensitive himself; most fully at home in the academy and, conversely, in nature; a loner with an abiding devotion to the idea of community; a Protestant who looked to Rome; a prophet who found peace in the sacraments: George Huntston Williams embodied in his own life much of what fascinated him in history. As difficult as it was rewarding, life taught him the taste of both triumph and despair. More than anything else, this depth of experience enabled him to bring church history and the passions of those who people it alive to others. His concentrated labor during the final decade of his life was his writing of a large manuscript being edited for publication: *Divinings*, a history of religion at Harvard University.

WILLIAM CARLOS WILLIAMS: PHYSICIAN AND POET (1883-1963)

By Patrick Murfin President of the Congregational Unitarian Church, Woodstock, Illinois

William Carlos Williams was born in a comfortably middle class home in Rutherford, New Jersey, in 1883. He would spend virtually his whole life in and around the environs of his hometown. His father was American, but his mother was born of a "respectable" Puerto Rican family, meaning they had almost pure Spanish bloodlines. An outstanding pupil at New York's Horace Mann High School, he excelled at writing poetry and in biology. He determined to pursue a dual career in medicine and literature. After graduating with a degree in medicine from the University of Pennsylvania and an internship in obstetrics and gynecology, Williams hung up his shingle and practiced medicine in his hometown and in the nearby industrial town of Paterson.

Many of his patients were Paterson mill girls, others were local prostitutes and desperate young mothers with too many babies. Yet he also saw the proper middle-class ladies of his hometown. The experience of his practice influenced his poetry and other literary endeavors.

While at the University of Pennsylvania, he fell in with the brilliant Ezra

Pound. Pound profoundly influenced the poetry Williams continued to write. He joined the Imagist movement, writing unsentimental poetry in evocative language and experimental forms. Pound arranged for the publication of Williams's second volume of poetry, *The Tempers* in London in 1913. Back in Rutherford, Williams continued to produce poetry, essays, plays, and fiction. He slowly built a reputation second only to Pound as an Imagist. This position would be challenged by the emergence of T. S. Eliot in the 1920s. By that time Williams was drifting away from the Imagists, considering them, especially Eliot, too bound to European culture, too elitist, and too obscure. He continued to experiment adventurously with poetic form and typography. This experimentation was evident in his *Complete Poems*, published in 1938 and his *Collected Poems* published in 1950. He began work on *Paterson*, his great extended poem of America in the Depression in the late 1930s. It was published over a period of years from 1946 to 1958. He also produced three novels during this period.

Williams's health began to fail after a heart attack in 1949 and a series of small strokes. He had to retire from the practice of medicine but continued to write. He received the National Book Award for Poetry in 1950. He published his memoirs the following year and continued to write bold, experimental poetry in addition to his *Paterson* books. His latter notable collections include *Pictures from Brueghel and Other Poems* (1962) and the posthumous *Imaginations* (1970).

He lived to see his reputation as a poet soar with the open admiration of a new generation of writers, notably Allen Ginsberg and the other Beats. Williams died in Rutherford in 1963.

UNITARIAN NOTE

William Carlos Williams was a lifelong member of the Unitarian Church of Rutherford, New Jersey, a community founded with the help of his parents.

CONRAD WRIGHT: HISTORIAN OF AMERICAN UNITARIANISM (1917-)

By Conrad Edick Wright, Ford Editor of Publications and Director of the Center for the Study of New England, Massachusetts Historical Society

A SON'S APPRECIATION

I'd like to share a small secret with you. But don't become too excited at the prospect of the revelation of a transgression hidden deep within some Wright family closet. It has to do with the professional discipline that my father and I both pursue.

The history Ph.D. is, of course, a research degree. It requires course work and a dissertation, and it prepares the recipient for a career as a scholar. But even most history Ph.D.s are unaware that the majority of people in the field never publish and that most of those who do write publish very little, often little more than an article or two or an occasional book review. Teaching, advising, and administration occupy most of the daily working hours for the great majority of college faculty members, who can never quite find the time or the energy to finish long delayed projects. Figures circulated a few years ago—which were so shocking that to this day I have trouble believing them—indicated that something like 5 percent of history Ph.D.s had published anything and roughly half that number had published more than infrequently.

What does this small secret have to do with my father's life? It is simply this: historians who are active scholars are rare enough; those whose scholarship is enduring, whose scholarship makes a difference, are even more uncommon. My father's writings have endured—have made a difference—in how scholars and Unitarian Universalists alike look at the Unitarian Universalist denomination.

There are two ways to make an enduring difference as a scholar. One is to write about an ignored subject and show us why we should care about it. In recent years, for example, talented historians have shown us why we should be interested in the stories of such groups as women, African Americans, Native Americans, and gays. From a professional standpoint, the discovery of these groups — how could we ever have ignored their existence? — has resulted in several growth industries, as energetic and committed investigators have explored previously forgotten byways. The other way to make a difference is to show us a new way to look at something that we think we already understand. Here is where we will find my father's major contribution both to historical scholarship and to his denomination.

In this series, we are asked to look at accomplished Unitarians in America between 1936 and 1961, but for the historiography of my father the key dates actually lie much closer together—1955 and 1961. *The Beginnings of Unitarianism in America* appeared in 1955, and *Three Prophets of Religious Liberalism* came out in 1961. These books, together with some titles by other authors that appeared at about the same time (notably *The Transcendentalist Ministers*, by William R. Hutchison, a long-time fellow member of the Divinity School's faculty) proposed two vital changes in our understanding of the history of American Unitarianism.

Ask a Unitarian parish minister in 1955 to discuss the origins of American Unitarianism, and if he were relatively young the odds are that he (it was almost always a he) would think back to seminary, where he had read Earl Morse Wilbur's *History of Unitarianism*. Wilbur's *History*, published in two volumes in 1945 and 1952, drew on themes he had first laid out in 1925 in *Our Unitarian Heritage*. Wilbur's writings, which drew on quite substantial research in primary sources, primarily traced the history of Unitarian beliefs in Europe, especially Eastern Europe.

When my father's *Beginnings of Unitarianism* came out in 1955, perhaps its central objective, at least for Unitarian readers, was to protect misguided enthu-

siasts from drawing the mistaken inference from Wilbur that to find our roots we had to look somewhere in Eastern Europe. A student of Perry Miller, the great Harvard scholar of American Puritanism, my father recognized the indigenous New England origins of American Unitarianism. These roots lay in the answer that provincial New Englanders offered to a frequently asked question. "What must I do to be saved?" The customary Calvinist answer to this question, informed by the doctrine of predestination, is "nothing." That is to say, your fate is in God's hands, and nothing you can do can affect the outcome.

The founders of churches such as the First Parish in Cambridge, Massachusetts, adhered to traditional Calvinist answers to questions about salvation, but even in the seventeenth century many New Englanders were uncomfortable at the stern and unyielding nature of the doctrines they espoused. The principal accomplishment of *The Beginning of Unitarianism* in America was to trace the indigenous origins of our movement, which the author found in the reaction of many New Englanders against Calvinist predestinarianism. The key figures in this story, including such Massachusetts ministers as Charles Chauncy, Ebenezer Gay, and Jonathan Mayhew—denominated then and since by the term Arminian—proposed that while the final decision on salvation was God's alone, men and women prepared themselves for a happy outcome by leading virtuous lives.

In this telling, American Unitarianism grew out of Puritan roots, not from an Eastern European origin. In scholarly circles, it is the account offered in *The Beginnings of Unitarianism in America* that has won the field of controversy. Outside the pages of the writings of some of our ministers, it is difficult to find anyone today who makes a serious attempt to connect Wilbur's European research to the origins of the American Unitarian movement.

The second important reinterpretation of Unitarian history in which my father played a central role by 1961 involved the relationship beginning in the 1830s between mainstream Unitarians and adherents to the Transcendentalist movement. Traditional wisdom emphasized the tensions between the two groups, the divisions that sundered them, but in their writings my father and William Hutchison both taught that mainstream and Transcendentalist doctrines nourished each other. In Hutchison's important 1959 book, *The Transcendentalist Ministers*, he went on to show that most prominent Transcendentalists also maintained a formal institutional relationship to Unitarianism. To be sure, Ralph Waldo Emerson, the best known of the Transcendentalists, left his pulpit in favor of an independent career as a lecturer, but his case was out of the ordinary. For the most part, leading Transcendentalists remained Unitarian.

The most important consequence of revisionist writings on the Transcendentalists was to recast them not as rebels against Unitarianism but as the reform wing of the denomination. All of a sudden, important links between the two groups became obvious. Perhaps the most important of these connections involved the doctrine of self-culture. In the tradition of the Arminians, who emphasized the individual's role in preparing himself or herself for salvation, such nineteenth-century writers as Emerson and William Ellery Channing made self-improvement the cardinal obligation of the virtuous man or woman.

Neither of the scholarly developments I have just described was solely my father's work. Like every historian, he built on the research of others, and he also depended on colleagues and students to engage with him in a cooperative effort to recast our understanding of the Unitarian past. Nevertheless, it is safe to say that in fundamental ways our knowledge of Unitarian history was shaped by his research and writing.

FRANK LLOYD WRIGHT: UNITARIAN ARCHITECT (1867- 1959)

By Max D. Gaebler Minister Emeritus, The Unitarian Society of Madison, Wisconsin
From an address delivered before the Friends of the Meeting House October 27, 1992

When I arrived in August of 1952 to take up my ministry in Madison, the congregation of the First Unitarian Society was still settling into its striking new Meeting House designed by its illustrious member Frank Lloyd Wright. The congregation had occupied the still unfinished Meeting House much earlier, having held the first service there on February 4, 1951. On that Sunday morning a special

dedicatory address was delivered by another distinguished member of the Society, the philosopher Max Otto, who chose as his title "To Own or Be Owned?" His words were a challenge to the congregation to be worthy of its new Meeting House, to match the imaginativeness and beauty of the building with a quality of congregational life that would reflect intellectual boldness and ethical sensitivity.

During that first year I met Mr. Wright on several occasions. While I have no claims to be an expert on Mr. Wright, surely not on his architecture, I did enjoy the great privilege of knowing him and of having been his minister during the last seven years of his life. Mr. Wright was not merely a member of our Society in Madison; he was part of a family with deep roots in Unitarianism on both sides of the Atlantic. His father, William Wright, was secretary of our Madison congregation when it was organized in 1879. Mr. Wright, a widower with three young children, had been, among other things, a music teacher and a Baptist minister. He had met Frank's mother, Anna Lloyd Jones, when she was a country school teacher and he the superintendent of schools for Richland County. Frank, their first child, was born in Richland Center in 1867. Three years later, now with a year old daughter as well, they began a series of moves that culminated in Mr. Wright's acceptance of a Baptist pulpit in Weymouth, Massachusetts.

When William resigned his pastorale in Weymouth after only three years, he did so as a Unitarian. William and Anna and their children returned to Wisconsin to be near the supportive family out in the valley near Spring Green. They soon settled in Madison, and it is scarcely surprising to find them among the little band who organized our congregation. Frank Lloyd Wright credits his mother with bringing the new light of transcendentalism, the work of Emerson and Parker, back with her from their years in Weymouth.

It was Uncle Jenkin and his friends whom the family back in the valley in Wisconsin listened to. Frank Lloyd Wright described listening to his uncle: "When Uncle Jenkin preached there was the genuine luxury of tears. Going gently to and fro in the rocking chairs below the pulpit as tears were shed and, unheeded, trickled down. His sermons always brought the family to emotional state—but then—so did readings from the transcendental classics or the singing of the children. Tears, too, when all rose in strength and in the dignity of their faith straightened themselves to sing—'step by step since time began to see the steady gain of man.' The faltering, the falsetto and the flat would raise that favorite hymn to the boarded ceiling and go swelling out through the open windows and doors and—to the young mind looking out toward them—seemed to reach far away and fade beyond the hills. This surrender to religious emotion was fervent and sincere!"

Although Mr. Wright did not come often to Sunday services, he stopped by unannounced to visit the building many times. Mr. Wright would come in, not on a tour of inspection but to experience the building yet again. He would sit quietly for a few moments on one of the benches, then go up to the prow and gaze out toward Lake Mendota over what was then a cornfield managed by the College of Agriculture. At such moments there could be no question of his special attachment to that place. It was in every way his church.

Mr. Wright died in 1959, and as minister of his church I was invited to officiate at his funeral. Several longtime associates carried his casket out of the house and placed it on a horse drawn wagon. Wes Peters, his son-in-law and principal assistant, and Gene Masselink, his secretary for many years, got up on the wagon and drove the horses down the hill and along the road to Unity Chapel. The rest of us, led by his wife, Olgivanna, and their daughter, Iovanna, walked behind the wagon. At the chapel a very brief and simple service ensued. The following paragraph comes from my personal tribute:

There is something very right in our gathering here in this chapel to pay tribute to Frank Lloyd Wright. His life and work spanned the globe, yet those most intimate bonds of loyalty and affection by which he was united with his native earth are poignantly focused at this place, a place as dear to him as it is filled for us with precious memories and with living hope. Here we cannot but sense something of that clean simplicity of thought and form, that unflinching honesty of word and deed, that unfailing sensitivity to the monitions of beauty which, like the tranquil loveliness of this familiar valley surrounded by the sheltering hills, provided the true setting for his life.

QUINCY WRIGHT:
AUTHOR OF *A STUDY OF WAR* (1890-1970)

By Karl Deutsch, Stansfield Professor of International Peace, Harvard University

Nothing less than this—the understanding of war and the possible ways to its abolition—is on the agenda of our time. War, to be abolished, must be understood. To be understood, it must be studied. No one man worked with more sustained care, compassion, and level-headedness on the study of war, its causes, and its possible prevention than Quincy Wright. He did so for nearly half a century, not only as a defender of man's survival, but as a scientist. He valued accuracy, facts, and truth more than any more appealing or preferred conclusions; and in his great book, *A Study of War*, he gathered, together with his collaborators, a larger body of relevant facts, insights, and far-ranging questions about war than anyone else has done.

Quincy Wright did more than pile up information about war. He developed a basic theory of war. Summarized and in drastically oversimplified form, it might be called in effect a four-factor model of the origins of war. Put most simply, his four factors are (1) technology, particularly as it applies to military matters; (2) law, particularly as it pertains to war and its initiation; (3) social organization, particularly in regard to such general purpose political units as tribes, nations, empires, and international organizations; and (4) the distribution of opinions and attitudes concerning basic values. These four factors correspond to the technological, legal, sociopolitical, and biological-psychological-cultural levels of human life, respectively. At each level, conflict is likely, and violent conflict becomes probable whenever there is an overloading or breakdown of the mechanisms of arrangements that have controlled the interplay of actions and actors at any level and that previously have preserved some nonviolent balance or equilibrium.

Violence and war, according to Quincy Wright, are probable and natural whenever adequate adjustments or controls on one or more of these levels are lacking. Peace, as he saw it, is "an equilibrium among many forces." It is unlikely to come about by itself. It must be organized in order to bring it about, to maintain it thereafter, and to restore it after it has broken down.

From *The Journal of Conflict Resolution* (Volume XIV, No. 4, 1970)

UNITARIAN NOTE

Quincy Wright, University of Chicago professor who was a member of the First Unitarian Church of Chicago, was a member of the Unitarian Commission on World Order. He was the brother of Sewall, the evolutionary theorist, and of Theodore, the aeronautical engineer.

SEWALL WRIGHT: DARWIN'S SUCCESSOR—EVOLUTIONARY THEORIST (1889-1988)

By Edric Lescouflair, Harvard College '03
From "Sewall Wright, the Scientist and the Man," *Perspectives in Biology and Medicine, 25, 2 Winter 1982*

Sewall Green Wright was born to Philip Green and Elizabeth Quincy Sewall Wright, residents of Melrose Massachusetts, on December 21, 1889. The family moved three years later after Philip accepted a teaching job at Lombard College, a Universalist college in Galesburg, Illinois. The ancestry of the Wright family could be traced through 16th century England to the 7th century reign of Charlemagne, and many of Sewall's ancestors were distinguished educated and innovative individuals. Wright would later profess a great interest in heredity; in the example of his life, he certainly manifested the genes of past success.

Wright and his brothers, Quincy and Theodore Paul, were very gifted children. Although they did not initially attend official schools, they were reading and writing at unusually early ages. Sewall entered the "publishing" arena at the age of seven with his pamphlet on various animals' physical characteristics. Also, he was then able to extract cube roots, to the disgust of the other children. The atmosphere at the school was not conducive to learning, and Wright had to avoid participation for fear of sparking the ire of the other boys with his knowledge.

From his youth, Wright was fascinated with math and mathematical models. He would often waste afternoons playing with his mother's balance in the kitchen, and she would in turn teach him arithmetical methods. The Wright parents were fond of reading to their children, and in the home a highly intellectual atmosphere was continually fostered. Wright, however, did not want to follow his father's suggestions to study poetry; he instead was enthralled by nature. Wright attended Galesburg High School, graduating in 1906 to enroll in Lombard College to concentrate on mathematics and surveying.

At the College, Sewall Wright's interest in biology was spurred by Professor Wilhelmine Entemann Key, one of the first women to earn a Ph.D from the University of Chicago. This interest led Wright to study at Cold Spring Harbor during the summers of 1911 and 1912, after which he entered the University of Illinois for graduate work in biology. After graduating with a Master's degree in 1912, he accepted an opportunity to work with Ernest William Castle of Harvard's Bussey Institution.

Wright joined the faculty of the University of Chicago to teach and research genetics. He embarked upon a distinguished career of publication at the university level, writing on genetics in populations and path analyses that could be applied to mathematical and social scientific models. Wright's achievements in these areas were groundbreaking.

Philip Wright, Sewall's father, was a polymath and was on the faculty of tiny Lombard College in Galesburg, Illinois. He taught mathematics, astronomy, surveying, economics, physical education, and English composition. He loved poetry and music and was disappointed that Sewall did not take to them. He had a printing press on which he printed his poems, as well as the College bulletins. Sewall and his brothers, Quincy and Theodore, printed the first poems of Carl Sandburg, who was a student in their father's composition class. Philip Wright later moved to Harvard and the Brookings Institution where he published a number of books on economics. One of them, *The Tariff on Animal and Vegetable Oils*, included an appendix by Sewall; Quincy went on to become a distinguished scholar in the field of international law, while Theodore was chief engineer at Curtis-Wright, a Civil Aeronautics commissioner, and acting president of Cornell University. He is said to have turned down the presidency because he didn't like raising money.

PHILOSOPHY

Very few geneticists have written seriously about philosophy. Wright is an exception. He discovered that his Chicago colleague, Charles Hartshorne, shared a similar view about the philosophy of organism, and they became lifelong friends. The philosophy is in the tradition of Leibniz. Wright's view is that there is no material basis for a mysterious "emergence" of new properties as systems become more complex. This being the case, one is forced to assume that such properties as consciousness must necessarily reside in the most elementary particles. He has developed this view in several papers; a good example is his presidential address to the American Society of Naturalists, published in 1953 under the title "Gene and Organism."

UNITARIAN NOTE

Sewall Wright was a member of the Unitarian Society of Madison, Wisconsin

THEODORE PAUL WRIGHT: AERONAUTICAL ENGINEER AND IDEALIST (1895-1970)

By Theodore Paul Wright Jr. State University of New York at Albany

Unlike his distinguished older brothers, Sewall Wright and Quincy Wright, "Ted" was a doer, not a thinker, an athlete, engineer and administrator who turned away from the academic life of his family to live in the world of business and government until he went to Cornell University as Vice President for Research in 1948. Yet he always admired the idealism of his ancestors, particularly two great-grandfathers, the noted abolitionists, Elizur Wright (1804-85) and Beriah Green (1795-1874). So there was a continual tension between the requirements of designing war planes and dealing with politicians versus the Socialist and pacifist ideals he received from his father, Professor Philip Green Wright (1860-1934). His family belonged to the Universalist church in Galesburg, Illinois; his mother's family, the Sewalls, descendants of Judge Samuel Sewall of Massachusetts (1654-1729), were Unitarians from Boston who had migrated to St. Paul, Minnesota, about 1855.

After graduating from Lombard College in Galesburg, Illinois where his father had taught (1892-1912) and fostered the budding plebian poet, Carl Sandburg, Ted went on to take another B.S. in architectural engineering from the Massachusetts Institute of Technology as his family were all living in Cambridge by then. His aunt, Bessie Wright of Medford, a teacher of Physical Education at Radcliffe College, paid his tuition. He especially admired the work of Ralph Adams Cram at M.I.T.

In 1917 after the United States entered the First World War, Ted enrolled in the U.S. Naval Reserve Flying program at M.I.T. He was given two months of instruction in aeronautical engineering by, among others, the brilliant young Edward P. Warner. Afterwards, he was assigned as a naval aircraft inspector to the Glen Curtiss plant at Garden City on Long Island. There in 1919 he was chief inspector for the Curtiss NC-4 flying boats which achieved the first crossing of the Atlantic by air. He apparently reconciled participation in the war despite his father's pacifism by believing that it was "the war to end wars". In December, 1918, he had married his college sweetheart, Margaret McCarl of Quincy, Illinois, whose father, Judge Lyman McCarl (1858-1920), a self-made lawyer, was a member of the Unitarian church. They had two sons, Douglas Lyman Wright (1920-1991), a civil engineer, and the author of this sketch.

Thus it was that in June 1940, in the wake of President Franklin D. Roosevelt's call for production of 50,000 military aircraft, Wright joined the National Defense Advisory Committee, an organization formed to coordinate the "defense" effort. The next year, he resigned from Curtiss-Wright to become assistant chief of the aircraft section in the Office of Production Management, and moved to Washington. After Pearl Harbor he served as chairman of the Joint Aircraft Committee, an Anglo-American body which scheduled delivery of all aircraft, director of the Aircraft Resources Control Office and member of the War Production Board. In all these positions, he played a key role in expanding aircraft production, especially in developing essential statistical tools that provided accurate information on industrial capacity and measured worker efficiency.

In the spring of 1951, Wright became Acting President of Cornell and indeed was offered the presidency, but turned it down because he didn't want to spend his time raising money from the rich, one of the chief duties of college presidents.

Wright retired from Cornell in 1960 and from the Aeronautical Laboratory presidency in 1966, but he continued to be active in aviation and community affairs, especially in environmental and conservation problems. He continued, for instance, to be a member of the National Advisory Committee on Aeronautics and was active in the Cornell Plantations in his retirement years. His collected technical papers were published in three volumes by the Laboratory and he wrote a final paper on the dangers of world overpopulation. Attracted by the sermons of Rev. Ralph Helverson, Ted and his wife had become active members of the Unitarian Church of Ithaca after they moved there. This was his first formal affiliation with a church since childhood.

N. C. WYETH:
ILLUSTRATOR AND PAINTER (1882-1945)

By Andrew Wyeth

Abridged from An American Vision: Three Generations of Wyeth Art *(Boston: Little Brown, 1987).*

MY FATHER

My father was a very robust, powerfully built man. Muscular. But strangely enough, his hands were very delicate. They weren't big. A lot of people like to think, since he was a great big man, that he ate enormous amounts of food. But he was a very delicate eater. He gave the impression of great power, physical power which was very obvious. One of the stories around Chadds Ford was about a milk train he would meet and how he would help the farmers lift their cans, these enormous ten-gallon cans—one in each hand—up onto the platform beside the tracks. That gives an idea of his physical strength.

But he had other sides to him also. He was a man who admired many arts—literary, dramatic, musical. From being hardly a reader at all in his youth, he had become a constant reader. He had a remarkable talent for writing. My mother's mother got him reading Thoreau. He also read Tolstoy. And he loved Robert Frost. He thought Keats was terrific. He loved Emily Dickinson. He was interested in drama. He went to see, and talked about it many, many times, *Mourning Becomes Electra*. He loved music. It was emotional. That's where we kids certainly learned about it. On Sundays after dinner we'd lie on the floor and listen to it. He loved Rembrandt. He admired George de Forest Brush and mentioned him often to me. He was a complex man in many ways.

I grew up and became mature under him. He had a marvelous way of never talking down to a young person. And I spent a lot of time with my father—much more than the rest of the children did. When I was a child I'd go out into the back room of the studio where he kept his drawings and paintings and many reproductions. Often I'd drag them out, wipe the dust off, and ask him about them. He told me so many things about these pictures that I got a pretty thorough knowledge of what he had done. I also spent hours in his studio going through his books of medieval armor, his historical books, and trying on costumes that he stored in his big chests. The costumes fascinated me. I was able to spend the time because I wasn't going to public school, I was being tutored at home. While all the rest were being shipped off to be educated, I was being educated by my father in a very direct way; I feel very lucky.

Illustration was already in my father's soul; he had his thoughts already in mind. All he really needed was the technical training. It's astounding how quickly he learned to paint under Pyle. I mean, it was a year and a half, and he just tore through the training and was off. Soon after beginning work with Pyle, my father received commissions for magazine illustrations. Within a few years he was a full-time illustrator. Some of his earliest commercial illustrations were of the West. Pa knew the Navajos; he lived with them.

Over the next fifteen years he received several important book commissions. Yet look at those books: he used a new style for almost every one. He was always groping for something new. He was experimenting in painting. But he began each book project in the same way—he read the story.

Pa's first and foremost interest was: Is it a well-written story? Is it a vital story? What he wanted to do was to bring air into those books that had been sitting in libraries for decades. People often refer to the books Pa illustrated as "children's classics," but I don't think you can call *The Last of the Mohicans* a child's book. And certainly *The Mysterious Stranger* by Mark Twain is not a child's book.

Pa was my only teacher. He taught me watercolors and oils. I remember one day when I was working in oil, doing a head of a man in strong light, and I started to get a lot of half-lights in the shadow side, reflected light. And he said, "You know, Andy, you've started out well, but you've lost your simplicity." He took his finger and he put it in some raw sienna and using his thumb just simplified that whole shadow. He made it sing. That's the painterliness that you find in pictures for *Treasure Island* and *Kidnapped* and in "Mowing." Another time I was drawing

an illustration. I guess I was about 18, and the image was of this man leaping out of a tree onto a man below. It was to be the perspective of looking down on the figure who was looking up and being leapt on. My father said, "You'll have to get a model for this, but you want to get this feeling, " and he quickly made a drawing of the figure looking up with his hands out, startled by this figure falling. It was a marvelous little drawing. Then I got a model and had him stand below me in that position as I got up in a tree. My father's drawing was absolutely accurate! But far better than that because it had an expression and expressiveness.

The 1920s and 1930s were a very social

period. My father enjoyed it. We kids never knew who was coming, I mean, they were always driving in with these enormous cars. I remember Scott Fitzgerald in a touring car with all these big straw hats, and oh, we kids had a great time with that. The Great Gatsby, right here! But of course, the Fitzgeralds lived nearby for a time. Joseph Hergesheimer was another big drawing card here and a very good friend of my father's. He'd bring down his manuscripts and stay up all night reading them to Pa. Other visitors were Hugh Walpole, Lillian Gish, John Gilbert, who played in *The Big Parade*—oh, the list is long. Richard Barthelmess, Paul Horgan, Eric Knight, who wrote *This Above All* and *Lassie, Come Home*. Of course, both Paul and Eric were friends of Pete and Henriette. I would almost call them students of Pa's literary side. Oh, yes, and Max Perkins, the editor at Scribner's, was always asking Pa to write.

He was still a keen observer of life. Just minutes before he died here in Chadds Ford, Pennsylvania, he was overheard talking to Nat's son about bundling shocks of corn: "This is something you must remember because this is something that is passing." It's an incident that is very compelling. A year or so later, Betsy picked up the woman whom he had been watching with the corn that day and drove her to Kennett Square. She told Betsy all about how Pa stopped and brought the little boy over and showed him what she and her husband were doing and talked all about the corn. Finally he said good-bye and returned to the car. She went back to work. About three minutes went by. They heard the train and this terrible crash. It's so ironic he was killed so close to home. He had talked to me a year before as we walked down that railroad track and he showed me the spring where the Howard Pyle students would stop along the railroad and get water. It was still running. And a year later he was killed near that spot. It was October 19, the same date that he had first arrived here to study with Howard Pyle.

The Wyeth family lived in Cambridge, Massachusetts in 1645.

On October 3, 1887 Newell Convers Wyeth was baptized a Unitarian.

Newell's family was active in the First Parish Church in the town of Needham, Massachusetts, where he went to High School. Newell declared: "It don't fit you for any practical college, such as Tech or Cornell. It only comes somewhere near fitting you for old, stale, rotten Harvard."

In 1906 Newell married Carolyn Brenneman Bockius in the First Unitarian Church of Wimington, Delaware, and it was the religious home of all five of their children.

RUTH YOUNG (JANDREAU):
LABOR UNION LEADER (1916-1986)

In the 1940s, Ruth Young was a prominent trade union activist in the United Electrical, Radio, and Machine Workers of America (UE).

Gerald Zahavi, *Professor of History, State University of New York, Albany*

MY STORY (SOME SPLINTERS OF A LIFE)

By Ruth Jandreau, 1979

A game which people often play is to ask one another—"if you could live your life over, what would you change, what would you do again"—or—one is often asked "what age would you like to be again"? I almost always have said my life was great when I was in my mid-twenties. Everything seemed to come together for me: I'd reached the pinnacle in my Union career; I finally gave birth to my lovely daughter Karen; I was healthy, attractive, traveling around the country, and doing many exciting gratifying things. This was in my "other life."

You see I feel I've had several distinct lives: my first life was one of poverty and great unhappiness when I was a small child. My second life was in the factory, the union, with the masses. My third life was begun when I married my second husband, my beloved Leo and became a housewife in a small community; had my second child; was stepmother to three including a young man only ten years my junior; and became active in community and church work. My fourth life began when I went back to work in an entirely new milieu—academe. And now—I do not know if my widowhood will lead to a fifth life, or a revision of the fourth. This is still in process, ever-changing and evolving.

I choose to write about the second life—or period in my life. I was pregnant—and so very, very happy. I had been married since I was not quite 18. I was going to have a child and a career I loved. Our factories were booming, the Union was growing. It was 1941. The United States was not in the war but we were lending all kinds of support to our Western European allies. Our union was in the Electrical, Radio and Machine industry. Many thousands of young women as well as housewives were entering industry. It was the era of "Rosie the Riveter." I was organizer and director of the Membership Activities Department. Besides organizing trade union training classes for new shop stewards, we also made a special effort to involve women at every level—organizing, negotiating, and even knitting for our men in service. We also had bus-loads of our girls go to Fort Dix for dances on base, and to USO sponsored parties. It was A-Z—organizing to mittens.

When my daughter Karen's birth was

imminent I finally decided to stay home and work by phone. One night the bell rang and there were the two young women, Jean and Mary who had taken over my job (they split it between New York and New Jersey—I had covered two states). Within the next hour about thirty more young women arrived—it was a surprise shower for my expected baby. She was literally showered with so many beautiful hand-made garments. These women who knit for the soldiers, knit for my baby. I still have the album they gave me and the baby book, over 37 years ago. I loved these people and they were happy for me . . .

After World War II ended all the CIO unions decided it was time to "catch up"—wages had been frozen for so long. Throughout the country, in the large organized plants, people struck. I was assigned to the Westinghouse Plant in Bloomfield, New Jersey. There were 10,000 people—mostly young women. We manufactured lamps and radio tubes. The night before the strike I slept in the small home of Dick Lynch, the President of the union. We were to begin the strike at 6 a.m., with the first shift. I was scared and awed by the responsibility thrust upon me. These people believed in me. I was at that time the only woman on the National Board of our union of 600,000, and the second officer in our District. I had wanted the position and now I had to deliver! We struck the plant.

For thirteen weeks I was with these people, going home to Brooklyn to sleep a few hours each night. On week-ends, when my housekeeper who lived with me had time off, I would sometimes bring little Karen with me. We had an Easter party and other parties for the children of the strikers. We set up soup kitchens, got welfare, had banks declare a moratorium on loans and mortgages, sent committees out to raise funds. I went to speak to large meetings in New York City—to maritime workers, transport workers, garment workers, pleading for money.

The Courts issued an injunction against our strike, and we answered by calling for a mass picket line of thousands. The sheriff came with bull horns and read the riot act (literally—the act dated back many years), calling on us to disperse. But we marched. I was frightened but was in front. I was angry at the men in the union office who left me alone. But—I'd asked for it—wanted to be a leader!

Once I went to Washington to a government meeting in the Women's Bureau of the Department of Labor—we talked about working conditions for women in our big plants, about day care centers, about shift differentials, minimum wage, equal pay for equal work, etc. Actually we addressed and moved toward resolving many of the questions current today, all over again, among women. I was young, articulate, filled with confidence in my people, a zealous woman with a "cause" and captured the attention of Catherine Filene Shouse. She invited me home for a week-end at her estate—Wolf Trap Farm. Today that estate is seen on TV as Wolf Trap Music Center—the Channel 17 carries concerts from there. It is similar to SPAC. Kay Shouse's father was Lincoln Filene, a Boston philanthropist and department store owner. I was introduced to how "the other half lived." A chauffeured limousine drove us to the estate in Virginia. A maid in uniform brought me coffee on a tray in the morning. To Kay Shouse I was an "oddity." She offered me a job in Washington. I had a husband, a child, a commitment to workers—people to be organized. We kept in touch for a while. When she came to New York City once I invited her to a large shop stewards meeting. Then it was her turn to see "the other half" and how we lived!

I remember the hard work and the hard times. But I also remember some of the fun. Cafe Society had opened—with many newly discovered jazz artists— Hazel Scott, Mary Lou Williams, Teddy Wilson, Helena (later Lena) Horne. After a meeting we'd go there—sit in the back—listen, talk, drink. We were free women, taking over for the men who'd gone into service—and we opened many doors. I worked among men on the outside I was rather tough, firm, aggressive, holding my own. Inside I was quite vulnerable, wanting so very much to be held, to be loved.... I was an aggressive leader, a good mass speaker, but I wanted to be cuddled and held. I seemed so self-assured, and in many ways I was—but I wanted someone to hold me. I'd been on my own for so long.... But that's another story.

I remember meeting with Eleanor Roosevelt. It was in the New York City apartment which she maintained at Washington Square. I had come to enlist her support for our working women and their organizing campaigns.

UNITARIAN NOTE

Ruth Y. Jandreau was a member of the First Parish Unitarian Church of Schenectedy. New York.

WHITNEY MOORE YOUNG, JR.: SOCIAL WORK ADMINISTRATOR (1921-1971)

By Edric Lescouflair, Harvard College '03

Whitney Moore Young, Jr. was born in Lincoln Ridge, Kentucky, on July 31, 192, into rather unusual circumstances. His family was black and lived in the South, but they were constituents of a black educated elite, as his father was the president of Lincoln Institute, the black boarding school that Young eventually would attend. His mother, the former Laura Ray, was a teacher at that school. Thus, as children, the Youngs never doubted that they could be educated and successful members of society.

After graduating from the Institute as valedictorian, Young continued on to Kentucky State Industrial College, a historically black institution, with the hope of becoming a doctor. His aspirations changed, however, after he had taken a year of premedical courses. He taught at a nearby school for a year, and then decided to join the Army. In 1944, after studying engineering for two years at MIT, he found himself in Europe in an all-black regiment with a white captain. More often than not, Young acted as a mediator between that captain and the troops, defusing the imminent racial

tension. Here Young's legendary skill as a "powerbroker" between whites and blacks was cultivated. The experience in the Army influenced him enough to lead him in to social work. On the topic, he commented to Joseph Wershba of the New York Post, "It was my Army experience that decided me on getting into the race relations field after the war. Not just because I saw the problems, but because I saw the potentials, too. I grew up with a basic belief in the inherent decency of human beings."

In 1946, he received his B.S. from Kentucky State Industrial College, at which point he headed to the University of Minnesota to pursue graduate study in social work. Minnesota, specifically St. Paul, is where Young was first introduced to the Urban League. Over the next three years he supervised fieldwork of University of Minnesota and Atlanta University social work students.

Young was known as an articulate and refined man, and this reputation allowed him to move relatively freely between various social circles. In Minnesota, he was acquainted with future vice-president Hubert Humphrey, who was mayor of Minneapolis from 1945-1948.

Upon accepting a position as executive secretary of the Omaha, Nebraska Urban League, Young was offered teaching positions at the University of Nebraska (1950-1954) and Creighton University (1951-1952).

Until 1954 Young had been fighting for the civil rights of blacks, but there was still a sense of incompletion in his work. The opportunity to become directly involved on the civil rights battlegrounds of the South arrived when he became dean of the Atlanta University School of Social Work.

At this point, Young also became a member of the Atlanta Unitarian Church, and thus forced it to face racism directly. The summer after he joined the church had planned its annual picnic, and it would take place in a park that did not accommodate blacks. Young was surprised, that the white church members had never thought about the possible offense in utilizing such a venue, and he protested. The church agreed that beginning with the next picnic, a different place would be used. Despite this bittersweet victory, Young would remain a Unitarian, joining the White Plains Church Community Church in New York.

Ironically, the effects of discrimination eventually convinced Young to leave the South. In 1960 he received a Rockefeller grant to study for a year at Harvard University, and in 1961 a golden opportunity presented itself. He was offered and accepted a job as president of the National Urban League, succeeding Lester B. Granger. As the president he revolutionized the inner workings of the League, using his connections to tap funding sources like the Rockefeller family. Under his presidency, the budget was increased tenfold, the staff was quadrupled, and the number of regional offices increased from 63 to 98. His "Operation Rescue" had in fact revitalized the Urban League.

The gross inequalities that Young dedicated himself to fighting were apparent but largely ignored. In a *New York Times Magazine* article, he articulated the discrepancy in earnings between the races. The average white family earned more than twice as much as the average black family. He observed, "For more than 300 years the white American has received special consideration or 'preferential treatment' ... over the Negro. What we ask now is that for a brief period there be a deliberate and massive effort to include the Negro citizen in the mainstream of American life." Urged on by his Unitarian faith, he was determined to make a difference.

The Urban League entered a rough period under the Nixon administration and was forced to implement government funding to stay afloat. Young continued to lead with creativity, even adjusting his rhetoric to be more in line with the Black Power movement in the late 60's without alienating whites.

Young authored two books: *To Be Equal* and *Beyond Racism: Building an Open Society*.

In 1968 the Starr King School for the Ministry in Berekley, CA honored him with an L.H.D. degree.

Whitney M. Young, Jr. suffered a heart attack while swimming on March 11, 1971, and died in Lagos, Nigeria, while attending a conference for black leaders. Young was married to Margaret Buckner in 1944, and they had two daughters.

Alphabetical index of Unitarians

www.ingramcontent.com/pod-product-compliance
Lightning Source LLC
Chambersburg PA
CBHW032038080426
42733CB00006B/119